EDWIN A. BURTT, who is Susan Linn Sage Professor of Philosophy at Cornell University, was born in Groton, Mass., in 1892. He received the A.B. degree from Yale in 1915, the B.D. from Union Theological Seminary, the S.T.M. degree in 1922, and the Ph.D. from Columbia in 1925. Dr. Burtt has been Professor of Philosophy at Cornell since 1941, and visiting lecturer at both Harvard and Stanford Universities. Dr. Burtt is the author of several books, among them *Types of Religious Philosophy*, of which Harper & Brothers published a revised edition in 1951.

Man Seeks the Divine

MAN SEEKS THE DIVINE

A Study in the History and Comparison of Religions

BY EDWIN A. BURTT

Sage School of Philosophy, Cornell University

Harper & Brothers . . Publishers . . New York

Contents

v

PART FOUR. RELIGION IN THE PRESENT AND THE FUTURE

Preface▫▫▫▫▫▫▫▫▫▫▫▫▫▫▫▫▫▫▫▫▫▫

This book is the outcome of my quest for wise insight in the area of man's religious seeking. No attempt is made in it to pile up masses of detail about the world's religions. Such materials contribute toward religious understanding only when they are seen in relation to the living core which makes this or that religious faith the unique affair that it is. And when that living core has been grasped, much detail is unnecessary except in the case of those who wish to become specialists in the history of certain religions. So I have tried in these pages to help the reader gain a sympathetic appreciation of the distinctive genius of each of the great religions—of that which makes it the unique way of meeting life and destiny that it has shown itself to be—and historical details are introduced only so far as reference to them seems needed to illumine this genius and make it intelligible.

The approach followed is in the broad sense a humanistic one. What this means is explained at some length in Chapters I and III. It seems to me presumptuous to suppose that we can know with confidence what God's ideas about man are, and could deal with the history of religion as though we were looking through His eyes. Many have made such an assumption, but in view of the variety of their reports it is hard to avoid the conclusion that however much or little of God is revealed through them the human fallibility of those who offer them to us is everywhere evident. This book proceeds on the modest assumption that while we cannot put ourselves in God's place and survey human history from His vantage

point, we can learn a great deal about how man has thought
of God. And this makes one of the most fascinating stories
that the records of human experience permit us to tell. Nothing needs to be left out because one proceeds on this humble
assumption—not even the inspiring belief that the very same
process which on the human side consists of man's sincere
search for God is on the other side the gradual self-revelation
of God to man. My own conviction that this is the case is
expressed in the final chapter.

For many years after I first began to teach the history of
religions I assumed that there was nothing particularly philosophical in such a study except for the selection of material,
which naturally reflected my philosophic interests. I have
now come to believe that this was a mistake. Just as a thinker
who wishes to be a discerning interpreter and critic in the
philosophy of science, or art, or history must first make himself a master of how scientists or artists or historians carry on
their work, so that his evaluations are based on a real understanding of the phase of human experience which they repre-
sent, so the first task of the philosopher of religion must be
to comprehend what religion is in the varied cultural settings
in which it has appeared, and to sense the significant role that
the great religious founders have filled in human history.
Only on the basis of this insight can he hope to deal adequately
with the problems about God, man's soul, faith, the church,
that especially concern a philosopher of religion. To approach
these problems on any narrower base would be like attempting to deal with the general methodology of science when
one is only familiar with the science of biology, or with the
general problems of art when one has only mastered modern-
istic American art.

It is a part of this conception of my task that only inci-
dentally do I deal with religion as popularly practised, with
its relics of magical rites, and its more or less superstitious
beliefs. I have tried to understand and present each religion

at its best—in the forms and teachings which express the most ideal insight that its founder achieved and communicated, as best he could, to his followers. This rich deposit provides the norm that continually criticises and gradually elevates whatever in the religion as a whole falls short of its living spirit.

It has been my purpose to avoid making positive statements on questions of fact which are under debate among scholarly historians. In view of my ignorance of much that is relevant in this vast field I have probably not wholly succeeded in this purpose. If any specialists who pick up this book find instances of failure in this respect I hope that they will let me have the benefit of their criticism.

It would be impossible to acknowledge my debt to all whose experience and thought have contributed toward what is now set forth in this book. But I want to express deep appreciation to the students and assistants in my course in History of Religions at Cornell, whose participation in this study over a period of more than twenty years has done much to shape my thinking in this field. I also wish to express my gratitude to Professor S. C. Lee of Michigan State University and Professor Horace L. Friess of Columbia University for giving me the benefit of their criticism on certain portions of the material.

Three specific matters need mention. One is the method adopted with footnotes in the present book. I have placed at the bottom of the pages in the text only those notes which the reader might find it clarifying to refer to immediately, but which do not seem to belong in the text itself. Other notes, particularly those indicating sources of quotations, etc., are placed in order under their several chapter headings after the last chapter of the text (see p. 527). The second concerns certain material from my *Types of Religious Philosophy*, which is used without substantial change. This material occurs in Chapter XI and XII where, in discussing certain topics, I could find no better way of saying what I wanted to than the way employed in that earlier book. A similar relationship will be noted in the case of brief parts of Chapters VIII and IX by those who have read the general introduction to my *Teachings of the Compassionate Buddha* (Mentor MD 131). The third concerns the pronouns which refer to God. Wherever it is the God of an explicitly monotheistic faith that is referred to, such pronouns are capitalized. Otherwise small letters are used. If the reader bears this in mind, what might appear to be a perplexing inconsistency will be explained.

Two further acknowledgments are thankfully made. On p. 136 f. I use a story which is taken from Lin Yu-tang, *The Wisdom of China and India*, New York, 1942, p. 1063 f. (Copyright, 1942, by Random House, Inc.). This is done with the kind permission of the publisher, Random House, Inc. And on pp. 291–293 and 298 I have quoted from *The Bhagavad-Gita: The Song of God*, Christopher Isherwood and Swami Prabhavanada (eds.), Harper & Brothers, New York, 1944. (Copyright, 1944, by the Vedanta Society of Southern California). Thanks are due to the Vedanta Society of Southern California for permission to make use of this material.

E. A. BURTT

Ithaca, September, 1956

Man Seeks the Divine

I

Guideposts in Our Quest for Religious Understanding

"Oh, Allah, may thy teeth ache like mine!" So speaks a Bedouin woman to her divinity, as she tosses with a sleepless twinge to which her prayer has brought no relief. And when her impatient resentment subsides she might perhaps attempt to shame the Deity by adding a line from a Vedic poet: "If I were you, and you I, I should certainly give you what you wish."[1]

Epictetus, on the contrary, says, "Dare to lift thine eyes to God and say, 'use me for what thou wilt. I agree, and am of the same mind with thee. I refuse nothing that seems good to thee. Lead me where thou wilt, and I will go.' "[2]

But such a prayer raises another question. Can we really follow it, from our hearts? Who is this God? How will He use us if we give ourselves to His leading?

"The God that holds you over the pit of hell," preaches Jonathan Edwards to his Northampton congregation, "much as one holds a spider or some loathsome insect over the fire,

I

abhors you, and is dreadfully provoked: His wrath towards you burns like fire. . . . You are ten thousand times more abominable in His eyes than the most hateful venomous serpent is in ours." The heads of wicked sinners, he goes on, "their eyes, their tongues, their hands, their feet, their loins and their vitals, shall forever be full of a glowing, melting fire, fierce enough to melt the very rocks and elements; and also they shall eternally be full of the most quick and lively sense to feel the torment . . . not for one minute, nor for one day, nor for one year, nor for one age, nor for two ages, nor for a hundred ages, nor for ten thousand or a million ages, one after another, but for ever and ever, without any end at all, and never, never, be delivered."[3]

Are we tempted by this fearsome picture to agree with Harry Elmer Barnes "that the orthodox religious complex is, in its multifarious ramifications, the most active and pervasive menace to civilization which confronts mankind today, compared with which war and poverty are unimportant details?"[4] But a little further searching reveals that not all religious people have thought of God in this way. De Joinville, in his account of St. Louis's crusade in 1248, tells of meeting a Saracen woman walking down a Damascus street with a pan of fire in one hand and a jug of water in the other. When asked by a monk of the crusading party what she intended to do, she replied: "Burn up Paradise, and put out the fires of Hell, so that men may do good for the love of God."[5]

It would not be surprising if, in the presence of such provocative contrasts, we decide that we cannot proceed without reaching a rational judgment, discriminating the good from the bad in men's beliefs about God. Such a judgment, we think, would give us sadly needed guidance. But as we seek it we hear Martin Luther's sharp warning: "It is Satan's wisdom to tell what God is, and by doing so he will draw you into the abyss. Therefore keep to revelation, and do not try to understand."[6] Here, too, however, decisive divergences appear instead of agreement. John Wesley holds: "It is a fundamental principle with us that to renounce reason is to renounce religion, that reason and religion go hand in hand, and that all irrational religion is false religion."[7] And should we look for a way between the sharp horns of this new dilemma, we may be cheered, while also perplexed, by words from Kahlil Gibran and from St. Bernard:

"If you would know God, be not . . . a solver of riddles. Rather look about you and you shall see Him playing with your children. And look into space; you shall see Him walking in the cloud, outstretching His arms in the lightning, and descending in rain. You shall see Him smiling in flowers, then rising and waving His hands in trees."[8] In any case, "He alone is God who cannot be sought in vain even when He cannot be found."[9]

Perhaps we can find light by pursuing the clue suggested in this paradoxical utterance of the medieval saint. What *is* the religious seeking that cannot be defeated no matter what its outcome? How can we identify it, and where does it find expression? Does it show itself in sincerity of prayer? This seems a promising possibility. But what constitutes true prayer? And how should it be employed? A devout Christian, or Jew, or Moslem would be horrified at the suggestion that men ought to pray to Satan rather than to God. But the Lepchas of the Himalaya valleys told the visiting Dr. Hooker that they did not pray to the good spirits. "Why should we? They do us no harm; [but] the evil spirits that dwell in every grove and rock and mountain, to them we must pray, for they hurt us."[10]

So we are dealing with a queer and paradoxical affair. What should we do in this maze of contradictoriness and confusion? How can we achieve a real understanding of religion? Clearly, the subject is too complex and tangled to justify any wholesale generalizations. There would seem to be two alternatives. Either religion must be left aside as beyond any sound comprehension or else we must gird ourselves for a far more careful and discriminating exploration than had at first seemed needed. It is highly likely that, not merely in the topics already mentioned, but in every theme that religion touches, there are puzzling contrasts which can only be clarified by a very patient and penetrating study. Are the rewards of such an effort enticing enough? For many, I am sure that they are. Not only is one's curiosity aroused by such an intriguing and perplexing subject; there is a special timeliness in a serious study of religion in our day.

The world is in the throes of a convulsive revolution. Old ways are passing, new ways are taking their place—in politics, in economic structures, in science, in military techniques, in education, in family life, in art, in morals. It is a drastic revolution, and it is world-wide. Perhaps we are as yet only in its early stages. And, among other things, it is a revolution in religion. New faiths are appearing on every hand; old faiths, in their effort to maintain themselves in the modern world, are undergoing radical reconstruction. It was in such a time of turmoil and anxiety and suffering and hope that all the great historic religions of the world were born, stirring their followers to a new faith and a new energy, a new confidence in themselves and in the divine source of goodness and truth. It may well be that religion on the surface of our planet has thus far only attained its adolescence—that the greatest part of its history does not lie in the past but is yet to come. At such a time it is especially important to understand religion as one of the major forces working in human life and human history. For it is a force of a unique kind, and in relation to other social changes it fills a unique role.

There are two ways in which an individual or a group can meet such a world-shaking revolution as we now confront. It can be met with frustration, foreboding, fear, and hate; and with the policies and acts which express such destructive emotions. Or it can be met with hope, trust, zest, and courage—as providing an unforeseen opportunity to realize a greater good for man than has ever before seemed possible. What is the role of religion in the face of these two alternatives? Well, each of the great religions has claimed that under its guidance men and women can discover the resources by which whatever happens can be met in the second of these ways rather than the first. And its history shows that this claim is not false. The founders and leaders of religion have been men who knew how to tap these resources. What could be more important in the threatening convulsions of our day than to master this secret—to learn how religion can bring integrity, peace, strength, and assurance to men even if all around them seems tottering toward disaster? Does it do this at the cost of fostering blissful illusions in place of realistic acceptance of truth? Or does it, in its best forms at least, fill this role by leading a man or a society to recognize reality for what it truly is, and to accept it with joy? What could be of more practical moment than to learn the answers to these questions?

I write these pages for those who would like to engage in such a study. I shall not presume to tell them what is true about religion, but shall rather sketch a map that I have found helpful in trying to understand it myself. Along with some basic facts, I shall throw out interpretative suggestions that will, I hope, prove clarifying to my readers as they thread their own way through this labyrinthine theme. And before we plunge into the heart of the subject, there are a few cautions and guiding lessons that I have found so valuable that it seems wise to state them at once. A brief pause over them will be sufficient; then we shall move ahead.

A. SOME GUIDING PRINCIPLES

First of all, my counsel is that we avoid the temptation to initiate our study by attacking the great theological questions of religion: Is there a God? Does man have a soul? Do we need to live by faith as well as by knowledge? What is it to be "saved"? These questions are indeed fundamental, and sooner or later everyone concerned with religion must square himself with them. But it will help a great deal if one can keep from being premature about it. Were we to plunge into such issues right away, we should inevitably take for granted the particular and limited setting in which they have come to be formulated, and have gained their meaning, in our part of the world and our temporal epoch. When we use such words as "God," "soul," and "faith," we should be assuming the meaning that these words have acquired in virtue of the particular religious background that is our treasured inheritance. When we try to answer these questions, we should be limited to the alternatives set by the long debates in Western Europe and America between the defenders of Hebrew-Christian doctrines and their agnostic or atheistic opponents. In brief, we should be presupposing some narrow notion of what religion must be, without having found out what in its wide diversity it actually is. The first step is surely—is it not? —to discover what it is and has been, not merely in the narrow area of our religious heritage but throughout the whole history of man and in all the geographical surroundings in which he has felt himself to be in living relation to the divine. A vast amount of material lies waiting for us here, much of which would be by-passed if we were to wrestle with the great doctrinal problems before exploring it.

In the absence of such a careful study, one who is concerned about this theme will almost inevitably take for granted a definition of religion which will be meaningful and valid to him, but which will flatly contradict the definition of many other equally sincere inquirers. He might find himself agreeing with Gandhi, who is reported to have said: "By religion I mean . . . that which brings a man to face creative reality."[11] But if so, then what will he do with the implied definition of Marx (which is accepted by many who are not Marxists): "Religion provides an illusory happiness. . . . It is the opium of the poor. . . . The idea of God is the keystone of a perverted civilization."[12]

How can such a pair of conceptions be reconciled? Just for fun, let us list the contrasts between these two definitions; they are pretty thoroughgoing. Gandhi holds that religion is essentially an individual experience; Marx that it is essentially a social affair. Gandhi is sure that it is a good thing; Marx that it is hopelessly bad. Gandhi prizes it because it points the path to reality; Marx condemns it because it is illusory. With Gandhi it is an expression of health; with Marx it is a symptom (perhaps a cause) of disease. And, remembering the quotations with which this chapter began, it is fairly evident that both Gandhi and Marx could make a good case for their conclusions simply by selecting from the vast panorama of religion those facts that would support their own definition and neglecting the rest.

It is clearly important to study religion, initially, in such a way that we can avoid falling into these contradictions. And one way surely is the historical exploration of religion, engaged in without any hampering advance commitments, aimed at finding out what it has actually been and now is— in the experience of people belonging to various sects and to various religions, holding different beliefs about religion, even beliefs as to whether it is a good or a bad thing. Especially would this be likely to help if we begin such a study, not with our own faith, but with religions as widely different from ours as possible—religions which provoke and enlarge our understanding by their startling divergence from what we are accustomed to conceive as religion. Indeed, by following such a route we might even find that not only has a broad foundation been laid for a deeper appreciation of religion, but that something even more significant has been achieved. Perhaps we will have also uncovered the main key to understanding the history of man. When we have in mind, not merely the immediate scene, but the long run, it may be that Max Müller is right in holding that it is not political or military or economic history, but the history of religion, that best reveals the deep-seated forces which shape the course of human events.

To my mind the great epochs in the world's history are marked, not by the foundation or destruction of empires, by the migration of races, or by French Revolutions. All this is outward history, made up of events that seem gigantic and overpowering only to those who cannot see beyond and beneath. The real history of man is the history of religion: the wonderful ways by which the different families of the human race advanced toward a truer knowledge and deeper love of God. This is the foundation that underlies all profane history: it is the light, the soul, and the life of history, and without it all history would indeed be profane.[13]

So much for the first lesson. The second is that if we are to study the history of religion with this purpose and this possibility in mind, a very difficult psychological feat must be performed—not impossible, but surely not easy. On the one hand, we must bring with us a warm and lively sense of the best in our own religious heritage, as it has come down to us from the prophets and saints among our own forebears. One who lacks this sense—who views the religious tradition of his own time and place with indifference or hostility —will find himself viewing the religion of other peoples with at best an amused curiosity.* He will lack the experience that gives it inward meaning; he will see in it everywhere only an external shell of superstitious rite or inherited dogma. On the other hand, we must free ourselves from such an exclusive attachment to our own sectarian forms of religion as would prevent us from appreciating religious insights and values in the different experience of others. One who lies under a hostile compulsion to deny all truth to every religion but his own, finding in others nothing but a mass of corruption and error, has failed indeed to discover the best in the religion that he professes, whatever it is. For all the great faiths teach that "love is the fulfilling of the law," and one cannot love his neighbor if he really holds that everything his neighbor deeply feels and believes is evil rather than good, false rather than true.

Now in describing this twofold attitude I have also laid

* Except in the case of the few who, in rebellion against their own tradition, rush to a naïve embrace of some other faith.

bare two basic characteristics of the method that is appropriate in the historical study of religion. Such a method must express, first, a sympathetic appreciation of the religious experience of others, and of the interpretative ideas by which their thinkers have given it meaning in relation to the rest of their universe. Without such sympathetic sharing, no understanding in the field of religion is possible. For religion is not just a set of social or historical facts, capable of being understood by observation from the outside. Deprived of its inner meaning to the devout believer, it is not religion at all. This can be realized at once if we imagine someone surveying our own faith in such a superficial way. Let us suppose that he has reached the point where he can describe the architecture of our church, recite our creed, tell the historical facts about our forefathers, even verbalize our theological arguments. Does this mean that he understands our religion? Not at all—unless along with this external observing and committing to memory he has acquired some living appreciation of what these things mean to us, some sense of how and why we find in them a way that gives hope and guidance to life and overcomes the anxious fear of death. So with our understanding of the religion of others. Unless it sympathetically penetrates beneath the shell to the living heart, so that we can realize what it would be like to face destiny in the way they do, we have not understood their religion. We have at best described uncomprehendingly its surface manifestations.

And the second characteristic is equally evident. The same considerations that require an attitude of sympathetic appreciation, in the interest of true understanding, require that such an attitude be expressed with inclusive impartiality. If it is good to understand any faith that diverges from our own, it is good to understand other faiths too; all alike reflect some deep experience of men in the presence of what to them is divine. Should we allow ourselves to be partial here—favoring in advance some religions and being hostile to others

—we would miss some areas of possible insight that the panorama of religious life as a whole is ready to disclose. And I as an author face the challenge of such impartiality for another reason. This book is not written merely for readers brought up in this or that sect of this or that religion; I hope that the quest upon which we have now embarked can be shared by all who are seriously concerned with religious truth, whatever their background and the initial emphasis set by it may be. If these pages were so couched as to win a participating response only among Baptists, or Christians, or Mahayana Buddhists, or agnostics, I should be sure that I had failed to understand the experience and perspective of other sincere religious men; I would then be discussing, as the genius of religion, what is in fact but the genius of some confined segment of this vast and intriguing field. To be sure, limitations of time prevent anyone from actually mastering all the manifold varieties of man's religious experience. But one who is open rather than closed on principle will at least be certain that his progress is blocked by no arbitrary exclusion. And honest awareness of his limitations, together with his essentially impartial attitude, will lead him to approximate the ideal inclusiveness in the way that he obviously can —namely, by making sure that he comprehends with sympathy some among the religions which diverge most sharply from his own. Readiness to exemplify in this way an unprejudiced spirit will reflect itself in his religious understanding, even while he is inevitably unable to apply it to the whole range of material at hand.

Now this sympathetic and impartial method, when conscientiously pursued, has revolutionary implications for the study of religion. How revolutionary they are will only gradually be revealed—as we endeavor to apprehend the meaning of primitive practices that arouse our moral abhorrence, as we face the challenge of the great Eastern religions in their distinctive spiritual ideals, as we recognize the obligation to apply to our own religious heritage the same principles of understanding that we shall take for granted when approaching the religions of others. So it will be well to pause at this juncture, and consider carefully the crucial objection that devout persons may feel when such a method is suggested. As I reply to it I shall also be explaining the third guiding lesson that seems to me important.

"Is not religion, in the very nature of the case, an exclusive affair? If a man sincerely accepts one faith, does he not thereby commit himself to the rejection of others? And does not this mean that it would be a mistake to recognize possible truth in other supposed ways of salvation? Does not a devotion to truth require condemnation of those who are propagating error?"

Two answers to the anxious feeling thus expressed may be made at this beginning of our quest; the third and more important answer can come only at the end, when some measure of the kind of understanding to which this method actually leads has been achieved. The first of these preliminary answers is this. The notion that religion is an exclusive affair, demanding faith in the form of dogmatic attachment to one creed and hostile repudiation of other creeds, is not a universal feature of religion. In general, it is characteristic of the Western faiths—Judaism, Christianity, and Islam—but by and large it is foreign to the Eastern religions. In their conviction, theological intolerance is a vice, and a tolerant hospitality toward the insights and interpretations of other religions is itself a religious virtue. In China, for example, it is almost always assumed that a person may be at one and the same time an adherent of all three of the great Chinese religions, Confucianism, Taoism, and Buddhism; none of them demands an exclusive loyalty. Now, one's religious understanding is incomplete unless one has mastered this difference between exclusiveness and inclusiveness in religion—how each of these attitudes arose, what conception of religion each reflects, how they have affected its historical development, how they are related to other important features of the religions in which they appear. To fail to understand both of these attitudes means inevitably that one will fail to understand a very significant contrast in the panorama of religion throughout the world. But it is clear that one cannot achieve such a wide perspective if his thinking is completely committed in advance to one of these contrasting convictions. If he takes for granted some exclusive loyalty, he may be able to realize sympathetically how another devout person can be equally loyal to a different religious faith (though even here there are difficulties that can be readily imagined), but he will hardly be able to grasp the religious attitude of those who reject such exclusiveness as essentially wrong. A capacity for appreciative understanding of both attitudes is required if we are to gain the broad comprehension we seek.

The second answer is that one of the basic principles of all the great religions of the world is the principle expressed in the Golden Rule: "Do unto others as you would that others should do unto you." In fact, it would be hard to find any earnest seeker for truth in religion who does not accept this as a valid law, which it is his moral and religious duty to obey so far as he can. Now, the Golden Rule can be practiced, or violated, in the study of religion itself. How would one need to proceed with an inquiry into men's religious experience, and the ideas through which it is interpreted, if one is to exemplify this basic principle in that quest? The answer is not difficult. Consider how any earnest religious thinker would wish others to do unto him when he tries to make clear to them the faith by which he lives. Would he be satisfied with a merely external response, with the absence of any effort to enter into the inner meaning of the words that he has been using (not to mention a hostile determination to view his faith with supercilious aloofness)? Obviously not. He would be conscious that such an attitude precludes any understanding of what his religion really is; it identifies his faith as a whole with its least significant part, and what is most vital in it is lost. If, then, he is to follow the Golden

Rule when he studies the religion of others, he must respond to their experience with the inward openness that he would like them to show when the roles are reversed. And this would require precisely the appreciative and impartial sympathy which has just been described.

We may be sure, then, that in studying the history of religion by this method and in this spirit, we are loyal to a central principle in religion itself, and will only thus be able to penetrate to its essential nature. No claim will be made that these pages fully exemplify this ideal; but where they fall short, it will not be through failure to make a strenuous effort to practice it. In the bewildering mass of facts that will soon be explored, and the diverging interpretations that have been proposed, we shall assume that the most clearly sympathetic and impartial interpretation of any given fact comes nearest to giving us the truth we seek.

A fourth caution is needed—and it is likewise a twofold one—in order to guard my readers against expectations that will not be fulfilled. For one thing, this is a *philosophical* exploration of religion. By using this adjective I mean that our study will not be concerned with the multifarious details of rite and ceremony, of ecclesiastical organization, of historical propagation and expansion, or even with the less central features of creed and theology. What we shall focus upon is the central idea, simple or complex, which reveals the distinctive genius of each religion as it emerges before us —the idea uniquely exemplified in the life and teaching of its founder, given form in the creed of his disciples, and systematically elaborated in the theologies by which keen minds have endeavored to make it persuasive. We shall try to grasp appreciatively its answer to the question: What is the nature and destiny of man in relation to the universe in which he lives and dies? With that answer clearly mastered, we may be quite content to let the mass of detail take care of itself. For the other thing, this is a *general* survey of the field only. We shall pass by many religions which it would be enticing and illuminating to explore, simply because the number of their adherents is not great enough to warrant including them along with faiths in which hundreds of millions of people find a satisfying way of life. But we shall assume that there is some enduring insight in each of the religions that have spread widely and continue in vigor to the present time, and shall try to discover in each case what the heart of that insight is. In accordance with our chosen method, we shall not allow ourselves to suppose, at least at the beginning, that any one of these faiths has a monopoly on religious truth. It will be our aim not to miss any true understanding, wherever it might be found.

B. *A CRITERION IS NEEDED*

So now we are ready for the next step. And what that step must be is decided when we cast a tentative glance over the kaleidoscopic field of religion in the light of what has been said. As we thus proceed, some logician will be knitting his brow and saying: "Even though you are postponing theological questions about religion in favor of an impartial historical understanding of it, you must realize that one difficult technical task must be carried out at the very beginning. You cannot avoid giving a satisfactory definition of religion. Without such a definition, you will not know what facts to emphasize as of crucial importance; you will not even know, in this vast and confused area, what facts to select as really belonging to the subject and what to pass by as apparently religious but not actually being so. Is Confucianism a religion, or only a system of moral teaching? Is magic a form of primitive religion, or should it be treated as something different from religion? You must have a criterion by which to answer such questions right from the start, and that can only be provided by an accurate definition of religion."

If we were to accept this plea and try to fulfill this requirement at the present stage of our quest, we should be lost. For, as the quotations earlier in the chapter show, sincere and keen inquirers have proposed or implied the most varied definitions of religion; in fact, probably no two would completely agree as to what is essential to religion and what is accidental. Not only has there been a radical disagreement as to whether religion is a good or a bad thing—some, like Gandhi, defining to bless and others, like Marx, defining to damn—but even among those who offer a neutral definition in this regard, there are serious differences as to what is fundamental in religion. E. B. Tylor thinks that its beliefs about the world occupy this place: "Religion," he says, "is the belief in spiritual beings."[14] F. D. E. Schleiermacher holds that feeling is what is basic in religion; it is, he claims, "the feeling of absolute dependence."[15] Matthew Arnold differs from them both in maintaining that what is central in religion is its bearing upon man's ethical conduct; his famous definition asserts that religion is "morality touched by emotion."[16] We could argue till doomsday about such proposed definitions and add to them without difficulty ourselves; and if it were necessary to resolve this logical quandary before gathering our facts and beginning to interpret them, we should puzzle forever in the anteroom of religion and never get into the subject itself. We should be hopelessly trapped in a peculiarly difficult problem in the philosophy of religion.

But our logician friend is right to this extent: it is imperative to have at the very start a tentative criterion for selecting and weighing the historical facts. We must have some preliminary way of telling what is religious and what is not. Fortunately, however, a reasonable criterion is available for this purpose that does not arrest us in any insoluble dilemma. If we turn from argumentative debates about what religion ought to be to the practices and ideas with which it is concerned in the actual life of men, there will be no serious doubt in our minds as to where an appropriate criterion lies. In that perspective "religious" is a significant and familiar classifying adjective. Just as certain phases and institutions of human life are naturally classified as political, others as economic, or scientific, or artistic, or educational, so certain phases and institutions are universally recognized as religious. Of course, there are borderline cases where one may be in doubt as to which of these adjectives is the most appropriate one to apply, or as to how two of them are related where they both seem to apply—is the research institute of a large industrial corporation a scientific or an economic enterprise, or both? But by and large one has no difficulty here. The major ways in which religion expresses itself in individual and social life are everywhere acknowledged as distinctively belonging to religion. People do not confuse a church with a scientific association, or mistake a prayer to God for a demand on one's employer for higher wages. And, what is more important for our purpose, there is no serious question as to what are the fundamental ideas that uniquely belong to religion. When one talks about "God," when he considers problems about man's "soul" and its destiny, when questions are raised about "faith" in its relation to scientific knowledge, there would be no hesitation in describing the discussion as concerned with religion. In short, it is known with general assurance what is religious and what is not—sufficiently at least to provide an initial criterion for selecting the relevant facts.

To be sure, we shall expect to improve upon this criterion as it is applied, and as we become more intimately familiar, under its guidance, with the variegated panorama that awaits our inquiry. Also, an intriguing problem will face us when it is employed in the field of primitive religion. It can be applied there as elsewhere; "religious" is a helpful classifying adjective in sorting out the activities and concerns of primitive life, just as it is for describing certain concerns of civilized life. But it is not so easy to use it confidently there. The various aspects that in a typical civilized society are sharply separated (or at least clearly distinguishable) from each other are in a primitive group more intimately intertwined; the same act may to the primitive mind be an expression of all these phases or concerns. When the members of a clan share in a totem sacrifice, this performance may at one fell swoop symbolize their political unity, their way of providing a regular food supply, their method of training the young in the traditions of the clan, their acceptance of established moral custom, their religious devotion. This intertwining poses a difficult and exciting problem for one who seeks to understand primitive religion. He finds that he must study it in this kind of social setting, for it is there that the realities of primitive religion lie. But he must overcome handicaps in identifying what is truly religious in this situation that he does not meet when dealing with religion in civilized societies; at least he does not meet them there in anything like the same degree. The clue that one has to follow in the presence of these handicaps is something like this: What is it in this or that primitive group that meets the same human needs which religion in our society meets? One cannot go far wrong when proceeding under the guidance of this question, and when he has become familiar with the significant details in the life of any group he will learn how to make that criterion more precisely appropriate, so that nothing distinctively expressive of what is religious will be missed. But this question will lead him without delay to much that is clearly relevant.

So far, then, as concerns the problem of a sound logical definition of religion, let us patiently wait till the outcome of our study. We shall be in far better position to attempt one then than now; such a definition should not precede a thorough understanding of the field, but should summarize its achievements at the end.

However, the difficulty just mentioned about primitive religion forces us to face another—a less formal technical problem—and we cannot postpone solving it. It concerns the organization and interdependence of the concepts that we will need to use, and the proper choice of words by which to describe the significant interrelations with which we must deal.

C. A LINGUISTIC PROBLEM AND ITS SOLUTION

To plunge at once into the heart of this problem, let us proceed with our rapid conspectus of the rich field of facts which we have set ourselves to explore. And the tripartite division of human conscious experience that was taken for granted by the older psychology will guide us in this enterprise.

First, among religious facts there are ideas and beliefs—facts having to do with the intellectual side of man's experience. The most fundamental ideas that are the distinctive concern of religion have already been mentioned; they are the ideas of God, of the human soul, of the church, and of belief itself—in the specific sense in which religious belief (or faith) contrasts with scientific knowledge. And the basic beliefs in the field of religion are beliefs about these ideas. They are expressed in statements in which something is affirmed about one or more of them—as for example, that God is a supremely perfect being, that He is the creator of everything in the universe except Himself, that He is the judge and redeemer of men, etc. Second, there are distinctively religious feelings or emotions. These are more difficult to separate clearly from feelings that are not religious, because there are few, if any, such emotions which we identify by a word that refers to them only in their religious form. And yet no devout person will have any doubt that there are such distinctive emotions and that they are very important. For instance, the word "reverence" refers to feelings that are not merely religious; it is quite appropriate to speak of reverence for an older teacher, or reverence for the flag as the symbol of all that is great and good in our country. But the religious man will be quite sure that reverence or awe toward God is a distinctive kind of emotion, similar in certain respects to other reverential feelings but not identical with them. Third, there are distinctively religious acts. The act of going to church is one example, and another is the act of worship through which one participates in its form of service. In the case of prayer, it is true that the word is sometimes used in a broad sense in which it is proper to speak of praying to a judge for clemency, or to a legislature for relief from an unjust tax. The act of prayer to God, however, has a specific character which these acts do not possess.

This is not, of course, an exhaustive list of the ideas, emotions, and acts that constitute religious facts; such a list would be a lengthy one and our present purpose does not require it. What I now wish to bring out by this conspectus is that the field of facts relevant to our inquiry is vastly greater and more varied than one is likely to suppose in advance of such a study of religious history as we are commencing, and that one cannot deal with that variety without raising and answering the linguistic problem mentioned. Consider a vivid illustration of this variety.

One of the great religious ideas—the central idea, in fact, in our Western heritage—is the idea of God. Just reflect for a moment on the meaning of this word "God." One can give a general identifying phrase that might be acceptable to many people—as, say, that God is the prime object of man's religious faith and sentiment—but what we are concerned about in the history of religion is its concrete meaning to the different religious groups, each of which has a distinctive conception of the divine object of adoration. And when this concrete meaning is examined, we find a vast diversity of ideas behind even such a simple word as "God." The most familiar conception to us is the one taken for granted by a "theistic" religion such as we have inherited, which means by "God" a single, supreme, personal being who created and controls everything in the universe outside of Himself. But even in the modern Western world this is not the only acceptable meaning of the word. The pantheist refers by it to an impersonal power expressed in the order and harmony of nature, and the mystic to a superpersonal being with which it is the destiny of man's soul to be ultimately merged.

And only a brief excursion is required into the wider territory in space and time that a systematic study of religion would cover to acquaint us with a kaleidoscopic variety of conceptions of God in addition to these three. The ones most nearly like our accustomed theistic idea are the "departmental polytheism" of ancient Greece and Rome, and notions referred to in histories of religion by the terms "henotheism" and "high god." Anyone who has studied ancient mythology is acquainted with the first of these three. Here many divine beings are recognized instead of one only, and they form a rather loose-knit hierarchy of status and function. Zeus (or Jupiter) presides over the council of the gods, and a certain superior dignity is attributed to him; but he has no effective control over the doings of the other gods, each of whom exercises a quasi-supremacy in his own sphere of operation. Poseidon controls the sea, Ares the vicissitudes of war, Demeter the fertility of the earth, Aphrodite the realm of love and beauty; and each of the others has his own department of activity in which he is the one to implore or appease.

A henotheist has a somewhat different idea. He grants that there are more gods than one, but he regards his own devotion as committed, either for a time or permanently, to a single deity among them. There is much evidence, as we shall see later, for the conclusion that the Hebrews were in general henotheists during the period between Moses and the great prophets; they recognized the power of the gods of neighboring peoples, such as Chemosh of Moab and Dagon of Philistia, but believed themselves to be the chosen people of their own god Jehovah and obligated to serve him only. In the religious literature of India one comes upon passages in which attributes are ascribed to, say, Varuna, which seem only applicable to a monotheistic deity; but he finds that at another time or under other circumstances the same worshiper will ascribe equally exalted epithets to Indra, or Agni, or Prajapati, and with no apparent sense of inconsistency.

For him, then and there, the divinity addressed possesses exclusive supremacy, but this must not be taken to mean that there really are no other gods at all, or that some other god may not tomorrow receive the unqualified adoration now given to today's object of reverence.

The "high god" concept is even more difficult to make intelligible to those familiar only with theistic religion, and some students have been led to the conclusion that it is a degenerate form of an original theism. A number of primitive (or at most semicivilized) peoples recognize a divine being whom they regard as the creator of the physical world and the guardian of the social order, but who is not worshiped; as in the case of the Lepchas, their prayers for help and their rites of propitiation are addressed to lesser beings, of whose dependability and moral rectitude there is more doubt. Such a divinity is called in current literature a "high god." Illustrations of high gods are Qat of the Melanesians, Dendid of the Dinkas who live in the Upper Nile valley, and Taaroa of the Polynesians.

We come to divinities less like those of our familiar heritage when we note that among many primitive peoples and one highly civilized nation (the Chinese) deceased ancestors are regarded as possessing divine powers. Most frequently, of course, such powers are attributed to great chiefs, priests, and heads of families, but the ascription is by no means limited to them. The ancestors are conceived as capable of blessing their living descendants in various practical ways, and also as ready to be dangerously hostile if their needs are not satisfied or their injunctions violated. "I do not know," Lowie quotes an Ekoi priest as saying, "if ghosts can do harm to the living, but I always sacrifice yams and plantains to my father's spirit so that I may not fall sick, and ask him to protect my farms. About once a year, too, generally when it is time to cut 'bush' for the farms, I sacrifice to my mother, for we know that ghosts are hungry just as we are."[17] It is not necessary for a man to die, however, to have divine properties attributed to him. Many peoples have deified human beings while they were still living. As in the case of ancestors, the more prominent instances of such deification are emperors, chiefs, high priests, and other individuals of special prestige or authority. The practice is not confined to primitive peoples; the ancient world accorded rites of worship to the Roman emperors, and as late as the seventeenth century kings of England were believed to possess the power to cure disease. Only as a result of the Second World War did the Japanese Emperor in our own day renounce the august attribute of being a divinity and insist on being accepted as an ordinary human being. If the reader marvel at this deification, all he need do is to visit one of Father Divine's "heavens"; he will realize that thousands of contemporary Americans accept as a divine being an elderly, somewhat unprepossessing colored man.

Divine power can be lodged in still more lowly creatures than living men. One of the most widespread forms of religion among primitive peoples, with relics pervading civilized religion as well, is totemism. Now in totemism the bearer of the most important divine powers is some species of animal or plant, with which the tribe or clan believes itself to be related by blood kinship. Periodic sacrifices are performed in which the members of the clan partake together of the flesh or blood of the totem creature sacrificed, and through which they thus share the new life and strength which come to them from the divine source. Another almost universal practice among primitive and civilized people alike is called in its starker forms "fetishism." The essence of fetishism is a religio-magical attitude toward small inanimate objects which are believed to exert supernatural potencies. Civilized people are familiar with this idea in the form of amulets and good-luck charms; but this form of it is impure, because belief in their supernatural power is not unqualified and because those who practice such magic have abstracted their higher religious feelings from these objects and focused them on a more august deity. Among primitive peoples, however, a fetish may be of extraordinary potency in its own right, in which case it will be approached by ceremonies that seek to win its favor and to avert its curse. The most common objects which fill this role are shells, gems, bones, feathers, hair, bloodstains, and sticks and stones of peculiar shape or color. And even yet the forms in which divinity may be conceived are by no means exhausted. Probably the most important form which has not yet been listed is the one usually referred to by the word "mana." Nearly a century ago Bishop Codrington found that the natives of the Melanesian islands believed in a vague, generalized power pervading the world by which unusual results happened or could be accomplished—a kind of diffused, impersonal medium through which magic operates to achieve its ends. He refers to it as "the active force in all they do or believe to be done in magic, white or black. By means of this men are able to control or direct the forces of nature, to make rain or sunshine, wind or calm, to cause sickness or remove it, to know what is far off in time and space, to bring good luck and prosperity, or to blast and curse."[18] Since Codrington wrote, a similar idea has been identified among many other primitive peoples, as in the "wakanda" of the Sioux and the "manitou" of the Iroquois Indians.

But our present concern is with a special problem posed by this kaleidoscopic variety of notions about the divine. It is a problem that must be resolved at the very beginning of our study because it has to do with the terminology which is to be used in describing and interpreting religious facts. When we are confronted by these manifold forms in which divinity is conceived by men, is it wise to use our familiar word "God" by which to describe and explain them? This is the most natural thing to do, and it is what Western students of religion usually have done when dealing with the religious cults they have examined. For instance, an account of a case of fetishism as described by the fetishist to a European is given in the following words:

I have a very large number of gods, and doubt not but that others have as many. For any of us being resolved to undertake anything of importance, we first of all search out a god to prosper our designed undertaking . . . a dog, cat . . . or, perhaps, any inanimate that falls in our way, whether a stone, a piece of wood, or anything else of the same nature. This new chosen god is immediately presented with an offering, which is accompanied by a solemn vow. . . . If our design prove successful we have discovered a new and assisting god, which is daily presented with a fresh offering; but if the contrary happen, the new god is rejected as a useless tool, and consequently returns to his primitive estate. We make and break our gods daily, and consequently are the masters and inventors of what we sacrifice to.[19]

Now I do not know what native word this speaker is rendering by our term "god," nor what its linguistic affiliations are. But the use of this English word throws us into confusion in grasping what he is trying to say, instead of being a helpful medium of understanding. We inevitably carry over into our interpretation of his statement the associations of a monotheistic concept of God, which are what naturally provide the meaning of that word to us. Hence our apprehension of his account is mingled, first with wondering pity that anyone would be so benighted as to identify the divine being with a petty inanimate object, and second with horror at the nonchalant claim that a god can be made and broken at the will of man. Suppose now that we reread the statement, substituting the phrase "good-luck charm" for "god" wherever it occurs. In that case these confusions and hampering emotional accompaniments will disappear, and the statement will become readily intelligible. To be sure, once this change is made, we will see the need of a similar change with some of the other words (such as "offering" and "sacrifice") if incongruity is to be completely avoided. Moreover, this rendering goes to another unfortunate extreme; it does not disclose the meaning in such a way as to prepare the reader for the possibility that the author does ascribe religious significance to these charms, and may have no religious objects that are more important to him than such fetishes are.

How is this difficulty to be met? What rule about our choice of words would establish a framework of language within which we can describe accurately and interpret objectively such facts as have just been sampled? Three answers to this question would seem to be possible.

One of them has already been mentioned, but we have not yet seen how grave the objections to it are. This is to use the words familiar to us from our own religious heritage, broadening their scope of application to cover all situations in which men believe themselves in the presence of a religiously significant object. This would mean extending our accustomed word "God" to all entities that people approach with religious attitudes, including deceased ancestors, totem plants, fetishes, and mana along with the deity of a monotheistic faith. If we do this we can hardly avoid carrying with us, in greater or lesser degree, the associations of these familiar terms. We shall imagine, in that case, that the primitive worshiper has the same notion in his mind that we do as to what it means for a being to be divine, but that he simply finds that divinity in different objects than the God we revere. Now such a carry-over has two consequences which obstruct, perhaps very seriously, our apprehension of the primitive man's actual experience. On the one hand, our judgment is confused with some measure of disgust at the degradation which seems to be disclosed, and this feeling is incompatible with sympathetic and impartial understanding. The totemist, we shall think, is worshiping as God one of the lower animals or plants—a creature inferior in dignity even to a human being—how ghastly! On the other hand, by blithely attributing to a primitive religionist the attitudes associated with our word "God," we prevent ourselves from discovering what attitudes are actually present in his mind, and thus from entering into the living meaning that they have to him. Presumably, his state of mind has something in common with the mood of pious devotion among ourselves, but there must be significant differences too, or he would not be able to feel that mood under the circumstances that he does; we need a terminology which will enable us to bring out clearly the differences as well as the similarities.

A second answer would consist in tossing aside all terms that carry any religious associations with us, and describing the facts in a different language altogether. Many today who take an agnostic attitude toward religion, or who regard all religious belief as superstition, are tempted to this procedure. In practice, this would presumably mean, at present, interpreting the facts of religion by the aid of a naturalistic psychology. "The only reality in the primitive divinities," one would say, in effect, "is the feeling in the worshiper's mind, which he is projecting into the outer world; hence his divinities can be accurately described in terms of such projected feelings." In fact, the language of Freudian psychology is already being employed by some investigators in this fashion. What is wrong with this answer? Well, the basic difficulty is that it implicitly assumes, in advance, that all religion is grounded in an illusion, and can properly be described on that assumption. But this is too much to take for granted at the beginning. A serious inquirer into the phenomena of religion may perhaps come to that conclusion after he has completed a careful study of the field, but he needs a framework of language in which to carry on the study that does not force him to it—an unprejudiced linguistic medium instead of a prejudiced one. And, besides this general difficulty, such a procedure would inevitably wed our thinking to some dubious contemporary theory in Western psychology, e.g., the theory of emotional projection above mentioned. We can hardly afford to presuppose the validity of any such theory; it is imperative to describe the facts in such a way that the description will not become meaningful or meaningless according to which school of psychology happens to be dominant at the moment.

Is there a third answer which avoids both these sorts of difficulty? I believe there is. It consists in employing what I have called elsewhere the method of "generic definition."[20] What would this method mean in the present context? How would it solve the problem?

It differs from the second answer by retaining terms which have traditional religious associations and are therefore not inharmonious with our religious attitudes and feelings. It thus permits a description of religious facts which does not appear to explain them away as mere superstition, but which enables us to enter into their inner meaning to those whose experience is in question. It differs from the first answer by supplementing the words which to us have become loaded with monotheistic significance by more general terms of similar derivation. It thus provides a terminology in which what is genuinely common to all forms of religious experience can be readily described and in which what is significantly different between them can also be revealed. The associations from our own religious heritage can thus be carried over to other forms of religion where they are relevant, and can be left behind where they obstruct true understanding. I shall illustrate this procedure, for to claim such virtue for it is to claim a good deal.

Suppose that instead of using the word "God," when discussing the objects of adoration in other religions than our own, we were to use the more general phrase "divine power." I am not sure that this is the best term to employ, but I have naturally used it in the preceding pages, and it will bring out the aim and role of a generic definition here. What we want is a word or phrase whose meaning will include the monotheistic concept of God as one of its species, but which will also include various other conceptions which religious people may entertain about their objects of worship. Now, whatever its limitations, this phrase is inclusive in that fashion. The monotheist does believe that the deity is a divine power. The ancestral worshiper is sure that divine power resides in the departed spirits whom he addresses. The totemist attributes divine power to the animal or plant that he sacrifices and whose substance he shares with his fellow clansmen. The believer in mana attributes divine power to the pervasive medium in which all things have their being and which he is confident can be magically controlled. Each of these kinds of religious object exemplifies a way in which divine power can be concretely conceived. In brief, what I am suggesting is that "divine power" become the generic term for our description of religious objects, and that its species be constituted by the particular ways in which, in different religions, this general idea takes more definite form. The logical relation that is assumed between the genus and its species can be represented by a table like the following:

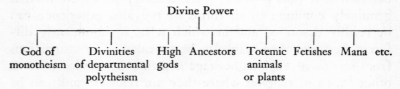

Divine Power

| God of monotheism | Divinities of departmental polytheism | High gods | Ancestors | Totemic animals or plants | Fetishes | Mana etc. |

It should be remembered that the relationships within such a table are purely logical ones, set up for their value in facilitating impartial description and comparison of religious facts. No suggestions of another order are intended, and they should be avoided. There is no implication, for example, that some vague "divine power" exists in the world of reality, and is somehow superior to the God of monotheism, the divinities of departmental polytheism, and the other divine objects believed in by various religionists. We are simply constructing a linguistic framework in which religious facts possessing a certain similarity to the fact referred to by the phrase "belief in God" can be sympathetically described and impartially interpreted.

The same principle applies to all the other concepts that seem basic in the classification and description of religious facts. It is because of this circumstance that the fetishist's statement above quoted still appeared somewhat incongruous after "god" had been replaced by another term, so long as parallel replacements of other key words had not been made. Consider the concept of "prayer." When the Ainu of northern Japan sit down to a meal of millet, they may address the prepared food as follows: "O millet, thou hast grown well for us. We thank thee; we eat thee." Is this a prayer? Or should we refer to it by some other term, and if so, which one? The difficulty is analogous in every respect to the difficulty about "God," and needs to be resolved in the same way. When the word "prayer" comes to our lips, we unavoidably tend to carry over into its use the attitudes that are taken for granted when one is addressing a monotheistic deity as Judaism and Christianity conceive Him. But there are many situations in other religions, especially primitive ones, in which a divine power (as divinity is there conceived) is being addressed, but in which these attitudes are not present. A feeling similar in certain respects is there; hence in this case, too, we should make a mistake if we were to describe it in nonreligious terms. None the less, the word "prayer" is misleading. It imposes upon this situation an interpretative context which is inappropriate, and which obstructs our apprehension of the attitude that is really present, in its differences as well as its similarities, with the attitude we are familiar with as "prayer." Here it is more difficult to find just the right phrase for the genus of which prayer is one species, along with invocation, recitation, incantation, magical coercion, and the like. Perhaps the phrase "religious address" will serve this purpose as well as any.

The reader will note that this procedure of generic definition, employed to provide a terminology for describing the facts and relationships that we seek to understand, is in harmony with—indeed, some such method would seem to be

required by—the ideal of sympathetic and impartial understanding in religion. The essential difficulty with each of the
two alternative procedures is that it attempts to describe the
field in a manner that is not impartially open to whatever is
there to be found, and is not sympathetically responsive to
its inner meaning in the experience of those whose religion is
being studied.

Enough, now, for these preliminaries. It is time to begin
our exploration with an excursion into the strange but
fascinating area of primitive religion. By starting here we will
be forced to transcend, at once and sharply, whatever limitations our minds have thus far been under because of the
special features of the religions we are most familiar with,
which have hitherto inevitably molded our ideas as to what
sort of thing religion is. If we can explore a few primitive
religions with real understanding our minds will be freed
from such hampering shackles. Then we ought to be ready
to wend our way among the great religions of the East and
come in due course to the impartial and sympathetic study
of our own religious heritage. These Oriental faiths are also
very different from ours in many respects, but they are
clearly civilized religions, not primitive. The religion of our
Western tradition will glow with a new and richer significance when we return to it toward the end of this exploratory
circuit.

PART ONE

How Religion Outgrows
Its Primitive Forms

II

Primitive Religion

A. WHAT IS PRIMITIVE RELIGION?

What do we mean by the distinction, confidently employed in the preceding pages, between primitive and civilized religions? And how do we tell which religions should be classified under each of these heads?

An easy answer to these questions was assumed when, as in the late nineteenth and early twentieth centuries, it was taken for granted that the history of religion could be written in accordance with the then dominant theory of evolution. It was a major feature of that assumption that the history of mankind essentially follows a line of progress from rude and simple beginnings toward the full achievement of the complex blessings of civilization. To be sure, there would be borderline cases, and a more detailed analysis might recognize intermediate stages between the two extremes; yet no one could doubt the real existence of an early stage that could properly be called "primitive," or of a later stage, like that of our own Occidental society, that may justly claim to be "civilized."

Such a blithe answer is no longer possible. For one thing, serious investigators of human history have now become capable of sufficient impartiality, and can appreciate enough of the sources of strength in primitive life, so that they

33

realize, albeit somewhat dimly, that from the viewpoint of what we call a barbarous society our own ways might well seem to be primitive and theirs, by contrast, more highly developed. We lack some values that they strongly prize, just as they lack some values that we highly prize. Is there, then, any way of life that can objectively be called primitive, or objectively pronounced civilized?* For another thing, except in the case of archaeological study, the peoples that to-day supply what information we are gaining about primitive culture are not peoples existing in the remote past; they are contemporary societies, just as well adjusted, perhaps, to the conditions of present-day existence as civilized ones. And while plenty of primitive groups have been almost or completely annihilated through the vicissitudes of time, the same is true of a number of civilized cultures such as those of ancient Greece or imperial Rome. To be sure—and that is a fact on which considerable weight may be laid—there does seem to be much evidence verifiably indicating that all the societies we would call civilized have passed through an earlier historical stage in which they exhibited many characteristics typical of societies we would call primitive. But one is readily tempted to exaggerate this circumstance; the theories prevalent a half-century ago pretty clearly did so. In short, we no longer know as well as we once thought we did what should be meant by the distinction between primitive and civilized cultures in general, or therefore between primitive and civilized religions—and we cannot tell so confidently which is which.

Nevertheless, the distinction is not only a very convenient but almost an indispensable one for our inquiry. When drawn in such a way that it is reasonably impartial instead of prejudiced, it provides a highly illuminating line of cleavage which definitely furthers our understanding of some major facts about religion. For, as we shall see, there are certain

* By "objectively" I mean "in a manner reflecting no prejudice that might vary from individual to individual or from group to group."

very important features which all the great civilized religions, despite their differences from each other, share in common, and which are lacking in primitive religions. Such a line of cleavage helps to reveal these, along with the contrasting features of primitive religion. What then should be meant by the distinction, and by what criterion shall we apply it?

The right solution to this question seems to be found by way of the following considerations. When one looks at the kaleidoscopic aggregate of human societies, with any major function of social life in mind, he discovers a provocative difference between societies which perform this function in a very simple way and societies where it appears in a more complex guise. To be sure, in the case of some of these functions it would be easy to apply this principle in too naïve a fashion. For example, all groups of human beings have some sort of social organization; but there seems to be a notable difference between those which are organized on the simple pattern of family and clan relationships and those revealing a more complex structure. In the former case, almost the sole differences that are obvious may be those between the adults and the young (usually with smaller councils of elders in a position of special authority) and between the men and the women,* whereas in the latter case there will often be an intricate network of classes. These can be grouped according to their vocational, military, political, religious, legal, and other functions, each with its own characteristic hierarchy of superordinate and subordinate responsibilities. But it may be that in this contrast our own notions of what constitutes significant complexity are reflected; perhaps if we viewed the matter through primitive man's eyes, recognizing all the economic, ceremonial, and educational activities through which his society carries on its life, we should find a complexity in his culture quite comparable with that of our own.

In many cases, however, a difference appears that does seem

* Secret societies of one sort or another are also common.

to be objective. All groups of men and women use language; but there is a marked difference between groups employing only a spoken language and those which have also developed symbols for its written expression. Again, all societies, even the rudest, employ tools of one sort or another in securing their food supply, in building their huts, and in battling against enemies. But there are some which are familiar only with relatively simple tools applied directly by human power to the natural objects which need to be dealt with—a plow for turning the sod, a spear for catching fish, a sharpened stone for skinning animals, and the like—while there are others with much more complex machines using nonhuman forces in their operation, such as windmills, catapults, steam engines, and water wheels.* And societies of the latter kind are likely also to possess some tools whose main function is not to produce effects in nature but to construct other tools—such as the grindstone, the lathe, the polishing disk, or more complicated instruments. Further, with the major economic processes of social life specifically in mind, one notes a pretty unmistakable difference between groups whose activities are limited to gathering roots and berries, fishing, hunting, herd raising, or the growing of some single agricultural crop, and groups exemplifying much more variegated economic functions of production, transportation, marketing, etc. Characteristic of the latter is a rather intricate division of labor, and such specialized institutions as banks, wholesale distributors, and carriers, which (so far as one can tell) are absent in the simplest forms of economic organization. In the former kind of culture the guiding purpose is to meet the immediate necessities of life directly, except for making sure (in an agricultural society) that seeds are preserved for the crops of the following year, whereas in the latter kind the aim includes the provision of whatever facilities are required to maintain and develop the entire network of recognized human activities.

* Not to mention the advanced inventions of modern Western civilization.

Now these differences, of themselves, would not yield a solution of our problem, but when taken along with two other important facts they do. One of these is the circumstance that, generally speaking, a society which falls on the side of simplicity when measured in terms of one of these factors also falls on the same side when measured in terms of any of the others; and the same is true of the opposite extreme of complexity. This is to say that a group which is only familiar with tools directly employed in fishing, hunting, yam raising, etc., will be highly likely also to show a very simple pattern of economic life; it will either have no written language or will not have developed it very far. There will be exceptional cases, of course, where complexity in some of these factors is accompanied by a simpler state of affairs in others, and there will be a middle area between the obviously simple forms at one extreme and the clearly complex ones at the other, which a merely twofold division will not be able to handle. But we shall find a large number of societies about which there will be no doubt as to where to place them. The other fact is that the kind of difference just observed in the case of these three factors is also noticeable in the field of religion, and that the same general parallel holds between what most investigators would identify as a relatively undeveloped form of religion and a relatively simple state with respect to each of those other aspects of cultural life. Since this second point will be illustrated in some detail later, it will not be necessary to dwell on it now.

But if this is the situation, an impartial meaning can be given to the words "primitive" and "civilized" when they are used to modify the noun "religion," and a practical criterion is available for applying them. The meaning is not as free from vagueness as one would like, and the criterion cannot be applied as universally as would be desirable, but both meaning and criterion are objective as far as they go. We can leave behind the plight in which it would be assumed, in effect, that the most civilized religions are those most like our own, and the most primitive religions those most different from our own. The word "primitive" will be applied to societies whose ways of living lie well toward the pole of simplicity in such features as have been mentioned, and by "primitive religion" will be meant the forms of religion that are characteristic of such societies. Likewise we shall apply the word "civilized" to societies that are clearly not primitive by any reasonable application of this criterion, and shall mean by civilized religion the kinds of religion that are found in such societies. This means that "civilized religion" will be a term covering a wide area of ideas and practices, ranging all the way from those that show relatively few differences from primitive religion to the great religions of our own day that claim a universal relevance to the needs of civilized man. It is with these latter religions that we shall be chiefly occupied after we leave the field of primitive religion. However, by this definition "civilized religion" will also include the religions of the ancient empires that have now passed away, such as Egypt, Babylon, Greece, and Rome. These cults preserved many of the features of primitive religion, but they also showed some significant differences that point toward characteristics of the civilized faiths which are still very much alive.

So far as concerns our immediate purpose, it quickly becomes evident that by applying the above criterion there emerge a large number of religions that we can unhesitatingly call primitive and can subject to detailed examination as such.

At this point it would be advisable for the reader to leave the perusal of this chapter for a while and soak himself in some of the summarizing descriptions, now readily available, of typical primitive cultures and of the religious ideas and attitudes that they reveal.[1] For our aim in this chapter is to advance as rapidly as possible to certain general conclusions about such cultures; but generalizations are pretty hazardous unless they are grounded in, and can be checked by, a wealth of well-attested facts. I shall proceed on the assumption that my readers have acquired or are now acquiring enough familiarity with the characteristic details of primitive religions so that they can follow with an independent judgment the data I shall now present and the inferences I shall draw from them. The special problems which need to be considered in any attempt to generalize in this field will be faced as they naturally present themselves in the course of the analysis.

B. ANALYSIS OF PRIMITIVE ADDRESSES TO DIVINE POWERS

As a result of many years' experience in studying comparative religion with college students, I have found that the distinctive features of primitive beliefs about "divine powers" emerge into clarity most readily when one examines a large number of typical primitive prayers, invocations, incantations—"addresses" to such powers, in short—and notes the basic similarities and contrasts that they show when compared with the beliefs of such a civilized religion as our own. What I am about to spread before the reader is a small collection of such addresses—a collection selected in such a way that, I hope, those who advance to a more thorough familiarity with primitive religions will find it to be on the whole a fair sample. Certain features of some primitive religions fail to appear clearly in any selection of this sort; we shall duly allow for that fact. Consider the following list:

1. *A Zulu prayer to ancestor spirits:*

"Our people! I pray to you; I sacrifice these cattle to you. I pray for more cattle and more corn, and many children; then this your home will prosper, and many will praise and thank you."

2. *A Papuan prayer, attended by a gift offering:*

"Compassionate father, here is some food for you. Eat it, and be kind to us on account of it."

3. *A Samoan prayer, accompanying an evening libation:*

"Here is *ava* for you, O divine powers! Look kindly on this family; let it prosper, let us be kept in health, let our food grow, let us be a strong people."

4. *A prayer of an Osage Indian, as he sets off on a raiding expedition:*

"Pity me, Wohkonda! I am very poor. Give me success against my enemies. Let me avenge the death of my friends. Let me take many scalps, many horses."

5. *A prayer of an Algonquin chief to the "Great Spirit," when setting out to cross Lake Superior:*

"You have made this lake, and made us, your children. Cause the water to be smooth while we pass over."

6. *A Nootka Indian prayer, offered when embarking on an attack:*

"Great Quahootze! Let me live, not be sick, find the enemy, not be afraid of him, find him asleep, and kill many of him."

7. *An address to the sun in New Caledonia, which is accompanied by the kindling of a fire and certain other preparatory rites:*

"Sun! I do this so that you may be burning hot, and eat up all the clouds in the sky."

8. *A prayer from one of the South Pacific islands, spoken at the beginning of a thieving expedition:*

"O thou divine Outre-reter!
We go out for plunder.
Cause all things to sleep in the house.
Owner of the house, sleep on!
Threshold of the house, sleep on!
Little insects of the house, sleep on!
Central post, ridge pole, rafters, thatch of the house, sleep on!
O Rongo, grant us success!"

9. *A prosperity prayer of the Khonds of Orissa, addressed to the Earth Goddess, ends as follows:*

"We are ignorant of what it is good to ask for. You know what is good for us. Give it to us!"

10. *Addresses to the sun by a Samoyed woman:*

In the morning—"When thou risest, I too rise from my bed."
In the evening—"When thou sinkest down, I too sink down to rest."

11. *A prayer of a Delaware Indian, as he goes out to fight:*
"O Great Spirit above! Have pity on my wife and my children. Let them not mourn for me. Let me succeed in this enterprise, slay my enemy, return in safety to my dear family and
friends, that we may rejoice together. Have pity on me, and
protect my life."

12. *An invocation of a group of Iroquois Huron Indians:*
"Spirit of this place, we give thee tobacco; so help us, save
us from the enemy, bring us wealth, bring us back safely."

13. *An Ainu address (already quoted):*
"O millet, thou hast grown well for us; we thank thee, we
eat thee."

14. *An Ainu invocation to the fire, into which at the same time
a libation is poured:*
"We drink sake to thee; we give thee the lees. Keep evil
from us; send us good."

15. *A prayer of a Watja Negress in Africa:*
"O divine power, I know thee not. But thou knowest me; I
need thy help."

16. *An invocation of an American Indian in great distress, as he
throws a handful of tobacco into the fire:*
"There, there, take and smoke! Be pacified, and do not harm
me!"

17. *A prayer by a sick Ekoi African, accompanied by a food
and drink offering:*
"Here is what you asked of me. Do not let me be sick any
more."

18. *A prayer from the African Gold Coast:*
"Divine power, give me today rice and yams, gold and agries;
give me slaves, riches, and health; and cause that I may be brisk
and swift."

19. *An invocation to the spirit of a deceased father, from the
Tchuvashes of Siberia:*
"We honor thee with a feast. Look, here is bread for thee,

and different kinds of meat; thou hast all thou canst want; but do not trouble us, do not come near us."

20. *A Dobuan incantation, spoken to prevent the speaker's yams from wandering away from his garden:*
"The yam *kulia*—
He remains inflexible, unbending.
He remains, he remains unmoved
In the belly of my garden."

21. *The above twenty addresses are all quite short. One longer prayed should be included, lest we draw some unwarranted inferences from this list. The prayer that follows is by a chief of the Blackfoot Indians spoken at a sun-dance ceremonial:*
"Great Sun Power! I am praying for my people, that they may be happy in the summer and that they may live through the cold of winter. Many are sick and in want. Pity them, and let them survive. Grant that they live long and have abundance. May we go through these ceremonies correctly, as you taught our fore-fathers to do in the days that are past. If we make mistakes, pity us!

"Help us, Mother Earth! for we depend upon your goodness. Let there be rain to water the prairies, that the grass may grow long and the berries be abundant.

"O Morning Star! When you look down upon us, give us peace and refreshing sleep.

"Great Spirit! Bless our children, friends, and visitors through a happy life. May our trails lie straight and level before us. Let us live to be old. We are all your children, and we ask these things with good hearts."

Before we proceed to analyze these miscellaneous addresses, it should be noted that the way they are rendered into English may in some cases be seriously inadequate. The trans-lators were people of varying degrees of competence in appre-ciating the spirit of a primitive religious group, and this cir-cumstance is undoubtedly reflected in their ability to convey the detailed meaning of a prayer or an invocation from the primitive tongue into their own. But the lessons that will be drawn do not depend on specific phrases that might be mistaken; they depend only on the fairly clear and definite general picture of primitive attitudes that these addresses would almost surely reveal through any translation, however defective. At least, if this limitation is kept in mind, we can be careful to draw only conclusions that are supported by the cumulative picture, irrespective of errors in this or that detail.

When one tries now to penetrate, sympathetically and impartially, the state of mind expressed in these addresses, what does he find?

Surely the basic thing that is revealed is this. The person making the address, almost without exception, is intensely concerned about some human need which he earnestly wants to have satisfied, but which, he realizes, may not be satisfied. It may be his own individual need (as in cases 4, 6, 7, 10, 11, 15, 16, 17, 18, and 20); it may be the need of a small group (as in 3, 5, 8, 12, and 13); it may be a need of the entire clan or tribe (as in 1, 9, and 21). As for the need itself, in all but a few cases it is a need for something on which the continued existence of the individual or group depends, or something which, if secured, will lift them (temporarily at least) above sheer destitution and give them a greater measure of physical well-being. The petitioners are asking for food, for health, for strength, for long life, for children, for slaves, for success in plunder or war, for safe passage across a dangerous lake, for protection against hostile threats, for prosperity in general. Now they evidently feel themselves dependent, for the satisfaction of these needs, on powers which are operating in the world around them, and the addresses express their attempt to win the favor of these powers and avert their hostility. Religion, as reflected in the vast majority of these beseechings, would appear to be a way of securing aid of this kind in the strenuous effort to assure continued existence and achieve greater well-being.

This, I say, is the most obvious disclosure of any such sample of primitive religious addresses. But the sample reveals two other important truths, which it will be essential for us to have in mind later.

One of these appears when we examine the few prayers in the above list (and occasional phrases in others) which do not reflect this preoccupation with the means of continued physical existence or prosperity. It becomes clear on such an examination that some of these cases express needs and motives which receive much greater emphasis in a typical civilized religion than they do here. They are present in primitive religion in a very simple form, but they are not entirely displaced from it by the insistent practical concern for help in the challenging exigencies of life. What are these further motives? Well, one of them is the feeling of gratitude for boons that have been received from the divine powers in the past. This is expressed in case 13, and by implication at least in two of the others. Another is a satisfying sense of identification with the divinity addressed, as in 10. Perhaps we meet here, in rudimentary form, the motive which, in a civilized religion, appears as the mystic urge to realize oneness with God. A third is very interestingly disclosed in cases 9 and 15, and in two sentences of 21. In these three addresses the worshipers are conscious of their own ignorance and limitations, as well as their weakness, and they ascribe to the divine being addressed not only power to aid them in satisfying their needs but also the greater knowledge which can correct their ignorance and transcend these limitations. Indeed, in case 21, confidence is expressed that any power which would be kindly disposed toward them would allow for such limitations and overlook the mistakes that might be made because of them; it would take the sincere will for the deed. A fourth motive is a sense of awe before the vastness and mystery of the universe; a touch of it is certainly present in the long prayer (21), and perhaps in 5, 7, and 9 also. Moreover, some quasi-religious feelings are not disclosed at all in this list, e.g., a delight in dramatic rhythm.

The other important point revealed here which will need

to be referred to later is the fact that primitive man typically lacks any sense of universal moral obligation, and that his religion frankly expresses this lack instead of aspiring toward its correction. This fact is brought out quite vividly in cases 4, 6, 8, 11, 12, and 18. In the situations in which these addresses were made, the speakers are sallying forth to war, to wreak vengeance, to obtain booty. Their immediate need is for divine help in carrying these enterprises through successfully. There is no hint whatever that the divine powers invoked might have a concern to protect those whom they are about to attack or plunder; the assumption is that these powers are just as ready to support them in such an aggressive undertaking as in any other activity aimed at attaining the means of continued existence and greater security for themselves. Whoever is their enemy is also an enemy of their divinities. Now at this point we meet one of the characteristic differences between primitive religion and the great civilized religions that have endured through the centuries. These religions recognize that man's moral concern and moral responsibility are properly universal. The divinity of such a faith (however that divinity be conceived) is impartially benevolent toward all men, favoring none against others; and he requires of his devotees that they express such an impartial benevolence in their conduct. "Love your enemies" is the principle in which this moral requirement comes to its clearest and most challenging formulation. Of course, civilized peoples, today as always, find it very difficult to live up to such a principle, and in time of war (hot or cold) they easily relapse into primitive attitudes in this regard. But they feel guilt when doing so, for the ideal of their religion is quite explicit and to some extent it has permeated their moral sentiments.

There is, to be sure, one interesting phenomenon in primitive religion that might seem to anticipate this sense of obligation to man as man: I mean the almost universal acceptance of the duty to extend protection and hospitality to any strangers who may visit a community as guests. But when one studies these cases with due attention, it becomes fairly evident that the main motive revealed in this feature of their religion is the feeling that a stranger brings a new and unpredictable potency into their home, which must be guarded against with special care; to appease it by providing for his obvious needs is the first requirement of cautious prudence. Rarely is there any indication of a sense of obligation to treat a visitor kindly just because he is a human being.

Now let us come to grips with the crucial question. In what terms shall we understand these challenging characteristics, revealed in such a sample of primitive addresses to divine powers? As we formulate an answer, it is important to recognize that our conclusion will not apply to every form of primitive religion; the main qualifications that are needed with regard to any generalization here will be noted in the next chapter. But we want the conclusion to hold good of these obviously prominent cases, since they provide a clarifying contrast with what is true about civilized religion. When I now speak, for brevity's sake, of "primitive thought" or the "primitive mind," I mean the mentality revealed in these striking and frequently met forms.

C. THE CATEGORIES OF PRIMITIVE THOUGHT

The primary step that must be taken in seeking a solution to such problems is to analyze primitive man's attitude toward his world, and the fundamental beliefs that he evidently entertains about it, as they are reflected in such addresses as the ones above quoted. This means bringing into relief what a philosopher would call the "categories" of primitive thinking—that is, the most general, inclusive, and basic ideas that primitive man ordinarily takes for granted in his dealings with the world around him.

And it would seem clear when we consider the matter carefully that there are three quite universal categories. Let us denote them, not by scientific terms that would suggest a refinement of thought of which primitive man is hardly capable, but by simple, unsophisticated words of daily speech. These three categories are "happening," "cause," and "power." Instead of the first of these terms we might have used a technical word popular in recent philosophy, namely, "event," but this would take us out of the simple-minded atmosphere of primitive thought; even the word "occurrence" has an aura of nonprimitive sophistication about it. "Happening" is a better word for our purpose.

Consider these categories in their basic interrelationships. To man's elementary experience, things are constantly happening in his world, and their happening is in many cases a matter of considerable concern because, directly or indirectly, it may affect the security of his existence. So "happening," in this simple sense, is a category of primitive thinking. "Cause" is another, and here we have a term of respectable usage in civilized science and philosophy as well as in primitive speech. Like ourselves, primitive man takes it for granted that every happening is caused by something, which has determined it to happen in the way that it does. If he can find a way to control the causes, he can control the happenings they produce—bringing them about if he wants them to happen, and averting them if their occurrence is painful—so, at least, he believes. And, in the third place, the cause of any happening that he is concerned about is always some "power." Again, I pick this vague and unsophisticated word in preference to the scientific term "energy" and even to the everyday word "force"; either of these has associations that are foreign to primitive man's attitudes, and either lacks some of the associations that must be preserved if we are to understand the religious as well as the quasi-scientific significance of this category in his way of thinking. The primitive mind is quite confident that what needs to be identified and induced to act aright if the happenings that concern him are to be controlled is always a power, resident either in the entity in which the happening is taking place or in some other being that determines how it occurs. If one surveys the addresses above quoted in the light of these assertions, I believe he will recognize the presence of these three categories in every case.

In order to reveal the further categories that are essential to our understanding of the primitive mind, it is best to present them in the form of a systematic division of "happenings" as primitive man confronts them:

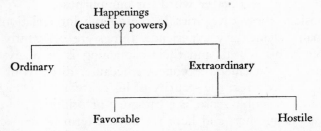

We thus meet four further categories, no one of which is universal, but which cover the field in pairs, after the fashion of logical alternatives.

The basic pair of alternative categories—"ordinary" and "extraordinary"—arise when we distinguish happenings in accordance with the intensity of their impact on man's experience, and with the degree of equanimity or confidence that he feels in their presence. Many things that happen in his world (as in ours) are ordinary, in the sense of being familiar, regular, predictable, and hence dependable; he feels secure when he observes them taking place; he senses no danger against which he must be on his guard. If we were to describe this phase of his experience in terms of the distinctions fundamental in civilized life, we could say that the area of "ordinary" happenings constitutes the realm of the secular, in contrast with the realm that is of religious concern. For example, so far as I am aware, there are no primitive prayers or rites aimed at inducing the sun to retain his fiery heat, or at making a river flow downhill, or at persuading a tree to grow branches instead of arms. Primitive man assumes, just as we do, that these things will continue to happen dependably in the fashion to which he is accustomed; he has never observed any case to the contrary and he has no anxiety about these occurrences. He uses them confidently to serve his ends, and feels no need of any special techniques to keep them from playing him false.

On the other hand, many happenings are extraordinary, in the sense that they are subject to strange, irregular, unpredictable vicissitudes. How they are going to come out is more or less uncertain, mysterious, and hence undependable. Consequently, in their presence he lacks the security that he feels with the ordinary occurrences just mentioned, and is under some measure of anxiety when he sees them in operation. The powers at work in this realm need to be taken seriously into account, and dealt with by procedures which will reduce the insecurity and apprehension that he feels in confronting them. The sun does not change his shape, but he does vary unpredictably in relation to the crops that men are trying to raise; sometimes his genial warmth nourishes them to fruitful maturity, while at other times he burns them up with his fierce and scorching heat. No river runs uphill, but rivers are very undependable in other respects; sometimes they bring abundance of fish and provide safe transportation for canoe and raft, while at times they yield no food and may sweep away a whole village in ruthless flood. The mysterious powers in sun and stream cannot therefore be taken lightly. They must be treated in whatever way proves to be required if their favor is to be won and their hostility averted.

And this consideration leads us to the remaining pair of categories. Their importance has already been implied in the preceding paragraphs. Of the extraordinary happenings, some work out in such a way as to favor primitive man's effort to satisfy his insistent needs. Others work out to his disadvantage. They disappoint his hopes, deny him what he has longed for, and may even cause his death. A happening may thus be lucky or it may be unlucky. Both of these possibilities have been illustrated in the case of the sun and in that of a river. They might have been illustrated in an indefinite number of other cases. Sometimes the rain falls gently and fruitfully, as often as is required during a long growing season; sometimes it fails entirely for months at a stretch, and sometimes it falls in violent storms that destroy or wash away the crops. Much of the time the moon goes through its phases in orderly fashion; but occasionally some celestial monster partially or wholly swallows it—which brings anxious forebodings of dire calamity. Often a thieving expedition comes off successfully; the hoped-for booty is lured or sneaked away in triumph. But sometimes it fails, perhaps at the cost of serious mishap to the raiding party. Usually, eating the flesh of an animal brings nourishment and renewed vigor to the hungry eater; but it may bring convulsive pain or other symptoms of illness. So this pair of categories is also fundamental in primitive man's mind.

D. THE GENERAL NATURE OF PRIMITIVE RELIGION

With these categories clearly mastered, in the way they are implied in primitive thinking, we are in a position to draw a tentative generalization about the nature of the chief powers recognized by primitive man. It is that they are essentially the powers working in and responsible for the extraordinary happenings that may be either favorable or unfavorable to his endeavors. They are the forces causing these occurrences, and thus showing themselves friendly or hostile to the persons who are dependent on them for the lucky or unlucky outcome. Hence they are treated by whatever techniques seem most likely to win their favor and avert their enmity. And the devices employed fall under one or the other of two general types. If the guiding idea expressed in them is that by some word-perfect incantation or ritual the powers can be compelled to do what men want them to do, the procedure is called a form of "magic"; if the idea is that they must be persuaded, in more humble fashion, to do the right thing by

the poor worshiper, we meet a religious attitude more akin
to that with which a monotheistic religion is familiar. We call
it the attitude of pious petition. And any particular address
to the divinities may express a mixture of these two attitudes,
antithetic though they may well seem to us; indeed, the civilized religionist often combines these same attitudes too. His
official belief is that God can only be persuaded, not compelled, to answer his supplication; none the less, the feeling
may lurk in his mind that some traditional form of prayer
possesses special potency which a spontaneous individual plea
would lack. Hence the powerful appeal of inherited petitions
with their satisfying associations.

Many of the insistent needs which primitive man attempts
to meet by winning the favor of the divine powers are shared
by some group—a family, a clan, or even a larger society. If
so, then the powers are recognized and appeased in a common
rite or group ceremony. A totemic sacrifice is a prime illustration of such a social rite. Some are individual needs, such
as recovery from illness, success in personal combat, protection against some immediate personal danger. If so, then the
powers invoked may be forces socially recognized or not, as
the case may be. Whatever power the individual feels his success to depend on, at that time and place, will be invoked. It
may be a new fetish, to which divine potency is now being
ascribed for the first time; it may be an individual patron who
takes the worshiper under his wing for the rest of his life. If
it is a need whose satisfaction involves harm to some other
person or persons in the same group, the technique of satisfying it is called a form of "black" magic, as in stealing a
neighbor's growing plants while they are still underground,
or fastening upon him some foul disease. As will be readily
appreciated, the arts of black magic have been under social
condemnation throughout human history, except in certain
cultures (like that of the Dobuans) which seem to have made
a virtue of hostility and distrust. These may not only place a
high valuation on competitive rivalry within the group but

also may recognize almost any wily trick as fair competition; in such a society those who fail as sinister magicians will not be approved but will rather be condemned as ineffective simpletons.

The divinities of primitive religion which fit this description most readily are the divine powers working in the major objects and processes of surrounding nature, on which man is so clearly dependent for the food supply which spells continued existence. When, after the long chilling rains of early spring, a priest accompanies an appropriate rite with the words, "Sun! I do this that you may be burning hot, and eat up all the clouds in the sky," he is recognizing a mysterious power in the sun which, in the interest of a good crop during the summer, he is concerned to get on the side of his people if he can. When the Ainu prefaces his midday meal by addressing the millet he is about to eat in the manner already quoted, he is expressing his awareness of a life-giving power in the food which might not have become available in the way that it has, and for whose past boons he is grateful. And a little reflection is all that is needed, I think, to show how the same conclusion applies to most of the forms of primitive religion noted above. In totemism, the worshiper is conscious of a mysterious source of life in the chosen species of animal or plant which serves as his totem and is somehow connected with his sense of emotional unity with other members of his clan. It is of vital moment to him that the power there present be so guided at all stages of his commerce with it that the nourishment and coöperative energy he counts upon are actually supplied.

Problems arise in the detailed interpretation of this totemic situation, not all of which are easy to answer. For example, in many cults whose totem is some animal, the sacred species, far from being the main source of the clan's food supply, is strictly taboo except on occasions of ritual sacrifice. But in a number of these cases there is an economic interchange with some neighboring people, each supplying the other with the article of diet it is itself forbidden to eat. And there is evidence that in other cases we may have come upon a society at an early stage in the evolution of a dietary habit. Flesh that is at an early time taboo, except for periodic sacrificial feasts, may at a later time become a regular item of diet if the animal in question is protected against natural dangers and propagates readily. All that is needed is a series of excuses for multiplying occasions of sacrifice, so that, instead of occurring, say, only once a month, they come to be performed once a week, and then finally once a day or even oftener. In such a process the accompanying ritual will be progressively reduced in scope and importance until it becomes nothing more substantial than our traditional "grace before meat."[2]

As for fetishism, the person who deals religiously with a bone or shell is aware of some unpredictable power that seems to him present in it, and which can spell the difference between success and failure in an important enterprise. The unusual shape, size, color, or what not that has attracted his attention to the fetish is vividly associated with the tense uncertainty that shrouds the outcome of the act on which he is embarking. It seems to him hence that there is some potency in the fetish which, if he can win its favor, will promise success in this larger undertaking—and also which, if it is hostile to him, will bring defeat and perhaps disaster. He does not, however, regard himself as permanently dependent on it as he is on the powers in the sun, the earth, or the rain; therefore if it disappoints him he will not scruple to throw it aside and turn to some other fetish object that seems to harbor more promising possibilities. But if his religion is so completely practical that he experiences no deeper reverential feelings toward any object than those expressed in this relation to a fetish, that relation will be as significant as anything else in his religion. It is of the same sort as his other religious attitudes except for the casual character of the particular attachment involved. In terms of his experience, then, the fetish cannot be reduced to the status of a mere good-luck token, as it is with civilized peoples who have developed a feeling of reverence toward some more august and ideal divinity which then can become the heart of their religion. Such people have separated their anxieties about good and bad luck, and the little objects on which they focus, from these deeper feelings, so that the former no longer constitute a part of their religion.

The phase of primitive religion which seems least easy to harmonize with this interpretation appears in the fact that primitive man typically feels himself dependent not only upon natural objects but also upon a large number of what seem to us purely mythological beings, and attributes to them, too, powers which can help or harm him. The Crow Indians, for example, recognize a host of such entities, which are disclosed in more or less vivid visions and are supposed to be the powers which bring them success in their subsequent enterprises. I cannot take the space to examine in detail the problem thus raised. There is considerable evidence, however, for believing that these powers may not be exceptions to the above generalization, after all. In many cases, at least, they seem to have been imaginatively conceived in the effort to trace an ancestry for familiar natural objects or by seeking anthropomorphically pictured causes behind the forces present in man's environment. This may be the origin of such potent entities as the Thunderbird or Old-Man-Coyote of the Crow Indians, which, once accepted as real, can be readily experienced in a vision or dream and easily associated with the subsequent occurrence of good or bad fortune.

The question, then, how widely adequate the interpretation above suggested will prove to be must be left open, to be decided by further evidence as it gradually accumulates. The next chapter will add supporting considerations of another kind.

E. CLARIFICATION OF SOME DIFFICULT PROBLEMS

There is no question, however, but that this interpretation throws helpful light on some problems concerning primitive religion that baffled investigators of a generation or more ago, and often led to serious disagreements among them. Let us consider a few of these problems.

One concerns the relation between magic and religion. Are these two different affairs? Or are they so related that we may properly call magic a form of religion—the dominant form in many primitive cultures, and probably absent from none? Sir J. G. Frazer, one of the redoubtable explorers in the field of religion, held that they are different, and are so related in time that magic has been the universal precursor of religion as religion, in turn, has been the precursor of science. According to Frazer, "the movement of the higher thought [of man, through history in general], so far as we can trace it, has on the whole been from magic through religion to science."[3]

Now this is a beautifully neat theory; it would be very nice if all the facts fitted comfortably into it. Some do, of course; societies which place a predominant emphasis on magical techniques are likely to be more primitive than others when judged in terms of such impartial criteria as have been mentioned, and if we trace the ancestry of the civilized religions there is much evidence that the farther back one goes, the more dependence on magical performances one finds. However, there are many facts which seem completely at variance with Frazer's proposed historical law. In some primitive cultures one discovers a mixture of magical techniques and persuasive prayers—the former used with some powers and the latter with others, the former used on certain occasions and the latter on others. In fact, there are many invocations in whose case it is difficult to tell whether they should be classified as magic or not. Consider, for example, case 7 in the list of religious addresses given above. Is it the belief of the speaker that if he kindles the fire and performs the rite correctly, the sun will be compelled to come out from hiding and dissolve all the clouds with his heat? If so, it would be a magical incantation. Is it his hope that he may induce the sun as a free and responsive agent to do what he wishes? If so, then we would classify it as a religious prayer. Or is there, perhaps, a confused medley of both attitudes and hopes in the speaker's mind? There is nothing to make this possibility unplausible.* And when we ponder this third alternative, we can see many reasons why it might provide the right explanation of many primitive addresses to divine powers.

After all, a sharp distinction between coercing and persuading is a distinction not of the primitive but of the civilized mind. It reflects the point of view of civilized religion, with its insistence on the appropriateness of humility on man's part when he stands before a divinity possessing superior perfection. From such a viewpoint, an address to God is always an expression of humble beseeching; any idea of bringing magical compulsion to bear upon the Divine Goodness would be fantastically impious. But is there any reason to suppose that primitive man has made this clear distinction? The very fact that he views so many inanimate objects in animistic or quasi-animistic terms shows that he has not clearly separated in his mind the kind of thing that can be mechanically controlled, if one knows the law of its behavior, from the kind of being that cannot be controlled but can only be persuaded by an appeal to its will. Each kind of object is refractory on occasion and responsive on occasion; his problem is the practical one of overcoming its refractoriness and securing its help by whatever procedures seem promising. If tradition has supplied him (as it normally has) with a number of formulas which he repeats under appropriate circumstances when he addresses the divine powers, there may be in his mind nothing more

* Frazer himself recognizes the presence of these possibilities. See *The Golden Bough* (one-vol. ed.), New York, 1940, pp. 56 f.

specific than an awareness of these phrases as hopefully facilitating the result sought through the responsive activity of the power addressed. He may not be conscious at all of any essential difference between facilitating by compulsion and facilitating by persuasion.

If and when this difference does come to be clearly recognized and is firmly grasped as a guide to human action in relation to the world, we have at that time the roots of technological science on the one hand and of civilized religion on the other. The one grows out of the magical aspects of primitive religion and the other out of its nonmagical features; but in primitive religion itself the two are not yet distinguished, but are typically intertwined. The most that we can say, perhaps, is that the farther a primitive group has moved in the direction of a reverent idealization of its divine powers, the more will its addresses to them express the attitude of deferent appeal; while the more its conception of these powers is lacking in ideal attributes, the more its invocations will express a mixture of magical and persuasive attitudes and the more dominant the magical element is likely to be.

Civilized man is not so far from this state as he might fondly suppose; indeed, a sudden practical emergency may be all that is needed to plunge him into it completely. I have already remarked upon the fact that when adherents of a civilized religion pray, they like to use some form of words that is hallowed by long tradition. This preference for word-perfect repetition not only gives them a sense of emotional comfort by reason of the cherished associations of the phrases repeated; it also often betokens an uneasy fear that the potency of the prayer would be lost if it were not repeated in just the right way. God is pleased, they cannot help feeling, not merely by sincerity of heart but also by correctness of speech; he is like a harassed and habit-ridden bureaucrat who processes only those applications that are filled out on the proper forms and rejects all that show the least variation from established rule. And it is especially easy to feel this in unanticipated practical situations where one's immediate need for help overwhelms the carefully articulated insights of his official theology.

With such considerations to ponder, it should not be too difficult for us to appreciate the possibility of a state of mind in which the distinction between the mechanical and the purposive, and hence the distinction between coercion and supplication, has not yet been clearly drawn, and which embodies features of both attitudes in a way that to us would be confusing.

Another feature frequently appearing in primitive religion, which can be readily understood in the light of the above analysis, is the presence of religious attitudes toward the tools whose successful operation is needed for assuring a food supply or the attainment of other important ends. In some cities of India a clerk may do obeisance to his pen before he starts to write with it in the morning, and in many parts of the world farmers practice quasi-religious rites directed upon the plow, the weeder, or the harvesting scythe. There is one passage in the Old Testament which refers to a similar practice: "He sacrificeth unto his net and burneth incense unto his drag, because by them his portion is fat and his meat plenteous."[4] And the last clause of this quotation gives us our interpretative clue. There is a more or less mysterious power in these instruments, revealed in the fact that sometimes they work efficiently in filling their important function, while sometimes they are awkward, ineffective, or bungling. The favor of such potencies, too, needs to be invoked, and as long as any remnants of magical or animistic belief are present, in relation to the physical objects on which man depends, he sees no reason why the same techniques that are employed elsewhere should not be used in dealing with these powers. Hence it is not surprising to find rites and addresses in primitive religions aimed at securing their help. Adherents of a civilized religion feel something of the same attitude, but with them it has become detached from their religion. A traveler who has returned from a long journey will experience an emotion of gratitude toward the ship or the plane or the car that has brought him safely to his destination, and he may at the commencement of a trip catch himself subconsciously invoking his carrier to give faithful service. He feels a somewhat unpredictable power here, vitally affecting his welfare. And if, as is the case with primitive man, there were nothing in his religion appealing to deeper motives than are present in that situation, such an attitude, expressed in appropriate words and acts, would constitute a part of his religion.

Consider now another problem. In civilized religion there is a clear separation between the mysterious power that is dependably seeking the achievement of good and the power (or powers) believed to be working evil. God and Satan are radically different beings. The former is constantly overcoming evil and pursuing his good aim for the world; the latter, assisted by his diabolical cohorts, is trying to frustrate God's high purposes in every possible way.* This separation is carried out in the sharpest possible form in Zoroastrianism, which pictures the course of history as a struggle between Ahura Mazda, who embodies in perfection the principles of light, truth, and goodness, and Ahriman, sinister chief of the forces of darkness. The divine and demonic are in complete opposition. And yet we find that in many civilized languages the words for "divinity" and "demon" are closely related, and sometimes are derived from the same root. In the Indo-European languages the original term was probably "deva" (which means "shining one") and at one stage of Greek thought the word "daimon," from which our "demon" is directly derived, meant simply supernatural beings superior in power and knowledge to man.

How are we to explain this peculiar circumstance, from our point of view so contradictory? Well, suppose that civilized emerges from primitive religion when men come to feel

* This does not mean that God may not at times use painful or destructive means to achieve His good ends.

that divinity must embody moral perfection and could not be sincerely worshiped otherwise. Then the mysterious forces which are responsible for evil must be conceived as entirely distinct from the divine and even as operating in hostility to it; and they, of course, cannot be worshiped, or even function as objects of positive religious feeling.* But if we reflect again on the addresses above quoted, it will be clear that this separation is foreign to the typical attitudes of primitive religion. To primitive man's experience, none of the mysterious powers on which he depends for survival and security always aids him in the way desired, or always disappoints. Sometimes it does the one, sometimes the other. It is the same unpredictable potency in the rain that often makes it fall in gently beneficent showers and occasionally turns it into a destructive torrent. It is the same strange mana in the magician that enables him to fasten a malady upon some enemy and to cure that very disease. So throughout the roster of primitive powers. In brief, none of them is always good or always bad, for to the primitive mind "good" means that which helps him in his struggle for success among the uncertain vicissitudes of nature; "bad" means that which thwarts him, bringing disappointment, deprivation, suffering, or death. The same power is therefore sometimes divine, sometimes demonic. Many factors may coöperate in the process by which, out of this situation, the contrasting civilized viewpoint slowly emerges. But the three essential factors are (1) the discovery that "good" cannot be identified merely with the satisfaction of urgent desires, (2) the formation of an ideal of moral rightness which functions as a standard for distinguishing good from evil conduct, and (3) the attribution of that ideal to some divine power who is conceived to be supremely worshipful because he embodies it. When this threefold transition has occurred, the significant contrast is no longer between

---

* It is true, however, that Satanic cults have occasionally appeared among civilized religions, and more often been suspected. See C. J. Ducasse, *A Philosophical Scrutiny of Religion*, New York, 1953, Chap. XI.

what satisfies dire need in a particular situation and what
frustrates it, but between what furthers the realization of a
clarified moral ideal and what stands in the way of such an
achievement. The power which essentially exemplifies the
former is for that reason a dependable power for good—it
is "divine" in the civilized meaning of the word; whereas any
power conceived to be always frustrating his efforts is a
power for evil—it is "demonic."

The radical difference between these two situations appears
when we note that what is clearly good from the standpoint
of primitive religion—the satisfaction of an insistent need—
may be evil from the viewpoint of an advanced civilized religion; for it may obstruct the pursuit by an individual or
group of the highest good for all men, which such a religion
will include in its conception of the valid moral ideal. The
history of conceptions of a "sky god" is exceedingly instructive to trace in this connection. Since the sky is not only a
universal canopy and protector for all people but also displays
the orderly motions of the celestial bodies, it comes readily to
symbolize an ideal of just, impartial, and kindly rectitude,
as that ideal slowly takes shape in the minds of the religious
and moral leaders of the race. Thus it is no accident that
whereas, for many primitive peoples, the power in the sky
is just one uncertain force among others in their universe,
God as conceived in civilized religions is often pictured as
dwelling in the sky and in several cases is clearly a personification of the sky itself. It is notable that several of the "high
gods" are apparently identified with the sky power; in view
of the distinctive features of a high god, such an identification
is very natural.

This consideration of "divine" and "demonic" in primitive and in civilized religion, revealing the permeation of the
latter in its more developed forms by the awareness of a
universal moral standard absent in the former, enables us to
examine certain other phenomena of primitive religion which
have baffled many students of the subject but are readily

understandable in terms of this analysis. The reader will re-call those addresses in the above list which seek the help of certain divine powers in carrying through a military or plun-dering expedition successfully. These indicate, as has been noted, the absence in the primitive mind of any sense of moral responsibility beyond the limits of one's own social group, and a confidence, so far as concerns the religious aspect of their behavior, that whoever is their enemy is an enemy of their divinities too. Now we are prepared to understand the ideas and practices of certain groups whose regular vocation is some form of crime—that is, an activity which from the standpoint of a broader social perspective would be branded as criminal. There have been groups in the hinterland of the Bombay Presidency in India whose caste occupation falls un-der this description. In most such cases it was believed that this occupation was assigned them by some divine power, and they accordingly held certain appropriate religious rites when embarking on or returning from their nefarious enterprises. In one case the tribe eked out a somewhat precarious living by making and circulating counterfeit coins; its members gave to their divinity, as a tithe, $12\frac{1}{2}$ percent of the gains won by this devious vocation.

With a civilized religion, its sense of universal moral re-sponsibility has become so deeply entwined with people's re-ligious attitudes that, except for war between nations or civil war, such practices as these would be quite impossible; it would be taken for granted that divine blessing never sup-ports antisocial acts. Hence groups which fall into criminal activity in a modern civilized society would not suppose that they could build a religious cult to give them support and assurance. But if the theory drawn from the above analysis is correct, there is no reason why such cults should not exist in primitive societies; in fact, we should expect them, for the same reasons that we should expect something like totemism, or practices designed to appease the powers present in the fructifying processes of nature. Primitive religion typically lacks a sense of general ethical responsibility; it fills its role in connection with whatever unpredictable forces affect favorably or unfavorably the vital activities of any individual or group. If, then, a particular group finds itself in a situation where it is struggling to satisfy its needs in ways that would be regarded as criminal from a broader social viewpoint, that fact does not at all prevent the rise of religious attitudes and acts focused on the mysterious powers that make for success or failure in their struggle. In time of war even the adherent of a universal civilized religion reverts, though with some qualms of conscience, to this orientation; he is confident that his battle is the Lord's battle and his enemy the Lord's enemy. In fact, an actual outbreak of war is not necessary for this to happen. Goaded by the frustrations, sufferings, and resentments which were the bitter fruit of the first world conflict, the leaders of Nazi Germany frankly abandoned the ethical internationalism of Christianity and adopted a tribal cult which openly glorified Germanic nationalism and gave religious support to an aggressive crusade for its promotion. And this reversion may appear in other forms than that of fanatical national feeling. One year, when Brooklyn and St. Louis were battling down to the wire for the National League pennant, a young clergyman knelt on the steps of Brooklyn's City Hall and prayed for the success of the Dodgers. In the heat of the struggle he apparently forgot that the Christian God is impartially concerned for St. Louis as much as for the borough across the East River; his eager petition assumed that the Deity could be persuaded to become a Brooklyn ally.*

Shall we examine in this same connection the Bacchic and phallic cults that are frequently found in primitive religion, but which the universal faiths of civilized life condemn as essentially irreligious? By a "Bacchic cult" I mean any form of religion which centers around some intoxicating drink, attributes sacredness to it, and encourages its use for religious

* St. Louis won the pennant.

purposes. By a "phallic cult" I mean any form which focuses religious attention upon symbols of the sex organs, male or female, and is likely to encourage, at certain times or under certain conditions, sacred prostitution.

Such cults are not only very widespread among primitive and some civilized peoples—witness Dionysian festivals among the Greeks and rites connected with the divine Soma in India—but new instances of them are constantly being born when social conditions happen to be propitious. As recently as the late nineteenth century a Bacchic cult arose somewhere below the Mexican border, which centered around a drink made from the button of a small cactus called the peyote. In some form it may have existed much earlier, but at this time it began to enlarge its reach, first to Indian tribes in Oklahoma, then to others farther north. At each expansion it was adapted to its new environment by some leader who had found religious significance in its capacity to produce a sense of intense exaltation and variegated visions. By 1912 it had spread very widely and had split into several sects, some of which attempted to combine it with Christian elements.

Now civilized man gets drunk too, and finds the experience more or less exhilarating, but he is at present unable to make a religious virtue out of it. For the advanced civilized religions have discovered that intoxication is dangerous; it removes the controls which guard a person against descent into moral laxity. A man under the spell of this potion has lost the possibility of intelligent self-control, so essential to an alert and sober devotion to the spiritual virtues of integrity, justice, and love. Hence several of the great religions have forbidden the use of intoxicating drink, as one of their basic commandments; they deeply distrust it as an enemy of all that is morally and religiously good. But this lesson primitive man has not yet learned. He feels intensely the need for excitement—for the seductive thrill that lifts him out of his humdrum routine and reveals emotional possibilities that are very intriguing. By swallowing this ready concoction he can at any time induce a trance, and produce visions of glorious achievement, perhaps even ecstatic hallucinations. They are not, however, hallucinatory to him, for the line between reality and fancy is not clear in his mind; and since he has not yet discovered his capacities as an intelligent moral agent, he cannot distinguish between ethically constructive forms of exhilaration and thrills that simply satisfy some vigorous need of the moment or nourish hope for wonderful boons in the future. Here, he finds, is a mysterious potency that is as significant as the power for renewed life in the totem animal or the power in a fetish to bring success in some hazardous plight. It is a potency strange, extraordinary, and unpredictable—not in the sense that there is uncertainty as to whether a queer effect will be produced, but in the sense that it is quite uncertain what form that queer effect will take. In any case, it will meet an insistent need, especially when the habit of using it has been formed, and it will give a temporary sense of vigor, hope, and happiness that is absent in the ordinary course of life.

The same principles apply to our quest for an understanding of phallic cults. These have horrified many students of primitive religion, who assume them to mean a religious encouragement of sexual license and the elevation of obscenity to the status of a religious value. Such a horror is natural enough when one fails to catch the real motive expressed in these symbols and their accompanying rites. Civilized religions have learned in the course of time how important and how difficult is a wise moral control of man's sexual impulses, and how easily their appeasement can be pursued in ways quite inconsistent with the spiritual mastery of the body's demands that is essential in a truly matured character. Hence the persistent attempt of civilized societies to develop and maintain institutions which, even at the cost of some prudery or asceticism, radically discipline these impulses. They do this not only in the interest of stable family relationships but also to the end of making sex serve rather than obstruct the higher moral potentialities in the relations between men and women. Now primitive societies, too, discourage promiscuity among adults, and in most cases their marriage institutions expect monogamy for the common man; only chiefs and other prosperous aristocrats can afford the varied pleasures of a harem. But divorce and remarriage may be very easy, and fairly uninhibited relations before marriage may be explicitly encouraged by their customs. In short, primitive groups accept the sexual drive as being the powerful force that it is, merely attempting to channel it in such ways as will secure the kind and degree of social stability through the succession of generations that seems to them essential. There is, however, much about its nature and its role in propagation that naturally calls for recognition in the form of religious rites with appropriate symbols.

On the one hand, there is the mysterious vigor of the sex urge, unpredictably but energetically asserting itself; and there is the ecstatic thrill of sexual union, with all its varied nuances of partial frustration or high fulfillment. To the primitive mind a "power" reveals itself here, more naturally symbolized by the erect male organ than in any other way, which may help or hinder the satisfaction of man's vital need just as truly as in the case of powers present elsewhere in the physical or social scene.

But this is only part, and perhaps the less important part, of the religious significance which lies in this range of primitive man's experience. For on the other hand there is the need of progeny, the fulfillment of which most primitive peoples have learned to be connected with the sexual act. The reader will have noted among the addresses above listed those which include a petition for children. Primitive man, for various reasons, is eager for progeny—to perpetuate family and clan despite the inroads of disease, to assure added help in the ceaseless struggle for the necessities of existence, to provide affection and care when he sinks into the senile weaknesses of old age. Now sexual intercourse may be followed by pregnancy and birth or it may not; the same strange potency that helps or hinders the urge for satisfying union also evidently needs to be coerced or appeased in order that the union may be fertile instead of barren. And it is not a difficult step of the imagination to associate the forces that make for human fertility with those which affect the productivity of the animals and plants on whose existence primitive man depends for his food supply. Here is a natural field for the operation of sympathetic magic, and many of the practices connected with phallic symbols or otherwise arousing the horror of civilized moralists are readily understood in terms of these motivations.

Among the Dobuans, for example, husband and wife by convention have intercourse in the yam gardens which are counted on to provide their food for the following year. This is made possible by the strict privacy with which each family's growing yams are guarded, but the main reason for the custom is undoubtedly the belief that thus the productivity of the garden is assured and enhanced. Agricultural festivals culminating in certain forms of sexual license, and the practice of "sacred prostitution" at the temples, especially at times of drought when the harvest is threatened with loss, are surely to be explained in terms of these concerns and magical assumptions. Primitive man is eagerly seeking in these special ways, which seem to him appropriate and promising, to secure the favor and avert the hostility of the potent forces which are the causes of fertility in man, beast, or vegetable crop. A spiritualized sexual ideal is as yet beyond his ken.*

F. THE WORLD OF PRIMITIVE MAN

At this point we may well pause to consider in what respects the typical attitude of civilized man toward the environing world of nature, grounded as it is in what we would call a more scientific orientation, differs from the attitude

---

* Hinduism is the one great civilized faith which has so reinterpreted phallic symbols as to harmonize them with high spiritual ideals.

of primitive man. Persons who have not patiently explored the realm of primitive experience are likely to run astray in answering this question. They readily suppose that the difference lies in primitive man's failure to believe in the ubiquity of causal order in the world, or—if this mistake is avoided —that it lies in his appeal to "supernatural" rather than "natural" causes to account for the occurrences that perplex him. These are, at the very least, misleading ways of describing the contrast. In general, the primitive mind believes even more unqualifiedly and trustingly than modern Westerners do in the ubiquity of causal relationships, and the distinction between supernatural and natural causes is a civilized distinction which has no meaning in primitive man's experience. All happenings, and the powers that cause them, exist in one and the same world for him. Sympathetically and more adequately understood, the difference is twofold.

First, civilized thinkers have learned to distinguish more clearly than primitive man between emotionally vivid associations and verifiable connections between events, and to picture the surrounding world predominantly in terms of the latter rather than the former. Primitive man also pictures "ordinary" happenings in this manner, so far as he takes time to picture them at all, but the vast and disturbing realm of the extraordinary he views in terms of a structure determined by what we have found to be subjective associations rather than objectively verifiable law. His world is a world in which manipulating names produces effects on the thing named, in which imitating rain causes rain, in which a malevolent incantation over a garment leads to some dire consequence to its wearer. And he can always rationalize the inevitable failures that occur by admitting the constant possibility of countermagic, by recognizing that he may have unwittingly omitted some essential condition of success, or by attributing strong resistance to the quasi-personal will with which he may be dealing. The causal powers which he sees operative everywhere are conceived in harmony with this perspective on the way in which things happen in his world; they are the obvious potencies in events, or the hidden forces behind them, through which these vivid associations assume in his mind undeniable reality. They therefore inevitably become the objects of practical attention in his effort to bend the course of events in directions more satisfying to his urgent needs.

Second, civilized man is the heir of much solid scientific achievement; happenings that previously seemed mysterious have been explained in ways which have eliminated the mystery. As a result of such success he can make predictions about them of the same sort that he confidently makes about the "ordinary" processes of nature. His forbears discovered regular laws governing lunar eclipses and also the rudiments of a science of meteorology, so that the occurrence of rain could be anticipated with high probability. Thus, such happenings as these have been for him transferred from the domain of the extraordinary to the realm of the ordinary, about which he usually feels no anxious concern; and the powers which he had previously invoked, and conceived in more or less animistic form, have disappeared from his picture of the cosmos. Once the laws of eclipses are known, there is no longer any place for the monster unpredictably devouring the moon; once the science of meteorology is well established, there is no longer any place for the capricious rain god whose favor can be supplicated or compelled by imitative magic. Images and feelings that arose with belief in such beings may still persist for a time and exert some influence on people's conduct, especially in times of drought or devastating storm. But as laws permitting verifiable prediction are more and more discovered, and knowledge of them is spread by education, these relics fade away and are replaced by patterns of order analogous to those exhibited in the realm of ordinary happenings. Moreover, for civilized man, in the West at least, the success of this achievement has been so great as to generate a confidence that, so far as physical nature

is concerned, whatever mystery still remains can and will be
cleared up in the same fashion. In virtue of this confidence,
the educated Westerner has extruded from his picture of the
cosmos even those divine powers previously supposed to be
present in the many phases of nature not yet scientifically
explained. Thus his total world has become a field in which
ordinary law is believed to reign, and whatever mysterious
force he still feels it necessary to assume has been pushed
outside the detailed happenings of nature to the position of
first cause, or ultimate goal of the cosmic process. Primitive
man, by contrast, gives little conscious attention to the realm
of ordinary law. He interprets causal relationships in terms
of his emotional reaction to the realm of the extraordinary;
hence his world is replete with powers which, without his
realizing it, are projections of subjective associations, as these
are determined not merely by his dependable observations
but also by his hopes, his fears, his feelings of gratitude, his
vengeful animosities.

In view of these pretty radical differences between the
basic attitudes of primitive and civilized man toward the
world, it is enticing to raise the question: What is the religious experience of primitive man like when viewed from
the inside? How does it compare with the religious experience of civilized man in the presence of the divine? It is much
easier to ask this question than to answer it. Our own feelings
have been so deeply affected by all that enters into a civilized
orientation toward the world that it is almost impossible for
us to make vivid to ourselves the typical reactions of primitive
man as he confronts the beneficent and threatening mysteries
of his universe. The one thing that can be confidently said
is that much of what forms the core of civilized religious
experience must be absent—the reverent awe before a Greatness conceived as creator of the world and determiner of its
destiny, as the source of all that is good and beautiful in our
experience, as the embodiment of wisdom and truth, as the

savior of man from wrongness and death. What can we affirm
to be present on the positive side?

Well, primitive man's state of mind must be a complex of
very varied factors, not all of which need to be present in
any given case and any one of which may be especially emphasized. The complex as a whole is almost certainly not as
clearly unified and stabilized as it would be with civilized
man; and it can probably run the gamut from hope to despair, from grief to joy, from humble supplication to aggressive hostility, more readily and quickly than would be possible
for him. If the above portrayal is on the right track, the
factor in the complex that usually plays the most vigorous
role is an anxious tension before the uncertainties of nature
that may spell luck and prosperity or mischance and disaster.
Intimately bound up with this feeling would be fear of the
threatening and the dangerous, and not far in the offing would
be a lively sense of what we would call the weird and un-
canny aspects of the world. Frequently associated with these
emotions would be gratitude for the boons, hoped for or unanticipated, that nature has brought, and a thrill of excitement spontaneously produced or stimulated by drama and the
dance. Occasionally, at least, there would be a sense of awe
or esthetic joy before the grandeur of the powers that are revealed; and when fate suddenly strikes, a dumb prostration
before unavoidable calamity or overwhelming force. Sometimes a wish to identify with some divine spirit must enter
into the complex, and not infrequently a bumptious delight
in manipulating a magical potency toward chosen ends. Rare,
but not completely absent, would be an encouraging trust in
divinities especially ready to show their beneficence—growing into a stably confident assurance in the case of the heaven-
power as the tested source of dependable order in the seasons
and the revolutions of the luminaries above. On the occasion
of special crises in the life of an individual—such as birth,
puberty, illness, death—the emotions naturally aroused by

these experiences blend with the more general feelings above described in ways that accentuate both, and give them a distinctive color that can be suggested but not easily described. Civilized man doubtless comes nearest to sharing this complex of feelings in those situations where his sophisticated adjustment to the world fails to give him the security that it ordinarily provides, so that he can hardly avoid reverting to a largely prescientific orientation. Or perhaps his best clue is a vivid recollection of the emotions of childhood, when—not yet having grown into the stable world of an adult—he sensed the presence of mysterious and magical forces.

III

From Primitive to Civilized Religion

But thus far our discussion of primitive religion has been couched in terms of a rather narrow setting. We have analyzed it in the light of certain characteristics that struck us vividly as we pondered typical primitive addresses, in their contrast with familiar features of our own religion. Accordingly, the kind of explanation achieved at this point is pretty limited; it accounts for primitive divinities merely in the sense of identifying them in their role in primitive man's experience as a whole, and in their obvious difference from the divinities recognized in civilized religion.

Can we develop a fuller and more significant explanation in the framework of a broad perspective on human history, religious and otherwise? Can we place ourselves in the position where an answer might be given with some confidence to such questions as: Why did primitive religion take the forms that it has taken? Why, when civilization arose in certain areas on the surface of our planet, did religion, instead of disappearing, become transformed into the great faiths of civilized mankind? If we can achieve a more comprehensive explanation of this sort, in harmony with everything that seems assured in our historical knowledge at large, it will be possible not only to understand primitive religion in this wider setting but also to anticipate what is distinctive in the civilized religions, and to see how natural those distinctive features are in the total growing experience of man in relation to his world. Such an explanation will inevitably be somewhat speculative, but speculative in a good sense, the sense required by a philosophical understanding of religion. One need not fear speculation as long as the comprehensive orientation he adopts is accepted tentatively rather than as a rigid dogma, is subjected to progressive correction by our growing knowledge, and its generalizations are properly limited. In fact, one can hardly think seriously in the field of comparative religion without having such a total perspective in the back of his mind; the important question is whether it is a naïve product of wishful and prejudiced thinking or is adopted with a sense of responsibility to the well-attested facts of history, and is guided by some familiarity with the ways of explaining the relation between primitive and civilized religion that have seemed persuasive to influential thinkers in the past.

A. WESTERN THEORIES OF RELIGIOUS HISTORY

Before we try to articulate such an inclusive orientation on our own, it will be well to examine briefly the speculative theories that have dominated previous Western thinking in this field, to make sure that our proposal profits by whatever virtues they can show and avoids falling into their errors. By and large, there have been two such views—one widely prevalent in European thought during the seventeenth and eighteenth centuries, the other dominating the late nineteenth century and the early years of our own. The former is appropriately called the "degeneration" theory of religion, while the latter is usually referred to as the "evolutionary" theory. Consider first the essential assumptions of the former of these views.

This theory arose in a historical situation in which explorers were bringing back to Europe from America, Africa, and the East reports of the strange religious practices they found in those regions, and European thinkers were trying to understand these descriptions in harmony with the general framework of ideas in which all social facts were being coherently interpreted. The crucial factor in this framework was the belief of many thinkers in an early "Golden Age" of history, antedating the social, political, and economic corruptions which they saw around them and which they were eager to bring to an end. This belief appeared in two forms in the period we have in mind; one held by devout Christians who accepted literally the story in Genesis about the life of Adam and Eve in the Garden of Eden before they fell into sin, the other by romantic naturalists who pictured primitive man as living in an innocence and simplicity not yet sullied by the evils which came with advancing civilization. Given a pre-suppositional pattern in which such ideas were uncritically accepted, it was natural that explanations offered by thinkers concerned with the history of religion exemplified the degeneration theory, and that they did so in these two ways.

One way was adopted by orthodox Catholics and Protestants who felt bound by their view of the Bible to interpret religious facts in conformity with its historical statements. From this standpoint, it seemed evident that the original religion of mankind—that practiced in the Garden of Eden by Adam and Eve—was a pure and true monotheism, uncontaminated by any form of error. But Adam and Eve sinned, and their descendants fell deeper and deeper into moral degradation. One consequence of this collapse of man's original virtue was that he lost his high ethical conception of God and began to entertain a cruder polytheism. He believed in a host of demonic powers which he thought might be persuaded to satisfy his selfish wishes through magic and sacrificial gifts. This tendency of religion to degenerate continued to display itself throughout human history except for those areas influenced by the work of the Hebrew prophets and of Christ. These teachers were specially sent by God in his mercy for mankind to combat this otherwise fatal trend toward idolatry and corruption. Thus Christianity is essentially a reëstablishment, through God's gracious and loving aid, of the early religion of Eden, when Adam and Eve lived in an intimate filial relation with God; the other religions exemplify the various barbarisms and pernicious crudities into which that pure faith has degenerated among peoples to whom God did not send accredited messengers. Among these, the so-called primitive religions exemplify them in an especially mischievous way.

The other form of the degeneration theory was adopted by many of the deists and those whom they influenced. They believed in a religion "of nature," which prevailed originally among mankind, and which instilled a simple and rational set of beliefs about God, moral obligation, and human destiny. This natural religion had, however, become corrupted, largely as a result of the machinations of clever priests who saw in man's susceptibility to superstition an opportunity to expand their authority and power. They taught that they were the special agents through whom the divine governance of man was to be exercised, and that access to God and influence over Him could only be secured by special techniques in which they alone were competent. From this standpoint Judaism and Christianity, as well as the other religions, illustrate the historic tendency toward corruption; all alike need to be purged from superstition and reduced to the rational religion of nature which had obtained in the beginning.

Neither of these forms of degeneration theory could, of course, maintain itself unchallenged in an age permeated more and more by the attitude of modern science. During the eighteenth and nineteenth centuries facts bearing on the historical and comparative study of religion were accumulated with increasing rapidity, facts which could only with considerable violence be fitted into the degeneration scheme.

Doubts about the Garden of Eden story and the supposed primitive Golden Age of mankind, together with the increasing influence of an evolutionary point of view in the study of human history, deprived the assumptions underlying the degeneration theory of their traditional supports and opposed them by other assumptions at least equally plausible. In fact, these old ideas have been entirely abandoned by naturalistic historians, whose framework of thought allows them no place; they are also quite uncongenial to presuppositions expressing the contemporary climate of anthropological study. The abandonment has not been so complete in the case of orthodox Christian thinkers. As would be expected, there are some well-attested facts about primitive religion which, if selected and emphasized, give a certain plausibility to the theory of degeneration. The most important of these facts are those which were mentioned in Chapter I when we were thinking of the "high god" cults. Such cults suggest the possibility that the peoples among whom they are found had at an earlier time known a more civilized form of theism, which had become corrupted by the infiltration of magical practices and by the notion that there are demonic forces operating in the world which must be placated if they are not to frustrate man's hopes. Among recent thinkers who have interpreted the whole history of religion under the guidance of such an emphasis are S. H. Kellogg, Andrew Lang, and Wilhelm Schmidt.[1]

With the general decline of the degeneration theory in the late eighteenth and the nineteenth centuries, however, the perspective that replaced it in the minds of the vast majority of serious thinkers was provided by the evolutionary theory. The central and distinctive idea in this approach reflected an assumption that in one fundamental respect was the direct opposite of the basic assumption of the degeneration theory. The latter held that the main cause which accounts for the significant changes evident in the history of religion is a tendency in man to degenerate—to fall away from the purer religious ideas that he has enjoyed in the past into cruder and more barbarous ones, dark with superstition. The assumption of the evolutionary theory, by contrast, is that the underlying cause of these changes is a tendency to develop from less adequate religious notions toward an ideally enlightened theology such as the highest achievement of civilized religion reveals. In the late eighteenth century this assumption was suggested and supported by the faith characteristic of the Enlightenment, that man gradually progresses through the centuries from ignorance to rationality—a faith specifically applied to the historical panorama of religion by such French optimists as Condorcet and such German idealists as Lessing and Herder.[2] In the early nineteenth century Hegel and his followers supplied a comprehensive and systematic philosophical structure into which this belief in religious progress could be coherently fitted; a little later, through the work of Darwin, a theory analogous to it so far as certain basic convictions are concerned attained scientific respectability, and seemed to give this evolutionary perspective both detailed articulation and a wealth of factual confirmation. Life itself, in all its manifold forms and phases, appeared to exhibit a process of development from very simple organisms, realizing few potentialities, to quite complex ones, able to express richer and far more varied capacities in their adjustment to environing conditions.

In the late nineteenth and early twentieth centuries it was almost universally taken for granted among Western students of the history of religion that this significant phase of human life could be rendered intelligible in terms of such a basic pattern, primitive religion exhibiting the relatively simple forms and civilized religion—especially, of course, Christianity as Western Europe had come to interpret it—exemplifying the more complex forms which indicate the goal toward which the whole evolutionary process is aiming. For, just as each of the degeneration theorists subtly assumed that his own conception of religion, being the true and highest one, must disclose the nature of the original faith from which mankind has historically fallen, so the evolutionary theorists were equally blithe in assuming that the religion they accepted must indicate the final end toward which the whole course of development is moving. The task of the student of religion, from this point of view, was to fit the kaleidoscopic facts of religious history into the pattern determined by this perspective, and most of the important contributions to the subject during this period were more or less systematic attempts to carry out this task.

A more specific clue to what this enterprise was conceived to require can be derived from the concept of the "tree of life" as it was applied at this time by many evolutionary biologists to a genetic explanation of this or that living species. These thinkers, for example, took it for granted—the great illustration is Darwin's famous *Descent of Man*—that if all the evidence could be marshaled and properly organized, it would be possible to trace the complete sequence of living forms which leads up to the emergence of man as the (thus far, at least) highest product of the evolutionary process. So, according to the thinkers who applied this clue to the field of religion, it should be possible to trace a unilinear sequence from the crudest form of primitive religion to the pure Christian monotheism which from their standpoint represents the highest attainment of civilized religion. In terms of this more specific assumption the task of the historian of religion was to determine what the original form of religion must have been, and then to indicate, by systematic appeal to the available facts, through what successive stages it developed from this rudimentary beginning to the particular type of Christian faith he picked as constituting the final goal of the process.

I shall not take the space to illustrate these evolutionary theories in any detail. In the course of the attempt to carry out their program certain serious difficulties appeared—many of them analogous to difficulties that are obvious in the degeneration theory—and as a result of these difficulties the evolutionary assumptions came to be pretty completely abandoned by responsible thinkers a generation ago in favor of a radically different approach.

What were these difficulties? Well, first and foremost there was the perplexing problem of determining in an objective and verifiable fashion what the initial form of religion was, and how it arose. Direct evidence on this matter seems to be lacking; the earliest peoples about whom anything is known are found to be already practicing some sort of cult, implying certain religious concepts and beliefs. Indirect evidence seems to be plausibly reconcilable with a large number of theories and to support no one of them decisively; in fact, the conclusion most naturally and impartially drawn from it is that different peoples, at different times and places, began to express what we would describe as a religious attitude in rather different ways, and that there is no one form of religion that can be definitely established as the prototype of religion everywhere. Herbert Spencer thought that ancestral worship was the earliest form of religion; Tylor that an animistic philosophy of nature provided its core; Durkheim, McLennan, and others that all other phases of religion grew out of totemism; Marett and Preuss that the idea of impersonal mana was the root of more specific religious forms; Max Müller, Tiele, and Reville that divine powers located in the striking objects and processes of physical nature were the earliest beings worshiped; Crawley and Van Gennep that mysterious forces that appear in the biological crises of life constituted the original divinities. And we have already referred to the theory of Frazer, according to which magic preceded religion, the latter replacing it when primitive thinkers became sophisticated enough to realize that magic did not produce satisfactory results. An imposing array of facts could be and was marshaled in support of each of these theories, and likewise an imposing array could be marshaled against each of them—when they were taken, that is, as offering a universally valid explanation of the way religion began in human history.

But, obviously, not more than one of them could be true; and as rival theorists contended with one another, each struggling to torture the evidence into harmony with his pet doctrine, it appeared more and more doubtful whether any such general evolutionary explanation could be securely established. Perhaps the truth is that there was no single original form of religion, and that the dogmatic demand for such a form is simply a misguided application to the field of religion of an idea which has found verifiable support in some other fields. No single original form of art has been discovered out of which all later types of art developed, and no single original set of moral customs or economic habits; why should there be a single initial form of religion?

Naturally, if different thinkers disagreed as to the guise in which religion originally began, they differed also more or less radically on the sequence of stages through which it advanced from that prototype toward its goal in the highest form of civilized religion. We need hardly, therefore, take the time to show what any of the detailed differences on this point were. But it will be profitable to note one of the challenging difficulties which arose in connection with the assumption of these evolutionary theorists that the process of development is aiming at a definite final goal and that they could tell what that goal is. Since most of the investigators who applied this idea to the field of religion were Christians, it is natural that they would identify the final stage of religious evolution with a specifically Christian conception of God and of spiritual truth. What, then, about Islam? By and large, the evolutionary supposition was that time itself is a significant factor in determining the line of historical progress; a later form, provided it has shown its capacity to survive and expand, is thereby proved to be a higher form in relation to those which it succeeds in displacing. Islam was obviously a serious embarrassment to a theory written in terms of the idea that Christianity is the highest product of the evolutionary process in the field of religion. Not only had this great civilized faith, with its several hundred million adherents all over the globe, arisen six hundred years later than Christianity; this was disturbing enough. But it was also the case that Mohammed was acquainted with Christianity and held it in high regard, that he thought of Jesus as the greatest of the prophets preceding him, that he conceived of Christianity (along with Judaism) as a definite historical precursor of Islam; and it is likewise the case that Islam succeeded in displacing Christianity from North Africa, southeastern Europe, and the Near East, never subsequently losing any substantial part of these geographical gains. In terms of the major assumptions of the evolutionary theory, these facts posed for Christian thinkers a puzzling problem. So embarrassing were they, in fact, that many Christian evolutionists in the history of religion reversed the actual temporal order at this point and placed Christianity above Islam in the developmental scale, while not a few of them felt it necessary to devise apologies for this arbitrary procedure. And of course Moslem historians have not been slow to use these considerations as grist to their own mill.

While such difficulties were giving serious trouble to conscientious students of religion during the early decades of the twentieth century, research in the more general field of anthropology was rapidly piling up relevant data and developing the rudiments of a more adequate method than the evolutionary theory provided. One of the major lessons embodied in this sounder method was that a human idea or custom may be superficially the same (or closely similar) in its appearance at different times and places, while its significance to the people who accept and practice it may be quite different as between one social group and another. A certain burial rite, for example, or the belief that some mysterious power is present in the seed of an agricultural product, may mean something radically different if there are differences in the whole pattern of accompanying practices and notions— that is, whether it is the pattern of a totemic clan, or of a society exemplifying some sort of departmental polytheism, or of a culture with a strong ancestral worship, or of a people whose main idea of divinity is like the Melanesian concept of mana. To understand the meaning of such a religious item, one must penetrate beneath the superficial likenesses and differences and see the distinctive role it plays in the whole setting of the society in whose life it is found. From this point of view, the evolutionary theorists could be judged guilty of having misunderstood many even of the facts to which they most confidently appealed—those facts, being "torn out of their cultural context," were used to justify conclusions to which they often lent no real support at all.

Recognition of such considerations led to the result that, for roughly a generation now, responsible research in the field of religious history in the Western world has been dominated by a perspective quite different from that of either of the general theories just described. It might be called the "specific culture theory," as applied to the study of religion along with other social phenomena. Viewed from the standpoint of the degeneration and evolutionary perspectives, indeed, this is not a theory at all—that is, it marks an abandonment of the attempt to set up any general historical scheme into which all significant facts in the history of religion can be industriously fitted. Instead, the aim is to study each social group in its own terms—in the context formed by the ongoing process of its own adjustment to the major conditions under which it lives. The basic task therefore is to analyze it in its own cultural setting, bringing out the meaning of each of its beliefs and practices, religious or other, in their relation to that unique whole. To this end, investigators have consciously sought to avoid carrying into their study of one human culture expectations generated by knowledge gained about another, in the thought that any such anticipation (except in special circumstances) is likely to be misleading rather than helpful; the important thing is to let each society tell its own story, and reveal the significance of each of its ways as the investigator sympathetically immerses himself in its distinctive assumptions and values.

But in a sense it is a theory, too—in the sense that it reflects a guiding general idea as to how the major facts in the history of religion (and of other social institutions) are to be adequately understood. The essence of this idea is that every cultural group has its own characteristic orientation—its own "pattern," to use a now popularized term—that each of its practices becomes intelligible only when its role in this total pattern of living is grasped, and that whatever larger generalizations may ultimately be possible can be securely reached only after many societies have been thoroughly studied in this fashion. Some tentative attempts at "cross-cultural" generalization have in fact appeared, but as yet they are very cautious. As a theory, this way of thinking has developed its own set of basic concepts for analyzing and relating the facts with which the study of religion deals—such concepts as "cultural focus," "integration," "function," "theme," "style," along with the one already mentioned, "pattern"—and these reflect the essential difference between this whole approach and that of the evolutionary theory with its radically divergent categories of interpretation and explanation. Students of cultural history in this period differ among themselves, of course, in the manner in which they have applied this guiding idea, but almost all the constructive contributions to the understanding of man's manifold social institutions in this generation have been written under the influence of this perspective.

So far as religion is concerned, it has proved an exceedingly fertile idea. It has encouraged thinkers to break free from the hampering limitations of previous assumptions as to what sort of thing religion must be, and to find out what it actually is as various peoples practise it in their own characteristic way. Prior to the appearance of this approach almost no one in the West had transcended the frank or subtle control of his thinking by the presuppositions of our Christian culture with respect to what kind of religion is true or false, good or bad; now it became possible to overcome this limitation and to realize what manifold forms religion can assume as it fills its place in the living activities of man. Among other things, it became possible to understand the real significance of such otherwise puzzling phenomena as the Bacchic and phallic cults (see page 63 ff.), without obstructive prejudices against them and also without any need to feel that civilized religion should make some positive place for them.

This outstanding gain in our orientation toward, and appreciation of, religion in its varied cultural manifestations and historical changes will, I trust, never be lost. But the "specific culture" theory, as such, gives no positive answer to one of the major questions which the degeneration and evolutionary theories answered (albeit in more or less erroneous fashion), and which a philosophical approach to the history of religion cannot help asking. How can we best understand the panorama of religion on the surface of this planet, including the civilized religions along with all these manifold primitive cults? Doubtless there is grave danger in premature conclusions on such a vast subject; doubtless any conclusions offered must be definitely conceived as a hypothesis, to be revised in the light of further facts rather than imposed as an a priori framework into which all facts must be willy-nilly fitted; doubtless, also, in the present state of our knowledge, useful generalizations must be formulated with proper limitations. But if these cautions are borne in mind, why should one not endeavor to articulate the most comprehensive picture that present knowledge seems to support? In fact, can any serious student of the subject avoid thinking in terms of some such picture, giving tentative meaning and value, in the way in which only a total orientation can, to every detail that he comes across in his investigations?

And a particular historical question of great interest is involved in this general problem. As was noted above, the available evidence seems to indicate that in at least one of its essential contentions the evolutionary theory was right: every civilized society has developed out of an earlier state exhibiting many of the characteristic features of primitive culture, and (since religion does vary in important respects with the general conditions of man's social life) every civilized religion has emerged from a situation in which many of the marks of primitive religion were present. Why and how did this transition take place? How can we explain it in harmony with the best-attested knowledge that is available about human history in general?

B. A SUGGESTED HISTORICAL PERSPECTIVE

I think that an answer to these questions can be given with a good deal of confidence, provided that we apply it with cautious good sense. This answer assumes that the major forces in the light of which human history becomes intelligible, in all its prime aspects, are the pervasive needs by which men at any given time are dominated. This, I submit, is a thoroughly justified assumption.* It is in harmony with the description of primitive divinities given above. It is supported by all that we know about human history in general. So far as one can judge, none of the major changes that have taken place in man's political, economic, artistic, or educational life can be adequately understood unless they are seen in relation to the growing needs and ruling concerns which required these changes for their fuller satisfaction. The rise, for example, of the "free enterprise" system in modern industry becomes intelligible when we note the increasingly vigorous demands which were frustrated by the detailed restrictions on medieval production and trade; and the more recent trend toward socialism likewise becomes intelligible when we see the new deprivations and insecurities into which large masses of men were plunged by this system when operating without

---

* In saying this I do not mean to imply, of course, that human needs constitute an ultimate factor in every situation in which they appear. In some situations certain needs can be helpfully explained in terms of their relation to physiological or other processes.

sufficient governmental control. I mention this illustration simply in the hope that it will give initial plausibility to the guiding assumption which I now propose to apply to the history of religion; its more systematic justification will come in whatever clarifying power it can reveal in that application itself. If it makes understandable the major features of that vast panorama in the reader's mind, it is so far confirmed; if it fails to do so, it is thereby proved incapable of filling its role, no matter what promising analogies it may show to fruitful ideas in other areas of human history.

But a few further words about the general nature of this approach are needed before I explain the main features of my hypothesis. The central aim is to see if we can formulate an acceptable notion of the long-range dominant needs that have revealed themselves in human history, and of the way in which one has succeeded another. We want to do this in such fashion that the outstanding changes that have occurred in the field of religion can be systematically explained by their aid.

Now many readers, I fear, will be disturbed at such a proposal. "Are you going to explain the history of religion in purely human terms," they will ask, "without recognizing the role of God Himself in this process?" Not at all. If God is real,* the long and tortuous course of man's search for the divine is also a process of the divine self-revelation to man. Whatever insight comes as we sincerely seek God is also a part of God's progressive disclosure of Himself to us. But I also believe that it would be presumptuous—even impious—to assume that we can explain religious history, in its detailed vicissitudes, *as* the process of God's revelation to man. This would imply the supposition that we can place ourselves in the position of God, thus being able to survey the course of the universe from His vantage point and describe the events of history as He would describe them. This is a

* I shall record my own conviction on this matter in the final chapter. See p. 523 f.

bolder supposition than I would dare to make, and I believe most of my readers will agree that we should not make it.

Well, if we reject that assumption, only one way of describing and explaining the history of religion seems to remain—the humanistic way that we have thus far been taking for granted. Without denying that the religious ideas we are studying are a gradual revelation of God to man, we have been aiming to understand them as man's ideas about God. This seems clearly possible. For whether or not they are God's disclosure to man, they are quite obviously man's notions about God, and as such it is feasible to examine them. We followed this lead in the preceding chapter; I propose to pursue the same route in dealing with the broad historical problem that now challenges us. It expresses nothing more radical than the recognition that we who are trying to understand the course of religion through the centuries are not God but men. It will be illuminating in many ways to pursue significant relationships between man's ideas of God and his concerns about other matters as he proceeds under changing circumstances with the adventurous business of living. These relationships we shall seek to discover.

But another comment also needs to be made before my hypothesis is expounded. It is that we must not let our explanation of religious history in humanistic terms take the form of a quest for some single basic religious need or instinct. A generation ago it was the fashion among psychologists to propose lists of original instincts in terms of which the recurrent features of human behavior might be explained, and many historians of religion looked among such lists for a distinctive religious instinct, by appeal to which this area of human life could be accounted for. These efforts have pretty generally been abandoned, and it is vital to see that even if they were successful our present purpose would not be forwarded by them. We wish to make intelligible, if we can, not only why man is religious but also why the outstanding changes have taken place in the way in which his religiousness has been expressed—such as the change, over many parts of the earth's surface, from primitive to civilized religion. The changes obviously cannot be explained by appealing to a factor which by definition has remained constant through the transitions which we hope to understand.

And when this essential feature of our task is clearly recognized, the limitations not only of the "instinct" theory but of any attempts to account for religious phenomena in terms of any single major cause become apparent. Followers of Marx, for example, have believed that religious institutions and their modes of operation can be explained in the same manner in which they explain all social phenomena—namely, by appeal to man's innate demand for economic security and economic power. Now, as the above analysis has indicated, there is overwhelming evidence to support the claim that the most striking features of primitive religion can be accounted for in this way, if the stress is on security rather than power and if the accompanying ideas of primitive man about the causal agents in nature are recognized in the essential role they fill. But can civilized religion be thus explained? If there are radical differences (as well as some continuities) between primitive religion and at least the higher civilized faiths, our natural supposition would be that whatever constitutes the main explanatory factor in the former will for that very reason not provide the true explanation in the latter. At least, the general framework in terms of which any serious study of religion proceeds should fully allow for this possibility, and not assume in advance that civilized and primitive religion be referred to precisely the same causes. As a matter of fact, I hope to show clearly that there are fundamental differences in the two cases, and that if they are not adequately recognized the true genius of civilized religion in its more developed forms is likely to be completely missed. So far as Marx is concerned, a mere glance at the living civilized religions suffices to show that in their pioneers the motive of economic ambition—and even the concern for economic security—is least influential; they are readier than any other group of men to subordinate such desires to the pursuit of other values that they have envisioned. And the same motive must be vigorous (though not necessarily *as* vigorous) in their followers, since idealization of and identification with the attitudes of the founder is a significant factor in the practices, sentiments, and doctrinal beliefs of the great civilized religions.

What, then, constitutes the core of a sound explanation? I shall outline the essence of my proposed answer first, and then elaborate a few of its major details. I hope that it will provide not only an acceptable interpretation of the features of primitive religion above emphasized but also an anticipatory clarification of the novel ideas of the civilized religions which we are soon to study.

When I survey the historical panorama of human life in broad perspective, trying to catch the contour of the forest without being distracted by the individual trees, I seem to see that two great human needs and two corresponding dominant concerns have been reflected in the course of human history, the second rising to this position only when and where the first has been basically satisfied. The first is man's need to learn how to master the subhuman forces of nature sufficiently to win an assured position in relation to them. Until about three or four thousand years ago this was the pressing need everywhere and among all peoples. Men were striving to secure the conditions under which they could survive in the presence of the perilous forces that surrounded them. Many were the cultures which came into existence, carried on the struggle for a longer or shorter time, and then failed, succumbing to some destructive power to which they were unequal when the crucial test came. And this is still the pervasive need and continuing problem of most of the contemporary groups which one would classify as primitive. They have managed to survive the dangers of the past; they have established cultural habits which enable them to keep on existing from year to year, from generation to generation, in face of the perils of the present; but they have not succeeded in satisfying this need adequately and dependably enough to be freed from the harassing burden of this absorbing preoccupation and to allow any other major concern to occupy the center of attention. But, beginning about three millenniums ago or a bit earlier, some societies did succeed in solving the problem posed by this need, with sufficient assurance so that it no longer aroused the pervasive and anxious fear that it had done before; the conscious attention of their leaders (and to some extent of others) was liberated from this preoccupation and given a chance to focus upon other concerns which hitherto had not been present or at least not so pressing.

And in their case one of these other needs became as insistent and dominant as the first had been throughout the long history of man preceding that successful achievement. This was the need for each group of human beings to learn how to live successfully and happily with other groups of men and women on the surface of this planet. The same factors which made possible a solution of the first great need thrust people into increasingly complex interaction with and interdependence on each other. This interaction and interdependence led to ominous conflicts between social groups, on a scale and of an intensity previously unknown. Efforts naturally were made to deal with these conflicts by the same techniques that had been employed to resolve hostile rivalry within a tribe and struggles between tribes for some crucial advantage. For the most part, down to the present, men have continued to pin their faith on this kind of effort; war—growing in destructive impact from the local clashes of twenty-five hundred years ago to the world catastrophes of the present day—is only the outstanding symbol in history of this fact. And during the last century civilized penetration of the planet has become so thorough and so persistent that even the primitive groups that would prefer to preserve their traditional culture in isolation from other people have found that they can no longer do so; they are swept willy-nilly into the network of this all-pervasive interdependence. They must adapt themselves successfully to its requirements or perish; they can no longer carry on their mode of life in terms of the presuppositions that were valid when all peoples still existed in the state of primitive adjustment to nature. But the attitudes and methods naturally employed in this situation have proved less and less adequate through this three-thousand-year period of civilized expansion. Instead of the joy of creating, man gives himself all too readily to the grim will to destroy, and it is now apparent that if no remedy is found civilization—Western civilization, at least—will efface itself, and perhaps sweep into annihilation with it all other forms of human existence.

Moreover, with the emergence into a dominant position of this second need and problem, new and breathtaking possibilities in man himself have been discovered—possibilities of a kind of satisfying fulfillment that were hardly glimpsed when men's minds were largely focused upon the uncertain, harassing struggle for the means of sheer survival. It was gradually learned that when he is in unresolved conflict with his fellows man is also in conflict with himself, and cannot realize the joy of free and integrated adjustment to the total universe that surrounds and enfolds him. The problem of these three millennia, then, has become, more specifically, how to learn this lesson of adequate social adaptation in such a way that the threat of universal catastrophe can be averted and these richer possibilities realized.

During the long period prior to the emergence of civilized life, the religious ideas and practices of men reflected, as has been already observed, the dominance of their lives by the first of these two needs. When, through the arts of civilization, men became liberated over large areas of the earth from the absorbing preoccupation associated with that need, religion did not perish (as it might have done) but became radically transformed in ways which reflect, equally clearly, dominance by the second of these two needs and the concerns which it essentially involves. Here lies our basic key to the understanding of the great living civilized religions, in the significant features which they have in common and by which they are readily distinguishable from primitive cults. Instead of seeing the divine through spectacles shaped by the first need, they envision the divine in the perspective determined by the second.

C. ITS CONFIRMATION IN SECULAR AND RELIGIOUS EVOLUTION

The gist of the proposed explanation will, I hope, be sufficiently clear from this brief sketch so that we may now proceed to fill in the main details. I shall not take the space to elaborate them in the manner that would be necessary in a philosophy of history, but only far enough to complete the above account of primitive religion and to prepare the way for an appreciative study of the great civilized religions.

The reader will realize that this interpretation does not depend on the adoption of any particular date as marking the first clear emergence of civilization. Archaeologists and historians will doubtless long disagree as to what conclusion the evidence supports on this matter. I have written as though this crucial transition took place somewhere between 2000 and 1000 B.C., assuming that prior to four thousand years ago people everywhere were living under the essential conditions of primitive society, and that by the later of those dates, at least, some communities had emerged from such conditions and were developing a form of civilized culture. This dividing line ought to be somewhat earlier if it can be established that a civilized adjustment to the environment had been definitely realized before that time in Egypt, China, India, Mesopotamia, or elsewhere. For our purposes the important thing is that such a salient event did occur, and that by the beginning of the first millennium B.C. several such civilized cultures were already successfully functioning and were beginning to absorb the primitive groups on their periphery. There is clear continuity from that time to the present in the transmission of the acquired arts of civilization and their evolution into new forms.

Before that transition (at whatever time it should be dated) men and women were carrying on their existence everywhere under the conditions characteristic of primitive culture,* and this has been the case since that time with groups that have been relatively protected from the impact of the civilized societies or have had the vitality to avoid absorption by them. What were the basic conditions of their existence?

The prominent features of primitive religion discussed in the preceding chapter suggested a partial answer to this question. Let us now complete it and note in what main ways it must be qualified. On the one hand, their major concern was with ways of meeting the elemental needs of physical life and health under the recurring threat of drought, flood, storm, famine, epidemics of disease, swarms of insects, forays of wild animals, or sudden attacks by neighboring groups of men. They built simple structures for protection against rain, sun, and cold; for their food they engaged in berry picking, grubbing for roots, hunting of animals, fishing, herd raising, rude forms of agriculture. Whatever they managed to secure was quickly consumed, except that seeds were preserved for the next season's planting, and (in the case of tribes living far from the tropics) sufficient supplies were stored away to carry them through the coming winter, when ordinary productive activities could not be pursued.

On the other hand, social problems (which occupy the center of the stage under the conditions of civilized life) took, for primitive man, relatively simple forms and were only sporadically critical. Groups of people living together were

* For some purposes it would be important to make divisions within this period, e.g., separating the time before the domestication of animals and the beginnings of agriculture from the later time. But, in the light of present evidence, such a division would have little significance for our understanding of primitive religion.

small, and most of the time each group was separated from others, hence problems caused by interaction between such societies only occasionally became challenging. Problems arising within the group were settled on the basis of tribal custom, except again for occasional cases of disruptive behavior that had to be met in some novel way. The major specializations of function were those due to sex and age; there were of course other class distinctions, giving rise to special privileges and special forms of authority; but they did not create the tense and divisive class consciousness that is a source of hostile conflict in civilized society. For the most part, each person felt his interest to be essentially one with that of his group.

Between one primitive group and another there was ordinarily little contact, even though they lived but a few miles apart. Only adventurous individuals braved the hazards of travel, except on a very limited scale, and commerce was carried on mainly through intertribal markets or trading circles whose procedures were governed by traditional rules. Above all, there was nothing corresponding to war, in the civilized meaning of that word. No tribal chief had the capital required to support an army, or the facilities by which it could be stationed and maintained over a wide territory; modern engines of mass destruction and annihilation of enemies at a distance had not yet been invented. Hence there was ordinarily no attempt to conquer neighboring tribes or reduce them to a permanent status of submissive obedience. Raids, of course, took place by members of one tribe on other tribes. But usually they were for some specific and limited purpose—to avenge an injury to a fellow tribesman, to capture an armful of wives, to steal away some attractive booty. Occasionally, to be sure, there were migrations of the whole clan in search of better hunting ground, grazing pastures, or agricultural soil—migrations induced by change of climate, long-continued drought, or some other persistent danger. When these happened there might well be a fight to the finish with the original possessors of the territory invaded;

if the aggressive newcomers were successful the former inhabitants would be either exterminated, expelled, or their remnants gradually assimilated.

Let us put the essence of the situation briefly and simply.
Primitive man's orientation toward the powers of nature is
determined mainly by his emotional associations rather than
by knowledge of her dependable laws. Because of this fact,
his effort to maintain the conditions of life and of physical
well-being is on the one hand very uncertain in its outcome
and on the other very time-consuming. There is little chance
for any other general goal to occupy the center of attention;
even the quest for power on the part of clever and enterprising
individuals can take only limited forms.

Under such conditions primitive religion naturally assumed
the character that it did, and found expression in the practices
and ideas that were seen in the preceding chapter to be prominent. Like most other early institutions, it was a major aspect
of this absorbing concern with the basic needs of life; the most
obvious modes in which it appears are indelibly stamped
with marks that clearly reflect this situation. Through magical
rites and incantations, through humble and hopeful appeals,
men sought the favor of the more or less unpredictable forces
on which success in this effort seemed obviously to depend; the religious addresses examined above are precisely
what we should expect to meet where religion is filling this
role in such a period of human history. The divinities recognized by primitive religion are the forms which these mysterious powers would naturally take when refracted through
the emotional concern of primitive man, and through the beliefs inevitably shaped under the stress of that concern,
while he remained ignorant of most of the natural laws that
civilized man succeeds in discovering. And we should expect
—what is likewise found to be the case—that other attitudes,
such as come to the fore and undergo significant development
in civilized religion, are not absent from primitive man's consciousness, but are so largely subordinated to the feelings
continually evoked by this consuming endeavor that they have

no chance to evolve or to make more than a feeble and sporadic contribution to the character of primitive religion.

The main qualifications that a person familiar with the facts of primitive society will emphasize in connection with these conclusions are the following. There are primitive societies that have been unusually blessed by nature or favored by accidental good fortune. Also there are societies which have acquiesced more or less contentedly in a truce with nature under the harsh conditions she has imposed, knowing no possibility of any better situation. In these cases no such anxious preoccupation with the conditions of continued existence appears to be present. But these societies have not developed the typical features of civilized religion, and when we view them in broad historical perspective it seems evident that they throw little light on the main forces that have shaped the evolution of religion.

Civilized society in general and civilized religion in particular began to appear in their distinctive quality when enough of the rudiments of what would now be called scientific technology had been mastered so that, in the societies achieving this result, man's anxious fears in the presence of the natural forces vitally affecting his life were radically reduced, except in times of crisis. They were gradually replaced by a confident feeling that he knew how to assure himself a regular supply of the resources on which continued existence depends. His technicians had invented dependable tools and discovered reliable methods for providing a sufficient food supply, season after season; usually he could count on adequate protection against cold, heat, and disease; fairly reliable safeguards had been established against the other major threats that render life precarious and the future insecure. In brief, man had found a solution, which was essentially within his own control, of the first great problem that he had to meet on the surface of this earth; so that his leaders, at least, could begin to give time and thought to other concerns that had either not yet emerged or had not been able to attract the consideration they deserved because of the primary and insistent nature of this first problem. Such a replacement of anxious uncertainty by settled assurance in the presence of the great forces of nature meant that his concern with mysterious powers that must be magically coerced or humbly persuaded to show him beneficence instead of hostility gradually faded away in favor of an awareness of nature as the scene of verifiable law, whose operations he could anticipate with some assurance and whose causes he could confidently control so that they would produce the effects desired.

One might expect, as noted above, that when this transformation has taken place in the minds of the leaders in a civilized society, religion for them would disappear. And indeed, in every generation of civilized history there have been thinkers who assume that it ought to disappear and who expect it to disappear; in their eyes, only a very powerful cultural lag keeps it in existence when, as they believe, the sole justification for it has long since passed away. Primitive religion, to them, is the only kind of religion that can be conceived; so that when science has done away with the need for it, there is no longer any real place for religion in human life. Frazer is the outstanding example, among historians of religion, of this point of view.

But it did not happen this way, and if one assumes that it *must* do so he will blind himself to some outstanding facts in the history of religion and render himself impotent to understand the true genius of the living civilized faiths. It is true that religion is very conservative, especially in its popular forms. One finds, hence, that in all the great civilized religions primitive relics are preserved, and that in time of unusual emotional stress they may well seem to determine the nature of the religion as a whole. The pious Christian today, as in the past, prays, "Give us this day our daily bread," but he has become increasingly sure through the course of history that he knows how to take care of this problem himself; the Deity is for him the ultimate creator of the natural forces on which his food supply depends, but is no longer really imagined, except in emergencies, as providentially determining their operation in detail. Such historical lags are due not merely to the conservative momentum of established habit, which is especially strong in religion, but also to the fact that the necessities of life and health are still very precarious for large groups of people, even in many civilized countries, and their religious feelings inevitably reflect this circumstance. But, as we shall see, the leaders of civilized society well know that this insecurity is not due to any lack of technical competence to provide for the world's economic demands; it is due to their failure, as yet, to solve the basic social problem which becomes man's major concern once he has successfully met the first challenge and established himself in a reasonably secure position against the subhuman forces of nature.

That second pervasive concern, to repeat, is this: How can the various groups of human beings that civilized life throws into increasingly complicated interdependence learn to live successfully and happily with each other? When a society emerges from its primitive state and develops the main arts of civilization, this is the basic problem that it inevitably confronts. Religion does not disappear, and does not remain the same; rather, it undergoes the radical and appropriate change in its character that this situation requires. It now locates its divine powers in whatever major forces are found to be mysteriously involved in the quest for a trustworthy answer to this novel problem. For, here too, while some features of the forces at work are obvious and dependable, some are hidden and uncertain. Man's orientation toward them will be analogous in this essential respect to his orientation toward the unpredictable powers of primitive religion; there will thus be a measure of continuity between primitive and civilized religion, despite their significant differences, and this continuity justifies our use of the word "religion" in both cases and renders it natural.

By thus describing the essence of civilized religion I do

not mean, of course, that its leaders consciously faced their task in these terms. They did not; none of them said, "We meet a drastically novel situation in human history—let us see how our ideas about divine power must be changed so that they will become suited to man's altered needs." No vital step in religion is taken in this way. What I mean is that, under the challenge of this altered situation, the leaders of religion discovered the divine in the mysterious powers present in this new range of human experience and aspiration. No longer could they find it in the typical divinities of primitive man.

How, more precisely, does this transformation come about? What are the major details of the process? Well, when a cultural group advances step by step toward the status of a fully civilized society, what happens, so far as concerns the accompanying revolution in religion, is essentially this. The establishment of dependable technological methods for assuring a regular food supply and guarding against the various threats to life and prosperity permits for the first time the rise of a stable and expanding agricultural community. More capital is accumulated than is needed for consumption before the next harvest is due to appear. This makes possible experimentation with new modes of production and of living in general; it supports a leisure class, which had little chance to arise before but which, once it arises, can engage in such experiments and can give reflective attention to the novel problems of which its inquiring members now become aware. Within any society, the rise of such a group marks the beginning of a process of specialization and of hierarchical stratification which soon makes the problem of happy social adjustment more insistent and difficult than it had been before. Distinctive functions multiply, and with them the corresponding class interests—economic, political, professional, scientific, ecclesiastical, and the rest. The various groups performing these functions and feeling these interests are dependent on each other for their continued existence and well-being, but the membership of each of them transcends the ties of family and clan which in a primitive society create a spontaneous sense of emotional unity. They and their members have to find some way of achieving coöperative harmony with each other, despite the absence of any feeling that they naturally belong to each other.

In any society's relation to the outside world the same problem appears in another form. More territory is needed to meet the requirements of an expanding population and an increasing diversity of productive activities; surrounding peoples are absorbed, and what had been a local clan now becomes a growing empire. Roads and canals are built, and it is now possible to maintain an army in the far-flung corners of the enlarging realm. Sooner or later two such expanding empires come into conflict with each other, and war in the modern sense appears for the first time in history—war for conquest and control of the larger area which each power needs for its prosperity and its growth. At first these wars are geographically small—they are fought for mastery of a limited area in the Near East (which is the arena where such conflicts seem to have first occurred)—but they gradually affect wider territory; today, such is the sobering destiny of our generation, they have become world wars from whose impact no people can hope to remain aloof. Weapons of more and more lethal power are invented and used; because of this fact, today there is no longer any radical difference between the perils of soldiers and those of civilians, and man has at last achieved the power of destroying, along with his enemies, the whole of civilization and perhaps of the human race. Reflection on this process in its historical sweep brings out very vividly the fact that while the basic source of insecurity for primitive man lies in his relation to environing nature, the great insecurity of civilized man lies in his relation to his fellows—in his and their aggressive urges and hostile acts. All his other hopes wait for realization on the removal of this insecurity.

The process of expansion beyond a civilized society's previous boundary adds to the class distinctions that are multiplying within it further ones of special emotional poignance. As conquered peoples are absorbed there appear the distinctions of citizen and slave, noble and plebeian, the luxurious wealthy and the downtrodden poor. In brief, what happens in such a transition is that, both within and without the boundaries of the social group, a much more complex and challenging network of social relationships emerges than primitive man is familiar with, and an intensified gamut of emotions expressing the fears and anxieties inevitable in this altered situation. Civilized religion reflects this shift; especially the founders of the universal religions are moved to respond to the general problem thus created, and their great concern is to envision and practice a way of life whereby it can be given a constructive solution.

Moreover, in the course of seeking such a solution, they discover new and tremendous possibilities in man for growth and happiness that had no chance to be discovered when people were mainly absorbed in the laborious effort to maintain their existence against the threats of physical nature. An ideal of peace and creative harmony between men everywhere is glimpsed, and a clarified understanding of the essential conditions on which its realization rests is sought. It becomes clear through the work of these pioneers that man is not condemned forever to domination by the attitudes and feelings that sadly limit him in primitive life; he is capable of a will to justice and to kindliness that is not limited by clan, race, or tradition, and of finding joy in the hopeful and friendly relationship with others which it brings. His true good, they discover, does not lie in the aggressive assertion of himself *against* other men—as if all outside the clan are nothing but obstacles to his blind drives, his own self-seeking desires—but rather in the realization of a happy oneness with them in virtue of which the good of each person becomes for that reason the good of all. Just as other adventurous spirits in civilized societies explore the vast geography of the earth, becoming acquainted with the varied resources of its most remote regions, so the equally daring adventurers of civilized religion explore the mysterious and tangled psychology of man, penetrating hitherto inaccessible areas in his capacity for fear and hope, anxiety and trust, hate and love, joy and despair, and learning how to achieve the glad freedom that integration around the constructive emotion in each of these contrasting pairs can bring. Indeed, without something of this moral achievement civilized societies could not have advanced very far in the absorption of alien people; a great empire cannot realize efficient unity over a far-flung realm merely by force, but must be able to appeal plausibly to the deeper loyalties of men. These can be won only when people see that in some sense its rule spells for them a security based on impartial justice and the chance to pursue their creative aspirations.

In essence, what it means for civilized religion to reflect this historical shift is that its greatest leaders envision an ideal moral order embracing all the human inhabitants of the planet, and that they exemplify, in their personalities and relationships with others, the virtues which are the basic conditions for realizing such an ideal order. Their implicit guiding motto is: 'Let those destroy each other who tragically must, but let those of us who can, begin to create the divine community of peace and harmony among men—remembering that hate arouses an avenging hate and that love can awaken a responding love.' For them, the divine is no longer found in capricious forces determining the weal or woe of man's physical existence, but in the mysterious powers of which they become aware as they engage in this process of exploring the richer spiritual potentialities of man. As a result of this vital and focal change, everything else in their universe becomes changed. Civilized religion in its advanced forms is the outcome of the radical reorientation which is gradually wrought in virtue of this transformation.

Although the masses of men are still largely preoccupied

with the first of these two historical needs, and therefore preserve many of the attitudes and feelings which such pre-occupation evokes, the leaders of civilized life—whose influence gives civilized culture its distinctive quality—know that man has learned how to live with assurance in face of the subhuman forces around him, and that the challenge which cannot now be avoided is the task of learning how to live successfully and harmoniously with his fellows. Throughout civilized history this task has become increasingly obvious, especially in modern times. In our day all people have become caught to some degree in its emotional impact; even those who have succeeded hitherto in preserving their traditional isolation can no longer quite do so. The need to fulfill this task is thus likely to be even more insistent in the foreseeable future than it has been in the past; all man's other interests and hopes will remain insecure and largely paralyzed until it has been adequately met. This situation provides our basic clue for understanding the religions of civilization, both in their continuity with and their radical divergence from primitive religion.

IV |||||||||||||||||||||||||||||||||

The Great Religions of Civilized Man

As one might expect, the first obvious form in which this second historical need was met consisted in the attempt to secure a sense of religious unity between the peoples who were absorbed into this or that civilized empire, as it expanded over wider territory, without any definite emphasis as yet on the universal moral responsibility of man to man. This form is exhibited in the religions of the ancient empires that achieved for a time the position of dominance in their part of the world but have long since passed away. As we follow the development of the religions of Egypt, Babylonia, Greece, and Rome, we see the gradual disappearance of many local godlings, or their merging in the pantheon of divinities recognized by the larger society that was extending its sway and in this fashion securing emotionally potent symbols of its unity.

A. DISTINCTIVE FEATURES OF THE LIVING FAITHS OF CIVILIZATION

But before the completion of this amalgamating process, men of a new stamp appeared on the scene—religious gen-

iuses who caught the vision of a world in peace and brotherhood, who emphasized as basic the moral virtues that must be
practiced if such a vision is to be realized, and who dared to
hold that the divine essentially embodies these virtues and
must no longer be conceived in terms of primitive ideas that
are inconsistent with them. Thus we meet the one God of
justice, mercy, and love, taking the place both of the local
spirits with their strange and threatening potencies and of
the national divinities, symbols of imperial authority. These
men are the founders of the great religions that have come
down to our day and still hold the allegiance of hundreds of
millions of men and women in the civilized world. The
processes that led to their appearance ran sufficiently parallel
in different parts of the ancient world so that a very interesting historical phenomenon confronts the student of religion
—the fact that several outstanding pioneers of this stamp appeared approximately at the same time, though without contact of any kind with each other or even knowledge of each
other's existence. What a century was the sixth before Christ
—the century of Buddha, Confucius, Zoroaster, Jeremiah and
Second Isaiah among the Hebrew prophets, and very likely
Lao Tse! That was the creative epoch in the history of religion, marked by the bursting of civilized religion into full
flower, after several hundred years of slow, halting, and
irregular germination.

Let me attempt now a description of the basic features
that are essential to this most highly developed form of religion—features present in each of the living civilized faiths,
in virtue of which they are sharply distinguished from primitive religion. I find four such common features, which it is
well to have in mind as we proceed to analyze the distinctive
genius of each of these faiths. First, they all accept a universal
moral responsibility as a religious duty of man, and reinterpret
the concept of divinity so as to harmonize it with such a
moral outlook; second, they exhibit a vigorous trend toward
monism in their picture of God and of the world; third, they

discover the soul of man in its essential character, as involving his moral capacity and as being an inward, nonmaterial reality; and fourth, they realize that true, enduring happiness for man demands more than merely satisfying the desires of which he is naturally conscious—it demands a new birth, a radical transformation of himself, so that he becomes capable of a different kind of happiness than primitive man has known. It will be worth our while to explore these four characteristics in enough detail so that their historical significance will be clear.

B. ACCEPTANCE OF A UNIVERSAL MORAL IDEAL

The first of these features is vitally important because it underlies and is the key to the other three. Primitive religion, as has been observed, shocks the modern student more than for any other reason because of the absence in it of any sense of universal moral responsibility. The only "good" that primitive man is conscious of, as such, is the good of his limited group; the only moral "right" that he feels responsible to practice is that which, through traditional rules of conduct, protects the existence and serves the well-being of his group. Members of other groups he is aware of mainly as external objects betraying modes of behavior which he must guard against, just as he is aware in the same terms of the animals in his neighborhood and capricious objects in physical nature. The divine powers that he recognizes are conceived to have no other moral orientation than he is conscious of in himself; they are neither moral nor immoral in the civilized meaning of these terms. They are "good" so far as they sometimes aid him in satisfying needs that he cannot confidently satisfy for himself, "bad" so far as they sometimes frustrate his efforts instead. If the satisfaction of a given need requires acts that harm some other human group—stealing its valuables, seizing its land, even slaughtering its members—the divine powers whose favor he seeks are assumed to be just as ready to help him in these exploits as in any others. If they are disposed to be kindly, his prey will be their prey, his enemies will be their enemies. In short, sympathetic and coöperative feeling reaches with him as far as the boundary of the social group to which he belongs but no farther, and his religious ideas and practices, like all others, express this limitation. It is no sin to act in hostile ways toward members of other societies; what is sinful is to violate any of the accepted taboos and customary rules, obedience to which is felt to be necessary to the stability and health of his own tribe. He must not neglect the traditional rites; he must not use magic on a fellow clansman to do him harm; he must not kill, or rob, or destroy within the group. And what is true of his concept of sin is true of every other concept that carries religious significance.

In the higher civilized religions this situation is left behind. A universal moral order is envisaged, and a conviction of moral obligation toward all men, simply because they are men, is born. The wall that circumscribed sympathetic feeling and kept it within the tribe is broken down, and the sense of community is encouraged to open out beyond that limit; the idea takes root that we are essentially members of a society embracing all human beings on the same terms and in which therefore all men are brothers. This involves a radical and decisive transcendence of customary morality and of the attitudes which pervade it. Only so far as its rules square with this sense of universal moral obligation are they now conceived to be good—wherever they lead to conduct inconsistent with it, they are for civilized religion wrong rather than right, and lose their traditional religious sanction.

For the divinities are now drastically reinterpreted too, so that their nature accords with this new orientation. The essence of divinity is no longer unpredictable power, as revealed in the processes of physical nature. It becomes rather the mysterious dynamic energy in man and beyond man that is disclosed in his quest for clearer insight into his nature as a moral being, and in his struggle to realize his aspiring potentialities against the resistance and inertia of the primitive elements in his make-up. The heart of the new perspective, so far as the divine powers are concerned, is epigrammatically and memorably expressed by the Greek tragedian Euripides: "If the gods do aught that is base, they are no gods."[1] This epigram brings out in striking fashion the radical feature of the new orientation thus achieved; it involves man's right and responsibility to judge candidates for godhood in terms of his own growing moral understanding and to reject those that fail to measure up to this standard. The basic reason why this right must be insisted on in civilized religion is that once man has clearly conceived a universal moral ideal and aspires toward it, he can no longer worship or reverence powers whose nature is not in full harmony with such an ideal; divinities that exemplify something less than the conduct it requires and appear to approve something less in his own behavior can no longer be divinities for him.

This step precipitates an emotional conflict in the civilized religions which at times becomes a serious one. For all members of a civilized society except its moral pioneers and prophets are likely to fear the divine powers so deeply, to retain traditional notions about them so persistently, and to respond so feebly to the appeal of an inclusive moral ideal that for a long time they easily succumb to apprehensions that divine punishment must follow any weakening of the ancient beliefs; they are unable to realize steadily that God must be unqualifiedly good if he is to be recognized as God. Hence a continuing clash is inevitable in civilized history between fundamentalist religion and a clarified ethical faith.[2]

Of course, this moral transformation takes place in somewhat different ways according to the varying basic concepts of the different civilized religions. The most striking difference appears when we compare a theistic theology with that of mystical religions. Since the former holds that God is a strictly personal being, the fundamental requirement in its case is that He be conceived to embody, in superlative and perfect form, the virtues implied by a supreme ideal—the virtues of sincerity, impartial justice, mercy, and love—instead of the capricious and biased foibles of a primitive divinity. But the latter conceives God, not as a personality, but as a metaphysical ultimate which cannot be defined in terms derived from human nature or experience; the divine even transcends all moral categories. In the case of mysticism, the ethical emphasis appears in the fact that the process of realizing oneness with God is so conceived that acceptance of moral responsibility toward all men and the achievement of loving unity with them are essential to it. It is impossible to become one with God except through friendly oneness with others. Each of these ways will be exemplified in the civilized religions soon to be explored.

C. A MONISTIC INTERPRETATION OF GOD AND THE WORLD

The second feature of high civilized religion is an acceptance of monism in its picture of God and of the world. Primitive man believes in many divine powers, each operating more or less independently of the others, and therefore his implied cosmology is pluralistic. There is no single order pervading the entire universe; there is no first cause or all-determining ground to which every event can be traced. Even in such civilized communities as ancient Greece and Rome, whose keenest minds had advanced to the idea of one ultimate principle behind all things, religion (except among the philosophers) did not fully adopt this monistic orientation —Zeus or Jupiter was the highest among the gods, but he lacked the power to control the activities of his colleagues in the areas thought to be under their sway. The civilized religions that have endured, however, are explicitly and unqualifiedly monistic. Their commitment to a universal and impartial moral order naturally leads to the notion that the universe itself is a coherent system, embracing all events and rendering them intelligible in terms of uniform law. Thus arises the conviction that is basic to the enterprise of science;

and one sees why science cannot develop in a primitive society, but is possible only in a community with a fully civilized orientation toward the world. I shall not try to answer the question, how far this conviction that all things are parts of a single network of causes and effects is due to the growth of intellectual curiosity as such, and how far it is simply a reflection, in man's quest for theoretical explanations, of the moral ideal of universal obligation and the impartial dependability it implies. The important and obvious fact is that a scientific attitude toward the world could only come to prevail when men had abandoned the notion that things happen through the arbitrary and unpredictable behavior of a plurality of powers in favor of the idea that they are all, directly or indirectly, the effects of one fundamental power whose acts express the virtue of impartial reliability.

This monism, too, takes different forms in the different civilized religions. Westerners are most familiar with the theistic form in which, in place of a number of quasi-independent divine powers, one personal God is recognized, and all things that happen in the universe are believed to be a part of His purposive plan. It may, however, take other forms, such as the pantheistic idea of an impersonal order in nature, or the Confucian extension to the cosmos at large of the moral harmony prevailing in a well-ordered family or state. When religion follows the first of these routes, the essence of the transition is that divinity becomes conceived as the One Father of all men, who treats them with equal justice and whose love flows without stint to all; the history of the world is the fulfillment of His all-inclusive plan.

It is important to note that these two characteristics of civilized religion, when adopted together, render inescapable a difficult problem that does not trouble primitive religion— the problem of evil. This problem is most sharp and harassing in a theistic faith, but it cannot be entirely avoided in any civilized theology. From the primitive standpoint there is no problem of evil. Each of the various erratic powers that are responsible for the way things happen sometimes acts in a manner which from man's standpoint is good, sometimes in a manner which is evil; and there is no expectation that it would be otherwise. Hence no theoretical puzzle arises from the fact that the course of nature includes frustrations and disasters, as well as blessings, for men who are virtuous and for men who are not—that it conforms to no general moral rule. But when the conviction has taken root that there is One God whose power is the ultimate cause behind all things and whose character exemplifies perfect love and justice, the problem of evil at once becomes challenging and very puzzling. If God is supremely good, it would seem as though all His works would clearly display His moral perfection; if everything that happens in the cosmos is the direct or indirect effect of His purposive power, how can He be honestly conceived as good? Each civilized theology has attacked this problem with keenness and vigor; some of the solutions that have been proposed will be noted in the following chapters.

D. DISCOVERY OF MAN'S SPIRITUAL SELFHOOD

The third feature of living civilized religion is its discovery of the soul of man as an essentially moral and nonmaterial entity. Primitive man does not lack the concept of soul, of course, but he has not yet discovered his true self—that is, the kind of self that civilized religion comes to envision as constituting the inner reality of man. For primitive thought, almost everywhere, the soul is a material or quasi-material entity, conceived after the analogy of a physical process and in intimate relation to the living body, although it is capable of acts that the rest of the body cannot perform. In many languages the word for soul originally meant "breath"—i.e., the process which most vividly marks the difference between a living body and one whose life has passed away. In some languages it meant "shadow"—i.e., the mysteriously changeable image which accompanies a body when light falls upon it and yet appears somehow detachable from it. In no primitive theory of man, so far as I know, is the soul supposed to have any essential connection with what we would call man's moral potentialities;* but of course it may be related, in specific ways, to the extraordinary powers by which a human being, living or dead, can bring weal or woe to his fellows.

Civilized religion abandons this physical conception of soul, although, here too, the abandonment is gradual and primitive ideas tend to linger, especially in the superstitious feelings of the popular mind. The abandonment becomes more rapid as scientific knowledge about man is developed, and such phenomena as breathing and the casting of shadows are explained in ways which have no religious import. By what is the primitive idea of the soul replaced? Here, as we might expect, there are considerable variations between the civilized religions—perhaps more variations of consequence than in the case of either of the characteristics already discussed. What can be said in general is that, instead of this physical notion of soul, what is essential in man from the point of view of an advanced civilized religion is his moral selfhood—his capacity to grow toward the realization of a supreme ideal, and to exemplify it with responsibility and understanding.

There are four general implications of this idea, which seem to hold good of all the living civilized religions despite their differences. The first and most basic is that every man *has* such a moral capacity, which constitutes his true self. No human being is condemned by nature to exist with no sympathetic feeling toward other persons and with no power to put himself in their place, appreciating their joys and sorrows; anyone who attempts to live on that basis is in conflict with himself as well as with those whom he treats as instruments to something other than their own good. Hence

---

* The first traces of such a connection perhaps appear in the idea, held by some primitive peoples, that a soul's destiny after death is partly determined by its virtue or vice during life.

the only way in which any man can achieve health and wholeness within himself is by accepting this status of brotherhood with all other men, and identifying himself more and more completely with his power to fulfill this role.

The second implication arises from the bearing of this idea on the nature of moral conduct—that is, on the way a universal moral ideal expresses itself in particular deeds of honesty, fairness, compassion. Primitive morality is essentially customary morality; it is supposed to be completely fulfilled in performing the various acts prescribed by tradition—obeying the taboos, administering the rites, repeating the appropriate incantations, executing the daily tasks which the community expects of its members.

With this notion of morality taken for granted, primitive thought is typically unaware of any distinction between an act and the intention or purpose expressed in the act. The most striking evidence for this is that primitive law typically recognizes no difference between an injurious deed which happens by accident and one which is done on purpose; the individual responsible for it is punished in the same way in both cases. The reason is that in a culture governed by merely customary morality no one has clearly discovered as yet the inward reality indicated by such words as "intention," "purpose," "spirit," and the like, and the extent to which there may be a contrast as well as a correspondence between that inner reality and the outward act through which it is expressed. It has not become realized that a person may intend one thing and do another. But when men have become conscious of a universal ideal, and of their obligation to practice it, the limitations of customary morality are transcended, and this distinction among others then becomes an object of clear awareness. The universal duty of justice cannot be equated with any specific set of acts which could be prescribed in advance. The individual who accepts it accepts the responsibility to realize the ideal of justice in any situation that might arise, novel or familiar, in relation to any human being with whom he might be thrown in contact, through whatever deed may be required to achieve it. The commitment to such an ideal constitutes an inward reality distinguishable from every act through which it finds expression.

Just how does this transformation take place? Well, when a universal ideal is accepted, thinkers become aware of the fact that there is always a gap between what the ideal demands and what any act performed under its guidance actually accomplishes, and that this gap may be pretty wide. There must be a gap, because there is always the possibility of a clearer moral insight and its fuller exemplification in action than the actor had been capable of at the moment. And the gap may be wide because the act performed may produce a quite different effect than the actor had hoped and expected. He intended, let us say, to give a friendly pat of encouragement; but he slipped while doing so, and the friend experienced the pat as a hostile blow. In these situations the distinction between a deed as such and what we call the "intention" or "spirit" expressed in the deed becomes recognized; the latter may be essentially good, deserving moral approval, while the former may, in any particular case, be unfortunate and bad.

Moreover—and here we meet the third implication—this disparity between intention and deed is of such a sort that we cannot think of the intention as a material reality. A deed, of course, is a physical performance visible to an external observer in the way any physical event is observable. But the spirit behind the deed is invisible—inexhaustible by and essentially different from any aggregate of physical acts, however extensive. And from the viewpoint of civilized religion the vital thing is not the deed but the state of this inward reality which underlies a man's behavior. Of course, an important lesson must be learned here, the lesson that a person may not continue to plead good intentions if he gives no clear evidence of them in his acts—for in the long run the test of the former does lie in the latter—yet this does not impugn the basic distinction between intention and act in its significance for religion.

In the theistic religions this transformation involves a consequence that is naturally absent in nontheistic ones. God is conceived by theistic theology as an ideal soul, guided in all His acts by a good purpose for the world and for man; He is believed to exemplify in perfection the virtues that a being so conceived would be expected to exemplify. Hence the heart of religion for such faiths (beyond its practical bearing on human conduct) consists in adoring reverence toward and trustful communion with God as so conceived. The primitive attitudes toward divine power are transcended and left far behind when this emotion takes root.

It is in this setting that Westerners can appreciate the essential meaning of their traditional words "spirit" and "spiritual," which are now so often used as vague edificatory terms that their historical significance has been almost lost. "Spirit" is the concept seized upon and reinterpreted by the late Old Testament thinkers and by the New Testament writers (especially John) for the sake of articulating in language the transformation just described. It originally meant "breath," but when they refer to man as a spirit they mean that he has the capacity of responding to an inclusive moral ideal and of living in the appropriate relation to God who essentially embodies it. To live the spiritual life, and to practice the spiritual virtues, is precisely to act in the way that a being endowed with such a capacity would act so far as he expresses his true nature. What this revolution means, more concretely, is that one leaves behind the idea that right religious conduct consists in obeying a host of detailed injunctions and taboos in favor of the conviction that it consists simply in fulfilling the two great commandments: "Thou shalt love the Lord thy God with all thy heart and soul and mind and strength; and thou shalt love thy neighbor as thyself." This does not mean that rites and ceremonies hallowed by tradition are to be abandoned if they are not repugnant to the new insight that has been won. But it does imply a realization that those which are retained have no value in themselves; they are religiously significant only when performed in the spirit which from the viewpoint of civilized religion they should express.

The fourth implication of this civilized idea of the soul is that while individuals vary greatly from each other in many respects, so that once they are freed from the bonds of customary morality no valid detailed system of rules can be set up for everyone to obey, yet there are certain general virtues, implied by this concept of "spiritual," that all must be expected to exemplify. Such is the virtue of justice, detached now from its original meaning of obedience to established law, so that it denotes the conduct of man to man that law would enforce if it were completely impartial and applied with full understanding. Such is the virtue of love, detached now from its narrow meaning as affection within the family and between friends, so that it denotes a constant care for the highest good of all men, rooted firmly in feeling and expressed in compassionate action.

Moreover, some very important virtues appear that could have had no meaning at all before this distinction between the spirit and the deed had come clearly to the fore. Such is the virtue of sincerity. Honesty and truthfulness, in some sense, are familiar to primitive man, but sincerity is a virtue peculiar to civilized religion. When there is a gap between intention and act, there may also be a difference between the real spirit behind a deed and the spirit that it seems to express—the spirit, perhaps, that the doer wants others to believe it expresses. And a person can deceive himself in this matter as well as his fellows, especially when the subtler motives of self-seeking and the need to be socially approved are strong. Now sincerity is an essential virtue in civilized religion—the foundation of all others—because it is a necessary condition of spiritual reality and moral growth. That a man is just can only be counted on with confidence when one knows that his commitment to justice is sincere—that he wants to be really just in all his dealings with others, and not merely to do what might appear to be just—and the same applies to every virtue of civilized religion. This becomes even clearer when it is recognized that one of the qualities implied by sincerity is readiness and competence in honest self-examination. The sincere man is eager to uncover any lurking forms of self-seeking that subtly obstruct his exemplification of the virtues to which he is committed; he searches inwardly to find them, knowing that only when they are uncovered and frankly faced can he grow away from unconscious domination by them toward a fuller realization of the moral ideal. Otherwise he stays spiritually where he is. And this means that he is really falling behind, because the true exemplification of any spiritual excellence consists in moving toward its completer expression; one who is not growing toward the ideal is inevitably lapsing more and more into bondage to the habits of his present limited self.

This consideration of the virtue of sincerity leads at once to the fourth general characteristic of the living civilized religions.

E. REALIZATION OF NEW POSSIBILITIES OF HAPPINESS FOR MAN

This characteristic is a clarified awareness that true happiness for man does not consist in finding more successful ways of appeasing his natural desires; it consists rather in a transformation of these desires so that he becomes capable of a different kind of happiness than primitive man has known—a happiness more secure and real than any pleasure arising merely from satisfying the longings that fill man's awareness before he undergoes this transformation. It was noted above that one aspect of the transition from primitive to civilized religion among the peoples who have achieved it lies in the discovery that man has magnificent potentialities that could not be known under the harassing pressure of the primitive struggle for existence, and in the exploration of ways by which these potentialities can be realized. It is hard for a person who has always identified happiness with the satisfaction of his natural desires to see that there may be a momentous truth in this insight.

But that the founders of the great civilized religions conceived the matter in this way there is no doubt. They were sure that the message they brought to their fellow men was "good news"*—news that the finest conceivable life is really possible for man. It is possible in the sense that a life of commitment to the universal good can be a truly rich and joyous life, not merely a successful repression of vigorous and persistent cravings by a dutiful conscience. Just before Jesus was arrested, tried, and crucified, he is quoted as completing his final message to his disciples by saying, "I have told you these things so that you might have the happiness that I have had, and that your happiness might become complete";[3] and such a statement gives vivid meaning to the more general remark in the same Gospel that "I came that you might have life, and might have it more abundantly."[4] Buddha is reported as having said:

We live happily indeed, not hating those who hate us! among men who hate us we dwell free from hatred! . . .
We live happily indeed, free from greed among the greedy! among men who are greedy let us dwell free from greed!
We live happily indeed, though we call nothing our own! We shall be like the bright gods, feeding on happiness![5]

It is in the light of this idea—that man may not only win a victory for his ideal self in its conflict with his primitive cravings, but may also terminate that very conflict and find an integrated joy in devotion to the ideal—that we must understand the meaning of the religious emphasis on "con-

* This is the meaning of the word "gospel."

version," on the decisive turning away from the kind of satisfaction with which primitive experience alone is acquainted to full identification with the spiritual self in its distinctive fulfillments. And by the same token we can appreciate the even more striking language used by several of the civilized religions in describing this process of conversion. It is a "new birth," analogous to the physical birth by which we emerged from our mother's womb—it is a passing, in terms of the spiritual criterion of real vitality, from death unto life.[6]

For primitive experience there is nothing else in life to be seriously desired beyond the fulfillment of those cravings whose satisfaction is necessary if the conditions of physical existence and customary well-being are to be maintained from year to year and from generation to generation. Civilized man, having caught the vision of a self with richer needs and potentialities, and having experienced in his prophetic leaders something of the joy that their fulfillment brings, gradually leaves this assumption behind, and commits himself to a more aspiring quest. And since what he now seeks is nothing less than a new birth, it brings a radical transvaluation of all his values, so that what had seemed before to be a real good becomes a deceitful appearance or illusion, in contrast with what he now knows to be the true good. What before had seemed to be strength—the power to make things and people serve one's primitive ends—is now revealed as weakness rather than strength; what had seemed to be knowledge and wisdom is now shown to be ignorance and folly; what had seemed to be love, freedom, activity, courage, even (in some respects) righteousness itself, is now proved to be the opposite of those virtues. Contrariwise, of course, what to the transformed soul is experienced as the reality of these values seems the opposite to those who have not yet experienced them. This circumstance would give rise to insuperable difficulties were it not for the fact that the stable joy of the twice-born cannot be wholly hidden from those who have known nothing but a more transitory and fickle happiness—nor can the fact that they understand the experience of the less mature as well as their own, and are thus able to inspire and guide others to share their richer achievement.

From this point of view, the historical significance of the founders of the living civilized religions is that in their exemplification of this joy in the experience of creative love they became pioneers in the quest for a greater sanity and health in human life than the rest of mankind would have discovered without them. They took the initiative in leading the way beyond the aggressive conflicts that disrupt the world, plunging individuals and groups into anxiety, fear, and hatred. In the light of the achievement of these men, those who came after them could really believe that nothing but the best as they had explored it is good enough for man, and could no longer rest until that best had been realized for all and in all.

F. A FEW REMINDERS ABOUT CIVILIZED RELIGION

It must not be supposed, of course, that when a great civilized religion first wins a people's allegiance it at once transforms their feeling and action into full accord with its central ideas. Rather, what happens is that the new religion takes root in the minds and hearts of their spiritual leaders and slowly percolates into the life of the more humble and custom-bound masses, while many features of primitive religion remain among the latter for a long time, perhaps permanently. Catholic Christianity has its saints, for example, who for many of its followers fill the role of primitive divinities; their images may even be given the rough and unceremonious treatment that is often accorded a primitive fetish. Frazer tells of a case where Italians prayed to St. Joseph for rain, but in vain; "at Palermo they dumped St. Joseph in the garden to see the state of things for himself, and they swore to leave him there in the sun till rain fell."[7] Magic is not only widely believed among civilized peoples, but is even practiced by some persons as a way of making a living, as the following news item, which appeared in *The New York Times* of March 26, 1939, indicates:

FROSTPROOF, Fla., March 25—Miss Lillie Stoate, who believes she has power to attract rainfall, established herself here today with the hope of ending a five-month drought in this citrus belt area.

She came yesterday from her home in Oxford, Miss., at the request of fruit growers who forwarded $25 for expenses and promised a reward if the drought were broken.

Miss Stoate said her method was to find a large body of water and sit beside it for several hours daily until the drops began to fall. She said it had been successful in more than four hundred trials, the time ranging from one to seven days. She was unable to give a reason for her success.

"Whenever I stand by water something begins to rise," she explained. "You can't see it, but it is there just the same. It continues to rise and the particles gather and draw together and that makes the cloud. This floats over dry areas and drops as rain.

"Where we find so much dry territory it is because the human beings draw away from the clouds and they do not fall there."

The phenomenon of Father Divine—his living deification and his "heavens"—has already been mentioned. Moreover, primitive features persist, at least for many centuries, in the official practice of civilized ecclesiastical bodies. Exorcism of demons was practiced in the Church of England as late as 1550, the following formula being used in cleansing infants before baptism: "I command thee, unclean spirit, in the name of the Father, Son, and Holy Ghost, that thou come out and depart from these infants."[8] This circumstance will make it easy for us to recognize that some quite basic teachings of each of the civilized religions reflect primitive ideas which are so deeply rooted that it has been impossible to leave them behind.[9]

Such survivals were even more prominent in the religions of the ancient empires of the Near East and the Mediter-

ranean world. And as we should expect, it is not difficult to
find expressions, in each of these religions, that reveal in germ
the four characteristics which distinguish the higher civilized
faiths. Consider in this connection a prayer of King Nebuchadnezzar to Marduk, the high divinity of Babylon in its
day of greatness:

> O Eternal prince! Lord of all being!
> For the king whom thou lovest, and
> Whose name thou hast proclaimed,
> As was pleasing to thee;
> Do thou lead aright his name,
> Guide him in a straight path.
> I am the prince, thy favorite,
> The creature of thy hand;
> Thou has created me, and
> With dominion over all people
> Thou hast entrusted me.
> According to thy favor, O Lord,
> Which thou dost bestow on all people,
> Cause me to love thy exalted lordship,
> And create in my heart
> The worship of thy divinity.
> And grant whatever is pleasing to thee,
> Because thou hast fashioned my life.[10]

Two particular illustrations of this general lag in the historical development of the civilized faiths are significant
enough to be mentioned.

One is that while the first three characteristics of high
civilized religion have succeeded, to some degree, in molding
other aspects of modern cultures into harmony with them,
the fourth has not yet done so. As far as it is concerned,
primitive and civilized cultures are still essentially alike. A
statesman must give lip service, at least, to the ideal of universal moral responsibility; he has to show if he can that
his policies serve the good of all mankind and not just the
interests of his own nation. Science and, for the most part,

philosophy assume that nothing in the universe is irrationally disconnected from other things; nature is pervaded by systematic law. The legal structures of civilized peoples have established elaborate precautions for discriminating between criminal acts that are premeditated, those that are accidental, and those performed on the hostile impulse of the moment. But except for the few persons in each generation who are especially sensitive to the religious insight expressed in the fourth characteristic, civilized cultures still take for granted the primitive viewpoint on this vital matter. Even their otherwise intelligent leaders identify the essence of human nature with the complex of desires and accompanying emotions that superficially seem to compose it. The idea that true happiness for man lies in a different dimension than that of satisfying these desires has not clearly dawned in their minds.

The other illustrative fact is that although the great civilized religions have clearly envisioned the ideal of human equality and in many respects have uncompromisingly taught it (however incongruous the conduct of their followers has often been), in one surprising respect their teaching itself has fallen short of full consistency. None of them has unqualifiedly recognized the equality of women with men. They have encouraged tender consideration for the weaker sex and have greatly elevated her status as compared with what it was before they came on the scene, but they have definitely expressed the belief that woman is inferior to man. High civilized religion thus betrays the fact that each of its faiths arose under the typical conditions of a patriarchal society. This feature is so out of touch with the more progressive equalitarian thought of today that we may safely presume, I judge, that any religions of the future that are destined to achieve widespread success will depart from tradition on this matter.

One more important thought before we turn to each of the civilized religions which have come down through the centuries and are powerful forces in the life of our day. There is a basic difference between the religions of the Far East and the religions originating in the West, which it will be helpful to keep in mind. In the patterns of thought which Western civilization has developed, the path of the human soul, in its quest for the real and stable happiness which constitutes salvation, is left largely in the realm of miracle and mystery, while knowledge about other processes, especially those occurring in the physical world, is organized into a systematic and impressive science. In the East (up till the present generation, at least) knowledge of these other processes has remained at the level of a rather primitive technology plentifully interspersed with magic, while the course of the soul in its search for liberation from bondage is made the object of detailed and rational understanding. As we shall see in detail, this assertion holds, though in different ways, of both India and China. Their great contribution to the world is a clarified and discerning understanding of the spiritual psychology of man.

PART TWO

The Religions of the East

V

The Native Religions of China

We begin our study of the living civilized religions with the native faiths of China—starting far in the East and moving slowly westward. And before we explore each of them by itself, a few preliminaries call for consideration. First, it will be necessary to sketch briefly the historical background of the work of the pioneering Chinese sages, with some reference to the survivals of primitive religion which, transformed to a greater or less extent through the influence of their moral insight, play a significant role in Chinese religion through the centuries. Then we shall attempt an appreciative survey of the distinctive qualities present in the attitude of the Chinese people toward life and destiny, as that attitude is reflected in their religion along with other aspects of their culture. These materials will prepare us for a systematic examination of the basic ideas which lie at the heart of the two major native religions of China, Confucianism and Taoism.

A. HISTORICAL BACKGROUND OF CHINESE RELIGION

From evidence now available—allowing some weight to Chinese tradition itself on this matter—we may conclude that it was during the period from about 2500 to 1100 B.C. that Chinese culture gradually emerged from primitive ideas and their accompanying institutions, and established a relatively stable agricultural civilization. The central plain of the Yellow River was the first area to complete this change; the capital of China in the last few hundred years of this period was Loyang. Later tradition looked back to an idealized Golden Age which was supposed to have existed about 2350 to 2200 B.C. This was the time of the great emperors Yao, Shun, and Yü, believed by the philosophers who came two millennia later to have possessed all the virtues which they hoped to see exemplified in the rulers of their day. Yü was regarded as the founder of the first dynasty which can be confirmed as such by sufficient evidence; the date of its founding can only be conjectured. It was brought to an end not far from 1600 B.C. and was followed by the Shang dynasty, which held sway till about 1027 B.C. Archaeological remains from the Shang period, along with records of later historians, indicate that ancestral rites (which were often very elaborate) were an important part of the religion of this period, and that the social structure was dominated by a hereditary aristocracy, the common people being heavily oppressed and their welfare counting for little.

The Shang dynasty was succeeded by that of Chou, which retained nominal rule for a period of nearly eight hundred years, i.e., till 256 B.C. For our purposes, this long era may be divided into three main segments of approximately equal length, the last of which covers almost exactly three hundred years and begins with the birth of Confucius in 551 B.C. I shall not attempt to draw a definite historical line between the first and the second segment, because the transition was apparently very gradual. The essential point is that for about two hundred years after the Chou dynasty was founded, it maintained a strong and effective central authority. This was accomplished through the formation of a political and social structure analogous to that of feudalism in medieval

Europe. But by 850 B.C. signs that this system was weakening were beginning to appear, and through the following centuries they gradually multiplied. Real control from the center was lost; more and more power was exercised by the rising heads of state in the loosely connected regions of the empire. Wars for supremacy among these aggressive chieftains became frequent; the people were impoverished by heavy taxation imposed to support these wars and to maintain the aristocrats in luxury, and many were ruthlessly conscripted for military service. The maintenance of law and order was precarious, insecurity was on the increase and anxiety was deepening, such moral coherence as had apparently been won in earlier days was disintegrating, while irresponsibility and selfish indifference were widespread among the leaders of society at all levels. This was the challenging situation faced by the philosophers and religious leaders of the creative epoch of ancient China, which constitutes the last third of Chou dynastic history. And what an epoch that was—counting among its pioneering thinkers Confucius, Lao Tse, Mo Tse, Mencius, Yang Chu, Hsün Tse, and Chuang Tse, to mention only the most illustrious of this galaxy of sages!

It will not surprise us to find that the basic character of this deepening social crisis, together with the essentially humanistic orientation of the philosophers who felt the call to meet it, left its impress on the nature of the religious ideas which they developed and which provide the key to an adequate understanding of their thought. As Latourette says in a trenchant summary: "It cannot be too greatly emphasized that the chief problem to which most of the thinkers of the Chou [period] addressed themselves was: How can society be saved? Cosmogony, cosmology, the nature of the gods— if any—and of man, were subordinate and ancillary to this question."[1] Such a statement is not quite as true of Taoism as of other religious philosophies of this period, but in an important sense, as will be seen, Taoism constitutes no exception.

We should remember that during this whole long period of China's emergence into the ways of civilization, with its significant gains, its threatening results, and its harassing problems, Chinese culture was expanding through the permeation and absorption of peoples on its periphery—eastward, westward, southward to the valley of the Yangtze River, and finally northward also. No such cultural expansion, once won, has since been lost.

In view of our survey of primitive religions in Chapters II and III, it is instructive to consider briefly the main primitive survivals which, gradually remolded during the prephilosophic period of Chinese history and then more drastically reinterpreted by the great sages, were preserved to play a decisive part in the religions which they founded. An appreciation of what happened in this regard in the case of the Chinese religions will facilitate our understanding of the process through which all high civilized faiths emerge from earlier foundations and primitive traditions. Six such survivals are worth mentioning.

One is the conception of Heaven as the creative and protecting power in the universe and the model of good order. We have observed that among many primitive peoples heaven came to be pictured as filling something like this role (especially in the "high god" cults). As moral and social problems thrust themselves into the focus of attention, its religious significance was more and more emphasized as against the appeasing of the spirits that seemed less benign and predictable. This process took place among the Chinese; the resulting concept of Heaven assumed a special quality in view of the way it was related to other phases of their growing moral insight. Another was the belief in *yang* and *yin*, providing a major clue to Chinese cosmology and such rudimentary science as the Celestial realm developed. It is probable that this belief came into Chinese thought from one of the surrounding peoples who were absorbed during the early Chou period. *Yang* and *yin* are the two basic forces through whose interaction things are produced and natural processes go on. Generally speaking, *yang* is the positive force and *yin* the negative—except that, while *yang* is akin to "love" in Greek cosmology and to "attraction" in later physical science, *yin* is not akin to "hate" or "repulsion." *Yang* is the active, initiating, creative factor of the pair; *yin* is the passive, receptive, diversely responsive factor. In the cosmological relation between heaven and earth, for example, heaven is *yang* and earth is *yin*. The idea which pretty clearly gave original meaning to these concepts, and whose associations still are significant determinants, is that of male and female as united in sexual intercourse.

A third is the emphasis on the family as the essential social institution. It provides meaning and motivation for the basic social virtues, and serves as a working model for all social institutions in which people are brought together in more than casual fashion. The Chinese conception of the family is different from that of the individualistic and mobile West, but exemplifies what most people are familiar with in the East. What they take for granted is usually referred to as the "joint family"—that is, a social structure in which each household includes the sons of a given pair of parents together with their wives and children, their as-yet-unmarried sisters, and any other dependent relatives. In this structure ultimate authority lies with the eldest male (as long as he is still physically and mentally competent); although in China sex equality is sufficiently accepted for this authority to be shared with his wife, and if the father dies before his wife, the eldest son will never exert authority over his mother. There is considerable flexibility, of course, in the degree to which such a joint family can expand before fission takes place and a new household, consisting of a group of cousins with their parents and children, is set up. If such new households remain in the same locality, a village may be formed, all of whose members belong to one clan; there are thousands of such villages in China today. Fourth, there is the very potent force of ancestral reverence, expressed especially in the seasonal and commemorative ancestral rites. This heritage of primitive religion in China is extremely important. Through it the family is united in a close emotional bond temporally as well as spatially; its deceased members, up to the third generation or longer, remain effective participants in the community of tender affection and in the family councils. Their needs are provided for; they are kept apprised of new developments and problems affecting the family's welfare; their experience and advice are sought. Through ancestral reverence, the virtue of filial piety in China gains an emphasis in morals and religion that it does not enjoy in most other parts of the civilized world.

A fifth survival concerns the general role and meaning of ritual, as it is revealed in the manifold ceremonies and taboos of a typical primitive cult. In China, as ritual is handed down into the context of civilized life, what continues to be emphasized is the idea that in every area of life there is a correct and proper mode of conduct which should be practiced, and that if it is disregarded dire consequences may ensue for the delinquent actor and for others. The very basic Confucian concept of *li*, which we shall later examine, is the heir of this idea in Confucianism, but it plays an important role in other religions too. Especially is this correctness of conduct essential for those who stand at the center of things and thus become the vital intermediary between man and the cosmic forces operating for good and for ill. Hence we meet at this point a sixth interesting survival—the distinctive place in morals and religion of the political ruler or emperor. He is not only the administrative head of the Chinese state, with responsibility to perform some of the major ceremonies; since he stands in the position of father to the larger family of his people and is the Son of Heaven, he is also the prime exemplar on earth of the moral order of the universe. If he behaves with meticulous propriety and exercises his authority wisely, all will go well with the country. If he fails to do so, not only will his vicious example undermine social order, but the flow of cosmic forces will be distorted; drought, storm, famine, and other calamitous tokens of Heaven's displeasure are likely to befall his people.

Why did the Chinese people prize these aspects of their earlier religious culture, and feel it important to preserve and spiritualize rather than to abandon them? Probably the best answer to this question would simply call attention to certain fundamental qualities of the Chinese mind which distinguish the people of that Eastern land from those of other great civilized nations. These qualities are reflected in the features of primitive religion which survived in China and in the teachings of the great Chinese sages. It will help us achieve a more penetrating understanding of the religions they founded to ponder, one by one, the chief characteristics that make up the Chinese cultural temper.

B. THE CHINESE TEMPER OF MIND

The most basic quality, perhaps, is a profound acceptance of reality, in cheer and in hope. There is little of our tense Occidental demandingness that the real world be other or better than it clearly presents itself as being; hence, as one walks the streets of a Chinese city or village, he does not see many of the anxiously furrowed brows that meet him at every step in a Western town. The prevailing attitude is: let's not worry because things are not better; one should accept the world as it is, and find what measure of poise and happiness and strength can be found in it. And the Chinese have discovered that a great deal can be found in it when life is taken in this way. There is obviously an important virtue in this attitude, which the West has largely missed. There lies in it also a vice—the vice of bearing too easily misfortune or exploitation, of refusing to take up arms amidst a sea of troubles and aggressively to make the world more just or righteous than it now is. Today this vice is becoming weaker; and human history may be profoundly affected by that change.

A second quality, which is equally important, is their never-failing touch of humor. The typical Chinaman always enjoys a good joke, even one of which he is the butt; thus he shows his capacity to avoid taking himself too seriously. It is in virtue of this quality that the Chinese have been relatively free from the dogmatism and fanaticism so characteristic of Western religion and Western politics—evils which arise from the insistent need that one's own convictions be taken with absolute seriousness, by everyone else as well as by oneself. The Chinese are not easily mobilized in a campaign to convert other people; such an enterprise shows, in their eyes, a failure to see the inevitable relativity of one's beliefs and to survey them with an appropriate touch of humorous skepticism. From their point of view, one should take nothing too seriously except the task of learning how to live the good life, and finding such adjustment to the ultimate nature of things as living the good life, responsibly and understandingly, can bring. Indeed, according to the Taoists, even this task can be taken too seriously; one may be so earnest in the search for moral truth that his conscientiousness stands in his own way and obscures the simple childlike insights that a spontaneous response to the world, detached from any dutiful zeal to be better than one is, can awaken in his soul.

There is a beautiful story about "Confucius and the Children" that illustrates this phase of the Chinese mentality. The reader will be interested to compare its jolly atmosphere with the yearning intensity reflected in the Christian story about Jesus and the children, which ends with the verse, "Suffer the little ones to come unto me, and forbid them not, for of such is the kingdom of heaven." The Chinese story is as follows:

Confucius was traveling east and met two children arguing with one another. He inquired what they were arguing about, and one child said, "I say the sun is nearer to us in the morning and farther away from us at noon, and he says the sun is farther away from us in the morning and nearer to us at noon." One child said, "When the sun begins to come up, it is big like a carriage cover, and at noon it is like a dinner plate. So it must be farther away when it looks smaller, and nearer us when it looks bigger." The other child said, "When the sun comes up, the air is very cool, but at noon it burns like hot soup. So it must be nearer when it is hot and farther away when it is cool." Confucius could not decide who was right, and the children laughed at him and said, "Whoever said that you were a wise guy?"[2]

A third major quality, which is in part a consequence of these two, appears in the fact that Chinese writers, in philosophy and literature, aim at suggesting fertile insights rather than at achieving analytic precision. The latter has not been absent from Chinese thinking, but those who exemplified it have never been accorded the top rank in the estimate of their successors, nor did they initiate any continuous development. Because of this quality Chinese thought appears to the typical Western philosopher to be vague, loose, and rambling. Not only does it center on questions of morals, leaving for sketchy and subordinate treatment matters of logic, metaphysics, and epistemology; even in that field its aim is to inspire and guide ethical action rather than to satisfy the intellectual quest for a close-knit moral theory. The genius of the Chinese mind is revealed most fully, not in its philosophical essays or dialogues, but in its poetry, where the suggestive nuances of thought can be freely expressed, unhampered by any need for meticulous distinctions or for coercion of the reader's thought through logical deduction. The reason for this, I am sure, lies in certain corollaries of the moral urbanity just described; it does not reflect any failure to understand the possibilities of systematic demonstration. One who writes in the fashion of a system-maker thereby shows that he is sure of having attained the essential truth he has sought, and that he is now endeavoring to fasten it upon his reader; his

unexpressed attitude is: "You will, of course, take my premises for granted, and I am now going to prove that you must
then adopt my conclusions." From the typical Chinese viewpoint such argumentation is not only largely futile (since any
keen and determined reader can always find an alternative
set of plausible premises); it is unseemly. For if one refuses to
take his own convictions too seriously, and approaches his
reader with proper respect for the latter's independent integrity, what he will be concerned to do is not to coerce
an acceptance of his assertions, but so to express them as to
elicit growth toward the reader's own more adequate insight. By its neat exactitude and seeming conclusiveness, logical argument can discourage and even block this growth. Let
us think and speak so as to guide constructive progress in the
experience and understanding of others, not so as to convert
them to some absolute which we have no business to regard
as such ourselves.

A fourth quality, likewise naturally arising from the ones
already mentioned, is a broad and urbane tolerance of novel
or heterodox ways of thinking. To be sure, this has by no
means been unqualified. More or less systematic persecutions
have from time to time occurred; the earliest historical instance on a large scale is the famous "burning of the books"
about 220 B.C., when many Confucian teachers were put to
death; and in later Chinese history there were less drastic
suppressions by the government of ideas felt to be undesirable
or dangerous. But such suppressions were sporadic and have
never led to long-continued or embittered religious wars. By
and large the Chinese attitude has been one of willingness to
live and let live in these matters—even one of open receptivity
to fertile and promising ideas, from whatever quarter they
might appear. This rests on certain characteristics which the
Chinese share with the Indians, who have also exhibited a
broad tolerance of religious belief; but in some respects it
reflects distinctive motivations. Deepest among these, perhaps, is the quality above mentioned of refusing to take one-

self too seriously—of realizing that however much one might be tempted to view his own ideas as absolute, they are really relative to his limited experience and therefore have no business to be enforced upon others who naturally will be led to more or less different ideas. Along with this general recognition of the limitations of one's own experience, there is a remarkable readiness to learn and profit from the contrasting experience of other people. Ordinarily, of course, it is assumed that the ways of the Celestial Kingdom will be superior to those of any group of barbarians, but in any particular area they may prove not to be so; why should we miss any truth that might enlarge our understanding of the world and guide us toward a happier adjustment to it? The Chinese have possessed a vigorous confidence, which seems to them confirmed by the whole course of Eastern history, that their culture can absorb and assimilate whatever is sound in the culture of others without losing in the process the basic values of their traditional heritage.

So far as I know, nothing has occurred elsewhere in human history quite analogous to the spread of Buddhism in China so that it became a major transforming factor in Chinese culture. After other great countries had achieved a civilized status and had adopted an advanced form of civilized religion, no other faith was able to win more than a small fraction of its adherents or to become more than a minor influence in their subsequent development. There might seem to be an exception in the case of some countries which in a late period of their history adopted Islam, e.g., Persia, but in these cases political and social decadence had created a vacuum which was yawning to be filled. Buddhism penetrated China after Confucianism and Taoism (not to mention other religions) had already achieved widespread acceptance, and during a period when, for the most part, Chinese culture was developing vigor rather than displaying weakness. It evidently contained insight that the Chinese did not wish to miss, and they were strong enough to be teachably open to that insight.

The same receptivity is being shown in our century to the scientific technology of Western culture.

A fifth quality of mind, revealed less in Taoism than in the other Chinese religions, is a practical "this-worldliness," and even in Taoism such an attitude is not absent. Again, this is a matter of emphasis in its contrast with prevailing attitudes in the West and in India; it is by no means a universal trait. In Chinese popular religion the quest for means of achieving immortality has been a significant factor, and one note in Chinese mysticism has been the search for oneness with the *Tao* in its transcendent nature. However, among the respected sages the dominant preoccupation is with a happy and constructive adjustment to the realities of society and nature as we meet them in the present world, and their religion has been pervaded by this preoccupation. There is little in their way of thinking which reflects the Western idea that this life is merely a prologue to an eternity beyond; likewise there is little which expresses the Indian eagerness to leave this world behind as a realm of deceitful appearance, and to become one with an ultimate reality conceived as indescribable in terms of such delusive phenomena. The task of life and of religion for the typical Chinese thinker is to make the most of the promising values that man and society here and now exhibit—not forgetting their transcendent dimension, to be sure, but not allowing its allurements to obscure the positive virtues, rich opportunities, and high responsibilities that the world of present reality opens before us.

A sixth quality of mind is revealed in the scale of values that underlies the traditional ordering of social groups in China. Although there has been no rigid system of caste, a hierarchy has been clearly present. The position of greatest respect and eminence in this hierarchy is occupied by the scholar and the sage—not by the aggressive business leader as in the West, nor by the contemplative saint as in India. The scholar who knows history and can guide his fellows toward moral insight has been really admired in China through the centuries, and by virtue of the respectful confidence inspired he has been able to exert a social and political influence far beyond that of any similar class elsewhere in the world. Next, for the Chinese, come the farmers, who provide the food supply for the nation, and are stably united to the productive soil of the earth as the sages are stably responsive to the creative and illuminating energy of Heaven. Next to them stand the artisans, who build the structures and make the instruments that men employ in their daily activities; and at the bottom among these major classes are the merchants, whose possessions are in unstable interchange and whose concern is with that which is profitable rather than with that which is good. Still lower than they, however, are the soldiers, who fill no constructive social role at all. It is provocative to observe that this hierarchical order is almost (though not quite) the reverse of that which obtains in the modern West, especially in America. Equally sharply does it contrast with the traditional caste system in India. There the agricultural workers constitute the lowest caste; above them are the merchants, next come the military and executive leaders, while the priests and religious guides stand at the top. In China no priestly class, strictly so called, has historically emerged, although some of its marks are exhibited by the Taoist or Buddhist monks.

It is obvious that a religious and theological orientation which reflects these characteristics will be rather different from the orientation with which we are familiar in the West, permeated as it is by contrasting attitudes in each of these respects. It is no accident that because of these differences Chinese religion (especially in the form of Confucianism) does not seem to many Westerners to be religion at all—it does not conform to all the criteria that the Jewish-Christian background naturally leads them to assume as essential to religion. But we who are pursuing the present study, having loosened such prejudices through our excursion in the field of primitive religion, will not be troubled or hampered by any rigid assumption. We have committed ourselves to a broad and open-minded conception of religion; we shall accordingly be ready to denote by this word whatever we find in Chinese experience and Chinese history to have met the personal needs and filled the social role that religion elsewhere meets and fills.

C. CENTRAL IDEAS OF CHINESE RELIGION

If one has mastered these background materials, and keeps in mind the general character of civilized religion as described in the preceding chapter, he will not find it difficult to appreciate the central ideas disclosed by an analysis of the living religions in China. These ideas, now to be considered, are common to both Confucianism and Taoism (not to mention other indigenous faiths that have perished); and when Buddhism spread in the Middle Kingdom, they largely account for the differences which its Chinese forms reveal as compared with the Buddhism of non-Chinese areas of Asia.

Perhaps the most central idea of all is that of the *tao*.* This idea is almost untranslatable into any other language than Chinese. Its original meaning is probably "path" or "road," and the least misleading English rendering is through our familiar word "way." But what it expresses in the mature trends of Chinese thinking is not too difficult to master, if one patiently explores its uses in the various contexts where it characteristically appears. To the Chinese, as has been noted, there is a right way for everything to happen. Nature spontaneously does things in the right way, although, because of man's capacity to fall into error, selective wisdom is required on his part to penetrate beneath the deceptive surface and apprehend this *tao* of nature. It is there, however, as a stable metaphysical reality, and it provides the norm whereby man can direct his own aspirations and order his own conduct. Now this statement implies a significant distinction which

---

* This word should be pronounced as a single syllable; the *a* and the *o* coalesce. The *t* is almost as hard as a *d*, the *a* is long as in "father," and the *o* is also the long English *o*. Neither the *a* nor the *o* is lost as the two are compressed into one syllable.

runs through Chinese thought about the *tao*. The *tao* of man
is not identical with the *Tao* of Heaven; it embodies, however, the moral lessons which the wise man can learn only
by discerning and accepting the *Tao* of Heaven. Besides these
metaphysical and moral roles (as the West would categorize
them), the *tao* also fills in Chinese experience a mystical role.
It is immanent, in nature and in man, but it is also transcendent; that is, it embodies more reality, value, and meaning
than any man, or all men at any given time, can apprehend.
In identifying himself with it, man becomes one with a source
and ideal of rightness lying beyond the definite forms of
good order that he can experience and cognize. By virtue of
all these aspects of its meaning, if we had to pick one single
idea as providing the distinctive clue to Chinese philosophy,
it would certainly be the idea of *tao*.

Next, the idea of Heaven as, having evolved through the
process described above, it takes shape in the religious thought
of the civilized period in China. There lingers here the primitive cosmological notion of heaven as the universal protector
of all who live under its canopy and as the creative power
which, acting on the passive receptivity of the earth, produces
the varied phenomena which man needs for life and well-
being—just as the male in fertilizing interaction with the
female brings forth the members of a new generation. But
the vital meaning in civilized thought is that Heaven is the
great cosmic exemplar of the *tao*. It fills this role in two
respects. On the one hand, in the regularity of its astronomical
motions and the succession of seasons which depends on them,
it is the prime model of dependable order in the universe. On
the other hand, in its creative relation to what happens on
the earth, it is the free giver of its goodness without demanding anything in return. All other things receive as well as
give; Heaven, being completely independent and needing
nothing that the rest of the universe has to offer, is the great
exception in this regard and is therefore the supreme example
of the moral ideal.

"Heaven pours forth his virtue, overspreading all things and feeding them. He gives, but takes nothing, therefore the spirits revert to him, and his virtue is supreme. Earth bears all things and lets them grow; she gives, but takes as well, e.g., when by death the body returns to her. Therefore her virtue is of a minor order. The virtue of heaven is the highest possible."[3]

At an early date Heaven came to be used interchangeably with *ti* (and, probably later, with *shang ti*), which is a more personalized term for God conceived as the cosmic "ruler." In virtue of this identification, Heaven combines for Chinese thought a personal and an impersonal—or, perhaps, "superpersonal"—connotation. Confucius expressed a serene trust, when misunderstood and persecuted, that "Heaven knows me"; at the same time the "decree of Heaven" is often used as a semimetaphorical phrase for the inescapable law according to which things happen in human affairs in the way they do. When the former connotation is clearly present, "Heaven" may be properly translated by the Western word "God" or, more specifically, "Providence"; when the latter connotation is dominant, it should rather be rendered by "law of nature" or, sometimes, by "fate."

In the third place, the conception of man in the developed religious thought of China is very important. We should expect this from its vigorous humanistic emphasis and from the central role which it gives to social ethics. On the cosmological side:

Man occupies an interesting place in this universe. He is . . . a natural and inseparable part of it, his acts affecting all the universe, and all the universe affecting him in a manner much more intimate than the Western world is accustomed to suppose. Yet he is also felt to be unique. . . . The *Liki* [*Book of Rites*] says:

Man is the heart and mind of Heaven and Earth,
and the visible embodiment of the five elements.
He lives in the enjoyment of all flavors, the

discriminating of all notes, and the enrobing
of all colors.

Here is suggested the idea, voiced many times, that man is a
microcosm, reflecting the universe. He is certainly in close relation to it.[4]

On the moral side, and in its relation to the metaphysical,
what this means is that man occupies a high and dignified
status in the scheme of things. Alone among the creatures
that exist under heaven, he has the capacity to understand the
tao, and to order his life in accordance with that understanding. It is his privilege and responsibility as an individual to
realize what this unique capacity involves. It is his duty (although here we have a specifically Confucian emphasis) to
apprehend the clue to the right relation between man and
man that can be found in the basic institution of the family,
and to grow toward a complete imitation of the *tao* from
the fulfillment of what it implies for his family duties.

Fourth, there is the idea emphasized in one of the primitive
survivals—unfamiliar to modern Westerners, though not to
their forefathers—of the political ruler as filling a religious
and moral as well as an administrative role. As has above
been noted, the ruler should be a moral example to his people;
if he fails in this regard, not only will the inevitable social
consequences ensue but also catastrophes in physical nature
affecting man's weal or woe. In virtue of this idea, a confusing
and anxious problem has arisen for Chinese religious thought
since the fall of the Manchu dynasty in 1912; subsequent to
that date no one has been accepted as properly occupying
this distinctive position, and therefore as capable of conduct-
ing the ceremonies on the Altar of Heaven that symbolize
in impressive form this mediating role between the divine
power above and his people. It may well be that this idea is
now moribund and that Chinese religion in the future will
be adjusted to its absence.

There is, fifth, the significant place of the sage in Chinese thinking. Other religions have their prophets and priests, their saints and theologians, but in place of all these the Chinese follow and revere the sage. His is the role of moral leader and teacher, counselor to the ruler, wise interpreter of the maxims of old in their bearing on individual problems and social affairs. One must not miss the significance of this fact for an understanding of religion in China. Sages have sometimes been elevated to the status of divine incarnations —Confucius has been so regarded by a few of his later followers—but in general they have been viewed simply as superior men, the superiority being measured by their moral and intellectual leadership. Even in Confucius' case the title usually assigned him in the Confucian temples is simply that of "the most revered teacher."

All the influential Chinese religions appeal, sixth, to a Golden Age in the past when, so it has been traditionally believed, the ideal social order was actually realized under the benign example and guidance of the great rulers of ancient time. That age, therefore, provides a historical norm to which we should turn in seeking a wise correction of foolish individual conduct and corrupt social practice. Usually the age idealized in these terms is the period preceding the emergence of the first dynasty, but sometimes it is the early years of the Chou that are mentioned for this purpose. In fact, the more conservative interpretation of Confucius makes it a vital part of his program to reëstablish the ideal feudal order which he believed to have existed before the calamitous disintegration of his own day had set in.

We must not forget, in the seventh and last place, a presupposition of Chinese thinking about man and the universe which contrasts sharply with the corresponding belief in Indian and in traditional Western thought. This is the assumption that all things are ultimately in process, rather than being grounded in some changeless absolute. The Chinese mind has naturally accepted a dynamic point of view in cosmology; there appears to be no word in the Chinese language by which to translate the Western concept of "substance," meaning an entity which remains the same through a period of time. Buddhism could appeal to the Chinese partly because it agrees with this dynamic emphasis. This conviction differs radically, however, both from the Hindu belief in the changeless Brahman and from the conviction of Western theologies that God in His essential nature is beyond all temporal vicissitudes—that however much other things may change, the divine being remains from age to age the same. "In such a thought-world as that of the Chinese it is process (as in the rotation of the seasons) which is stressed; perfection is a dynamic, not a static, ideal. Harmony, as the *summum bonum*, must be a highway to follow, not a temple in which to stop."[5] It is easy to appreciate how, in this dynamic framework of thought, the Chinese should think of ultimate reality as a "way" rather than as an ontological entity.

Each of the two indigenous Chinese religions that remain influential today—Confucianism and Taoism—takes for granted these fundamental ideas, and its philosophical interpretations move in the setting which they provide.* In each of them, these concepts are freed from the obstructive superstitions of primitive thought (at least in the minds of their leading thinkers), and infused with the spiritual insight and moral vitality essential to a religion teaching a way of life

---

* H. G. Creel gives a brief summary of most of these ideas in their significant interrelationships (*Sinism*, Chicago, 1929, pp. 63 f.):

"First, the conviction that there exists a potential and preëstablished pattern according to which all existing things ought to be arranged and regulated, that all things are good in their proper place, and that all deviation from this pattern is unnatural and the result of perversion. This is the belief in the *tao*.

"Second, that the emperor is the center of all things on earth (including human and animal society), that he is the earthly viceroy of more than human power, and that it is only necessary for him to adjust perfectly to the *tao* in order to bring about earthly harmony; conversely, all disorders on earth are caused by failure of the emperor to follow the *tao*. The sage has special knowledge of the *tao* and should be employed to advise the emperor.

"Third, that in remote times the "Holy Emperors" of the "Golden Age" knew and followed the *tao*, and it is therefore only necessary to learn and follow their formula in order to bring about universal felicity."

appropriate to the needs and problems of civilized society. I mean by saying this that in each of them this framework of thought is so construed and developed that it gives the individual systematic guidance to real and dependable happiness, and society a way leading to stable peace and brotherhood.

But each of them does this in a different fashion and under the direction of a different central principle. The Taoist philosopher says: "Purge yourself of the desires that can be seen to lead to unhappy futility!" The Confucian philosopher says: "Harmonize your desires, so that the happiness they promise can be dependably realized!" This difference is not a radical one on the metaphysical side, but in its bearing on the practical way to the spiritual goal it cuts pretty deep. Consider in this regard the significance of the concept of *tao* in these two religions. Metaphysically, in the case of both of them it stands for the universal order of harmony and perfection, which is ultimately real and is also the norm under whose guidance man can realize his moral ideal. As a concept of method, it signifies the way in which this ideal is to be wisely pursued in the present social world, and on this point they reveal sharply diverging convictions. For Taoism, the proper way is that of gaining detachment from the evil corruptions in oneself, in the faith that a virtuous character will then arise and express itself with a simple naturalness. For Confucianism, the proper way is that of earnest cultivation of what is already good—one's fellow-feeling and sense of social responsibility—in the faith that what is discordant with it will through this process gradually fade away and a more stably virtuous character will thus be built. In both religions, the needed reform of society is achieved through the prior appearance of individuals able and ready to exemplify in their relations with others the virtues which create and preserve a sound social order.

It is in virtue of this difference that some of the generalizations about religion frequently made by non-Chinese theologians and philosophers do not strictly apply to Confucianism, and need revision if they are to cover the whole field of the great civilized religions. Sir S. Radhakrishnan, thinking of religion as it has been exemplified in India and in the West, offers the following trenchant criticism:

"Religions as they have come down to us . . . emphasize the individual, rather than the social, side of life. By exaggerating the values of personal development, they discourage the growth of social sense and imagination. They stress contemplation more than action, theory more than practice. By their conceptions of the Kingdom of God they turn men away from their efforts to secure a better life on earth."[6]

Confucianism is the outstanding civilized religion of which this description is definitely not true. It is, to be sure, as keenly alive as other great religions to "the values of personal development"; no one familiar with its genius and history would be likely to reproach it as defective on that score. But Radhakrishnan's negative assertions flatly contradict what is most distinctive and significant in Confucianism. Far from discouraging, it strongly encourages "the growth of social sense and imagination," and this on religious principles that are central to it. It will soon be our task to see in some detail how this is so.

D. FROM CONFUCIUS TO THE PRESENT DAY

Before we plunge into the major features of Confucianism and Taoism, an anticipatory survey of the course of religion in Chinese history after these two faiths had become established will be in order.

By the end of the third century before Christ each of these religions had absorbed the main factors that its pioneer thinkers had contributed, and had entered the stream of Chinese history as a more or less systematized philosophy and a distinctive way of life. Beginning with the Han dynasty, which came to power in 206 B.C., Confucianism became the dominant orthodoxy, and through most of the subsequent period it continued to occupy that role. Taoism, however, exerted a powerful appeal on many Chinese minds in every generation, and occasionally rose to the position of an effective political force; this happened, for example, in the third and fourth centuries A.D. In A.D. 67 Buddhism was introduced from India; its influence gradually spread and reached its peak during the sixth and seventh centuries of the Christian era. At this time it might well have seemed to an impartial observer that the foreign faith had swept all before it and was destined to replace the native religions. But there was too much vitality in Confucianism and Taoism for this to happen; instead, Buddhism became a third major force in shaping Chinese culture and the development of Chinese religion. In the twelfth century the philosophy of Neo-Confucianism arose, synthesizing traditional Confucian doctrines with much that was central in the spirit and teaching of Buddhism. For several centuries this more inclusive Confucian philosophy was the dominant intellectual and spiritual trend in Chinese thinking, only gradually giving way to the factors which have converged in the current turbulent upheaval of the Celestial Kingdom.

The revolution in China which the world is now witnessing is a matter of the last fifty years, though forces beneath the surface that lead in the same direction have been stirring for a much longer time. It is a social and political as well as an intellectual and spiritual revolution. That it is the former is revealed in the political convulsions that have been apparent to the most casual observer—the revolution establishing the Republic under Sun Yat-sen in 1912, the rise to dominance of the Nationalists under Chiang Kai-shek in 1926–1928, and the transformation of China into a communist state under Mao Tse-tung in 1949. That it is an intellectual revolution too is evident in the growing eagerness to absorb Western science and technology, and the readiness to take Western philosophies as serious competitors with Chinese ways of thinking; on the negative side it is apparent in the fact that the intellectual and spiritual coherence that had been so long established under the guidance of the Confucian tradition has been lost. For half a century the young leaders in China have been searching for a new center. Many of them now believe that this new center has been found in the communist ideology, as it has been adapted to the major social problems of present-day China. One who takes a long-range view of human history, however, will be assured that the philosophies of the past will not disappear; China will modify communism far more than communism modifies China. That this is, indeed, already happening is indicated by the differences in the attitudes and policies of the Chinese communist leaders as compared with those of the Kremlin.

The crucial question, which only the future can answer, is: How profoundly will the communist social ideal and philosophy of history remold the inherited Chinese patterns of thought and ways of life, and what form will the product of their interaction take—in China's culture as a whole and in her religion? Would that we might confidently guess what the answer will be!

But our task is to understand Chinese religion as it has been and is, not as it will be in the future. Which of the two great native faiths should we study first? If this book had been written a generation ago (or even somewhat less), I should naturally have described Taoism before Confucianism. The traditional dates for the life of Lao Tse—reputedly the philosophical founder of Taoism—make him an elder contemporary of Confucius. Since historical sequence provides the most impartial order in which to explore religions that have enjoyed any significant interaction with each other, it would naturally follow in that case that we should give priority to Taoism.[7] But it is now frequently held, especially among the younger and bolder sinologists, that this dating is a mistake, and that if Lao Tse was a historical individual he could not have lived earlier than the fourth century B.C. And no careful student of the famous *Tao Teh Ching*, the early classic of Taoism, can fail to detect that in its present form, at least, it takes for granted the currency of certain Confucian ideas, which it subjects to merciless criticism. A possible solution of the problem, to which some scholars incline, is that Lao Tse lived at the time to which he was traditionally assigned, but that the *Tao Teh Ching* is only in part his work—that it is a collection of thoughts gradually accumulating from the sixth to the third century B.C., and perhaps longer. Although the Confucian literature exhibits a similar process, the dates for Confucius' life are fairly secure. Accordingly, I shall expound Confucianism first; this order of presentation will also have the virtue of enabling us to relate Taoism directly to Buddhism—the Indian religion which spread in China largely because at certain vital points it was in harmony with Taoist principles.

VI

Confucianism

A. CONFUCIUS' LIFE AND PERSONALITY

Confucius was born in the state of Lu, now a part of Shantung Province, in 551 B.C. and died near his birthplace in 479 B.C. There are readable and instructive biographies of him; for our purposes, it is unnecessary to dwell upon many details of his life. He was brought up by his mother, his father having died when he was a baby. In his youth he showed a strong interest in study and in the traditional religious rites. He rose in his fifties to several responsible ministerial positions. But failing to find (in his native state or elsewhere) an administrative post which really gave him opportunity to achieve the political and social reforms which he saw to be desperately needed, he traveled about for some fifteen years, making contact with men in positions of authority and spreading his ideas among all who were responsive. His late years were spent in teaching his disciples—the activity which he had already become convinced was of first importance in paving the way for the regeneration of society. For he was sure that any such regeneration, to be genuine and enduring, must be based on the moral and spiritual renewal of those who were to carry it through.

What was it in Confucius' personality that appealed to his disciples and followers, so that subsequent generations of

Chinese could look back to him as "the most revered teacher" in their illustrious past? Well, if we accept as essentially dependable the complex picture handed down by tradition, there was much in his make-up that India, with her ideal of the ascetic saint, and the West, with its ideal of the fiery and aggressive prophet, find it hard to associate with a religious leader. He was very meticulous in matters of dress, food, and social deportment. He was an eager and studious historical scholar, and believed that both constructive moral insight and sound political strategy must be based on a wise understanding of the lessons of history. There is a deep note of conservatism in his constant appeal to the model supposedly displayed in the righteous ways of the ancients, and in the significance he attached to the preservation of ceremony and ritual.

. . . true filial piety consists in successfully carrying out the unfinished work of our forefathers and transmitting their achievements to posterity. . . .

To gather in the same places where our fathers before us have gathered; to perform the same ceremonies which they before us have performed; to play the same music which they before us have played; to pay respect to those whom they honored; to love those who were dear to them—in fact, to serve those now dead as if they were living, and now departed as if they were still with us: this is the highest achievement of true filial piety.[1]

But these characteristics were combined with others. Like most Chinese, he was full of jollity and humor, and was always ready to enjoy a joke on himself. He loved music, and was no mean player on the *ch'in** himself. More important still, he loved people—especially those who seemed capable of intellectual effort and were responsive to the practical challenge of whatever moral insight they had gained. He hated insincerity and hypocrisy. He was modest about his own attainments, and yet always maintained a dignified self-respect. He was at ease in the presence of all manner of folks— high and low, serious and flippant, hostile or friendly. He

* A stringed instrument popular in China.

was always ready to learn from experience and to raise the most searching questions—even questions about his basic convictions. He was at peace within himself. And finally, there was in his soul a deep and abiding trust in Heaven as the prime exemplar of the moral order of the universe; he serenely left in the hands of Heaven whatever tasks could not be fulfilled through his own untiring and devoted effort. It was in virtue of this last quality that it would not be sufficient to describe Confucius as a moral philosopher; he was also one of the spiritual pioneers of civilized mankind. In sum, he reflects and carries far toward perfection the most distinctive and endearing characteristics of the Chinese temper as it has revealed itself to the rest of the world through the centuries.

This description may be rendered more concrete, and several of these significant qualities illustrated, by reference to a particular occasion in his life as it is described by the great Chinese historian Szu Ma Chien.[2]

It occurred in 489 B.C., during the middle period of his wanderings from state to state. Certain basic features of his character and philosophy had just gained clarified expression. His disciple Tselu had been asked by the Duke of Ch'u to give him a description of Confucius and Tselu, too baffled to reply, reported his quandary to the master. Confucius said at once, "Why didn't you tell him that I am a man who seeks the truth untiringly and teaches others unceasingly, who forgets to eat when he is enthusiastic about something, who loses all his worries when he is happy, and who doesn't know that old age is coming on?" The same Duke asked Confucius directly what constitutes the essence of good government, and Confucius replied, "Good government consists in [such policies as are likely to succeed in] winning the loyalty of people at home and attracting those who are abroad." A little later a group of thinkers had been met who had abandoned all hope of improving society, and one of them had challenged Tselu: "The world is full of people wandering about [as you are doing], but who is ever going to change the state of affairs? . . . Why not follow a leader who avoids society altogether?" Again Tselu reported to Confucius, who sighed and said, "Birds and beasts [and those who wish to imitate them] are not the right company for us. If there were a moral order in the world as it stands, I wouldn't try to change it."

It was soon after this that the revealing event occurred. One day Confucius and his party found themselves surrounded by a battalion of soldiers who held them in close custody, permitting no one to leave the area. According to Szu Ma Chien, the ministers of two neighboring states had plotted together and had decided, "Confucius is a very able man. He has pointed out the weaknesses of the rulers of the different states. Now he has remained for a long time around here and he doesn't seem to like what we are doing. Ch'u is a powerful state and is thinking of using Confucius, and if Confucius should ever get into power in Ch'u, our countries would be in trouble and we ourselves the ministers would be in danger." It is not clear just how serious the threat was, but the historian reports that the party was getting short of food and that several members had fallen sick. Confucius' disciples began to behave in ways that expressed their anxious fear, but Confucius himself, serenely trustful in Heaven, continued to study as usual and to sing, accompanying himself on the *ch'in.*

Tselu angrily reproached the Master, "Does a superior man sometimes realize when he is in dangerous circumstances?" "Yes," replied Confucius, "a superior man is sometimes aware that he is in dangerous circumstances. But when a common man finds himself in danger he forgets himself, and does all sorts of foolish things." The remark sank home, and Tselu was silent. But some of the other young men were impressed, and Confucius added, "What have you been thinking about me—that all I've been trying to do is to learn as many details as possible [about history and moral conduct] and commit them to memory?" "I have thought so," replied one of the young men; "isn't that true?" "No," said Confucius, "there is a central thread which runs through all my knowledge." What he referred to was the basic principle of the Golden Rule: Do not do to others what you do not wish them to do to you. And the implied corollary was: In my study and meditation I have been seeking such general truths as this—truths by which a man can live whatever the circumstances into which he may fall, truths expressive of his deepest insight and his full moral integrity, truths in following which he knows himself to be in tune with the way of Heaven—truths therefore in commitment to which a man can overcome all anxiety and fear.

But the disciples could not quite apprehend his meaning; they were still baffled and apprehensive. So, seeing their state, Confucius decided to share with them, one by one, without reserve, the troubled question that had been going through his own mind since the perilous event had befallen them. "It is said in the *Book of Songs*, 'neither buffalos, nor tigers, they none the less find themselves wandering in the desert.' It *is* strange that we are in this situation. Does it mean that my teachings are wrong?" Tselu, who had been called in first, replied, "Perhaps we are not great enough and have not been able to win people's confidence. Perhaps we are not wise enough and people are not willing to follow our teachings." "Is that so?" said Confucius. "Ah Yu, if the great could always gain the confidence of the people, why did Poyi and Shuch'i have to go and die of starvation in the mountains? If the wise men could always have their teachings followed by others, why did Prince Pikan have to commit suicide?"

Tselu came out and Tsekung went in, and Confucius said, "Ah Sze, it is said in the *Books of Songs*, 'Neither buffalos, nor tigers, they wander in the desert.' Are my teachings wrong? How is it that I find myself now in this situation?" Tsekung replied, "The Master's teachings are too great for the people, and that is why the world cannot accept them. Why don't you come down a little from your heights?" Confucius replied, "Ah Sze, a good farmer plants the field but cannot guarantee the harvest, and a good artisan does a skillful job, but he cannot guarantee to please his customers. Now you are not interested in cultivating yourselves, but are only interested in being accepted by the people. I am afraid you are not setting the highest standard for yourself."

Tsekung came out and Yen Huei went in, and Confucius said, "Ah Huei, it is said in the *Book of Songs*, 'Neither buffalos, nor tigers, they wander in the desert.' Are my teachings wrong? How is it that this plight has now come upon us?" And Yen Huei replied, "The Master's teachings are so great. That is why the world cannot accept them. However, you should just do your best to spread your ideas. What do you care if they are not accepted? The very fact that your teachings are not accepted shows that you are truly a superior man. If the truth is not cultivated, the shame is ours; but if we have already strenuously cultivated the teachings of a moral order and they are not accepted by the people, it is the shame of those in power." And Confucius was pleased and said smilingly, "Is that so? Oh, son of Yen, if you were a rich man, I would be your butler!"

The story has a happy ending: the King of Ch'u, hearing the news of Confucius' imprisonment through one of the disciples who escaped through the lines, sent an army to rescue him. But we must not miss the lesson which the sage taught his disciples in this dangerous situation—imparting it as much by his fearlessness and his readiness to share his own questionings with them as by the words which he elicited or spoke. One must not assume that true greatness and wisdom will at once succeed in winning converts, nor should one, in his eagerness for public approval, dilute his message or fail to express the deepest insight he has gained. His task, while he remains always open to criticism and eager to achieve a completer wisdom, is to sow the seed to the best of his ability and trust Heaven for the ultimate harvest. If he did not do this, the failure would be his; if when he does this a public response does not quickly come, the failure is on the part of the rulers who have not given him the opportunity to make his teaching influential. And we must not miss, too, the remarkable illustration, given by this story, both of Confucius' method of moral education and of the third quality of the Chinese mind mentioned above—the readiness to use language not as a technique of systematic demonstration but as a medium of eliciting moral insight in the hearts and intuitive judgments of others. The essence of the lesson here is not spoken by Confucius himself but by the young men who have grasped it under the stress of his searching questions and the clarifying power of his example.

B. THE CENTRAL IDEAS IN CONFUCIAN MORAL PHILOSOPHY

Before we endeavor to penetrate more fully the secret of his way of thinking and to master his message, it will be well to pause for two rather dry but necessary considerations. The Confucian literature, as traditionally conceived, consists of the so-called Five Classics and Four Books. The Five Classics—*Book of Rites, Book of Change, Book of History, Book of Poetry*, and *Spring and Autumn Annals*—were, with one exception, in existence before Confucius' time. But they were edited by him and his followers, so that in the form in which we now have them they definitely reflect a Confucian perspective. The exception is the *Spring and Autumn Annals*, a history of the Chou era from 722 to 481 B.C., which has traditionally been ascribed to Confucius himself. The Four Books are the more distinctively Confucian sources. Foremost among them is the *Analects*—disconnected sayings of Confucius that were preserved by his disciples. Then there are the *Golden Mean* and the *Great Learning*—expanded chapters from the *Book of Rites*, as interpreted by Confucius and refracted through the understanding of his early followers. These two books are collections of essays on basic Confucian themes, such as the superior man; the nature of true manhood; the significance of ritual, of education, and of music; the art of government; the moral order of the universe. The last of the four books is the *Book of Mencius,* containing the doctrines of a great Confucian thinker who lived two centuries after Confucius. Mencius' work comes closest, of these varied materials, to exemplifying what the West would expect in a systematic moral and religious philosophy.

Now, since Confucianism is the first of the living civilized religions that are the object of our study, it is important to note—for the initial strangeness of these documents is apt to obscure it to a Western reader—that with this literature we are in a different atmosphere from that of primitive religion. The basic concern is no longer the struggle for life, for the precarious requisites of continued physical existence; it is, instead, the quest for the good life—for the finest moral and spiritual realization of which man is capable under the complex conditions that a civilized society confronts. With Confucianism we are in the midst of the harassing and threatening social problems that man has created for himself when civilization emerges; we are beginning to glimpse the new and wonderful potentialities that he reveals in this altered historical situation. The demands of mere existence are now subordinated to the vision of something greater and more appealing than had loomed as a real possibility before, but which now is believed to lie open to men if they but dare to rise to the challenge of a clarified moral ideal.

One can reconstruct the course of Confucius' thinking with fair confidence if one does not succumb to the temptation of trying to do so in too great detail. He began with the worsening political and social situation of his day, rendered more poignant because his historical knowledge led him to believe that at an earlier time human life was happier and justice more fully realized. The anarchy, callousness, and oppression that he saw around him on every hand had not obtained then; the traditional proprieties were recognized and practiced, and the rulers governed the people as true Sons of Heaven should. And it seemed clear to him that at the root of this general social problem lay an individual and personal one. Those who were regarded as "gentlemen" did not show the responsible moral leadership that this term ought to connote and for which the times desperately called; far from taking the initiative and pointing the way by their example toward the true social order, they were giving themselves to luxury and dissipation, and were using their power of inherited wealth to plunge the common people into even greater subjection, poverty, and despair. Where lies the solution of this deepening social and personal confusion—a solution that would really be adequate and assure increasing and lasting success? He saw that it must be fundamentally a moral solution—hence Confucianism has the character of a constructive ethical philosophy; but he saw also that it would not be complete without the cosmic overtones and implications that make it a religion as well. This solution would begin to reveal itself when men appeared who were really gentlemen (i.e., superior men in the true sense of the word)—men endowed with moral insight, men ready to assume the responsibilities of moral leadership without waiting for others to fill such a role first. In fact, a basic characteristic of the superior man, for Confucius, is the kind of independence that initiates the regeneration of society, and does so by accepting the task of self-renewal—of making oneself, through moral understanding and moral commitment, capable of filling this creative role. And one who steadily pursues this course will naturally be responsive to the divine harmony in the universe at large, of which the ideal order in men's social relationships is a reflection and with which it is intrinsically continuous.

I shall expound the genius of Confucianism by elaborating in some detail on the nature of this solution and by attempting to clarify the basic concepts in which it is expressed. To none of these concepts is there any precise equivalent in Western languages; an Occidental can understand them only by gradually mastering their meaning to the earnest Confucian as he uses them in the context of his moral experience and his spiritual aspirations. Of these basic concepts, three are primary; other important ideas gain their meaning largely in and through their relation to these three. *Tao*, of course, is one of these, but in the case of Confucianism it is best to introduce it last; the other two, which we shall examine first, are *li* and *jen*. In the following exposition I shall not attempt to distinguish between the thought of Confucius himself and ideas that soon became a part of the Confucian tradition.

Confucius was sure that the deepening social problem of his day was largely caused by the loss of *li*, and that its restoration was an essential requisite to any sound solution. Lin Yu-tang, attempting to explain this difficult term to Westerners, says:

> In the narrowest sense, it means "rituals," "propriety," and just "good manners"; in an historical sense, it means the rationalized system of feudal order [that was supposedly realized in the early Chou period]; in a philosophic sense, it means an ideal social order with "everything in its place"; and in a personal sense, it means a pious, religious state of mind, very near to the word "faith." . . . Among the Chinese scholars, Confucianism is known as the "religion of *li*," the nearest translation for which would be "religion of moral order." It subjects the political order to the moral social order, making the latter the basis of the former. . . .[3]

It is obvious that the unifying core of meaning here, by which this term has implications different from those of the *tao* as discussed above, lies in the idea expressed in English by the adjective "proper" and the noun "propriety." The conservative side of Confucianism is revealed especially in this concept; one of its basic emphases is reverence for the best that has come down from the past.[4] That is, certain modes of conduct have gradually been established, through tradition and custom, which smooth our social relations, express our pious emotions, and satisfy our need to feel that we live in harmonious continuity with the ways of those who have gone before; let us preserve them, faithfully practice them, discipline the rebellious impulses which would lead us to neglect them, realize the unity of spirit which a community enjoys when all its members are governed by respect for these proprieties.

If one catches this central thought, with all its implications, he will see why a translator of *li* in its varied contexts will need on occasion to use all the English terms that Lin Yu-tang's definition has employed. And he will see, too, how a religion that emphasizes *li* will naturally adopt the belief that no human act is so lacking in importance that the manner of its doing is morally indifferent. Everything will be done either in a spirit of respect for *li* or in the absence of such a spirit; hence even courtesy and good manners in the least significant situations of life gain a moral value and are among the modes of conduct implied by this word. When we pass from these practical meanings to the general religious attitude which is bound up with them, the word "reverence" probably comes closest in English to conveying the Confucian idea.

But the concept *jen* is equally important; it is needed to balance the essentially conservative emphasis of *li*. A religion of *li* alone would quickly become nothing but a way of clinging to established tradition, with a strong aversion to all change and a lack of responsiveness to the novel needs of a living situation. *Jen* provides the complementary emphasis at this point: it saves Confucianism from the rigidity and fundamentalist inertia that would otherwise threaten it, and it does so in a special and significant way. This term, again, is untranslatable, in the sense that there is no English equivalent; a rendering that in most cases is fairly close is the one preferred by Lin Yu-tang—"true manhood." Dr. E. R. Hughes chooses a translation which brings out the etymology of the Chinese character for *jen* (仁). The left-hand part of this character is the symbol for "man"; the right-hand part is the number "two." This derivation suggests—at least, when the

typical uses of the word in various settings are kept in mind—
that the root idea is something like this: "the proper way in
which a true man would act, in relation to any other man."
Dr. Hughes, accordingly, translates the term by "man-to-
manness," thus explicitly coining an English equivalent for
this concept.

Now, in my attempt to express the root idea, I have used
the word "proper," which implies that in some sense *jen* includes the meaning of *li*, while conveying a further meaning
too. I think this is the case. No one can exemplify *jen* without practicing *li*, while it would be possible, to a degree at
least, to show respect for *li* without living up to the full
meaning of *jen*. And this relationship between the two is
clearly implied by one of the memorable sayings attributed
to Confucius: "True manhood consists in realizing your true
self and restoring the moral order (or *li*). If a man can just
for one day realize his true self, and restore complete moral
order, the world will follow him."[5] It would indeed seem obvious that one could not express man-to-manness without
exhibiting courteous consideration of others or without respecting the proprieties that have become rooted in their feelings and habits.

In what essential respects, then, does the meaning of *jen*
reach beyond the implications of *li?* Both of these concepts
presuppose that man is fundamentally a social being and that
he accepts the responsibilities which fall upon him in virtue
of that fact. But *li* assumes in general that what those responsibilities involve is already known (since it consists in maintaining the traditional forms of proper behavior), whereas a
basic implication of *jen* is that it is not fully known and in
the nature of the case cannot be. There is flexibility involved
in the meaning of *jen;* a part of what it implies to the reflective Confucian is that one must be intelligently adjustable
to the needs of each new human situation and not allow himself to be rigidly bound by any traditional routine. He is expected to express wise moral discrimination in his realization

of man-to-manness in any given case—knowing when to be sternly just and when to show kindly compassion, when to be trustful and when to be cautious, when to assert a dignified firmness and when to give way to the wishes of others. In brief, he must realize the Golden Mean of true manliness as compared with the various pairs of extremes, such as foolhardiness and cowardice, callousness and sentimental pity, into which a person who lacks the virtue of *jen* is likely to fall.[6]

Now this wise adaptability, together with the basic meaning of *jen*, suggest that there is some general principle by which the person committed to the way of true manhood will be guided in all his decisions and acts. It must be a principle which cannot be fully expressed in any customary routine and through which the superior man creates, so far as in him lies, the moral order that will bring enduring harmony and mutual fulfillment when practiced by others as well as by himself. As we have seen, Confucius taught such a principle; it is symbolized by the term *shu*, which is usually translated "reciprocity." The West is familiar with it as the Golden Rule, here stated in negative form: "Do not do unto others what you do not want others to do unto you."[7] This form of the universal rule of moral conduct has been criticized by Westerners as falling short of the positive form taught in the gospels by Jesus: "Whatsoever you would that men should do unto you, do you even so to them." There are other passages in the Confucian literature, however, which make it plain that Confucius was clearly aware of its positive meaning. In one of the many statements modestly recognizing his own imperfections, he is reported to have said:

There are four things in the moral life of a man, not one of which have I been able to carry out in my life. To serve my father as I would expect my son to serve me: that I have not been able to do. To serve my sovereign as I would expect a minister under me to serve me: that I have not been able to do. To act towards my elder brothers as I should expect my younger brother to act toward me: that I have not been able to do. To be the first to behave towards friends as I would expect them to behave towards me: that I have not been able to do.[8]

This quotation, clarifying Confucius' interpretation of the rule of reciprocity as providing guidance to one committed to the ideal of true manhood, is important in two further respects. It shows, first, that the central point in his mind about the role of *shu* was that the man who practices it puts himself understandingly in the place of the other person whom his conduct affects, and acts in the manner which, he realizes, the other person would wish to have exemplified in that relationship. It is taken for granted that it will also be a manner in which his own self-respect and equality are maintained; the moral man will not conform to any demand that he act in a subservient fashion or allow himself to be exploited. It brings out, second, the way in which Confucianism makes use, in this regard, of the social relationships with which all people are acquainted as a foundation on which the comprehension and practice of *shu* can be stably achieved. In view of the common core in these relationships every normal person can appreciate how a just sovereign ought to treat a subject, how a wise father ought to treat his son, how a considerate elder brother ought to treat his younger brother, how a true friend would treat a friend. In fact, in some of these cases one vividly knows this from his own experience. Every father has been a son, and knows the feelings of a son; every ruler has been (during his younger years) subject to authority, and knows the feelings of those who are subject to authority. The major social relationship not mentioned in this quotation, among the five traditionally emphasized in Confucian philosophy, is that between husband and wife. But the significance of this intimate bond is by no means forgotten; in fact, there are passages which attribute to it unique importance in the achievement of spiritual insight.[9]

In the main, however, marriage is treated as only one of the cardinal relations in a normal life; and it is noticeable

that two of the five relationships explicitly involve a difference of age—that of father and son and that of elder and
younger brother—while in the case of four of the five, special
honor and authority rest on one of the pair in comparison
with the other. It is no wonder, then, that the father-son relationship, which exhibits each of these features in familiar
and vivid fashion, serves as the key to the moral and social
attitude which Confucianism prizes as of basic importance.
The relation between ruler and subject is conceived as
definitely analogous to that between father and son; something of the same note appears in the husband-wife relationship and that between elder and younger brother; moreover,
the honored ancestors are approached by the living in essentially the same attitude of respectful and dutiful affection that
good children show toward parents still alive.[10]

In view of these circumstances we are not surprised to
find filial piety (*hsiao*) treated in the later Confucian literature and in Chinese tradition as the focal and distinctive moral
virtue, concretely embodying *jen* in its inclusion of *li*, and
infusing all other virtues and modes of social conduct with
something of its own quality. The family is the important
economic and social unit in China; in many villages it is
essentially a political unit, too. The attitudes and emotions
that are characteristic of happy family life are stable and
strong; they naturally pervade all one's human relationships.
The basic concepts, then, which order the intercourse between man and man and disclose what true manhood implies
in this or that situation, derive their meaning in the last analysis from the pattern of a model family, and especially from
the mellow harmony between a wise father and a respectful
son. In ideal, this harmony should expand to include all humanity, on the principle that "within the four seas all men
are brothers"; and one of the results of accepting this ideal
(in view of the emphasis on filial piety) is the high degree to
which honor and tender consideration are shown the aged
generally—who for this reason have occupied in Chinese cul-

ture a unique position of dignity and respect. It is in the cheerful, warm, and secure enfoldment of family life in general and the relationship of father and son in particular that men are expected to learn the habits of thoughtful kindness, dutiful care, and spontaneous affection that are appropriately expressed in any exemplification of true manhood.

We may say in summary that from the fully developed Confucian point of view the enduring stability of society must be grounded in the stability of the family, which in its turn must be rooted in the stable moral integrity of each individual.

The truly superior man then, for Confucianism, is a person of sensitivity to *li*, whose virtues are perfected in *jen;* the rule of conduct which he practices (*shu*) is no abstract principle but is a generalization of the ideals whose meaning and validity are clear in the daily life of a happy family. He will have other virtues too, but they are either corollaries of those just described or are conditions of their effective exercise. He will be sincere in heart, that is, unqualifiedly devoted to the right; this virtue is expressed by the Chinese concept *yi*. He will not fail in moral courage. He will be responsible in action and always worthy of trust. He will be friendly toward all. He will prize wisdom and understanding, acquiring the insights of the past and being open-minded to any new lessons that the present can teach. He will be serene and cheerful in mind, for he has accepted the universe without demanding more than it is likely to give, and he knows that whatever may betide he has realized his own moral integrity—the ultimate value that can be achieved by any man. He has fully accepted Shakespeare's maxim: "to thine own self be true, and it must follow, as the night the day, thou canst not then be false to any man."[11] In this sense he is sure that goodness is its own reward, and he is content with the decree of Heaven which has so ordered life that, with all its vicissitudes and pains, this achievement of spiritual reality is open to man.

How are the insight and virtue of the superior man communicated to others—and especially to those of the younger generation who are expected to assume the mantle of moral leadership when it falls from his shoulders? In two ways, both of which are emphasized again and again in the Confucian classics: by education and by example.

We need not pause long over the former; its role and importance have been implied in the above exposition. The one point which needs explicit mention—because it is not a part of the prevailing Western idea of education—is that for Confucianism this process is not just the sharing of intellectual information but is spiritual training, and its intellectual aspect is profoundly affected by the fact that the ultimate aim is moral growth and preparation for moral leadership. All things—so the guiding assumption runs—are truly understood in their relation to the social realities and spiritual possibilities of man; and these are dealt with not from the viewpoint of satisfying a theoretical curiosity, but from the practical standpoint of realizing through them the finest quality of life that is open to man. More specifically, the underlying aim in education is gradually to establish in the pupil a basic accord between the motives expressed in his conduct and the moral law which all right conduct exemplifies. Only by appreciating this will we understand what Confucius means when he says, "Education begins with poetry, is strengthened through proper conduct [li] and is consummated through music."[12] The role of poetry is to instill an inward taste for discrimination in thought and refinement in conduct; the central lesson in the *Book of Poetry*, according to Confucius, is that one should "keep his heart right." To master this lesson is to acquire a stable foundation of moral behavior. The role of the other two disciplines consists, as described in the *Book of Music*, in bringing "the people's inner feelings and their external conduct into balance (or harmony)." Or, more concretely, the inculcation of *li* "gives a well defined sense of order and discipline, while the general spread of music and song establishes an atmosphere of peace in the people."[13] The influence of music is to unite people in a spirit of friendliness toward one another, and so to achieve this that poise and calm within the soul of each person are generated, capable of being preserved in any social situation. Other studies, such as history and natural science, are pursued in the context of their significant relationships to the growth of men toward spiritual perfection.

As for communication by example, we have already noted the constant emphasis in Confucianism on the responsibility of the ruler to set his people a high moral example. "If a ruler rectifies his own conduct, government is an easy matter, and if he does not rectify his own conduct how can he rectify others?" And the reason for this maxim is that "when the ruler himself does what is right, he will have influence over the people without giving commands, and when the ruler himself does not do what is right all his commands will be of no avail."[14] But the principle here expressed is accepted as universally sound; it applies to the responsibility of parents, elder brothers, and teachers as well as to that of rulers. Confucian thinkers have little confidence in preaching as a way of instilling moral rectitude. If the preacher practices what he preaches, the important thing is not his exhortation but his example, although it is true that the example can be helpfully clarified by wise instruction. If he does not, his words will have no power as compared with the effect of his conduct; and before he can hope to rectify others he must rectify himself. The special importance of the teacher or sage in this situation is that his exercise of moral leadership is guided by the distinctive insight and social wisdom that he has gained. He must be prepared for probable rejection by the people of his own day, who may not be able as yet to share his insight; but if he truly understands the moral laws of the universe, his example and teaching will be confirmed by posterity. "Wherefore it is that it is true of the really great moral man that every move he makes becomes an example for generations; every act he does becomes a model for gen- erations and every word he utters becomes a guide for gen- erations. Those who are far away look up to him, while those who are near do not decrease their respect for him"[15]

Through education and example, thus conceived, moral un- derstanding and moral habits of conduct are believed not only to become more and more firmly established through time but also to spread, in widening circles of constructive in- fluence, from the ethically creative individual to the whole of mankind. In virtue of this conviction, moral duties them- selves are conceived in terms of four social contexts, in each of which they are guided by a distinctive aim as well as by the basic ethical values common to them all. First, every per- son has a duty to and for himself, namely, to cultivate a sound personal and social character. Second, he has a duty toward his family, to work unceasingly, in whatever role has fallen to his lot, for its harmony and happiness. Third, he has a duty to his country and his cultural heritage, to con- tribute toward their preservation and orderly growth. Fourth (increasingly emphasized in recent times), he has a duty toward all mankind, namely, to strive for the realiza- tion of a world community exemplifying the principle of reciprocity in the relations of all men to each other, without distinction of race, color, vocation, or creed. In this fourfold pattern of obligations the social ideal of Confucianism comes to its full expression.

C. THE RELIGIOUS DIMENSION

Thus far, the major details of Confucianism have been expounded with no reference to the cosmic dimension men- tioned above, without which it might be plausibly main- tained that we have here an appealing moral and social phi- losophy but no religion. However, the cosmic dimension is essential; any description of Confucianism which leaves it out would be grossly inadequate. And when this phase of human experience is considered, we confront the meaning for Con-

fucianism of the other basic concept that has hitherto been
left in abeyance—the concept of *tao*. And the essential point
can be stated very briefly. When one orders his life in accordance with respect for *li* and in commitment to the ideal
of *jen*, practicing the other virtues that are involved, he is by
that fact realizing the *tao* of man and relating himself harmoniously to the *Tao* of Heaven. It is now our task, with
this idea in mind, to explore more fully the cosmic dimension as interpreted in Confucianism, and to catch the significance of this concept in its metaphysical as well as its
moral implications. We must grasp sympathetically the Confucian faith that when one adopts the principle of reciprocity
and exemplifies it wisely in all his human relationships, he is
adjusting himself to cosmic as well as to social reality—he is
finding oneness with the universe as a whole. In the Western
world the traditional belief has been that one discovers the
moral truth about man by first apprehending God and His
will for the world; for Confucianism the relation is reversed
—one first gains insight into the moral truth for man, and
then in virtue of the cosmic significance of the moral order
thus envisaged he realizes a trustful and sustaining harmony
with God.

The key passages on this aspect of Confucian thought occur in the classic called the *Golden Mean*. One of them reads:
"The moral man finds the moral law beginning in the relation between man and woman; but ending in the vast reaches
of the universe." The most comprehensive statement of the
basic idea in a single passage is as follows:

Confucius taught the truth originally handed down by the ancient Emperors Yao and Shun, and he adopted and perfected the
system of social and religious laws established by the Emperors
Wen and Wu. He shows that they harmonize with the divine
order which governs the revolutions of the seasons in the Heaven
above and that they fit in with the moral design which is to be
seen in physical nature upon the Earth below.

These moral laws form one system with the laws by which

Heaven and Earth support and contain, overshadow and canopy all things. These moral laws form the same system with the laws by which the seasons succeed each other and the sun and moon appear with the alternations of day and night. It is this same system of laws by which all created things are produced and develop themselves each in its order and system without injuring one another, and by which the operations of Nature take their course without conflict or confusion; the lesser forces flowing everywhere like river currents, while the great forces of Creation go silently and steadily on. It is this (one system running through all) that makes the Universe so impressively great.

But in order to interpret these statements with assurance a third passage must be added, which is found in the introductory paragraphs of this classic: "Our central self or moral being is the great basis of existence, and harmony or moral order is the universal law in the world. When our true central self and harmony are realized, the universe then becomes a cosmos and all things attain their full growth and development."[16]

We might as well plunge at once into the major difficulty which these assertions pose for the Western reader, and clarify them by saying what can be said to meet that difficulty. No such perplexity would have been felt by a Westerner of several centuries ago, who would have approached the study of Confucianism from the perspective of Stoic or Aristotelian thought. These ancient philosophies did not sharply separate nature as fact from nature as norm of moral order and moral value; any value that man is moved to seek—so they believed —is shown thereby to be a natural cause of the changes that the seeking brings about. But modern thought in the West, profoundly influenced by the basic assumptions of modern science, has rejected this perspective. As a result, the realm of moral value and the order of natural fact have been separated. Any valid moral norm is not believed to have become such merely because of factual considerations, and the predictive relations between factual events, in terms of which they

are causally explained, are supposed to have nothing to do
with moral values. Hence any attempt to think of the moral
and factual orders in the universe as constituting a single system seems grotesque and absurd to the typical Western
thinker of today—it is a mixing of things which, in the interest of clear understanding, need to be carefully disjoined.

Now the Confucian thinker (and indeed the Chinese
thinker in general) takes for granted the Stoic and Aristotelian
presuppositions on this matter. Moreover, he approaches the
world of nature with a further assumption in his mind. He
has little interest in the way things happen in the universe
when considered without reference to the values their behavior symbolizes and the moral lessons it can teach. It is
thus inevitably to him a part of the moral realm, with which
man as a moral being must deal. That such an orientation is
present can be most clearly seen if we consider what is said
about heaven in the longest of the passages just quoted. When
the Confucian thinker looks at the celestial phenomena he
does not see just what the Western astronomer sees—a complex system of physical motions whose future course can be
mathematically predicted on the basis of what has been accurately learned about their past behavior. What he sees is
heaven as a protecting canopy over the earth and as the self-
giving source of the light and heat which nourish all things
on its surface. What he sees when he looks at the detailed
astronomical revolutions is the regularity of the processes
there taking place, which accounts for the fructifying succession of the seasons and the dependable alternation of day
and night; he sees a celestial model of the trustworthiness of
the man who can be counted on to fulfill his social functions
with a dutiful conscience. In brief, he sees the orderly relations of fact as symbols of the moral harmony and integrity
that are present in nature.

Besides—and now we come to the insight expressed in the
last of these quotations, an insight that has not been missed by
the keenest thinkers of the West—it is a matter of experience

that power to discover a systematic order in the world (and in basic respects the kind of order discovered) depends upon the achievement of a harmonious order in oneself. "Our central self or moral being is the basis of existence itself, and harmony or moral order is the universal law in the world." In just what sense is this true? Simply in the sense that if one has failed to attain an ordered harmony in himself, he will be unable to discover any stable, systematic order in his world; whereas, "When our true central self and harmony are realized, the universe then becomes a cosmos and all things attain their full growth and development." In this fundamental sense, the universe that man is capable of discovering is relative to the moral state of his own soul. If there is integrity within, a unified cosmos is discoverable without; if the moral harmony of a mature personality is in process of realization within, one finds himself part of a universe in which all things are moving toward the goal of full growth and development. When this fact is added to the one mentioned above, the order without becomes literally an extension of the order within, not merely an inspiring model for it.

From this perspective, then, there is genuine continuity between the moral pattern realized in human life at its best and the harmony of heaven and earth that is displayed to an observant objective view. And the key to the order without is found in the order within. It is in the light of these convictions that one can understand the bold and rugged humanism in epistemology and metaphysics that Confucius ventured frequently to express. "It is man that makes truth great, and not truth that makes man great. Truth may not depart from human nature. If what is regarded as truth departs from human nature, it should not be regarded as truth."[17]

So a deeply religious note enters Confucianism by this route. It shows itself specifically in two ways. On the one hand there is a simple and hopeful trust in Heaven—whose will is ordering all that happens toward a good end even when we with our limited vision cannot see that this is the case. Hence the devout Confucian has an abiding confidence in the ultimate rightness of things and accepts with calm acquiescence the divine decree, whatever it may involve for himself. On the other hand, there is a mystic note in Confucian piety, arising from the fact that while the moral law of the universe can be known in part, it yet reaches beyond what even the most spiritual man can fully apprehend. "The simple intelligence of ordinary men and women . . . may understand something of the moral law; but in its utmost reaches there is something which even the wisest and holiest of men cannot understand."[18] Hence a vital aspect of the spiritual life is a quest for responsive accord with a greatness in the universe which is immanent in the moral order of human life, but which also transcends it in the awesome mystery of its ultimate nature.

Were we to develop the moral theology of Confucianism in greater detail, one of our interesting tasks would consist in tracing its view of the spiritual significance of music and ritual in their relation to the primitive cosmogony which by Confucius' time had become moralized and freed from its grosser superstitions. According to the early cosmogony of *yang* and *yin*, heaven as the male and *yin* as the female principle interact to produce the world—heaven being the active, creative power, the source of growth and change, while earth is the passive recipient of its seed, generating thus the diversity of its visible phenomena in all their varied potentialities. In Confucianism the essence of this cosmological idea still remains, although heaven has become, in its beneficent self-giving and stable order, the prime model of moral perfection, and earth, in fulfilling its proper duties in their manifold forms, depicts the responsiveness of the rightly disposed man to the creative harmony of the divine.

Now Confucian thought explicitly interprets music and ritual as the characteristic media by which these cosmic norms communicate their beauty and appeal to man's emotional life. In this doctrine it makes a rather distinctive contribution to civilized religion. A crucial passage in the *Book of Music* expresses this idea thus:

> Music rises from heaven, while rituals are patterned on the earth. . . . Music illustrates the primordial forces of nature; ritual reflects the products of the creation. Heaven represents the principle of eternal motion, while earth represents the principle of remaining still; and these two principles of motion and rest permeate life between heaven and earth. . . . Truly great music shares the principle of harmony with the universe, and truly great ritual shares the principle of distinctions with the universe. Through the principle of harmony, order is restored in the physical world; and through the principle of distinctions, we are enabled to offer sacrifices to heaven and earth. . . . Rituals teach piety under different circumstances, and music teaches love in varying forms. . . . Therefore the sage creates music to correlate with heaven, and creates ritual to correlate with the earth. When rituals and music are well established, we have heaven and earth functioning in perfect order.[19]

When such passages are pondered in their historical context, and in their relation to what has been said about the role of ritual and music in education, the central idea becomes clear. Music and ritual are the ways in which man naturally and spontaneously expresses the response of his heart to the unifying harmony and the ordered variety displayed in the universe. Music expresses his emotional attunement to the distinctive role of heaven in the cosmic process—creating peaceful concord and a cheerful, sincere friendliness wherever its benignant power reaches. Ritual expresses his emotional acceptance of the manifold proprieties which are the correlate, in daily social life, of the ordered diversity of earth's products as she responds to heaven's influence and the tokens of her differentiating fertility appear. In the light of these facts, one comes to realize that in Confucianism music and ritual not only have an important meaning in the moral life of man; they also have a metaphysical significance of a distinctive kind—they constitute a medium through which the wise and responsible person achieves harmony with cosmic reality.

What does Confucianism teach about immortality? Well, when Confucius was asked, "What about death?" he is reported to have replied, "We don't know yet about life; how can we know about death?"[20] Philosophically, then, a realistic agnosticism is its teaching here.

But what gives the devout Confucian the emotional support he needs in the expectation and presence of death? The answer to this question lies in the attitudes developed through the centuries in connection with the ancestral rites. As he participates in these rites, honoring those members of the family who have gone before, including them in the family councils, preserving a living sense of continuity with them, he realizes that he too will be warmly and affectionately enfolded in the same way after his life is over. This for him is enough. He needs no assurance of any other form of future existence, for himself or for those he loves; whatever further destiny may await he resignedly leaves to the will of Heaven.

D. THE PSYCHOLOGY AND THEOLOGY OF MENCIUS

We shall deal with only one Confucian thinker who came later than the master, namely, Mencius, who was born in 372 and died in 289 B.C. As a teacher and leader he has by subsequent generations been placed second to Confucius, and his book is one of the four Confucian scriptures. In his role as a philosophic thinker he was a more systematic analyst than his great predecessor, and partly for this reason it is sometimes difficult to tell how far he is developing in his own way ideas already present in Confucius' teaching and how far an original viewpoint is finding expression. As a personality, he exhibits the main qualities of the Chinese sage and also something of the aggressive righteousness of the Hebrew prophet; to his wise and gentle counsel to the rulers of his day, that "if you govern with love, then the people will love all above them and will die for their leaders," he adds a fearless denunciation of all who are guilty of injustice and exploitation—

if they do not mend their ways Heaven will cast them from their thrones.

Among the many treasured passages from his book is one in which the childlike simplicity, freshness, and responsiveness of the moral man are stressed—"The great man is he who does not lose his child's heart"[21]—and one in which the ancient Chinese ideal of a virtuous character is beautifully expressed: "To dwell in the wide house of the world, to fill his correct place in the world, to walk in the great *tao* of the world; when he obtains his desire for office, to practice his principles for the good of the people; and when that desire is disappointed, to practice them alone; to be above the power of riches and honor to make him dissipated, of poverty and low status to make him swerve from principle, and of power and force to make him bend—such is the man who may be called truly great and courageous."[22]

Were I to give a brief characterization of his philosophy, bringing out both its continuity with earlier Confucianism and his originality, I would say that his central theme is the moral potentiality of man. For Mencius this is the greatest and most sublime thing in the universe, as it moves toward fulfillment under the guidance of an idealistic trust and a wise realism. This combination of moral faith and sober respect for fact appears most strikingly in that feature of his teaching that reminds us of the "Love your enemies" in the Christian gospels. Confucius had said, when asked whether one should repay evil with kindness, "Repay kindness with kindness, but evil with strict justice."[23] Mencius expresses the deeper insight that evil can and should be overcome by love for the evildoer, but he is careful to add that one must be realistic in his commitment to this principle. "Love overcomes its opposite just as water overcomes fire. Those, however, who nowadays practice love [do it] as though with a cup of water they could extinguish a whole wagonload of faggots on fire, and when the flames are not put out say that water cannot overcome fire. Such a course is the greatest aid to what is contrary to love, for the final outcome will simply be this—the loss [of that small amount of love]."[24] That is, it is true that love can overcome hatred, and the moral leader will courageously put this principle into practice, but he must be intelligent about it. Knowing the power of hostile passions, he must not expect too much at any given time or place. If he does, he will become disillusioned; his faith in the power of love will be lost, and he will thus sow the seed of moral distrust among others as well as in himself.

We may best bring out the most original aspects of Mencius' teaching by commenting briefly upon three topics: (1) his moral psychology, (2) the democratic corollary which to his mind it involved, and (3) his approach (in this perspective) to the problem of evil.

The basic truth about man, according to Mencius, is that he is by nature good, and only becomes bad under the influence of unfortunate circumstances. Confucius was ever ready to recognize the goodness in those who showed a capacity for moral growth, but he likewise condemned the badness in those who exhibited stupidity, inertia, hypocrisy, and malice. Mencius was not blind to the facts in this area of human conduct, but his emphasis was definitely that of a morally optimistic faith.

If you let them follow their original nature [he affirmed], then they are all good. That is why I say human nature is good. If men become evil, that is not the fault of their original endowment. The sense of mercy is found in all men; the sense of shame is found in all men; the sense of respect is found in all men; the sense of right and wrong is found in all men. The sense of mercy is what we call benevolence or charity. The sense of shame is what we call righteousness. The sense of respect is what we call propriety. The sense of right and wrong is what we call wisdom, or moral consciousness. Charity, righteousness, propriety and moral conciousness are not something that is drilled into us; we have them originally with us, only we often forget about them (or neglect or ignore them). Therefore it is said, "Seek and you will find it, neglect and you will lose it." This moral consciousness is developed in different persons to different degrees, some five times, some ten times and some infinitely more than others, because people have not developed to the full extent what is in them.[25]

The fundamental moral valuations, he is saying here—the assured approvals and disapprovals—are common to all men, however much some may seem to flout them. The moral task of life is the full development of the character which expresses itself in these virtues, in an abiding trust that they constitute a stable foundation on which spiritual progress in the individual and in society can be achieved.

The outstanding corollary which Mencius drew from this basic principle is the democratic conviction that all men are essentially equal. Being the same in their intrinsic moral endowment, i.e., in that which is most important, any man is really equal to any other man, however they may differ in the accidental features that life has brought. "All men," he says, "may be Yaos and Shuns"—i.e., on a par with the ideal rulers of ancient time who were looked upon as paragons of wisdom, filial piety, and true devotion.[26] The political implication of this conviction is that the common people are the most important element in a country, the ruler being least significant, and that the voice of Heaven is revealed in the voice of the people. "Heaven sees as my people see, Heaven hears as my people hear."[27] The general philosophical implication is that the mind of the common man is the ultimate court by which true insight is distinguished from falsehood—not, of course, the common man as he now is, but as he is capable of becoming through following the moral example and guidance of the sage. The philosopher must allow himself no aristocratic confidence in his intuitive judgments as such; they prove to be true only when gradually confirmed by universal experience. Confucius was rather impatient with the dullness of many men's minds; Mencius, however, dared to say, "The sage and we are of the same species." "The sages only apprehended before me that which I and other men agree in approving."[28]

By making these convictions his foundation, the moral leader, for Mencius, can realize a universal perspective, not limited in place and time; he shares and serves the unfolding experience of all men who, like him, are participating in the spiritual quest. In such a perspective all problems of a moral philosophy and a sound religion can find, he is sure, their solution. To Western thinkers his treatment of the problem of evil is especially illuminating, in its balanced realism and its preference for practical moral insight instead of a merely theoretical doctrine.

When the right teachings prevail, the morally inferior serve the morally superior, and the mentally inferior serve the mentally superior. When the right teachings do not prevail, the small serve the big and the weak serve the strong.

Both these cases are (the law of) Heaven. They who accord with Heaven are preserved; they who rebel against Heaven perish.[29]

The unspoken practical corollary here is that those who see these truths, in the setting of a wise perspective, will live their lives in such a way as to bring it about (so far as in them lies) that right teachings *shall* prevail—and this outcome also is in accord with the law of Heaven. Both good and evil are actual in the world, and have the inevitable results that they do; but a true understanding of them in those who achieve it also has its consequences and these are entirely on the side of good, for they are the expression in action of an inward integrity in which the moral man realizes and preserves his own true self.

The genius of Confucianism may be helpfully summarized by a brief description of the distinctive way in which it exemplifies the four major characteristics of high civilized re-

ligion discussed in general terms in Chapter IV. Its acceptance of universal moral responsibility is essentially expressed
in the concept of *jen*. The truly superior man, striving to
realize the ideal of *jen*, obeys the principle of reciprocity in
all his conduct, whatever social relationship may be involved;
and this means that while recognizing his special duties toward those bound to him by family or other ties, he follows
this principle with all men because they are men. Its sense of
ultimate unity in the cosmos is expressed in the conviction of
the reality of *tao*, and especially in the assurance that the *tao*
of man is continuous with the *Tao* of Heaven, so that one
who realizes the harmonious order implied in the former by
that same process also achieves oneness with the latter in its
transcendent as well as its immanent nature. Its awareness of
the spiritual inwardness in the soul of man is expressed in the
belief that man's true nature is not found in the quest for
wealth, reputation, or power, but in unreserved commitment
to the moral law and to the realization of the rugged uprightness that can only be realized through such commitment. To
be one's own true self is the greatest achievement of which
man is capable, and one who is conscious of inner rectitude
of heart is serenely content, whatever may come or fail to
come of the external gifts of fortune. The fourth characteristic is less radically expressed in Confucianism than in the
other great civilized religions, but it is there. It is less radical
because no "new birth" is felt to be needed—no drastic transformation as a result of which the soul moves in the direction
of another goal than that toward which it has previously been
aiming. There is a core of goodness already present in the nature of every man; what is needed is its wise unfolding, in the
course of which the foolish and irresponsible impulses that
conflict with it are gradually weaned away. But the process
involves, at the end, a thoroughgoing remolding of character
that is just as complete as it is in other religions. Confucius is
reported to have summarized his own spiritual growth thus:
"At fifteen I began to be seriously interested in study. At

thirty I had formed my character. At forty I had no more perplexities. At fifty I knew the will of heaven. At sixty nothing that I heard disturbed me. At seventy I could let my thought wander without trespassing the moral law."[30]

It is noteworthy that the final achievement is here described in terms of complete unity of mind and heart and deed; he could live in accord with the *tao* without there remaining any longer the slightest desire in any part of himself to live otherwise. What at an earlier stage had been performed as a more or less painful duty, because his heart was not really in it, had now become the free and spontaneous expression of his integrated self.

VII

Taoism

Every great religion, when it spreads widely, becomes corrupted, and it is necessary to distinguish between the insights of the pioneers who founded it and the popular superstitions which arise through mingling their teachings with persistent primitive notions or through interpreting their basic ideas so as to satisfy childish demands on the part of their followers. This distinction is especially sharp in the case of Taoism. As a philosophical religion, centered in the deep wisdom of Lao Tse and Chuang Tse, and preserved in the beautiful Taoist monasteries by their philosophically minded followers through the centuries, Taoism is one of the most provocative and profoundly instructive among the civilized religions of the world. In it something of the Chinese spirituality that escaped the moralizing meticulousness of Confucianism comes to full and rich expression. As a popular religion, practiced by the priests, many of whom cater without scruple to the perennial weaknesses and foibles of the masses, it has degenerated into a system of magic, preserved through the generations because of man's incorrigible belief that there must be some simple way of gaining prosperity and immortality by applying the right techniques. In the following sketch I shall pay no attention to the second form of Taoism; our concern is with the major ideas of its great originators.

A. THE MORAL PHILOSOPHY OF THE TAO TEH CHING

By the fourth century B.C. (some historians would place the date a little later) the unique classic known as the *Tao Teh Ching* had been composed and was molding philosophical and religious thought in China; a century or so later the bantering humorist Chuang Tse added his contribution to the life-giving stream that flowed from it. Traditionally, the *Tao Teh Ching* has been attributed to the authorship of "the old sage" (Lao Tse). Nowadays scholars are debating not only the date but also the composition of this profound work; whatever conclusions they reach on matters of detail, the responsive reader will rest assured that its central ideas express the insight of a single keen personality who was one of the outstanding thinkers and religious teachers of the world. When in the following pages I speak of "Lao Tse," I mean that personality, whenever he should be dated and irrespective of whether or not he should be identified with the Lao Tan of tradition, supposed to be an older contemporary of Confucius.

In attempting to master this classic, the Western reader faces again the difficult problem of translating key terms of Eastern thought into a Western language; perhaps the best procedure is to do so only very gradually, after one has become familiar with their basic implications in the Chinese context. Its teaching centers around two concepts—*tao* and *teh*—and we may initially translate the title (since the word *ching* poses no serious difficulty) as "the classic of *tao* and *teh*." *Tao* we have already explored in preliminary fashion, and it is important not to forget the associations suggested by the guiding idea that we are dealing here with a "way." But, as over against the Confucian interpretation of *tao*, it is essential to bear in mind that in the *Tao Teh Ching*, *tao* explicitly fills the role of "ultimate reality" in a mystical metaphysic. This does not mean that its primary significance as a moral concept is lost; it does mean, however, that to understand it one turns to nature at large rather than to the social relations of men, and that the moral doctrines are definitely grounded in a metaphysical theory—which could not be asserted in the same fashion of Confucianism. As for *teh*, when considered out of context, it is very similar to the Latin *virtus*, which means the intrinsic power (of a man) on the one hand, and true virtue on the other; although these two meanings may seem antithetical to us, they are fused in the thought of this book, and we shall see in the sequel how that fusion is conceived. Provisionally, one may think of *teh* as that moral energy in man which finds integrated expression when his realization of oneness with the *tao* is achieved.

Whether one is already familiar with any Chinese characters or not, he should not miss the lessons that can be learned from examining the opening couplet of this brief classic:

名　道
可　可
名　道
非　非
常　常
名　道

Note the complete parallelism that obtains between these two lines; only one character is changed as we pass from the first to the second. They have been variously rendered by the many translators of the *Tao Teh Ching*; I shall suggest my own rendering as follows (avoiding any attempt to provide an English equivalent for *tao*):

The *tao* that can be *tao*'d is by no means the real *tao*;
The name that can be named is by no means the real name.

What does this mean? One is tempted—succumbing to the presuppositions that could be taken for granted in analogous Western assertions—to interpret it simply as the statement of a mystical metaphysic; reality transcends all the categories of human experience and human language. And this thought is indeed present, as later assertions in the opening stanza and in the work as a whole clearly indicate. But when one absorbs the full message of the classic, making sure of its relative emphases and remembering the essentially practical orientation of Chinese thinking by and large, he comes to see that the primary meaning here is a moral one, and that the mystical metaphysic is to be understood in relation to that moral idea.

Lao Tse is beginning in these two lines with the basic plight of man, from which he needs to be saved. And this plight he conceives in very different terms from those which the Confucian moral philosophers would use (although there is a common core of convictions, namely, those described in Chapter V); in fact, Lao Tse is sure that man needs salvation from the misguided efforts of the Confucian teachers as much as from various other evils that are leading him astray. The essence of man's plight is that he is caught in a competitive struggle for prestige, honor, wealth, and power. In this effort to "keep up with (and get ahead of) the Joneses" he aggressively follows his self-seeking impulses and is driven by his need for social approval; he becomes the prey of worry and fear; he trusts to the faculties he finds within him—especially his sense of duty and his reason—to lead him to success in this anxious endeavor. But all this is a mistake. It does not lead to contentment or happiness or inward peace; to pursue this route is to miss the *tao* rather than to find it. It is the way of distorted artifice and ignorant convention; it is not the way of simple naturalness and integrity. Moreover, it is futile. It does, to be sure, often lead to a transitory success in its own fashion—to the kind of success people hope to achieve by following it—but the higher one climbs by this route the more precarious his position, the more certain and disastrous his ultimate fall.

Now when one begins to see that this is the case, the first and basic lesson taught is that one should renounce this silly and pathetic struggle, giving up the idea that anything is accomplished by hectic rivalry with others for these supposed goods of life, and turning in the direction of a different goal which will actually bring peace and true happiness. And this practical lesson at once involves a theoretical one. The person who has thus come to question an erroneous way of life finds that he has been mistaken in accepting the conventional meanings of the concepts in which that way of life is expressed; and that he must abandon them also—all of them. What he has thought to be happiness is not real happiness; what he has thought to be strength is not real strength; what he has thought to be knowledge is not real knowledge; what he has thought to be virtue is not real virtue; what, even, he has thought to be effective action is not real action. The way he has been using these names is all radically wrong. "The name that can be named (by one still in bondage to convention and aggressive self-seeking) is not the real name." Indeed, the real name never can be named; for when one turns away from basic error in these matters toward basic truth, he finds that although he is now on the right track the full truth always eludes his grasp—the real meaning of all these names transcends his experience even though it is also an immanent guide to his converted understanding.

At this point we begin to catch our central clue to the meaning of *tao* in Taoism—and can see how its primarily moral significance leads to and is grounded in its metaphysical setting. To generalize from this description of the human situation: what we inevitably, in view of our immature experience and inadequate insight, regard as real is not real; the only order of relationships which we can conceive in life and the world is not the right order; the way that we find ourselves traveling (and alone can travel until we achieve a keener insight) is not the true way. Expressed in terms of the problems that emerge everywhere when man commits himself to the complexities of civilized life, it is clear that all the anxious and contentious bustle that these complexities have plunged him into—with the fear, hostility, loss of peace and contentment, that are the inevitable consequence—is an evil rather than a good. Only a very radical moral and metaphysical solution —a "transvaluation of values"—can cure it.

So the first step toward such a solution is to become clearly aware that our compulsive pursuit of the conventional goals of civilized life is misguided and futile, and that the ideas in terms of which such action has been conceived and justified are hopelessly perverted.

What, then, to do?

> Oftentimes, one strips oneself of passion
> In order to see the Secret of Life.

Or, more fully,

> Curtail thy desires,
> Check thy selfishness,
> Embrace thy Original Nature,
> Reveal thy Simple Self.[1]

In brief, understand and conquer yourself. Realize that your self-centered and aggressive passions are the essential source of your mistaken action and your false notions. Lay them aside. Accept all things in your universe, not just those that your distorted ambitions lead you to notice and to clutch at. Understand all things in their own pattern and order—not just in the order determined by your impulsive hopes and loves, hates and fears. Then you can begin to catch the clues that the world reveals to the true nature of *tao*. You had missed them before, but now you will be able to observe them and, in the measure of your power, to imitate them.

Here, for example, is the simple and familiar substance, water.

> The best of men is like water;
> Water benefits all things
> And does not compete with them.
> It dwells in (the lowly) places that all disdain,—
> Wherein it comes near to the Tao.[2]

That is, water is what all things depend on for their nourishment and growth, but it does not compete for high position and exalted rank. It is quite content to settle in the hollows that other objects struggle to avoid: in this one can see the nature of the *tao*. Or, looking out upon things in the large, consider the universe as a whole.

> The universe is everlasting.
> The reason the universe is everlasting
>   Is that it does not live for Self.
> Therefore it can long endure.
>
> Therefore the sage puts himself last,
>   And finds himself in the foremost place;
> Regards his body as accidental,
>   And his body is thereby preserved.
> Is it not because he does not live for Self
> That his Self achieves perfection?[3]

The universe, too, exemplifies the *tao* because it does not compete against anything, but instead gives life to all things through the unceasing transformations that go on within it. When one has become open to such lessons he can begin to imitate the universe in this respect. He can abandon the struggle against others for the position and power that not all can attain, allowing the preferred places to those who ambitiously seek them; he can give himself to others instead of demanding prizes for himself. Then he discovers that, by following this way of modesty and selflessness, the kind of selfhood that he really wants is gained rather than lost; and he is even freely accorded by others the exalted position that he refused to climb for against them.

It is hardly necessary to assemble further parables from this wise classic. Toward what conclusions does the thought in all of them converge? Still sticking for the moment to the practical moral lessons, they are as follows: when you truly understand the *tao* in the light of such revealing processes in nature, and begin to imitate it in your own conduct, you find

that instead of becoming weak, crushed, empty (as might
have been expected) you gain a new strength and wholeness
which you realize is the only real strength and wholeness.
You achieve a knowledge that is the only real knowledge, a
freedom and happiness that alone truly deserve these names.
By nonaction—that is, by abandoning the aggressive self-assertion that alone seems effective action to others—you find
that in reality you are accomplishing all the ends that are
worth accomplishing. In brief, by discerning and following
the *tao* you achieve a positive, assured, dependably satisfying
relation to the universe and to everything in it; indeed, you
will even gain as an unsought reward the worldly values that
you had vainly striven for in the days of your childish blindness.

> [The sage] does not reveal himself
>   And is therefore luminous.
> He does not justify himself
>   And is therefore far-famed.
> He does not boast of himself,
>   And therefore people give him credit.
> He does not pride himself,
>   And is therefore the chief among men.
>
> It is because he does not contend
> That no one in the world can contend against him.[4]

The way of true success, then, of genuine achievement, is
not the way of contentious self-assertion that people mistakenly follow—the way of pressing demands and claims, the
way of pursuing wealth, honor, knowledge, cleverness—it is
rather the way of giving oneself to others, the way of modest
yielding, of patience and nonviolence, of tolerance and impartiality. For "gentleness overcomes strength," and only
"love is victorious in attack, and invulnerable in defense."[5] A
summarizing description of the nature of *tao* as a moral norm,
well worth pondering, is given in Chapter XXXIV.

The Great Tao flows everywhere,
(Like a flood) it may go left or right.
The myriad things derive their life from it,
And it does not deny them.
When its work is accomplished,
It does not take possession.
It clothes and feeds the myriad things,
Yet does not claim them as its own.
Often (regarded) without mind or passion,
It may be considered small.
Being the home of all things, yet claiming not,
It may be considered great.
Because to the end it does not claim greatness,
Its greatness is achieved.

The wise ones of old understood the *tao* and followed the right way.[6] If we are to be wise in our age, concludes Lao Tse, we will do the same; for it is the loss of that way that has brought the disintegration and corruption rampant in the world today.

B. ITS MYSTICAL METAPHYSIC

Thus far our concern has been with the central moral teaching of the *Tao Teh Ching*. Now we must consider its metaphysical foundations, which indeed for Chinese thought are not separable from the moral insight, but which to the Western mind need a separate exposition. The *Tao Teh Ching* recognizes three basic strata, or metaphysical levels, in the structure of the universe. The primary and ultimate of these, of course, is the *tao* in its transcendent character—that which lies beyond all names. If Lao Tse has to give it a name, he says he will simply call it "great."[7] Various passages assume, however, that certain other attributes may be ascribed: it is also one, changeless, and eternal. Second, there is the "Named . . . Mother of All Things."[8] We are left in considerable darkness about the nature and role of this second level. Perhaps it is merely the ultimate *tao* as it assumes describable form in the fabric of the observable universe; perhaps, more specifically, it is the dynamic interaction between Heaven and earth which produces and nourishes the aggregate of worldly phenomena. In the third place, there are the "myriad things" which are born of the *tao* and which constitute the variegated detail of the world as we know it.

Now the manner in which the dynamic operation of the universe goes on is essentially simple. The myriad things arise out of the *tao;* they aggressively assert themselves in their separateness, trying to maintain and expand their position at each other's expense. This is the source of the fundamental problem of life from which salvation is needed, for men, like other creatures in the universe, assert themselves in this fashion too; each tries to preserve his separate status, nay even to win a high place and superior power at the cost of forcing others into inferiority and servitude. But however much a temporary or apparent success is achieved in this endeavor, the struggle is really futile, and the futility unfailingly reveals itself in the end. In due course, sooner or later, all lose their separate existence and are once more merged in the great Mother from which they came. This is the process that endlessly goes on in the cosmic economy.

To man, however, belongs a distinctive dignity and privilege in comparison with his fellow creatures among the myriad things. He can come to understand this situation; he can accept the universal process for what it really is; and in the light of that wise acceptance he can consciously hasten and guide his return to the *tao.* He can abandon the self-seeking passions that obstruct him and to which he has been enslaved; he can discover and follow the eternal law of the universe; he can replace his false conceptions of power, freedom, knowledge, virtue, and action by the true ones; he can thus, in secure adjustment to reality, gain light, love, peace, and immortality.

Yes, immortality. For there is a radical difference between returning to the *tao* in the fashion exemplified by the true sage and the inevitable return that is the destiny even of those who fight against it. The latter perish; the separate existence that they had struggled so hard to preserve is simply brought to an end. They are lost in the *tao*. But the former, through conscious acceptance of the *tao* and willing identification with it, achieves a living union with that which is everlasting in the nature of things; and through this realized oneness he is immortal. When, like the *tao*, a person gives himself freely and demands nothing in return, he no longer has any separate existence which he is trying to maintain against other forms of existence. He has freed himself from the self-centeredness that perishes; he has discovered that and how "to yield is to be preserved whole."[9]

Such is the central teaching of this profound little book. Were we to follow all the illuminating corollaries that are briefly developed in its pages, more space would be stolen from the other great religions than can be allowed. But we must not leave it without pondering one of its most instructive corollaries, namely, the application of its basic idea to problems of government.

Like Confucianism, Taoism is convinced that virtue and wisdom spread, not by indoctrination or any sort of compulsion, but by example. They must be realized first in oneself, by observing and imitating the great models of the *tao*, which do their work not by possessive control of others but by effortless self-giving. Then, so far as true virtue has become realized in any person, it can be counted on to spread—to his family, his village, his country, the world.[10] Peace in the world will come as a consequence of the peace thus won in the souls of individuals, who gradually persuade others by the attractive power of their exemplification of the *tao*. This much, in general, is common to the two native Chinese religions, although the Confucian thinkers do not interpret it in quite such extreme form as the Taoist does.

But the *Tao Teh Ching* is prepared to apply this principle, without qualification by other considerations, to the problems of government. The ruler—so far as he is a true ruler—is one of the prime models of the *tao*, and he will govern simply by being such a model. He will avoid coercive legislation and any use of punishment beyond the minimum that cannot be avoided; he will refuse to interfere in the lives of his subjects, for this would be inconsistent with the basic principle of non-action. And the reason for this conclusion is brought out in various chapters, especially XXXVII and LVII. If he is ready to interfere, that would testify to the continued presence in him of an unfortunate desire to dominate others, whose consequences would inevitably appear in the kind of control he exercises and their rebellious reaction to it. If he has become completely purged of any such desire, he will no longer be willing to make his subjects do this or avoid that; he will know that in the long run more will be accomplished by the silent influence of his virtuous example than by any form of restrictive obtrusion in their lives. The Confucian thinker, in his strong sense of responsibility to establish social justice in the here and now, could not commit himself to such an apparently anarchical doctrine.

This contrast betokens in Lao Tse a courageous trust in people that has been very rare in religious history—a deep trust that they will respond to truth and goodness wherever it is really exemplified, and hence that compulsion and punishment are not needed and are dangerous devices, likely to lead to evil rather than to good. Suppose that the object of your chastizing interference imitates your example instead of cowering under your command! Mencius shared something of this confidence in the moral responsiveness of people, but to Confucianism in general it seemed too unrealistic to be politically practicable. The depth of this faith, and its spiritual significance in Taoism, are best revealed in one of the most suggestive stanzas of the *Tao Teh Ching*:

> The honest ones I believe;
> The liars I also believe;
> That is the faith of Virtue.[11]

It would be contrary to the whole tenor of this classic to interpret such a passage as recommending a gullible simple-mindedness that could be easily imposed upon by a crafty liar. The thought is surely this: if you do not reject the dishonest person any more than the honest one, and are prepared to "requite hatred with virtue," you will be able to understand why the liar lies, just as you will understand why the honest man is honest. In the light of this understanding you will see that there are possibilities of a deeper truthfulness in both, to be brought out by your resolute trust. Not that you will respond to both in quite the same way—you will know that the one is lying and the other is not—but you will also know that the path toward a better relationship lies not in rejecting the liar as hopeless, but in believing that he too is truthful in his natural selfhood and can be led by that faith beyond the suspicious and self-seeking impulses which made him lie.

The *Tao Teh Ching* concludes with a summarizing chapter which also contains profound insight on the uses of language:

> True words are not fine-sounding;
> Fine-sounding words are not true.
> A good man does not argue;
> He who argues is not a good man.
> The wise one does not know many things;
> He who knows many things is not wise.
> The Sage does not accumulate (for himself);
> He lives for other people,
> And grows richer himself;
> He gives to other people,
> And has greater abundance.
> The Tao of Heaven
> Blesses, but does not harm.
> The Way of the Sage
> Accomplishes, but does not contend.

C. THE DISTINCTIVE CONTRIBUTION OF CHUANG TSE

I shall deal briefly with the contribution to Taoist thought of the second great thinker of this school, whose dates are approximately 360–280 B.C. and who was thus a contemporary of Mencius. Chuang Tse's general Taoist orientation and approach to life and destiny are strikingly revealed in his reported reply, when nearing death, to his disciples, who wished to give him a sumptuous funeral: "With heaven as my canopy and earth as my coffin, with the sun, moon, and stars as my regalia, and the whole of creation to escort me, is not everything needed for a splendid funeral at hand? What more should I wish?"[12]

This sage was a witty, jovial, and searching mind, elaborating the basic Taoist themes in keen philosophical essays, which never lose a bantering touch. He loved to pillory the Confucian thinkers for their proud claims to wisdom and superior rectitude; he teased them with amusing stories about Confucius which are on a par with his Aesoplike tales about the "Spirit of the River" and "General Clouds"—the point of many of the stories being that Confucius was really a Taoist in disguise. He laughed at the emissaries of the King of Ch'u who came to offer him the premiership of that powerful state. He wrote an analysis of current philosophical schools, in which he discussed his own speculations in the same critical and humorous vein that he used with other philosophers. "With unbridled fancies, facetious language, and sweet romantic nonsense, he gives free play to his spirit without restraint."[13] He dreamed of being a butterfly fluttering among the flowers, and on awaking asked, "Now am I Chuang Chou who has dreamed of being a butterfly, or am I a butterfly dreaming of being Chuang Chou?"[14]

But so far as concerns his serious contribution to Taoist thought, we shall confine attention to two major ideas. Chuang Tse gives in trenchant form the answer of philosophical Taoism to the two most serious objections to this religious philosophy that were raised by Chinese critics two thousand years ago and are raised by Western thinkers today. One is: Does not commitment to the way of nonaction mean the abandonment of all effort to fulfill our social responsibilities? The other is: If we recognize the relativity of all our current uses of names, and renounce as mistaken our conventional ideas of power, knowledge, happiness, and virtue, by what standard can we tell the true meaning and value that we seek? How will we know when we find it? Will we not be lost in a hopeless skepticism?

Chuang Tse's answer to the first question is, in effect: What *is* responsibility? If it is what people who have not found accord with the *tao* take it to be, then the less we have of it the better. In that case, what we call "conscientious endeavor" is a blind attempt to force ourselves and the rest of the world into a pattern determined by our confused and distorted ideas of wisdom, rectitude, duty, and action. It is substituting the artificial way of misguided man for the free and simple way of nature. This is what the Confucian sages are zealously seeking to do; but the result is only to increase the moral deformity of the world. Don't try to make people into something other than they would become by their spontaneous, original nature. It is not necessary that all be alike. Don't assume that you know what's good for them! Leave them alone, "to find the even tenor of their lives" in their own way! Trust the intrinsic integrity of all things, including man; his heart when unspoiled is good. Realize your own virtue, through self-knowledge and intuitive union with the *tao;* others can be trusted to realize theirs, whether it conforms to what is conventionally called virtue or not. To be sure, there is a relative value in what established custom regards as justice, charity, propriety, and knowledge, which the impatient rebel against it may miss; one cannot advance from the *tao* of man (which is inevitably limited) to the *tao* of God without respecting these current ideals. But when one gains insight into the truth he will understand their relativities and perversions also, which have obstructed the discovery of his natural self. He will then leave their confusions behind. This alone is true progress.

His answer to the second question again rests at bottom on

faith in the competence of men to find the right way if others refuse to impose any strait jacket upon them and allow them full freedom to find their natural norm—freedom from all who would like to control them as well as freedom from every other artificial obstruction. By what standard are we to guide our choices and acts, if we accept the relativity of all values and abandon the standards that are current in the world, seeing that they do not reflect nature but mere convention? The answer is implicit in a trenchant passage in Chuang Tse's chapter entitled "Autumn Floods." The passage is difficult to interpret when removed from its context, but the attentive reader, even without familiarity with Chuang Tse's subtle style, will be able to catch the drift of his thought. He speaks through a dialogue between "Uncle River" and the "Spirit of the Ocean"; the latter holds the floor first.

"Rulers abdicated under different conditions, and the Three Dynasties succeeded each other under different conditions. Those who came at the wrong time and went against the tide are called usurpers. Those who came at the right time and fitted in with their age are called defenders of Right. Hold your peace, Uncle River. How can you know the distinctions of high and low and of the houses of the great and small?"

"In this case," replied the Spirit of the River, "what am I to do about declining and accepting, following and abandoning (courses of action)?"

"From the point of view of Tao," said the Spirit of the Ocean, "how can we call this high and that low? For there is (the process of) reverse evolution (uniting opposites). To follow one absolute course would involve great departure from Tao. What is much? What is little? Be thankful for the gift. To follow a one-sided opinion is to diverge from Tao. Be exalted, as the ruler of a State whose administration is impartial. Be at ease, as the Deity of the Earth, whose dispensation is impartial. Be expansive, like the points of the compass, boundless without a limit. Embrace all creation, and none shall be more sheltered or helped than another."[15]

The key idea here expressed is: Don't be so ready to call this "high" or that "low," this "long" and that "short." The standpoint from which you judge is not absolute, but relative to your perspective and your limited experience. Be impartial and inclusive in your acceptance of men and your good will toward them; and trust whatever standard naturally emerges in virtue of that impartiality and inclusiveness. Don't be anxious if it is a different standard from what you had expected in advance; don't be concerned either if in this process your ideal of normal naturalness itself needs revision. Truth always lies beyond our present conventional prejudices; have faith in the path which leads toward it, and in the competence of other people to find it if you no longer stand in their way.

We need hardly take space to state explicitly the distinctive form in which Taoism exemplifies the first three of the four major characteristics of civilized religion; they are obvious from the above description of Taoist principles. But in the case of the fourth characteristic it is worth noting that here is a religion in which this factor is present in vivid and challenging form. As man stands, before achieving oneness with the *tao*, Taoism maintains that he is incapable of true happiness. The best that he can achieve is a limited and relative well-being. He is in bondage to the perverted, customary notions of where happiness lies and how to find it; only a radical conversion, guided by penetrating self-understanding, can save him. There must be a decisive revulsion from the mistaken and futile struggle for competitive success, and the equally mistaken ideas about knowledge, virtue, strength, and action, by which men have sought to justify that struggle; through such a new birth alone, and a realization of the true natural values of life, can he find the selfless tranquillity which is expressed in effortless action.*

---

* An effortless action that to the world, of course, appears as nonaction.

VIII

The Background of Hinduism and Buddhism

Two peoples in the history of human civilization have revealed a special genius in the field of religion. Just as the Greeks have shown an aptitude for philosophy and art, the Romans for law and for efficient patterns of social organization, Britain for political liberty, and America for industrial engineering, so these two peoples have found in religion an area which challenged their capacities to the full. The leaders who stand out in their history have been consumed by a passion for the divine, and this passion has sufficiently permeated their culture so that the persons most respected, most looked to for guidance in its development, have been the religious saints and prophets.

One of these is the Hebrew people. A small nation it has been numerically, never numbering more than a few million persons and never in control of more than a small part of the geographical surface of the globe—in fact, during most of its history it has been without political independence and even without any national home. But its prophets were fired with an enthusiasm for God and His righteousness such as gave it an influence on religious history out of all proportion to its insignificant size. From Judaism emerged two of the great faiths of civilized man, whose adherents include well over a third of the earth's population and whose influence dominates all of the continents except Asia—indeed, they dominate a rather large segment of Asia too. We shall deal later with the religious genius of this remarkable people. The other inhabits the Indian subcontinent. It too has been distinctively responsive to the divine. However, India, unlike Palestine, is one of the most populous countries in the world; for this reason the extent of its influence is more easily understandable. Here too the individuals most admired, most looked to for guidance, are the religious saints and sages; millions of people will gather to experience "darshana"* in the presence of a "mahatma," or for a special religious festival. And from India too a spiritual power radiated far and wide—in Lin Yu-tang's words, "A trickle of Indian religious spirit overflowed to China and inundated the whole of Eastern Asia."[1] Out of early Hinduism there likewise grew two of the great world religions of today, whose adherents number somewhere near a fourth of the world's population. This is the people whom we shall now begin to study.

But, happily for the full realization of the spiritual possibilities of mankind, the genius of these two peoples has led in somewhat different directions and has made of religion, as they have developed it, two somewhat different things. To grasp this difference, we must avoid the temptation to pay much attention to their priests. There have been, of course, priests both in Judaism and in Hinduism, and they have occupied an influential position, but in neither case is it the priesthood that reveals what is religiously distinctive about these peoples. Among the Jews the true religious leader is the prophet; among the Hindus he is the saint. Now a saint may also be a prophet—witness Sankara eleven hundred years ago and Gandhi in our own day—but he need not be a

---

* That is, a deeper "vision" or spiritual realization. "Mahatma" means "great soul."

prophet to exemplify the traditional character of the saint. He must be an individual of a different type than that which appears in the Jewish prophet, and the unique nature of this type is one of the major things that we shall need to understand. The Jewish prophet is a man burning with zealous devotion to a moral God, whose will he believes to be expressed in a righteous plan for the world and for all His children. The Indian saint, even if he be a theist, as many have been, is not this kind of person, and such a consuming zeal does not, for him, constitute the essence of religion. His passion is the passion of the fragment for the whole—the longing to throw off the hampering limitations of finite existence and to achieve union with the infinite.

A. GENERAL CHARACTERISTICS OF INDIAN RELIGION

One of the most popular prayers of the ancient Hindu Upanishads reads:

> From the unreal lead me to the real;
> From darkness lead me to light;
> From death lead me to deathlessness.[2]

Here speaks the spirit of Indian religion. The problem of life, for this way of thinking, is rooted in the here and now of our daily existence, but the envisioned solution reveals an unquenchable metaphysical audacity. There is a sense of the limitless possibilities of man, in comparison with which everything that he has experienced before he becomes aware of them appears illusory rather than real, darkness rather than light, death rather than life. The task of man is to leave behind the cramping world of his present acquaintance, leave behind his limited self and all that is bound up with it, and become one with ultimate reality—with the divine source of all that is great and good and true. Religion reveals the way of this arduous ascent; anything that does less than this will not, for the Indian mind, deserve to be called religion. Its role is to discover, and make available to men, a new dimension of human potentiality which apart from the insight of religious pioneers would never have been glimpsed.

Plato's famous allegory of the cave[3] presents in poetic and philosophic form the Indian concept of the way to salvation —as a tortuous passage from the darkness of unreality to the brilliant light of the truly real. But a reader of Plato might be left with the impression that this process of emancipation is a purely intellectual one, and that it can be accomplished only by those endowed with high philosophic gifts. To the Indian theologians a theoretical insight is indeed necessary, but the realization as a whole is by no means merely intellectual. It is a remolding of the whole personality—a new birth, except that it cannot be achieved suddenly but only as a result of long and patient discipline. Its essence is liberation from attachment to the unhappy demands and longings that now hold us captive, and from the fearful self that erects a protective wall of separation between itself and all other forms of life; for it is these that pose the formidable obstructions that stand in the way of our realizing the Infinite and Eternal Being that we truly are. What the world thinks of as life is really death; our task is to escape from it to that which is truly life —the kind of life of which man is intrinsically capable and for which he is destined.

To most Westerners—even those deeply permeated in thought and feeling by the Jewish-Christian tradition—this sounds very puzzling and even incredible. It looks like a call to abandon life rather than to realize a higher quality of life; many Western thinkers, indeed, propose to explain it as symptomatic of a loss of nerve in the presence of too baffling social problems, or even of a loss of vitality under the enervating heat of the Indian sun. We shall, however, make a serious mistake if we brush it aside on any such suppositions. It rather points toward the typical way in which the Indian faiths exemplify the fourth characteristic of the living civilized religions—the conviction that true happiness for man does not consist in satisfying the urges by which, in his natural state, he is dominated, but requires a radical reshaping of his personality so that he finds true well-being in something else, which without that transformation would never have been glimpsed. In the Indian interpretation of this principle it means, on the negative side, a renunciation of all that obstructs this conversion—all the cravings that express the blind ignorance of our finite selves, so that we may then realize a limitless capacity which as long as it was hampered by those cravings could never even be discovered. To leave these behind is true liberation. The feature in Christian thought which most nearly parallels this aspect of Hinduism and Buddhism is the doctrine, already mentioned, of the second birth in the Gospel of John and the letters of Paul. The two major points of difference between Christian and Indian ideas on this matter are that the Christian concept holds that the rebirth is brought about by divine grace and often (for Protestant Christians, at least) takes the form of a sudden conversion, while the Indian concept holds that man should be an effective agent in the process himself* and that it is usually a slow and gradual growth.

It is because of the emphatic place of this idea in Indian religion that the mystic and the ascetic emphases are exemplified as sharply as they are. Mysticism is found in all the great religions, but on the whole it is a secondary trend in China, in Europe, and in Islam. In Indian religion it is the primary and basic trend. Salvation, so the mystic is convinced, consists in renouncing the separate, fearful, self-centered individual that each of us now is and becoming one with the universal and Absolute Self—leaving behind the realm of the illusory and unreal and becoming identified with the ultimate source of reality. And because it is our self-centered cravings that stand in the way of salvation, it is imperative to lay them aside—to refuse them the satisfaction they now demand, in order that this union with something greater and more real

---

* The degree to which this is the case, however, is a matter of disagreement in India, too.

beyond our present selves may be possible. A certain essential asceticism is therefore required by this whole religious standpoint. But from the point of view of the saint who has experienced the greater reality, this refusal is not rightly pictured as renunciation. A disciple of Bhadura Mahasaya, who had abandoned great family wealth for the sake of religion, said to him one day, "Master . . . you have renounced riches and comforts to seek God and teach us wisdom!" To which the sage is reported to have replied, "You are reversing the case! I have left a few paltry rupees, a few petty pleasures, for a cosmic empire of endless bliss. How then have I denied myself anything? I know the joy of sharing the treasure. Is that a sacrifice? The shortsighted worldly folk are verily the real renunciates! They relinquish an unparalleled divine possession for a poor handful of earthly toys!"[4]

When one refers to the asceticism of Indian religion he is, then, describing an essential intermediate stage in a person's spiritual progress. It will lead in due time to a state in which he is no longer attached to the enticing objects of the present world because he has found his true self and a greater joy beyond them. What shall his attitude at that time be toward the ordinary and apparently innocent pleasures of life? Shall he still reject them as evil? Or shall he enjoy them without being in bondage to their lure? Here is a question to which different answers have been given as the Indian religions developed; we shall note the crucial differences in the following chapters.

B. THE BASIC CONCEPTS OF INDIAN THOUGHT

In dealing with the faiths originating in India it will be necessary to follow a somewhat different procedure from that employed with the Chinese religions. Hinduism and Buddhism are so related historically that we shall need first a brief picture of their common background in ancient Hindu thought. Then an account of the rise and distinctive genius of Buddhism will naturally follow, and finally a sketch of the emergence and development of later Hinduism, drawing as it did both upon its early sources and upon certain major Buddhist insights.

As for the ancient historical background of both of these religions, much remains obscure; scholars are still debating many questions concerning the process by which the subcontinent became settled by its present inhabitants, and the way in which they adventured beyond their primitive religious ideas. For our purposes it will be sufficient to note that somewhere between 1500 and 600 B.C. the four Vedas made their appearance. The oldest of these is the *Rig-Veda*, which presents a picture of religion very similar to that with which we are familiar in the classic epoch of Greece and Rome. The divinities celebrated are Indra, Varuna, Agni, Soma, Prajapati —mighty powers revealing themselves in the storm, the sky, the sacrificial fire, the intoxicating potion, the creative process in nature—and turbulent are the emotions which contemplation of their exploits calls forth. But a note of eager metaphysical search appears even here, closing with the agnostic query:

Who verily knows and who can here declare it, whence it was born and whence comes this creation?
The gods are later than this world's production. Who knows, then, whence it first came into being?[5]

This note prepares us for the daring new trend in the Upanishads, the last of the Vedic writings, which were written between 800 B.C. and several centuries later. In these, about a dozen of which are recognized as especially important, the basic attitudes and convictions of Indian ways of thinking that subsequently became dominant are clearly expressed and their major concepts are formulated. The *Brihadaranyaka Upanishad*, for example, introduces us to the sage Yajnavalkya, who teaches the philosophy of life and destiny that many later religious and philosophic leaders of influence took for granted.

What are these major concepts? Let us run over, in order, those whose comprehension is essential to the understanding of Hinduism and also of Buddha's doctrines. For a short time I must ask for the reader's close attention.

First and foremost is the concept of Brahman, the metaphysical absolute. Out of Brahman come all things; to Brahman all things return. In himself, Brahman is unknown and unknowable, but as taking form for human experience he is *Sat-chit-ananda*—the source and embodiment of reality, knowledge, and bliss. Second, the concept of *atman*, the soul or self. And the very meaning of this concept is determined by the essential Hindu conviction that the true self of each human being is identical with Brahman, and that when that identity is realized the quest for salvation is fulfilled. When the individual soul that has not realized its oneness with Brahman is discussed, it is referred to as "jivatman" or by the entirely different term "purusha." The crucial stage in the process of gaining this realization is *moksha*, which means "release" or "liberation." The central idea here is that what makes possible the realization of union with Brahman is the freeing of the self from control by longings which bind it to the needs of the body and to other self-centered concerns. Now only in rare cases will a person be sufficiently purged of these cravings in his present existence so that he can hope for *moksha* before the death of the body which his soul now tenants. But his soul will survive this event and continue to exist, taking new forms one after another until the purging is complete; in fact, it has existed in innumerable forms in the past. This continued transmigration in the "ocean of births and deaths," which inevitably goes on as long as any taint of self-demandingness is left, is *samsara*. And what determines the form that will be taken in each new existence is the law of *karma*. By this concept Indian thought expresses the idea that the principle of causality operates in man's moral and spiritual experience, and does so in a particular way. The state of one's achievement at the end of his previous existence is the cause whose effect is the form taken by his present existence; similarly, the state achieved at the end of the present existence will decide the form to be taken in the next. Or, stated more generally (so that it will apply within the sequence of events in each existence as well as between one incarnation and its successor), *the law of* karma *is the principle that wise choices, earnest efforts, good deeds build good character, while bad choices, inertia, and evil deeds build bad character.* In the latter case, one is lengthening and making less hopeful the round of successive existences, for there is no magical way in which an evil character can be suddenly transformed into a good one; whereas, in the former case, one is shortening it and making it more hopeful. He is systematically doing what each person can do to eliminate the moral obstructions that bind him to the cycle of birth, suffering, and death. Thus he makes the law of *karma* work toward his ultimate release and his blissful union with Brahman.

It will be noticed that from this point of view virtue is its own reward and its own effect. The proper consequence of a virtuous deed is no externally bestowed blessing; it is simply greater virtue—i.e., a stronger aspiration toward the spiritual ideal and a greater power to practice it.

To these five basic concepts should be added a sixth, *dharma*. This is as difficult to translate into a Western term as the Chinese concept of *tao*. Indeed, in one of its ranges of meaning it is the Sanskrit correlate of *tao*, in the sense in which the Chinese speak of the *tao* of man alongside the *Tao* of Heaven. It is the way that man should travel in order to fulfill his nature and carry out his social responsibilities. But there is also in it an element that is expressed in the different Chinese concept of *li*. In this dimension of its meaning it betokens what is right and proper, either in general or in some particular context of functions and obligations. If one had to pick a single English word by which to hit off as many as possible of its implications, he would very likely pick the word "duty," by which both ranges of meaning just mentioned are in some measure brought together. But this word leaves out much that is conveyed by the Indian term, as indeed any single word would do.

C. THE RISE AND EXPANSION OF BUDDHISM

Just as the sixth century before Christ was a momentous period of creative discovery and reconstruction in China, so was it in India. It was at this time that two pioneering leaders appeared who rebelled against the corruptions into which, as it seemed to them, religion had fallen and struck out on a somewhat novel path. As a result two new civilized faiths started on their career, with one of which we shall need to deal at some length.

Mahavira was the elder of these two great men. The religion he founded is known as Jainism, which emphasizes asceticism and pacifism as basic religious principles. In its original form it rejected the concept of deity and offered an essentially humanistic way of salvation; as in other cases its great heroes, historical or legendary, later became quasi-divinities for many of its adherents. And Jain philosophy has made distinctive and significant contributions on more than one topic, especially in connection with the problems arising from the relativity of human knowledge. The number of Jains has never been large in comparison with the followers of Hinduism or Buddhism, but the religion has maintained an established place in India through the centuries, and has exercised an influence out of proportion to its numerical strength. Some of the most beautiful religious edifices in the Indian cities today are Jain temples, whose rich purity and symmetry both delight the beholder and infuse an atmosphere of contemplative peace. But in accordance with our self-imposed formula of selection in the present book, we must forego the temptation to elaborate further on this interesting development of religion in India.

Prince Gautama, who later came to be known as the Buddha, was the younger of these outstanding men. With Mahavira, he inherited the religious, philosophical, and psychological heritage of the Vedas and Upanishads, and accepted the basic presuppositions reflected in the six ideas just explained.* He was probably born a few years earlier than Confucius (about 562 B.C.), and the situation which he faced, much like that of the Chinese sage, was one of radical social readjustment and deepening religious need. Wars were frequent between the petty princes and rival clans in northern India, and the organization of society was moving more and more in the direction of a rigid caste system. The struggle to rise above one's present social status and win a larger sphere of opportunity in life was becoming increasingly difficult. Religious insight was being obstructed by the dead hand of the past; the Vedas were frequently taught as a collection of authoritative texts rather than as living truths to be tested and reinterpreted (if need be) in the present. Heavy and probably increasing emphasis was placed on the correct performance of rite and ceremony. Religious thinkers, in the attempt to satisfy their metaphysical curiosity, were championing varied cosmological systems, each visionary claiming truth for his pet theory and heaping argumentative scorn on the theories of his opponents. Worst of all, perhaps, from Buddha's standpoint, religion was straying through these and other vices away from the insistent, poignant, practical needs of men and women. It was not leading them toward true fulfillment and more dependable happiness; it was becoming mired in lethargic tradition, repetitious rite, and dead or cantankerous dogma. He conceived it as his task to break through or sweep away these obstructive tangles and to bring India and the world a saving message of light and life and love. That message we shall study in some detail in the next chapter.

Given its initial push by his dynamic personality, Buddhism spread rapidly. In a little more than two centuries after Buddha's death, Asoka, the first Buddhist emperor of India, came to power. Through his influence the new religion not

* Although some were modified rather drastically. See pp. 224 f., 235 ff.

only swept large areas of India but spread to Ceylon and other neighboring regions, especially to the east and the northwest. For a millennium it was the most powerful force in molding the religious, moral, artistic, educational, and social life of India. But by the end of that thousand-year period its decline in the subcontinent had begun, and in another five hundred years it had practically disappeared from the land of its birth. We shall soon raise the challenging question posed by this circumstance. But Buddhism lived and continued to grow because of its missionary fervor. The eagerness of its followers to carry the saving way to others had by this time spread it far and wide through northern and eastern Asia. In the west and northwest it was in time met and checked by the surging tide of Islam, but it remained the dominant religion of Ceylon, Burma, Siam, and some other areas in southeast Asia; it became one of the living religions of China and Korea; it won Tibet and competed successfully with Shinto for the soul of Japan.

In this process of missionary expansion it was itself profoundly transformed, and the most significant steps in this transformation we shall attempt to follow. In general, the farther it ranged, in space and in time, from the locus and date of its origin, the deeper the remolding which it underwent.[6]

D. THE DEVELOPMENT OF LATER HINDUISM

As Buddhism weakened in India its place as a major factor in shaping the religious aspects of Indian culture was taken by Hinduism in its later form. In fact, the growing strength and appeal of this revised Hinduism, which have enabled its influence to remain dominant in the subcontinent to the present day, were one of the forces that hastened Buddhism's decline.

There are many reasons which help to explain why Hinduism gradually replaced Buddhism in this way; the more essential ones we shall try to formulate as we deal with each of these religions in the two following chapters. The only rea-

son which it is especially important to appreciate in advance
is that Hinduism learned much from Buddhism, so that in its
matured form it met the same deep religious needs that Buddhism had met. One of its basic characteristics is a tolerant
hospitality to religious truth wherever it might appear, and
this open-mindedness stood it in good stead in the historical
situation created by the challenge of Buddhism. Its saints were
responsive to the spiritual truths that had proved their validity in the experience of earnest Buddhists, and its thinkers
made a place for them in their systematic interpretation of
life and the world. The influence of Buddhism on Sankara,
the greatest of the later Hindu philosophers, was so profound
that some critics have regarded him as a Buddhist in disguise.

But this teachable receptivity does not mean that Hindus
became unavowed converts to Buddhism; it means that they
selected from it what seemed to them to be true, and fitted
that precious core into a revised interpretation of the Upanishadic perspective which had come down from ancient
times. Where Buddhism had seriously departed from that
perspective it was not followed. This newly resurgent Hinduism is grounded securely in the mystical philosophy of the
Upanishads and never abandons its basic presuppositions. At
the same time it has come to recognize the legitimacy of
varied conceptions of ultimate reality, as required by varying
experiences of the divine; this flexibility is also expressed in
the belief that there are manifold ways to salvation, each
meeting the needs of a certain type of human personality.
All ways must be generously provided for, so that all men
and women may find their appropriate path toward the supreme goal.

These basic presuppositions of the early philosophic writings are accepted in the six speculative systems which arose
in post-Upanishadic times and which are known as the "orthodox" systems in contrast to the "heterodox" Buddhism
and Jainism. They are orthodox in the sense that they recognize the authority of the Vedas and interpret the universe in

harmony with the basic ideas of ancient tradition. They are regarded as complementary orientations on philosophic problems rather than competing schools between which seekers for wisdom must choose, as in general is the case with Western philosophies. This is possible because each centers its attention upon a somewhat different problem from that of the others, and because the aim of all of them is to solve its problem in such a way as to clarify the progress of the soul toward its final goal.* Of these six philosophies the most continuously influential and the most important for an understanding of present-day India are the Sankhya, Yoga, and Vedanta; their basic ideas, so far as we need to master them, will be explained in Chapter X. Other speculative systems have of course appeared from time to time, but for our purposes they may be passed by. The most challenging and important difference among these various philosophies which bears on theological issues is that between the superpersonal conception of the divine, which is most congenial to a strictly mystical religion, and the conception of God in strictly personal terms required by a religion of devotion to a divine savior. This difference appears throughout Indian history; it breaks out in very provocative form in the Vedanta philosophy itself, the Advaita (non-dual) Vedanta of Sankara representing the former of these two positions, while the Visistadvaita Vedanta of Ramanuja (who flourished two and a half centuries later than Sankara) is the best-known representative of the latter.

During the eight hundred years since Ramanuja's time one of

* To explain this point more fully: the Nyaya philosophy devotes itself to an analysis of logical inference; the Vaisesika builds a pluralistic cosmology of the phenomenal world; the Sankhya clarifies the common and contrasting properties of the soul and matter, together with the dynamic process of their interaction; the Yoga philosophy applies psychological analysis to the problem of achieving the spiritual control of body and mind required by systematic progress toward *moksha;* the Mimamsa provides guidance in adapting the Vedic tradition to the manifold duties and ceremonies of daily life; and the Vedanta is a metaphysical theology which draws upon each of the other systems and offers an answer to the ultimate problems about the universe that speculative minds in all ages raise.

the chief problems of this revised Hinduism has been to adjust itself to the invasion of Islam and of the Christian West. This invasion has meant not merely a serious threat arising from the missionary zeal of vigorous religions that had been only locally significant in India,* but also the political domination of the subcontinent by rulers giving special protection and encouragement to those faiths—the Islamic Moguls in the one case and Christian Britain in the other. The Mogul rule was founded by Baber in the late sixteenth century, and the British Empire established control over a large part of India two hundred years later. The spiritual leaders of Hinduism have characteristically met this situation by a cheerful welcome to the distinctive ideas of these religions—in many cases, e.g., Ramakrishna and Gandhi, by an open-hearted eagerness not to miss any insight into truth that such ideas might express—but they have also been confident, partly because of this dynamic openness itself, that Hinduism harbors infinite resources for the meeting of man's deeper needs and can absorb whatever spiritual truth it may have lacked in the past.

* Christianity has existed in South India since early Christian times.

IX

Buddhism

A. GAUTAMA THE BUDDHA

Buddha was born a prince of the Sakya clan, which at that time (the first half of the sixth century B.C.)[1] inhabited a part of the territory now embraced by Nepal and the adjoining area of north India; its capital city was Kapilavastu. His family name, as we know, was Gautama, and his given name Siddhartha. Few people, however, now know about these names, or make any use of them. Just as Jesus of Nazareth became to his devoted followers and to later generations in the Western world the Christ—the "Anointed One" of God, born to be the Savior of the world—so this great religious and philosophical pioneer of India became to later centuries the Buddha—the "Illumined One," destined to bring light and hope to a large fraction of civilized humanity. And we shall need to be familiar with two other titles that are likewise derived from his religious significance in history. One is easily understood; he is Sakyamuni, the sage of the Sakyas. The other is haunted by much mystery; he is Tathagata. What this title means is more fully determined than any of the others by devout Buddhist feeling, as it lovingly centers upon him and gradually becomes enriched through time. We may render it, "He who has fully come through," or, more simply and briefly, "the Perfect One"—the one who has attained spiritual perfection.

How glad the student of religion would be if it were possible to penetrate the mixture of legend and history that partially discloses, partially shrouds, the life of this great man! In Buddhist tradition an idealizing and moving story confronts us, filled with all the detail suggested by grateful projection and pious imagination. If the reader wishes to follow such a story, let him turn to the pages of Sir Edwin Arnold's *Light of Asia*, based on the life of Buddha as portrayed by a Buddhist thinker who lived five to six hundred years after the time of Buddha himself.

What do we know that can be set down with confidence as sober fact? Very little; but that little is deeply significant. Siddhartha grew to young manhood amid scenes of luxury and surrounded by all the paraphernalia of sensuous enjoyment; he was protected by his father from learning about the sorrows and frustrations and perplexities to which ordinary flesh is heir. Somehow, when in his middle twenties, he became acquainted with the sad facts of old age, of disease, and of death; for the first time he knew the major miseries to which human nature is inevitably subject in a world of decay and dissolution. This experience moved him to anxious and puzzled reflection, and then—having also met a monk of wisdom, insight, and serenity—to determined, undiscouraged action. He must learn the meaning of life in such a strange world. At the age of twenty-nine he left his father's palace with its constant stimulations to self-centered indulgence, left his beautiful wife and new-born son, and wandered into the forest—the accepted haunt in India for those who have found the ways of ordinary life spiritually cramping. His purpose was to discover the truth—the essential and saving truth—about life and death, about sorrow and happiness. For seven years he sought and struggled, in relentless, torturing self-experiment. He inquired of renowned hermit sages. As would be the case in India, with its traditional insistence on the necessity of renunciation, he tried ascetic denial of the body's demands in extreme form, finally succumbing to the dull blankness of a starving swoon. When he returned to consciousness he was convinced that this was not the right way—such radical punishment of the body brings, he saw, not spiritual illumination and peace, but exhaustion, torpor, and impotence of mind.

Gradually he found more successful clues to the understanding and liberation he sought. After being persistently tempted by the clever demon Mara, his quest reached its culmination in a long period of meditation under a spreading tree,* not far from the present city of Gaya in northeastern India. In the joy of assured enlightenment he rose and, after a brief delay, wandered slowly toward the sacred city of Benares, two hundred miles or so to the west. How could he make his discovery intelligible and persuasive to others, so that it might guide them also toward true happiness and peace? Apparently there was a strong temptation to keep his insight to himself, but it became clear that he must make the attempt. It meant formulating the basic truths about life in the halting, inadequate medium of human speech; and then it meant speaking those truths in love, so that others capable of responding to them would sense the answer to their living need too, and would not rest until they had mastered its promise and its power. At Sarnath, a few miles from the river near Benares, he preached his first sermon and won his first converts. Then for forty-odd years he continued to proclaim his message, explaining its bearing on the problems that sincere inquirers raised, and adapting it to the special needs of all who found hope and cheer in his presence. At the age of eighty he passed away in the arms of Ananda, his beloved disciple, with the words: "Decay is inherent in all compound things. Work out your own salvation with diligence."[2]

What sort of person did the man whose biography has thus been briefly sketched impress others as being? Well, Gautama the Buddha seems to have combined in high degree two qualities that are rarely found together and each of which is rarely

* Which became for that reason to Buddhists the sacred Bodhi tree.

exemplified in high degree. On the one hand, he was a man of rich and responsive human sympathy, of unfailing patience, strength, gentleness, and good will. His friendliness, to all who came to him in sincere search, was full and unreserved. He therefore aroused in his followers a wondering, eager, affectionate devotion such as only the greatest leaders of men have awakened. On the other hand, he was a thinker, of unexcelled philosophic power. His was one of the giant intellects of human history, exhibiting a keenness of analytic understanding that has rarely been equaled. He probed through the virtues and the deceptions of the philosophic thought of his day, adopting it where it seemed to him clearly sound and abandoning or radically revising it when he saw that it was missing the true and the good. It is in virtue of this characteristic of the Master that Buddhism is the only one of the great religions of the world that is consciously and frankly based on a rational analysis of the problem of life, and of the way to its solution. Buddha was a pioneering lover of men and a philosophic genius rolled into a single vigorous and radiant personality.

When his followers in the centuries that succeeded his own looked back upon his role as a religious leader, they saw, in addition to these basic characteristics, two facts about him that vitally affected their theological interpretations. On the one hand, there was his complete renunciation of worldly interests, activities, and responsibilities, in his concern to attain as quickly as possible the illumination and liberation of *moksha*, and his refusal, when the attainment had come, to participate again in those activities and reassume those responsibilities. On the other hand, there was his whole-souled commitment to the salvation of others as well as himself, in a sense of loving oneness with the weal of all living creatures which he might further by sharing his insight with them. We shall see later how an emphasis on the first of these aspects of his life led in later centuries to the formation of one of the two main schools of Buddhism, and how an emphasis on the other led to the formation of a different school. For the present, it is important to note that these differences of emphasis affect the question as to what writings compose the reliable scriptures of Buddhism, one school accepting as authentic certain sutras which are rejected by the other as containing serious distortions of the Master's message. The following summary of his major teachings rests upon scriptures generally regarded by impartial scholars as substantially true to his original discourses.

B. HIS CENTRAL TEACHINGS

With the strongly philosophic quality of his thinking in mind, we shall be prepared for the fact that he explicitly rejected all the criteria of truth to which most religious enthusiasts have appealed, and grounded his teaching on the common reason and the common experience of men. He rejected all appeals to authority—not only submissive acceptance of the Vedic tradition but even the tendency of his disciples to rest on his own authority. "I am only a way-shower," he is reported to have said on one occasion, "and you as wayfarers must walk in the way of your own choosing."[3] He rejected all claim to any special revelation of truth. He refused to perform miracles for the sake of gaining adherents. "I despise and reject the miracles of magic power and divination. I and my disciples gain adherents only by the miracle of instruction."[4] The whole spirit of the Buddha's teaching on these matters is clearly brought out in his reply to an inquirer who was puzzled by the conflicting claims of dogmatic sectarians.

The son of Kesa, from Kalama, came to the Buddha, and said: "Master, every priest and teacher extols his belief as the only true one, and condemns that of others as false. I am worried by doubts. I do not know whom to believe."

The Buddha answered: "Thy doubts are well-founded; oh Kesaputta, listen well to my words. Do not believe anything on mere hearsay. Do not believe traditions because they are old, and have been handed down through many generations. Do not believe anything on account of rumors, or because people talk a great deal about it. Do not believe simply because the written testimony of some ancient sage is shown to thee. Never believe anything because presumption is in its favour, or because the custom of many years inclines thee to take it as true. Do not believe anything on the mere authority of thy teachers or priests—Whatsoever, according to thine own experience, and after thorough investigation, agrees with thy reason, and is conducive to thine own weal and welfare, as well as to the weal and welfare of other living beings, *that* accept as true, and shape thy life in accordance therewith."[5]

Let us examine briefly the criterion of religious truth with which this statement closes, for it would be difficult to find a comparable statement in the teaching of any other religious founder. Since authorities differ, one must turn to the clearest testimony of one's own experience, interpreted by reason as it also makes sincere use of the experience and testimony of others. And testimony about what? Not about matters calculated to satisfy a metaphysical curiosity; Buddha was practically minded above all else, though not in any narrow sense. "Whatsoever is conducive to thine own weal and welfare, as well as to the weal and welfare of other living beings." We are to use experience and reason, in short, to determine the conditions of dependable happiness—not for ourselves alone, but for all men. Now it takes the clearest exercise of our cognitive powers, playing upon all the lessons of life, to distinguish between apparent happiness and true happiness—between the happiness that weakens those qualities of the soul which make for well-being in oneself and others, and the happiness that strengthens them.

"Happiness I declare to be two-fold, according as it is to be followed after or avoided. And the distinction I have affirmed in happiness is drawn on these grounds: when in following after happiness I have perceived that bad qualities developed and good qualities were diminished, then that kind of happiness is to be avoided. And when, following after happiness, I have perceived that bad qualities were diminished and good qualities developed, then such happiness is to be followed."[6] What a confidence, here, in the power of experience and reason to learn the major lessons of life, and to discriminate the way that leads to the highest values man is capable of attaining! And in proposing this method Buddha is speaking, rightly or wrongly, in universal human terms, unhampered by any presuppositions limited in time or space. It is the natural accompaniment of this confidence that Buddha rejected, in favor of an equalitarian individualism, the hierarchical structure of society which he found prevailing in his day.

This rationalistic and generous humanism vitally affected the message of Buddhism when it became a missionary religion and sought converts all over the world. Obviously, it could make no dogmatic claim to absolute truth, valid without change for everyone, as has been made by such missionary faiths as Christianity and Islam. At the other extreme, it could not be satisfied with an easygoing acquiescence in error; so clear was it that the mass of people in every country were missing the priceless boon of true happiness. And Buddhism was confident that it could supply this need—that it had come nearer than any of its rivals to finding the key to the universal problem of man. So when inquirers asked for proofs and assurances, the natural answer of the Buddhist preacher was: "Come and see. Don't come blindly, just because of *our* testimony. Mobilize your experience as clearly as you can; use your reason to the full; and come and see if the way of the Master is not, in its fundamentals, your way too."

What basic truths about the world do reason and experience clearly teach, according to Buddha, that vitally affect our understanding of the common problem of life? His answer to this question is that everything as we know it, participating in finite existence as we find ourselves doing, is in constant change. The universe of our experience is not a static affair but a dynamic process. Things arise through the interaction of the factors necessary to produce them; they precariously maintain themselves for a longer or shorter period; sooner or later their existence ends when these factors separate. This means that decay and dissolution are inherent in the very nature of finite existence, and they bring, to us as to other forms of existence, the ills that are bound up with these phases of change. More concretely, all of us and those whom we love are subject to illness, old age, and death, and to the sorrows, anxieties, and frustrations that these inevitable experiences thrust upon us. No solution to the problem of life can be adequate that does not include a genuine acceptance of these inevitabilities and a thoroughgoing adjustment to them —an adjustment of such a sort that it encourages a similar solution on the part of others. No security is really possible that is not grounded in such acceptance; no happiness is dependable and enduring that is not grounded in such an adjustment.

Now this orientation meant that, while Buddha preserved much of the framework of thought that Indian thinkers had been slowly developing, two of the basic concepts discussed in the preceding chapter had to be rejected. These were the concepts of Brahman and *atman*. However much we might like to believe in an eternal reality that is the source of finite beings and to which they ultimately return, experience gives us no clear justification for such a belief. We have to start our quest with the changing process in which we find ourselves, and use our power of reason to discover what is constructively possible with it. Likewise with the belief in a changeless self supposed to form the substantial core of each individual. Such a belief is the expression of wishful thinking; experience discloses nothing in ourselves that is not in a process of composition and dissolution. Hence the famous *anatta* ("no soul") doctrine of early Buddhism, so difficult for other Indian thinkers as well as for Westerners to appreciate. The bearing of these rejections on Buddha's religious teaching we shall in due time examine.

It might be thought that in view of these conclusions he could not retain the doctrine of transmigration, so vital to Indian ways of thinking. If man has no substantial soul, what transmigrates from one form of bodily existence to another? But he did retain it; however, the doctrine had to be drastically revised. What transmigrates is not a soul but the moral and spiritual achievement of an individual at the moment of his death, so that another individual can begin with that achievement (his *karma*) and build upon it, for good or for ill, in the course of his own existence. Buddha retained also the ideas expressed in the concepts *moksha* and *dharma*, though in each case, as with *karma*, giving it a more or less radical reinterpretation so that it would harmonize with his new philosophy as a whole. The form taken by that revision we shall soon see.

Now we are ready for the kernel of Buddha's teaching, as he developed it on these foundations. What, for him, is the essence of a true understanding of the problem of life as people, generation after generation, find themselves facing it? The answer is given in the "four noble truths," which according to tradition he first enunciated in his opening sermon at Benares. The meaning of these truths has been unfortunately obscured by those who have translated them into Western tongues, either because their ponderous conscientiousness required a literal rendering or because they persistently looked for something deep and recondite instead of something clear and simple. I shall begin by stating the heart of Buddha's reasoning in what seems to me the briefest and simplest form, and then proceed to a more detailed consideration of each of the four doctrines, guided by his own reported commentary on them.

1. Existence is unhappiness.
2. Unhappiness is caused by selfish craving.

3. Selfish craving can be destroyed.

4. It can be destroyed by following the eightfold path.

What strikes the Western reader as most surprising in this analysis is the complete omission of anything savoring of a metaphysical theology. There is no reference to God, no reference (of course) to soul, no reference to anything transcending human experience, no reference to the possibility of any superhuman aid in resolving life's perplexities. These omissions are intentional and well considered. What Buddha is trying to give the world is a way to meet the difficult practical problem that men and women universally confront, freed from any unrealistic hopes and any cosmological theories that lie beyond experiential verification. He is offering a systematic dissection of the problem of life in such terms as will, he believes, give men and women dependable guidance in finding their way from the confused mixture of misery and unstable happiness in which they now exist to a state of true and secure well-being. And he was sure, as his rejection of the concept of Brahman indicates, that this quest is obstructed rather than aided by doctrines claiming truth about metaphysical ultimates. Why? Well, there are honest disagreements about such matters, incapable of being decided by conclusive evidence; if they are allowed to clash in contentious argument they will engender a spirit of strife and dogmatic bluster that at worst is a source of hostility, and at best distracts men's attention from the real problem that can only be solved by steady, undistracted concentration on what it involves. An inquirer is recorded in the *Sutta Nipata* as asking the Master:

> Fixed in their pet beliefs,
> These divers wranglers bawl—
> "Hold this, and truth is yours;
> Reject it, and you're lost!"
>
> Thus they contend, and dub
> Opponents "dolts" and "fools."

> Which of the lot is right,
> When all as experts pose?

To which the Buddha replied:

> I count not that as true
> Which those affirm who call
> Each other "fools." They call
> Each other so because
> Each deems his own view "Truth.". . .
>
> There's one sole "Truth" (not two)
> To know which bars men's strife.[7]

The completely practical orientation is obvious here. True knowledge is the knowledge under whose guidance men are drawn away from strife and contention and the other conditions which foster unhappiness, not the supposed knowledge that leads them into it. Or, negatively expressed, nothing is true that cannot be spoken in love—nothing whose speaking promotes discord rather than harmonious understanding. Truth is insight into true values, as well as into true relations among the facts which must be taken into account in the quest for those values.

Let us now ponder the four noble truths, one by one. And in expounding their meaning I shall express Buddha's basic convictions in terms that, I hope, will make them as intelligible as possible to the experience of Western people today.

The first, Buddha is reported to have clarified in his opening sermon at Benares thus: "Birth is painful, old age is painful, illness is painful, death is painful; contact with what we dislike is painful, separation from what we like is painful, failure to attain what we crave is painful. In brief, all the conditions which make up bodily existence are painful." The word that I am translating by "painful" in this passage is *dukha*, which is variously rendered, according to the context, by such English words as "suffering," "sorrow," "misery," as well as "pain" —it means the opposite of happy well-being. What is it that Buddha is saying here? Is it that all people are in conscious

misery most of the time? I don't believe so. He is not denying that many find much gladness in life. What he is saying is
that, by virtue of being born into the realm of finite and
changing existence in which events follow their own laws, no
one escapes the conditions that bring pain, and therefore that
the problem of unhappiness is the universal problem of life.
If existence were such that all people naturally found real
and continued happiness in it, there would be no such problem calling for a way of deliverance. Even if by lucky accident a person escaped every other source of pain and frustration, death is inevitable for himself and his loved ones, and is
painful to face; moreover, one who has not adequately dealt
with this problem will be sure to crave from life more than
he can attain, and thus to meet frustration in other ways.

The second noble truth locates the basic cause of unhappiness. If we are to understand anything in such a way as to
deal successfully with the problems it poses, we need to
identify its universal cause, control of which would enable us
to control the effect. And Buddha locates this universal, con-
trollable cause in *tanha**—another of those Eastern terms
which are difficult to translate simply and straightforwardly
into a Western tongue. It is usually rendered in English by
"desire" or "craving." But if such a translation is accepted
without qualification, the popular Western criticism of Buddhism is encouraged and justified—namely, that this religion
expects us to annihilate the whole range of drives within ourselves that are covered by the Western concept of "desire."
So I have supplied the crucial missing factor in this translation
by the adjective "selfish." For it is consonant with the meaning of the Western term "desire" to speak not only of a desire
for food or for sex fulfillment but also of a desire for oneness
with God or for the true good of all men. But the Buddhist
interpretation of *tanha* assumes that it is always a craving of
the limited, individual living creature, seeking to gratify itself

* This is the Pali form of the Sanskrit *trishna*. Its original meaning is
"thirst."

in its separateness and to use the surrounding world as a means to its own self-centered ends. The aspiration to rise beyond domination by such demands and to transcend this separateness is not a form of *tanha;* it is the active expression within the self as it now is of the purified self which it is destined to be. This should be referred to by some other term, lest we confuse the childish state which must be left behind with the mature state which the man of insight hopes to achieve.

But why pick upon *this* cause of unhappiness as the cause uniquely significant in a basic analysis of the problem of life? There are many conditions that contribute to human misery, such as the vagaries and convulsions of nature, accidental misfortunes, and the inescapable impact of death. Buddha was not unmindful of these. Why, then, the crucial emphasis upon *this* cause? Because, I take it, this is the cause about which alone the following important things can be said: (1) it is a real cause; (2) it is within our control, something effective can be done about it; (3) everyone must do something about it in his own case if it is to be controlled; (4) control of it is sufficient to destroy unhappiness, irrespective of how much or how little one succeeds in doing about the other causes. Let us examine these four assertions. The first has already been commented on; only a moment's reflection on the meaning of what Buddha is saying about this truth would seem to be necessary. The second does need further proof, but the proof is given in the fourth noble truth, which indicates the path by which *tanha* can be brought under control; and in the meantime the confirming example stands before us of those who have followed that path—notably Buddha himself—whose character shows the selfless peace and joy which liberation from *tanha* can bring. We must consider then the third and fourth assertions, which I shall take in reverse order.

Why is elimination of *tanha* sufficient to end unhappiness, as well as necessary, in a sense in which this is not the case with the other conditions that make for human suffering?

Because some of the other causes cannot be eliminated, e.g., death. They can therefore be dealt with successfully only by transcending the state in which we are slaves of the cravings they frustrate, and by identifying ourselves with values to which they are irrelevant. In this way and in no other can we find a happiness unaffected by death, whether it be our own death or the death of those we love. Moreover, even in the case of the causes of unhappiness that might be overcome by science, such as the sudden calamities of nature, the victory cannot come at once but only through the quest for knowledge over many generations, and there is no way of telling in advance how successful at any given time this effort will be. True happiness for a man must be possible irrespective of any particular degree of triumph in this process during his lifetime.

So we are brought back to the third assertion. Because of these circumstances, it is essential to the adequate conquest of unhappiness that every human being become aware of the problem posed by them and resolutely face it from the focus of his own experience. No one can remove all the causes of unhappiness for anyone else; no one can make a present of true well-being to another person. At best one can only remove for another some of the external sources of misery and pain; the internal sources, expressing an inadequate emotional adjustment to the realities and possibilities of life, can only be destroyed by each for himself, as he gains alert and constructive awareness of such handicaps within. So if Buddha is right, this *is* a peculiarly fundamental cause; if it is not dealt with soberly and persistently by each person, the problem will remain unsolved.

The third noble truth is that *tanha* can be destroyed. Again, if proof be demanded that this is so, appeal can only be made to those who have succeeded in destroying it in themselves and who exemplify the spiritual perfection that results. But this is the convenient point at which to clarify the Buddhist convictions that are so frequently challenged or misunderstood in the West, and which are sharply reflected in this doctrine. Why not find ways of satisfying *tanha* as fully as possible instead of rooting it out? Or, if we sense our lack of power and skill to carry this program through successfully, why not aim at a judicious balance between self-gratification and prudent regard for others, so that on the whole the maximum of canny well-being will be achieved that a sensible man might hope to achieve?

Buddha's answer to this plea, when we gather all in his teaching that is relevant to it, can be set forth pretty clearly under four heads. First, once more, there are some cravings that cannot in the nature of the case be satisfied—for example, the craving that existence in its present form might be endless for ourselves and our dear ones. No strategy for dealing with the problem of life can be adequate which does not adjust us, with equanimity, to the realities of death and bereavement. Second, even in the case of the cravings that an ambitious man might hope to satisfy, this strategy reflects a fatal ignorance of oneself. When one adopts this way of meeting the challenge of life, he finds that his desires grow faster than his power to satisfy them. One aims at amassing a hundred thousand dollars, but by the time the goal is within his grasp he must have no less than a million; one sets out to be the best mountain climber in his neighborhood, and when he succeeds he is unhappy because he is not yet the best in the country. Third, these cravings focus upon objects that are craved by other people too; as they expand without limit we compete against our fellows, making our happiness depend on victory in a struggle in which either we or they are bound to meet defeat. But defeat for ourselves is painful, and their defeat is our guilt. Fourth, and most important, the satisfaction realized by whatever partial success we might win is not real satisfaction. Human beings are capable of a better and greater achievement—a kind of happiness that is not based on unrealistic hopes of evading the inevitable frustrations of finite existence. Our true happiness must and can rest on a thorough understanding and acceptance of ourselves and the world, making possible a stable, growing joy that is incomparable with the confused and transitory pleasures of gratifying this or that impulsive urge.

The implication of these considerations is very drastic; what the Western world in general thinks of as freedom—namely, emancipation from external obstructions to our power of action—is really a peculiarly tragic form of bondage. For what could be more hopeless slavery than the state in which one struggles without restraint for the satisfaction and multiplication of his ignorant cravings? As for the strategy of discreet compromise mentioned above, as an alternative to the blind quest for gratification, this might guide one in avoiding the conflicts with his fellows that otherwise would arise, but it could not lead him to peace within himself. He would always be craving things which he could not, for reasons of caution, allow himself to have; when he eschews self-seeking behavior it is because he is accepting an irksome duty, not an opportunity for happy self-giving. A solution of the problem of life is needed which enables us to find real inward peace, not merely an anxious adjustment to the limitations of our aggressive powers.

The fourth noble truth specifies the path by which the earnest aspirant may gradually succeed in eradicating *tanha* and thus achieving the goal of true happiness. This path includes eight steps, or systematic requirements, which may be indicated in English as follows:

1. Right understanding
2. Right purpose (aspiration)
3. Right speech
4. Right conduct
5. Right vocation
6. Right effort
7. Right alertness
8. Right concentration

I shall not take the space to explain this eightfold path at
length; but a brief clarification will help us grasp the significance of each step, and also what the path as a whole can reveal about the genius of Buddhism. The first two requirements
constitute the preliminary essentials; without them one is unable even to make a serious start toward achieving the goal. In
the absence of a true understanding of what the problem of
life is, and an unflagging aspiration toward the right ideal, one
would not know in what direction to turn, or his steps might
be so feeble and wavering that there is no reason to hope in
his case for any real achievement.

The third, fourth, and fifth requirements are conditions
necessary if we are to be assured of the aspirant's sincerity,
determination, and power of self-control in adhering to what
he sees to be right. Even before one has climbed many rungs
of the long ladder of spiritual growth it is possible, if one is
earnest, to exert a minimum degree of self-discipline, and it is
necessary that it be exerted if one is to avoid paralyzing moral
confusion. One can scrupulously tell the truth instead of
using judicious falsehoods, and without a determined habit of
truthfulness how could one hope to lay bare the unpalatable
truths about himself that must be honestly laid bare if he is to
grow beyond them? One can follow the basic rules of moral
conduct, refusing to be a cause of harm to other living beings
or to himself; he can eschew killing, stealing, meat-eating,
intoxication, and similar evils. If he is so completely the slave
of *tanha* that he cannot follow these rules, how can he be
expected to renounce impulsive gratifications when they conflict with the more rigorous requirements of spiritual progress?
And one can abandon any mode of gaining his livelihood
that places him in daily contradiction with the goal toward which he is professedly aspiring. A believer in the sacredness of life will not realize power for spiritual growth if
he earns his living in a slaughterhouse. These three steps
then constitute a pledge of one's readiness to order his daily

acts in a manner consistent with his chosen aim—to maintain the moral foundation on which his progress can be built.

The last three requirements turn our attention to the basic conditions of systematic growth toward the goal of completed self-conquest. They culminate in the achieved power of "right concentration." In this form of self-mastery all eight steps reach their fruition. To those unpurged of *tanha*, controlled attention is impossible; the mind is pulled hither and yon by enticements which it cannot steadily resist. As one grows in disciplined awareness of himself, and rejects *tanha* in all the varied forms in which he discovers its presence, he gains more and more in power of concentration. First, he conquers the distraction that comes by way of the itches of the body, the pulsations of the physiological functions, the seductions of interesting objects around him. As this is achieved, he masters the wanderings of mind itself, its tendency to follow this or that intriguing image as fancy suggests it. Gradually he becomes free from all the promptings and unpredictable flittings due to blind and selfish craving. He can see steadily, as it is, whatever he chooses as a worthy object of attention—life, death, the good, the bad, reality, illusion. He is capable of fully absorbed meditation, of completely identifying himself with truth and whatever the unqualified acceptance of truth brings in its train. With this achievement of *samadhi* (the Sanskrit term for "concentration") the goal is reached. He is no longer subject to rebirth in the ocean of *samsara*. He enters Nirvana.

C. THE GOAL OF NIRVANA AND THE IDEAL OF LOVE

Confronting this crucial and distinctively Buddhist concept,* we enter the next stage of sympathetic and impartial exploration. The main thing that is now essential to understanding the genius of Buddhism is to clarify certain puzzling questions that the Western thinker inevitably raises, and to

---

* Distinctive, that is, after it was taken over in Buddhist philosophy. It had been used in earlier Indian thought.

which he is prone to give a mistaken or at least inadequate answer. And the central question is: What is Nirvana?

It is well to begin this part of our study by reminding ourselves that Buddha adopted from previous Indian ways of thinking those basic ideas which seemed to him adequate to a realistic understanding of human experience, along with some more dubious ones to which his critical attention was perhaps never directed. Thus he accepted as valid the concepts of *moksha, samsara, karma,* and *dharma,* though in each case reinterpreting them sufficiently to fit them into his own philosophical convictions. He explicitly rejected the concepts of Brahman and *atman,* and we have briefly considered the reasons which led him to these drastic conclusions.

But now, in the case of Brahman, we must ponder his problem more fully. If we can understand clearly the grounds for his elimination of this concept, we shall be in a good position to appreciate the meaning of Nirvana, and also to master his whole philosophical perspective. Brahman filled two roles in Indian thought. On the one hand, as the ultimate source and essence of everything in the universe, it provided a basic principle of metaphysical explanation—it was the Absolute Reality. On the other hand, it was the goal of the religious quest, since the wise man finds salvation in leaving behind his finite selfhood, confused by ignorance and thrown in turmoil by *tanha,* and realizing union with Brahman. Now Buddha's agnosticism in metaphysics, resting on the theoretical and practical grounds mentioned above, required the abandonment of any concept claiming to fill the first of these roles. And this abandonment made it necessary to replace Brahman by some other concept so far as the second function is concerned; this function, of course, was vital to him as it is to every religious teacher. Well, the concept of Brahman as filling this role was in effect replaced by that of Nirvana; the goal of spiritual attainment for Buddhism is not the realization of oneness with Brahman, but entrance into Nirvana. What does this replacement signify, and what were the crucial considerations that led Buddha to adopt this concept?

"Nirvana" means, literally, a state of nothingness, of ceasing to be, of extinction. Is this what is actually meant by the Buddhist "Nirvana"? Many Western thinkers have taken the answer to be yes (though with some lingering puzzlement), and there have not been wanting Buddhist thinkers who seem to have accepted, without flinching, such an interpretation of this key term.[8] Is this a sound interpretation? Is Buddhism a sheer religion of escape—escape from the unbearable sorrows of life into nothingness?

Let us first be quite clear that any such interpretation is at least very unplausible, when one keeps the whole history of this religion in mind. One who gives this answer must face the exceedingly difficult task of explaining how a great religion that seeks sheer nothingness could make a successful missionary appeal to men and women of varying cultural backgrounds under quite different climatic conditions, and how a sense of joyous fulfillment could be found in annihilation. There are, of course, passages in the Buddhist scriptures which, taken apart from other statements, appear to support this interpretation. Listen to a *Psalm of the Sisters*, which pictures a Buddhist nun as saying:

> One day, bathing my feet, I sit and watch
> The water as it trickles down the slope;
> Thereby I set my heart in steadfastness,
> As one doth train a horse of noble breed.
> Then, going to my cell, I take my lamp,
> And seated on my couch I watch the flame.
> Grasping the pin, I pull the wick right down
> Into the oil . . .
> Lo! the Nibbana of the little lamp!
> Emancipation dawns! My heart is free![9]

If for a moment we pay no attention to the last line of this selection, it seems clear that Nirvana can mean nothing other than extinction. As the quenching of the flame is the Nirvana

of the lamp, so the extinguishing of one's personality would
be its Nirvana. And this is true if we remember that the
entity which is extinguished is the finite, changing self controlled by obsessive cravings, and that in Buddhist literature
the most popular analogue of such cravings in the physical
world is flame or fire. But to stop here would be a mistake.
For the last line intimates that Nirvana does not mean sheer
annihilation—there is in it the realization that one has achieved
an ardently sought emancipation, a hitherto unexperienced
freedom.

So we must pause. And when we examine other passages,
seeking to know what it is that one is emancipated from and
what in him therefore is extinguished, a basic Buddhist doctrine that has now become familiar looms before us. Buddha
is reported in the *Dhammapada* to have described his own
attainment of Nirvana thus:

> Painful are repeated births,
> O house builder! I have seen thee;
> Thou canst not build again a house for me.
> Thy rafters are broken,
> Thy roof timbers are shattered.
> My mind is detached;
> I have attained to the extinction of desire.[10]

Here the Master seems to be saying that what is extinguished
is selfish desire, and the need, as long as such desire is present,
of continued rebirth in one limiting bodily prison after another. But it is clearly disclosed that this experience does not
mean the extinction of the essential personality; what is meant
is its detachment from *tanha*, and this provides our interpretation of the emancipation to which the above psalm referred.
And thus we are ready for a more explicit answer to our
question in another quotation attributed to Buddha:

> When the fire of lust is extinct, that is Nirvana;
> When the fires of hatred and infatuation are extinct,
>   that is Nirvana;

When pride and all other passions and torments are
    extinct, that is Nirvana . . .
There is only one thing I preach now as before—
    suffering, and the extinction of suffering.[11]

No statement on this vital point could be clearer or more
definite. If something then is left to make up the core of one's
personality after the annihilation of craving, what is it? And
why does Buddha choose the word "Nirvana" to refer to the
spiritual goal instead of some word or phrase with a more
positive meaning? If we can confidently meet these questions,
we will understand him on this crucial matter pretty well.
Let's try.

As for the first question, it is necessary to bring together
passages from far and wide to answer it, and when this is
done it is clear that at least five major qualities of conscious
experience (not to mention minor ones) are left to give
positive content to the state of Nirvana; one of these has already been mentioned. They are liberation, peace, joy, insight, and love. The liberation is freedom from control by
blind and compulsive passions; this freedom brings the inward
peace only thus attainable, and the joy of realizing that the
most abject and unhappy slavery to which man is subject
has in one's own case been ended. The insight is the intuitive
comprehension discussed earlier—the true understanding of
reality which is impossible as long as the perceiving, relating,
and theorizing activities of our minds are subtly dominated
by cramping desires and the objects that arouse them. The
love is the free and compassionate outpouring of ourselves
to others and to the world, of which we first become capable
when self-centered yearnings and demands disappear. To express this Buddhist idea in the Christian terminology which
has already been found helpful: when our "old man" has
been crucified, the "new man" which takes its place will
manifest itself by the fruits of the spirit, which are "love,
joy, peace, patience, kindness, faithfulness, gentleness, self-
control."[12] In brief, all that is dependably real and good in

human experience and human relationships remains when *tanha* has been extinguished, and only then is it placed on a secure foundation.

Now for the second question. Why did Buddha feel it essential, as he evidently did, to avoid dwelling hopefully and encouragingly upon these positive qualities? Why did he often talk as though spiritual perfection were sheer nothingness?

Before we answer this question it is well to become vividly aware of the way in which Buddha's intensely practical concern dominated his thinking and his teaching. Even theoretical perplexities are dealt with in such fashion that, irrespective of whether or no the curiosity expressed in them is satisfied, the answer promises the greatest practical help in leading people away from unhappiness toward true well-being.

This concern is emphatically revealed in one of the sutras in the *Majjhima-Nikaya*, which describes a disciple coming to Buddha with his mind made up to cease following the Master unless he is given a definite answer to certain metaphysical questions—Is the world eternal or not eternal? Does the liberated person exist or not exist after death?, etc. The Buddha replies, in effect:

Would you be like a man who has been wounded by a poisoned arrow, and when his relatives and friends procure a skilled physician says to them: "I will not have this arrow taken out until I have learned what caste the man who wounded me belongs to, or what his name is, or whether his color is light or dark, or how tall he is, or what kind of bow he used?" That man would die, Malunkyaputta, without ever having learned this.

In exactly the same way, Malunkyaputta, any one who should say, "I will not lead the religious life under The Blessed One until The Blessed One shall explain to me either that the world is eternal, or that the world is not eternal . . . or that the liberated person either exists or does not exist after death"—that person would die, Malunkyaputta, before the Tathagata had ever explained this to him.

The religious life, Malunkyaputta, does not depend on the

dogma that the world is eternal; nor does the religious life, Malunkyaputta, depend on the dogma that the world is not eternal. Whether the dogma obtain, Malunkyaputta, that the world is eternal, or that the world is not eternal, there still remain birth, old age, death, sorrow, lamentation, misery, grief, and despair, for the extinction of which in the present life I am prescribing. . . .

Accordingly, Malunkyaputta, bear always in mind what it is that I have not explained, and what it is that I have explained. And what, Malunkyaputta, have I not explained? I have not explained, Malunkyaputta, that the world is eternal; I have not explained that the world is not eternal. . . . And why, Malunkyaputta, have I not explained this? Because, Malunkyaputta, this profits not, nor has to do with the fundamentals of religion. . . .

And what, Malunkyaputta, have I explained? Misery, Malunkyaputta, have I explained; the origin of misery have I explained; the cessation of misery have I explained; and the path leading to the cessation of misery have I explained. And why, Malunkyaputta, have I explained this? Because, Malunkyaputta, this does profit, has to do with the fundamentals of religion, and tends to aversion, absence of passion, cessation, quiescence, knowledge, supreme wisdom, and Nirvana; therefore have I explained it. Accordingly, Malunkyaputta, bear always in mind what it is that I have not explained, and what it is that I have explained.

The principle revealed in this discourse is quite general. All questions raised for the purpose of satisfying curiosity are dealt with in this spirit; they are answered in such a way that, in Buddha's judgment, satisfaction of the need expressed in the question will also promote liberation of the questioner from the unhappy cravings to which he is now in bondage. Sometimes the need should not be satisfied at all; "It is not the time to discuss about fire for those who are actually in burning fire; but that is the time to escape from it." Theoretical understanding is good only when it is a constructive part of the inclusive self-realization which marks true growth toward the spiritual goal.[13]

Let us return now to our question. Why did Buddha emphasize the negative concept of Nirvana instead of the positive qualities which, if we are right, entrance into Nirvana intrinsically brings?

I think that the right answer runs as follows. Each of the words by which the five qualities above mentioned are referred to has two basic meanings, which point in a different direction and lead to a different course of action. On the one hand, they have the meaning that they would naturally have to a person who has passed through the course of spiritual discipline that leads to their realization, and who has therefore come to experience them in their full and true significance. On the other hand, they have the meaning that is naturally suggested to a person who is still more or less controlled by self-seeking desire, and who therefore envisions them as qualities which he hopes to experience through the satisfaction of longings that he now feels.*

In the latter case the meaning of each of these words will be, to a greater or less degree, distorted; it will reflect the guise in which he imagines these qualities while his imagination is influenced by whatever self-centered yearning is still a part of his make-up. They will be projections of his frustrated hopes and demands. He will picture liberation, not as freedom from his immature cravings, but as freedom from the external forces that prevent him from fulfilling them. He will picture peace, not as the termination of an anxious and exhausting inner conflict, but as a hoped-for contentment arising from the satisfaction of this or that urgent desire. He will think of insight, not as an impartial contemplation of reality undistracted by the push and pull of his blind impulses, but as the kind of knowledge that results when one's selecting, relating, and interpreting of objects is subtly determined by the urge to achieve this or that desired end with the objects thus perceived. He will construe love, not as the compassionate giving of himself to all living beings, in a happy concern for their true well-being, but as a dependent attach-

* In Sanskrit and Pali some of these differences are often indicated by using different words for the two meanings.

ment to this or that person whose affection he needs to provide him the gratification, the comfort, and the security
which he craves.

It is not that he interprets these words in this unfortunate
way because of any wish to miss their true meaning. In each
case he attributes to them the most ideal meaning that he is
able to glimpse, in view of the limitations of his experience
to date. But none the less, not only is the interpretation a distorted one, but the distortion is of such a sort that it seriously
threatens his progress toward the spiritual goal. If he is encouraged to dwell hopefully upon freedom, joy, truth, and
the rest while he inevitably thinks of them in this way, he
will be tacitly enticed to strive more eagerly to satisfy his
immature desires, when what he really needs is to lay them
aside and advance as quickly as possible toward the experience that will give true meaning to these important words.
Under these circumstances, to emphasize the positive meaning
of Nirvana—i.e., of the qualities expressing spiritual perfection—is to place further handicaps in the path which people
must follow to attain it, not to give them helpful guidance.

So what answer could Buddha give to questions about that
goal, other than that it is Nirvana? For, whatever else it is or
is *not*, it *is* Nirvana—the Nirvana of passion and grief, of
blind demandingness, of anxiety, fear, and hatred, of ignorance, turmoil, and despair; the Nirvana of the enslaved,
craving, suffering self. It is best that people who have not
yet attained the goal think of it simply as Nirvana, for it is
the Nirvana of what they now largely are, of that with
which they now unfortunately identify themselves. The
process of attainment *is* an emptying, extinguishing process.
And so far as they need any hint as to the positive nature of
the goal it is better that it take the form, not of verbal description, but of exemplification—in the persuasive person of the Tathagata (who has "come through to perfection") and in the persons of others who have progressed
farther than they have done along the path. Words can be

misleading, even distorting, but there is nothing misleading in the example of those who reveal in feeling and action what liberation truly is, and what the other qualities that follow in its train truly are.

Freedom is the crucial mark of spiritual attainment when it is viewed in relation to the earlier state which it succeeds. Its very essence consists in liberation from that state. Love is the crucial mark in the sense of being that quality in which all other qualities find their convergence and culmination. This fact was not fully realized in the early history of Buddhism; perhaps it was not fully realized by Buddha himself. And there are difficulties to the Western mind in the Buddhist ideal of love whose clarification will go a long way toward making the basic convictions of this religion yet more intelligible.

The major problem confronts us vividly in the words which Buddha is reported to have spoken to a bereaved grandmother, who came to him hoping for comfort in her sorrow: "Those who have a hundred dear ones have a hundred woes; those who have ninety dear ones have ninety woes . . . those who have one dear one have one woe; those who hold nothing dear have no woe."[14] This not only seems to be cold comfort; it suggests that what is desirable in our human relationships is to withdraw from emotional attachment, to forbid ourselves depth of affectionate feeling, in order that we may be spared the woe that comes from the death of those we love. One might suppose that Buddha has missed the deep lesson expressed so poignantly by George Eliot when she wrote, "We can only have the highest happiness . . . by having wide thoughts, and much feeling for the rest of the world as well as ourselves; and this sort of happiness often brings so much pain with it that we can only tell it from pain by its being what we would choose before everything else, because our souls see it is good."[15]

But this interpretation would be a mistake; it arises from failing to draw fully and clearly the distinction mentioned above between two kinds of love. That such a distinction is needed for adequate understanding appears from a pair of passages in the *Dhammapada*. In Chapter XVI of this great classic we are told: "Let no man love anything; loss of that which is beloved is evil. Those only who love nothing, and hate nothing, have no fetters." This, if taken by itself, would seem to confirm the impression just drawn from Buddha's cold comfort of the bereaved. But in the very next chapter we read: "Let a man overcome anger by love, let him overcome evil by good; let him overcome the greedy by generosity, the liar by truth!"* It would hardly seem possible to harmonize these two passages without recognizing that from the Buddhist point of view there is an unfortunate kind of love, and also a good kind—there is a love which expresses ignorant *tanha* not yet overcome, and a love which expresses creative spiritual attainment. The usual way in which, in the East, these two emotions are contrasted is to describe the former as love of "attachment," the latter as love of "detachment." But these words are hardly self-explanatory to a Western mind.

By "love of attachment" a Buddhist thinker means the kind of feeling which involves the making of emotional demands upon the person or object loved. A child's love for his parents is largely a love of this sort; it is the expression of his insistent need for their attention and approval, for the security and comfort that he depends on them to give. And a parent's love for his children is often of this sort too; it reveals an urge to control the child's way of life instead of an eagerness that the child find his career and guiding aim in his own way. In contemporary discussions in the West it is frequently described as "possessive" love—love which seeks to possess the loved one in the sense of making him do this or that which the lover yearns for him to do. It is the kind of love referred

---

* In the original, two different words are used here. But the fact that each of them can be rendered by the English word "love" creates precisely the problem for the Western mind which needs clarification.

to in *The Bridge of San Luis Rey* when Thornton Wilder says of the Marquesa de Montemayor: "She persecuted Doña Clara with nervous attention and a fatiguing love."[16] It is the love which may easily turn to hate when the dependent clinging or selfish aggression which is essential to it remains unsatisfied.

"Love of detachment," on the other hand, is free from all demandingness, all need to control the loved one, all dependence upon him. It is detached, not in the sense of withdrawing from emotional concern for others, but in the sense of gladly accepting them as they are, not requiring them to be different from their present selves as the price of one's friendly affection. It is detached, not from caring for others, but from preoccupation with oneself, and from the need to make others serve the cravings of the self. It is the compassionate giving of oneself to the world without asking for anything in return—the compassion radiated by Buddha himself after his enlightenment. Now it is the conviction of Buddhism that, as our emotions are progressively purged of all blind demandingness and self-seeking, we do not just pass into a psychological vacuum but become more and more the vehicle of such an outgoing compassion toward others. As the subtle elements of possessiveness and aggressive hostility are destroyed through poignant recognition of their presence, what takes their place is not sheer nothing but a positive emotion for which there was no room before—a joy in the well-being of others and an eagerness that they too win the undisturbed peace that such love experiences in itself. This love will be free from dependence on anything external, for it is guided by a realistic understanding and acceptance of whatever happens. It will be aware of the inevitability of death, and in the presence of the death of a dear one grief will be overcome by the joy that the loved one had lived as long as he did, and by a sense of compassionate oneness with all others who, like ourselves, must face the sorrows of death. The first of these two kinds of love is by its very nature bound up with the *tanha* which must be left behind in the process of spiritual growth; the second is the high-water mark of the spiritual attainment itself.

The way in which, for Buddhism, this realization of a deeply satisfying compassion is related to an unqualified acceptance of death and dissolution in a world of ceaseless change is clearly disclosed in the parable of Kisa Gotami.* Westerners naturally wonder why such acceptance would not more readily lead to a frustrated bitterness toward the world, or a numbing withdrawal from emotional involvement with persons and objects that must inevitably perish. The Buddhist answer is that indeed it would do so if it were not part of a transforming process in which our unrealistic cravings are being left behind—our blind demands that the universe give us and those we hold dear more than it is prepared or able to give. A full emotional adjustment to life and death, achieved through such a process, does culminate in a loving oneness with others and the releasing joy that it brings. Kisa Gotami was a young girl who married and bore a son. But while still at a tender age her son died. In her overwhelming grief she could not accept the reality of his death. Carrying the little body on her hip, she inquired of people for medicine that would cure her son. Most of them laughed at her, but before long a discerning person directed her to the Buddha. Sensing that she might be ready to learn the spiritual lesson needed, he said to her, "You did well, Gotami, in coming hither for medicine. Go enter the city, make the rounds of the entire city . . . and in whatever house no one has ever died, from that house fetch tiny grains of mustard seed."

"Very well, reverend sir," said she. Delighted in heart, she entered within the city, and at the very first house said: ". . . . Give me tiny grains of mustard seed."

"Alas! Gotami," said they, and brought and gave to her.

* This parable is included in my *Teachings of the Compassionate Buddha* (Mentor MD 131), New York, 1955, p. 43 ff.

"This particular seed I cannot take. In this house some one has died!"

"What say you, Gotami! Here it is impossible to count the dead!"

"Well then, enough! I'll not take it. . . ."

In the same way she went to the second house, and to the third. Suddenly she thought: In the entire city this must be the way! This the Buddha, full of compassion for the welfare of mankind, must have seen! Overcome with emotion, she went outside of the city, carried her son to the burning-ground, and holding him in her arms, said: "Dear little son, I thought that you alone had been overtaken by this thing which men call death. But you are not the only one death has overtaken. This is a law common to all mankind." So saying, she cast her son away in the burning-ground.

The profound spiritual truth here taught is that as long as in the presence of death one is absorbed in his own sorrow and loss, no liberating peace or happiness is possible. But when one can give up the demand for special protection for himself against the inevitable dissolutions that existence brings, he realizes an emotion of loving unity with all others who suffer because of such grief and loss—an emotion so intrinsically satisfying that when it is born and becomes the core of his being, the sorrow previously experienced is transmuted into joy. For death can then be fully accepted because it has become a means to the realization of this supreme good.

When the difference, then, between these two kinds of love is fully mastered it will be evident, I think, that there is no real contradiction in Buddha's thought on this vital theme. And it will be clear also that, to Buddhist insight, the quest for Nirvana is not an escape from life and reality, but rather a process of achieving victory over the painful aspects of existence through the discovery and fulfillment of those that are dependably good.

This second kind of love is beautifully revealed in a passage in the *Sutta Nipata*,[17] which may well be described as the Buddhist "Thirteenth Chapter of First Corinthians":

> May creatures all abound
>
> In weal and peace; may all
> be blessed with peace always;
> all creatures weak or strong,
> all creatures great and small;
>
> Creatures unseen or seen,
> dwelling afar or near,
> born or awaiting birth,
> —may all be blessed with peace!
>
> Let none cajole or flout
> his fellows anywhere;
> let none wish others harm
> in dudgeon or in hate.
>
> Just as with her own life
> a mother shields from hurt
> her own, her only, child—
> let all-embracing thoughts
> for all that lives be thine,
>
> An all-embracing love
> for all the universe
> in all its heights and depths
> and breadth—unstinted love,
> unmarred by hate within,
> not rousing enmity.
>
> So, as you stand or walk,
> or sit, or lie, reflect
> with all your might on this;
> —'tis deemed "a state divine."

Besides Buddha's abandonment of the concept of Brahman, the other main respect in which he departed radically from traditional ways of thinking is his rejection of a permanent soul or *atman* in man. This is known historically as the *anatta* (or "no soul") doctrine. It also has been mentioned above; now we are in a position to probe more fully its meaning and to throw further light on the motives expressed in Buddha's adoption of it.

In the first place, he was convinced that observation of ourselves and of others discloses nothing that is not in a process of ceaseless change. If therefore one accepts the idea that over and above these transient states there exists a permanent entity like the *atman* as traditionally conceived, he would be insisting, without evidence, that there must be in the self something analogous to a changeless metaphysical ultimate. But, in the second place, as we have seen, he distrusted all metaphysical reasonings that issue in conclusions incapable of definite proof. It was not, almost surely, that he had any objection to speculation as such. But he was sure that to indulge in it is usually to evade the primary responsibility of so using our minds that we will understand better the problem of life and learn how to guide ourselves and others toward its solution. Let us not succumb to the temptation of metaphysical stalling when we need all the intellectual energy of which we are capable to lead us toward the spiritual goal. Furthermore, to proclaim that our pet beliefs are true when other thinkers reach quite different and equally defensible notions about the same matters is to encourage an argumentative bickering, a warring of sectarian dogmatisms, that is inconsistent with inward peace and outgoing love. Such contentiousness is a sign of self-seeking desire not yet overcome—the desire to gain victory in debate, to impose one's own darling dogmas upon others. When Buddha sensed that an inquirer was possessed by this argumentative zeal, so that any answer would be taken as giving support to some metaphysical theory, he refused to answer at all. "Is there the ego?" he is asked on one occasion. He replies with silence. "Is there not the ego?" He replies with continued silence; and the questioner departs. His beloved disciple Ananda ventures to ask what the silence meant. "If I had said there is an ego I would have confirmed the belief in the permanence of what is really transient. If I had said there is no ego I would have confirmed the belief in annihilation."[18] It was better then to avoid answering either way. And finally, he was sure that such an understanding of *samsara* and *karma* as guides us successfully toward *moksha* does not require the assumption that an unchanging soul passes from each existence to the next. It does require the conviction that there is a continuity of moral character and of spiritual development between successive existences, but no substantial *atman*. Hence he taught that the accumulated *karma* in one form of existence is passed on at death to the succeeding form as the flame is passed from one candle to another when the first candle is about to flicker out. No substance is handed over from one to the other—only the property of being aflame.

D. THE SPIRIT OF EARLY BUDDHISM

The spirit of early Buddhism, as communicated by Buddha's energetic and winsome personality to his followers, was one of constant alertness in face of the temptation to sloth and inertia, of hopeful pursuit of the path of self-conquest, and of eager enthusiasm to share with others whatever saving insight has been won. This missionary zeal, which points toward the characteristic emphasis of Mahayana Buddhism, soon to be explicitly examined, is well revealed in one of the passages in which Buddha is reported to have commissioned his disciples to spread the good news: "Go forth, disciples, and travel, to the salvation and joy of much people, out of compassion for the whole world—to the blessing, salvation, and joy of gods and men. Go not two together on the same way. Preach, disciples, the doctrine which is salutary in its beginning, its course, and its consummation, in its spirit and in its letter; proclaim the pure way of holiness."[19] The insistent stress on alert responsibility for one's own steady progress toward the spiritual goal is best revealed in the Buddhist classic known as the *Dhammapada*, characterized by Lin

Yu-tang as "a great spiritual testimony, one of the very few religious masterpieces in the world, combining genuineness of spiritual passion with a happy gift of literary expression."[20]

Rouse thyself by thyself; examine thyself by thyself—you yourself must make an effort. The Tathagatas are only preachers. . . . If anything is to be done, let a man do it, let him attack it vigorously! . . . By oneself the evil is done, by oneself one suffers; by oneself evil is left undone, by oneself one is purified. The pure and the impure stand and fall by themselves; no one can purify another. . . . For self is the lord of self, self is the refuge of self; therefore curb thyself, as the merchant curbs a noble horse. . . . If one man conquer in battle a thousand times a thousand men, and if another conquer himself, he is the greatest of conquerors. . . .

Earnestness is the path of Nirvana, thoughtlessness the path of death. Those who are in earnest do not die; those who are thoughtless are as if dead already.

In other words, to summarize the message of this classic as a Westerner who had absorbed its spirit might do:

I bring you great and good news. There is a way from the crushing miseries of life to real happiness, and it is open to all. But the way is hard, and there is no magical method of making it easy. It means strenuous and constant self-examination; it means renouncing all that you foolishly prize now—your present self, in fact, with all the ignorant cravings and blind urges that now compose it. No one can tread this path for you, neither god nor man; you must tread it for yourself. So begin now. Be alert, and steadily alert. Make the most sustained effort of which you are capable. Let nothing entice you to dally by the wayside—neither self-indulgence, nor the mistaken urge to self-punishment, nor vain metaphysical curiosity, nor the desire for companionship with those not yet ready to enter upon the path. Face uncompromisingly toward the goal. And victory over self—the greatest of all victories, and the key to true joy in this life and beyond—will be won.

E. THERAVADA BUDDHISM

In discussing Taoism and Confucianism we found it necessary to pay some attention to their historical development, at least to the extent of noting how Chuang Tse supplements the original message of the *Tao Teh Ching* and how such documents as the *Great Learning* and the *Book of Mencius* add novel elements to Confucius' teaching. With Buddhism such a historical perspective becomes even more essential. The main reason for this is that a few hundred years after Buddha's time, while Buddhism was rapidly spreading throughout southern Asia, a major divergence among his followers appeared. Each of the two groups appealed for support to certain elements that it found in his teaching, but each expanded and developed those elements to the point where the interpretation of the one became irreconcilable with the interpretation of the other, so that a cleavage had to result. An analogy would have occurred in the West if early Christianity had split in terms of the loyalty of one theological school to the picture of Jesus and his teaching given in the Synoptic Gospels, and of another school to the rather different picture in the Gospel of John. The concepts generally employed by which to refer to this division are *Mahayana* (the "greater vehicle") and *Hinayana* (the "lesser vehicle"); Mahayana being the form in which Buddhism spread to Tibet, Mongolia, China, Korea, and Japan, while Hinayana Buddhism became the dominant religion in Ceylon, Burma, Siam, and a few other areas of southeast Asia. It will be observed that these terms reflect the Mahayana viewpoint, which is held by some three-fourths of living Buddhists today. A less prejudicial way of referring to the followers of Hinayana is to call them *Theravada* Buddhists—those who preserve "the way of the elders." From their own standpoint this is essentially what characterizes their form of Buddhism.*

---

* The term "Theravada" sometimes refers to a particular Hinayana school active in the early centuries of Buddhism.

I must not take the space to deal in any detail with Theravada Buddhism. In general, it is the more conservative of the two trends. It retains the characteristic emphases of the early period of Buddhist enthusiasm, especially as expressed in the *Dhammapada*. Theravada Buddhists stress the individual's responsibility to undertake the path of strenuous self-discipline, expecting no one else to save him; they think of Buddha as the great teacher and master who first showed the way, not as an incarnation of a cosmic power working through all ages for the salvation of the world—as he became for Mahayana thinkers. He is the one whom we must emulate, especially by as radical a renunciation as we are ready to undertake; the ideas expressed in *samsara, karma, anatta, moksha,* and Nirvana are retained essentially in their original form. Accordingly, the followers of Theravada interpret the basic vow by which they "take refuge in the Buddha, the Dhamma, and the Sangha" in a manner that is consistent throughout with these emphases. The Buddha for them is the original exemplifier of the way who has now entered Nirvana; the Dhamma is the body of doctrine which he taught, centering around the four noble truths; and the Sangha is the community that he founded, looking for its leadership to the monks who are farther along the path of renunciation than the laymen and therefore serve as their counselors and teachers. The outstanding Theravada thinker was Buddhaghosa, who lived and wrote in north India about A.D. 400, but who made a memorable and influential visit to Ceylon at one period of his career. It will be desirable, after we have followed the significant new developments in Mahayana, and especially the criticisms of southern Buddhism which they involve, to return briefly to the Theravada philosophers and note their answers to these criticisms.

F. *MAHAYANA BUDDHISM*

The ideas which became central in Mahayana thinking began to be formulated in northern India in the second century

B.C., and in the course of three hundred years had attained clarified and systematic elaboration. Several outstanding theologians appeared during and after this period of rapid growth; if one had to pick a single thinker as most important historically, the choice would fall either on Ashvaghosa, who taught in Oudh late in the first century A.D., or on Nagarjuna, who probably lived about seventy-five years later. Among Ashvaghosa's varied writings are a *Life of Buddha* (already mentioned) and a work entitled *The Awakening of Faith*, which is a systematic and also stirring exposition of the essentials of Mayahana doctrine. Nagarjuna is one of the great dialecticians of history, using logic to demonstrate the limitations of rational thought and the need of transcending it by a spiritual realization that is superrational.

Mahayana Buddhism is a rich aggregate of ideas and practices, with the coherence of a living religious development articulated by keen idealistic and dialectical systems of philosophy. I cannot attempt to cover, even in outline, the varied forms which it took. What I shall try to do is to bring out the dominant spirit reflected in its main trends and some of its characteristic ideas. From the point of view of Theravada Buddhism the key feature of Mahayana—which makes it a heterodox doctrine—is that it is a metaphysical doctrine *about* Buddha instead of being the faithful preservation of the religion *of* Buddha—the way of salvation set before men by his original teaching. And it is true that Mahayana Buddhists found in Buddha's personality something much greater than was clearly reflected in his doctrines as contained in the most authentic sutras. To this something they gave a religious and speculative interpretation, and that interpretation became a guide in the understanding of everything else that was significant in their faith; it even found expression in a number of sutras in which we find Buddha proclaiming that the major Mahayana ideas constitute the culmination of his teaching. To Theravada Buddhists Gautama was primarily their inspiring leader and, as such, their master; to Mahayana Buddhists he became, in addition to these, their savior, and the divine object of adoring faith. As Theravada Buddhists looked back upon the events of Buddha's life on earth, their attention centered upon his renunciation of the world and the basic doctrines which had shown the way to truth and to effective spiritual self-discipline; as Mahayana Buddhists did so, their attention focused in loving reverence upon the princely heir of pomp, luxury, and power who had given up all for the sake of truth, in pity for suffering mankind, and upon the Buddha who upon attaining enlightenment refused to hug his great discovery to himself but shared it with others and devoted the rest of his life to teaching them the saving path that he had found.

We plunge into the heart of the theological issues reflected in these divergent emphases when we raise the question: Was the fact that Gautama devoted the years after his attainment of Buddhahood to preaching the way of salvation to others an accidental or an essential expression of the spiritual perfection thus achieved? From the standpoint of Theravada Buddhism it must be regarded as an accidental expression. Gautama had gained his illumination, and had become fully purged of all the *tanha* which obstructs one from entering Nirvana and makes necessary his continued entrance into new forms of existence. He was then ready for Nirvana, and what could keep him out of it? To be sure, he would show a pitying compassion for mankind, since this is a necessary consequence of eliminating all blind self-seeking from one's nature. But he would be entirely free to express this compassion in whatever manner his spiritual insight might lead him to adopt; no one would have the right to insist that it must take the form of actively preaching the truth to others and giving them continued guidance. His example would be quite sufficient, with such explanation as would enable those who respond to follow it. If others are to be saved they must follow that example; there is no other way.

From the Mahayana standpoint, as it came to be more and

more clearly formulated, what Buddha did was not an accidental but an essential expression of his achieved liberation. The love that constitutes the supreme mark of spiritual perfection is not just a compassionate pity for the mass of men and women who wander in ignorance and misery, as experienced by one who through long effort has emancipated himself from their follies; it is an acceptance of and commitment to ultimate union with them, with the consequence that his own destiny and salvation are felt to be intrinsically bound up with theirs. This, they were sure, is the significance of the spirit in which Buddha sought the saving truth, and of the happy eagerness to share it with others that he revealed after his insight was gained. If he had not exemplified this radiant love for others, that would have shown that he had not really been purged of all self-centered *tanha;* he had not yet really attained Buddhahood, had not yet come through to perfection. The basic conviction of Mahayana thought at this point is the conviction beautifully expressed in John G. Whittier's little poem "The Meeting":

> He findeth not who seeks his own;
> The soul is lost that's saved alone.[21]

In the Buddhist framework of thought two very searching questions were thus brought to the fore, to which the Theravada and the Mahayana thinkers gave different answers. One is the question: In what form is self-giving love an essential mark of spiritual realization? The other, which at once proved to be bound up with it, is the question: Can one enter Nirvana by himself? The Theravada answer to the first question is: in whatever form it finds expression in the individual who, through persistent self-discipline after the Master's example, has extinguished *tanha* and gained liberation. The answer of Mahayana philosophy is: in the form required by a deep sense of oneness with all who suffer in pain and darkness and are blindly groping for the saving way. To the second question the Theravada answer is yes; it cannot be otherwise, for one's readiness to enter Nirvana depends only on conditions present in himself, not on the degree to which others have achieved liberation. The Mahayana answer, however, is no; at least, the highest form of spiritual realization shows itself in a conviction that one's own salvation is incomplete, nay even impossible, as long as any other creatures have not yet found salvation too. Naturally, each school sought and found justification for its answer to these two questions in sayings attributed to the Buddha, and so we find a number of sutras appearing, and gaining popularity in the Mahayana countries, which are not recognized as authentic by Theravada historians. They present Buddha as expounding typical Mahayana doctrines; among the most influential of them, besides those already mentioned, are the *Diamond Sutra*, the *Lankavatara Sutra*, the *Lotus of the Perfect Law*, the *Surangama Sutra*, and the *Sukhavati-Vyuha Sutra*.

How did the Mahayana thinkers deal with the fact that many obviously early sutras taught a religious ideal and a conception of salvation quite different from the one they had come to accept? Some, apparently, were not disturbed by this question. But others frankly confronted the problem posed by these sutras, and did so in a very natural and revealing way. This way is developed especially in the *Lotus of the Perfect Law;* according to it, Buddha taught to each group of his disciples at each stage of their development the highest truths that they were able to grasp. The Theravada teachings were adapted to the needs of those who had made some progress and had gained partial insight, but the Mahayana doctrines could only be revealed later to those who had reached the point where they could understand and follow them. The main purpose of some of the famous Mahayana parables is to explain and justify this idea. In the parable of the "burning house," the householder realizes that his small boys, who are at play in the building, unaware of danger, will be caught by the fire if he does not entice them to run out of the house to the gate at once. He has a present of incomparable value to give them, but they do not appreciate its worth and would not be attracted by it. So he must call to each of them that he has for him the trinket that would be most appealing to a child of his years and his degree of understanding. He does so and all are lured away from danger. Was he deceiving them in doing this?

So with the Buddha in relation to his followers. He has salvation to give, after the Mahayana ideal, but he leads the immature *sravakas** and *pratyekabuddhas*† toward it by teaching them the highest form of insight that they can as yet apprehend. In the tradition of Zen Buddhism in China and Japan this concept is carried to the extreme. The Zen teachings are held to be superior even to the other Mahayana doctrines; they were revealed by the Master only to the single person among his disciples who could comprehend them, and they have been handed down through the line of Zen patriarchs, upon whom rested the special responsibility of preserving them for the sake of those in later centuries who could respond to their meaning.

It will be clear from this that the Mahayana trend of thought, as compared with that of the Theravadins, envisioned a somewhat altered spiritual ideal, that this vision needed certain novel concepts for its adequate expression, and that at certain points definite divergences of doctrine appeared when measured by what had apparently been taught by Buddhism in its earlier forms. The altered spiritual ideal has already been briefly described. As over against the emphasis on rugged self-reliance, shown when one leaves behind all dependent attachment to worldly things and achieves freedom from anxiety about other people, we now have an emphasis on the sense of loving unity with all men and women, expressing itself in an eagerness to partake in their

* "Hearers"—those who listen to preaching but lack spiritual initiative.
† "Separate Buddha"—one who wins enlightenment only for himself, independently of others.

struggles and vicissitudes and to find fulfillment in devoted sharing with them even while they remain in their imperfections. Only when this transformation is fully mastered can one who has become acquainted with Buddhism in its Theravada guise understand Anesaki's description of what the Japanese people saw in Buddhism when (in its developed Mahayana form) it was introduced to them:

Whatever the Western critics may say, the influence Buddhism exerted everywhere lay in its practice of love and equality, which was an outcome of its fundamental teaching of the unity of all beings, and of its ideal of supreme enlightment (*bodhi*) to be attained by all. This *bodhi* amounts to realizing, in the spirit and in life, the basic unity of existence, the spiritual communion pervading the whole universe. This was exemplified by the person of Buddha, not only in his teaching of all-oneness but in his life of all-embracing charity. Those united in the faith in Buddha and his teaching form a close community of spiritual fellowship, in which the truth of oneness is embodied and the life of charity is practiced. . . .

Now the Buddhism brought over to Japan was a developed form of this religion, demonstrated artistically in ceremonies and supported by a system of idealistic philosophy. . . .

The central idea in Buddhist teaching is the gospel of universal salvation based on the idea of the fundamental oneness of all beings. There are in the world, Buddhism teaches, manifold existences and innumerable beings, and each of these individuals deems himself to be a separate being and behaves accordingly. But in reality they make up one family, there is one continuity throughout, and this oneness is to be realized in the attainment of Buddhahood on the part of each and all, in the full realization of the universal communion. Individuals may purify themselves and thereby escape the miseries of sinful existence, yet the salvation of anyone is imperfect so long as and so far as there remain any who have not realized the universal spiritual communion, i.e., who are not saved. To save oneself by saving others is the gospel of universal salvation taught by Buddhism.

A prayer commonly used by Japanese Buddhists is:

> There are beings without limit,
> Let us take the vow to convey them all across.
>
> There are depravities in us without number,
> Let us take the vow to extinguish them all.
>
> There are truths without end,
> Let us take the vow to comprehend them all.
>
> There is the Way of Buddha without comparison,
> Let us take the vow to accomplish it perfectly![22]

It will be evident from this quotation that the ideal of love taught by the Mahayana Buddhism introduced to Japan is a bolder and more mystic concept than that which Theravada Buddhists found in their spiritual heritage. And this ideal not only became theoretically conceived but was also concretely embodied, especially in the cosmic Buddha Amitabha and in the compassionate Bodhisattvas. Amitabha is mythically portrayed as having gained Buddhahood on the express condition that all mortals who call sincerely upon his name will be received at death in his Western paradise, where they can continue the process of liberation under far happier and more encouraging auspices than would be the case if they remained tied to the wheel of existence on earth. Here it is evident that Buddha is not thought of as simply identical with the historic Gautama who lived and died some hundreds of years ago. That individual was one incarnation of a transcendent cosmic reality, the Buddha-nature, which is working in all ages and in innumerable worlds for the salvation of all sentient beings. Amitabha is one celestial exemplification of Buddhahood, thus conceived. A Bodhisattva is one who, having attained the goal of purification and emancipation, refuses to enter Nirvana, out of devoted love for those who still remain behind and a consuming zeal to help them. He postpones his own entrance into perfect bliss because his sense of spiritual oneness with others leads him to prefer to wait with them and lovingly serve them until all are ready to enter together. In Anesaki's words, he feels that his own salvation would be imperfect, and even impossible, as long as any living beings remain unsaved.

How did the Mahayana philosophies explain and justify this more radical ideal of love?

A full answer to this question would be rather complex; it would have to allow for several important variations of Mahayana doctrine, especially between those who accept a definitely idealistic metaphysic and those who believe that ultimate truth transcends the possibility of any rational formulation. One very influential line of thought, illustrating the former of these two types, may be briefly summarized as follows: the law of spiritual growth, culminating in the realization of loving oneness with all living beings exemplified in the personality of Buddha, is not merely the law of progress for individuals seeking liberation—it is also the key to ultimate reality; it is the true essence of the universe and of every particular form of existence when seen in its pure and unclouded nature. Now this general conviction has both a metaphysical and a religious aspect, each of which needs elaboration if it is to be adequately grasped.

On the metaphysical side it means that the particular objects of the phenomenal world that are discriminated by our senses and interpreted through analytic thought, while genuine when viewed as relative to ordinary perception, are not ultimately real. What is real is the Buddha essence or Buddha mind with which one becomes identified when he throws off the obscuring dust of *tanha* and recognizes his true nature for what it is. But this Buddha mind is not something that exists apart from the realm of changing phenomenal events, to be attained by leaving that realm behind; it is just that realm itself when realized in its essential unity and its inner meaning. The implications of such an idea are of course very radical. Among other things it involves the conclusion that Nirvana, as the principle and goal of spiritual growth, is not separate from *samsara*, the ocean of births and deaths in which all who have not yet achieved liberation are wandering; Nirvana and *samsara* are one, and are seen to be so when the latter is grasped in its true nature and accepted in the spirit of the Buddha.

On the religious side it means just the clarified and trans-figured ideal of love that has above been described. The aim of the true spiritual seeker is not merely to follow Buddha's example but to become one with his perfect essence. Now that essence was revealed, not in his leaving the world and pursuing the path of self-discipline as such, but in the loving concern for the salvation of others to which that path led and which marked his complete conquest of *tanha*. Accordingly, Nirvana must not be conceived as a state into which one can escape in self-sufficient isolation, abandoning the imperfect world in which others struggle and suffer. One who believes that salvation can be attained in this way shows thereby that there is still a taint of self-seeking and proud aloofness in him—that unpurged *tanha* remains in his nature. Nirvana is achieved just through the transforming realization of a sense of devoted oneness with others that is characteristic of the Bodhisattva. The person who is filled with this love ex-presses it by preferring to share the woes of his suffering fellows and to help them onward in the path, instead of en-tering any state of bliss in which he would be separated from them. He is sure that the truly enlightened person, being purged of all unworthy desires, can associate freely with all, even the lowest sinners; far from being tempted into their vices he will inspire them to emulate his example. Of course, until he has become purged he must guard against temptation; but the ideal is to become like the pure and fragrant lotus, which shoots up from the muddy bottom of the pond through the unclean water and lies white and un-smirched on the top.

Certain passages in the *Lankavatara Sutra* are of special interest because of the way in which they formulate and ex-plain this Mahayana religious insight in the framework of the idealism above described. The problem which provides the

theme of these passages arises from the fact that if the Theravada concept of Nirvana is accepted it would appear to
follow that for the Buddhas and Bodhisattvas there could be
no Nirvana. According to the Theravada philosophy, Nirvana is essentially the state into which one enters when
through independent self-discipline he has completed his liberation from *tanha*. But the seeker who has accepted the
Bodhisattva ideal of sainthood prefers to give himself in loving concern for others who are not yet free from *tanha*,
and therefore postpones his own entrance into Nirvana until
they are ready to come with him. And he is sure that such
postponement, in this spirit, is a truer mark of the attainment
of spiritual perfection than would be a willingness to enter
while other struggling mortals remain behind. In other words,
according to this altered perspective, those who most deserve entrance into Nirvana do not achieve it, because of
their continued compassionate renunciation of its rewards.
But this would be an intolerable dilemma, and analysis of it
leads to the needed Mahayana redefinition of Nirvana.[23]

The key passage begins by listing four approaches to the
meaning of Nirvana, of which the first two may be neglected for our present purpose. The third is the meaning
given to it by those who seek in Nirvana eternal bliss for
themselves—i.e., those whom we are already familiar with as
the *pratyekabuddhas*. But, as Buddha is reported here to insist, this willingness to enjoy self-realization in solitude shows
that they are still clinging to a form of egoism. They have
not yet attained the state of true self-giving, and so the bliss
that they gain still reflects the qualities of the individual mind
seeking to preserve its independent separateness. The Nirvana
of the Tathagatas is something different; it is won by transcending all thoughts of personal gain and devoting themselves "to helping those who have not yet attained the truth
attain it."

But how can this be? As the inquirer with whom Buddha
is reported to be speaking here (Mahamati) says, such devo-

tion would rather mean that the Bodhisattva loses all assurance of Nirvana; by his voluntary choice he makes himself spiritually one with his fellow beings, in whom there remain unpurged evil and unmatured *karma*. They cannot while in this state realize Nirvana; neither then can he. The answer given is twofold. The first part of it is this: just as the enlightened mind perceives that the Buddha-nature is realized not in some separate metaphysical realm but in the unity of all particular forms of existence, so the insight of the heart tells the Bodhisattva that the egolessness arising from the destruction of *tanha* is not expressed in any isolated bliss but rather in the deeper compassion and more complete oneness with others which are revealed in his loving devotion; he is sure then that he makes no mistake in believing that true spiritual perfection lies in this direction.

The second part is that when one adopts this perspective he sees that Nirvana itself must be redefined in harmony with the insight it brings. If, having gained this "noble wisdom," we were still to think of Nirvana as a state which can be achieved by a pilgrim in solitude, for himself, there would indeed be no escape from the conclusion that "for Buddhas there is no Nirvana." But this conclusion is obviously unacceptable. Whatever else Nirvana means or does not mean, it must mean the state of perfect self-realization; it must denote the goal of true spiritual achievement. Rightly conceived, it must be, then, that stage in the maturing process in which, all taint of the ego being left behind, aspirants find themselves committed to the Bodhisattva ideal; "they are moved with the feeling of love and sympathy due to their original vows made for all beings, saying, 'As long as they do not attain Nirvana I will not attain it myself.'" And the essential reason is that such an active, sharing love for all suffering creatures, whatever their weaknesses and however serious their imperfections, is now recognized to be the supreme spiritual state, greater than any realization that could be achieved for oneself. As Buddha is described here to have stated this vital point: "The fact is that they are already in Nirvana . . . because of their attainment of the inner insight that belongs to the stage of Tathagatahood." In other words, to express the conclusion in the form of a clarifying para-dox, the renunciation of Nirvana for oneself, for the sake of realizing a devoted oneness with suffering men and women everywhere, *is* Nirvana in its true meaning. Nirvana is not separate from *samsara;* it is realized just through a loving identification with those who are struggling in the ocean of *samsara*—through sharing their woes and helping them find the saving way.

G. SUMMARIZING REFLECTIONS

Perhaps it would aid our understanding to construct a brief hypothetical debate between a Theravada and a Mahayana thinker on this issue.

"I am not denying what you emphasize," the Theravada champion might say, "since love for others surely is an essen-tial mark of genuine spiritual perfection; if it is lacking, we may be sure that the achievement is at least incomplete, some obstructing *tanha* is still present. But *how* the one who has realized perfection expresses his love is for him to decide. He has insight that the rest of us lack; we have no right to insist that his love must take any particular form. We can trust him to be compassionate in his own fashion. And in any case he would not want to express his love in such a way as to encourage others to be dependent on him and to find a comforting security in his love. That would not be a concern for their true well-being. They must be roused to take re-sponsibility for their own spiritual progress, and to find such support as they need in the process of their own active and disciplined self-conquest. No one can give salvation to an-other. The primary task of the religious pioneer is to provide others an inspiring example of one who boldly renounces the entanglements of the world for the sake of the true values that can only thus be achieved."

To which the Mahayana defender might reply: "I am not denying what you emphasize. But we can say something more about love than that it will express itself in its own way. If it is true love it will be revealed in an active self-giving to others, moved by a sense of unqualified oneness with them. It will prefer to share their life under all the conditions in which spiritual sharing can be realized, rather than to hold aloof from them in isolated self-sufficiency. They will be more likely to follow a saint's example if he be such a person as this. It therefore follows that the true saint will accept the Bodhisattva ideal of perfection, in contrast with any ideal that does not include this sense of loving oneness with his suffering fellows."

Which of these interpretations comes nearest to what Buddha himself intended to teach? The evidence is not clear or conclusive on this question. Both emphases seem to be traceable to him, and both found exemplification in his life. It may well be that his own position was modified in the course of the years with his expanding and deepening experience. In any event, the task that remains for us is to note certain further consequences of the Mahayana position which gradually became apparent in the course of its historical unfolding.

I shall limit our consideration to one very instructive consequence; it concerns the ascetic aspect of Buddhist self-discipline. All Buddhists recognize that one must renounce all indulgences which express the appeasing of unpurged *tanha*. Buddha himself was clear and consistent on this point, even though he rejected extreme mortification of the body because it brought spiritual torpor rather than spiritual strength. But is it possible for the saint to reach the point where renunciation of the satisfactions that other people childishly demand is no longer necessary? Is it possible to transform the pleasures of normal relationships between husband and wife, for example, so that instead of being an expression of passionate self-indulgence they become an expression of happy, mutual self-giving? Theravada Buddhism distrusts any such idea. One is likely to fool himself if he supposes that he has transcended so soon the need to curb his sexual lust. There is no hurry. He will have all the time he requires for his spiritual progress. The important thing, so far as one's present existence is concerned, is to make sure that rejection of the world and its enticements is as complete as one's settled determination permits. He will be assured then that his progress toward the goal is proceeding as rapidly as it can, and that he is setting the best possible example for others, who without such an example will find it hard to take even the initial steps on the path toward Nirvana. Hence in the Theravada countries the Buddhist monk is expected to be a consistent model of the way of renunciation, and there is a clear distinction between those who are ready to pursue this way and the laymen who are not yet able to leave the world but can only practice the vows which express their moral preparation for such a step.

Mahayana Buddhism accepts this principle too, so far as it indicates certain basic conditions and essential stages of spiritual growth. Indeed, the central note in the Bodhisattva ideal is that one who illustrates it is lovingly in the world but not of it—as Gautama was when he actively preached the saving way to others while avoiding any resumption of family life with his wife and son. But it is an implication of the ideal of devoted oneness and mutual sharing that the world and its pleasures, so far as they are not inconsistent with true love, can be spiritually transformed into harmony with it, and do not need to be renounced as hopelessly evil. Several Mahayana sects adopt this conclusion; in the Shin sect of Japanese Buddhism, for example, it is revealed in rather extreme form. The monk who abandons the world is judged lower in the scale of spiritual progress than the man who lives with his family and makes family relationships a means for the expression of a devoted love.*

* Zen Buddhism also finds a place for this idea, as do certain trends in Tibetan Buddhism. It takes some forms which are quite different from those of the Shin sect in Japan.

I shall leave it to my readers to express in their own way how Buddhism illustrates what I have described as the four essential characteristics by which the living civilized faiths are sharply distinguished from primitive religion. It is obvious that each of these four will need to be portrayed differently, according to whether we have in mind original Buddhism or the Mahayana religious philosophy.

X

Hinduism

A. HINDUISM AND BUDDHISM

We return now from this survey of the evolution of Buddhism to what happened in India, the land of its origin. In sketching the background of Buddhism we became acquainted with the basic ideas of early Indian philosophy as they were formulated in the Vedas and the Upanishads. We have seen how Buddha adopted certain of those ideas and revolted against others; we have followed his new religion as it gained influence and became the dominant faith of India for nearly a thousand years. But then it gradually lost its hold in the country of its birth, being saved in its position as a great religion by its successful missionary spread throughout eastern Asia. In India it was replaced by modern Hinduism, which was likewise a development from Vedic and Upanishadic thought but in a form which proved in the long run more congenial to Indian mentality and Indian culture.

How is this interesting historical phenomenon to be explained? This question was broached in Chapter VIII, and we may well begin our attempt to understand the distinctive genius of modern Hinduism with a fuller consideration of it.

The reader will appreciate, of course, that it is one of those puzzling questions which no one can adequately answer. But a partial answer can be ventured, and if it is on the right track it will throw much light on the nature of modern Hinduism and the forces revealed in its historical success. And the answer I shall give consists of two general considerations: on the one hand, Hinduism learned from Buddhism enough of the latter's basic insights so that it was able to meet in its own way the same spiritual needs that Buddhism had successfully met; on the other hand, it did this without departing as radically as Buddhism did from the treasured cultural heritage of India. It preserved the social setting that would appear to be necessary if a religion there is to enjoy a secure foundation and maintain the essential conditions of survival and growth. I shall briefly elaborate each part of this answer.

Because of the characteristic eagerness of the Indian mind to profit by whatever spiritual insight is anywhere gained, Hindu seers and thinkers learned a great deal from Buddhism. From early Buddhism they came to accept the basic doctrine that the essential key to *moksha* is destruction of the self-centered craving (*tanha*) which as long as it is present in any soul prevents it from realizing its oneness with Brahman and achieving unity of love with other living beings. Buddha's teaching was not the only source of this idea, but it was a powerful factor in its rise to the dominant position that it came to occupy. From Mahayana Buddhism many of them also gained the conviction that this sense of loving union with others is the supreme mark of spiritual perfection, and they came more and more to interpret the true meaning of love in the light of the Bodhisattva ideal. Again, Buddhism was not the only source of this conviction; nothing could express it more clearly than a verse from the *Bhagavata* (presumably antedating the Mahayana thinkers) which reads: "I desire not the supreme state with its eight perfections, nor the cessation of rebirth. May I take up the sorrow of all creatures who suffer and enter into them so that they may be made free from grief."[1] And the same spiritual forces leading in this direction also brought about a gradual change in the Indian conception of the saint, the truly "holy man." Prior to the growth of Buddhism, no one seems to have been recognized as exemplifying this concept unless he became a hermit sage— sharing, of course, his insight with any who might come to him, but not zealously seeking to save other individuals or to transform society, because his main concern was to prepare himself for a favorable rebirth in his next existence. After the rise of Buddhism, especially in its Mahayana form, this ideal had to compete with another which through the centuries has become increasingly strong in Hinduism. Many of the greatest leaders of Indian religion have imitated Buddha in actively preaching the saving way to others, and some have founded vast enterprises whose aim is to penetrate social life in all its phases with the spirit of true religion. Sankara in the eighth century and Gandhi in our own day are only two of the great figures who exemplify this transformed ideal.

So far as popular Hinduism is concerned, as contrasted with the religion of the philosophical thinkers, the influence of these forces in their specific relation to Buddhism appears in the fact that Buddha came to be accepted as the eighth incarnation of Vishnu—thus being given a respectable place in the pantheon of divine beings that the common man might worship and adore.

But Buddhism also, in many ways, called for too radical a departure from India's traditional cultural heritage, and in course of time lost the healthy contacts with society that were needed for its vigor and preservation. Perhaps this would have happened even if Hinduism had failed to absorb its main contributions to man's spiritual life; it is clear at any rate that Buddhism's continued vitality in India would have demanded a more drastic transformation of the Indian social structure than the subcontinent was ready to accept. Hinduism made the essential accommodations in this regard. They were of several sorts; only the most important of them can I mention.

Buddhism rejected the authority of the Vedas, boldly appealing to the common experience and reason of men for discovering what the deepest problems of life are and how they can be successfully solved. Now, since few Hindu schools conceive these ancient scriptures as an absolute authority comparable to the authority of the Bible for orthodox Christians or of the Koran for Moslems, this might seem unimportant. None the less, to turn away completely from the Vedas as a valid source of truth seemed to most Hindus unjustified as well as too drastic. Experience and reason are needed to apply their truths wisely to the living problems of each generation, but must never presume to take their place. Moreover, the conviction was strong that, so far as the majority of human beings are concerned, their own experience is too limited and superficial to constitute an adequate criterion, and their own reason too feeble and biased to serve as a dependable guide. Men need to understand what life brings home to them in the light of the deeper experience of the great seers of the past, and to assume that there is vital truth in the lessons they have handed down. Where an individual finds himself diverging from them he is more likely to be in error than they. As one would expect, different thinkers and schools of orthodox Hinduism interpret this attitude toward the Vedic scriptures variously, but all maintain the appropriateness of humble acceptance of them in some form, and all distrust the rebellious self-confidence (as it seems to them) that is expressed in the complete rejection of ancient authority.

Buddhism also assumed that it could decline to accept any responsibility for the structure of Indian social institutions and the way they work. It called individuals out from society as soon as they were emotionally ready for the renunciation required; thereafter, as monks, they were to devote themselves single-mindedly to the task of their own purification and self-realization. To be sure, in relation to Buddhist laymen they filled the important role of giving religious instruction and moral guidance, but social institutions were left as they were except so far as changes in them might follow as a consequence of these spiritual preoccupations. The danger of a widening cleft between the meditating seekers in the monasteries and the everyday life of the laymen was minimized during the early years of Buddhism by the dependence of the monks on the constant and generous support of others for their daily food. But in course of time many monasteries were freed from this dependence by the bountiful patronage of rulers and by gifts of substantial endowments from wealthy aristocrats. Then the danger became very real. The monastic seekers for Nirvana became isolated or even an appendage of the top political structure of society, involved in its vicissitudes and subject to whatever internal or external forces vitally affected its continued existence or its collapse. In this situation, laymen turned increasingly to the spiritual leadership of those who were more closely integrated with the whole pattern of social life in which their daily activities went on. And, generally speaking, these were the Hindu priests, in their important relation to the other functionaries of evolving Indian society.

For Hinduism avoided this mistake. Despite the important and revered role which it gave to the ascetic saint who retires to the forest, Hinduism developed its characteristic modern form in close and effective contact with the living social institutions—political, economic, educational, legal—through which the variegated culture of the Indian people found expression. Religion was thus integrated with the rest of life instead of being perilously detached from it. This integration is revealed in many ways; I shall mention two outstanding illustrations: the place of caste, and the concept of the four *ashramas*.

Instead of rejecting the caste stratification of society, Hinduism accepted it and endeavored to give it appropriate religious significance. The supremacy of religion in Indian culture is recognized in the fact that the spiritual leaders and teachers constitute the highest caste (that of the Brahmins). The actual operation of the caste system, in its tendency toward a rigid hierarchy in which the lower castes were sadly exploited, was periodically criticized in terms of the moral ideal that caste was supposed to realize—expressed in the Platonic concept that each major group in society is responsible to make the contribution toward the social good that in virtue of its talents and training it is best able to make. Caste was bound up with the concepts of transmigration and *karma* through the pervasive belief that one's present social status is determined by the accumulated *karma* of previous lives and by the further conviction that only through faithfully fulfilling the duties of one's caste can a higher vocation be won in the future. However, against the conservative effect of these beliefs must be set the trenchant criticism of the evils of caste made by the humane and prophetic spirits of Hinduism. This criticism more and more clearly expressed the ideal of an essential equality of individuals in their right to worldly as well as ultraworldly opportunity. Today, under the impact of the democratic West, such prophetic criticism has become bolder than ever and is leading to a wholesale weakening of the most serious inequalities of caste.

The concept of the four *ashramas*, in one of its main aspects, might be described as a way of reconciling the ultimate goal of *moksha* and the saintly ideal of spiritual perfection with the necessities of ordinary social life, without disrupting the accepted ways of satisfying the latter. A man should give himself whole-souledly to the task of spiritual self-realization, but he should take no premature steps, and the task should be so carried out as to build upon his fulfillment of social responsibilities rather than upon an evasion of them. The expectation then is that he will proceed through the successive stages indicated by the four *ashramas*. From the age of five (when he has outgrown the needs of a small child) to that of twenty-five he lives the life of a student, under the guidance of a teacher who is responsible for his moral as well as his intellectual growth. At twenty-five he will marry, and for another quarter-century or so will fulfill the duties of a householder—perpetuating his family name and heritage, and doing his share to meet the economic and professional obligations of social life. When his sons and daughters are married and his first grandchild is born, he is freed from these duties; he will retire to the forest (with his wife if she wishes to accompany him) and through meditation and reflection he will devote himself to the self-understanding and self-purification that could not quite have been his steady preoccupation earlier. When the requisite detachment has been gained he will enter upon the last stage, that of the *sannyasin*. This requires complete renunciation of all social ties; it will complete, so far as possible in the present life, his spiritual preparation for a desirable rebirth in the next one. Of course, this fourfold scheme is for the average person; in each generation there will be exceptional cases of those who can move toward the spiritual goal more rapidly than this schedule allows, and whose progress must not be hampered. They will feel the call of renunciation at an early age, perhaps while still in the career of a student, and if accepted by a *guru* (spiritual guide) they will skip the ordinary duties of life and become *sannyasins* after a brief period of training as novitiates.

In the light of these comparative considerations one can begin to understand the victory of Hinduism over Buddhism in India and can gain further insight into its distinctive characteristics as a living civilized religion. What are the outstanding ideas that express the genius of this triumphant Hinduism, as it develops from ancient times through the intervening centuries to the present day? What are the special emphases which are not so centrally present in other great religions?

B. THE GENIUS OF HINDUISM AS REVEALED IN ITS HISTORICAL DEVELOPMENT

The primary fact that can never be ignored in any answer to this question is that Hinduism is grounded in the mystical philosophy of the Upanishads and never abandons its basic presuppositions. Ultimate reality—the ground of all metaphysical explanation and the goal of the religious quest—is a unity transcending all differences and leaving behind all distinctions. The true self of each of us is identical with that reality; salvation consists in realizing this identity, with one's whole personality, and the practical task of religion is to teach the way to that liberating realization. Since, however, these convictions have been discussed in general in Chapter VIII and their historical evolution will be traced in the present chapter, they need no elaboration at the moment.

The second fact that stands out in the development of Hinduism is the hospitable tolerance and teachableness which its leading representatives have shown. In contrast with the claim to the exclusive possession of saving truth which has been characteristic of the Western religions, Hinduism has made open-minded responsiveness to truth, wherever it is found, a religious principle and a spiritual virtue. This is because its leading thinkers have been convinced that individuals vary in their spiritual needs and in the way in which such needs are effectively met. Many, too, have come to believe that much can be helpfully shared between individuals pursuing one way to salvation and individuals pursuing another. The religious attitude reflected in the first of these convictions is a deep respect for the right of each person to progress toward spiritual maturity in the way that meets his need, and a willingness to help him in such progress instead of attempting to convert him to one's own way. The attitude reflected in the second conviction is an eagerness not to miss any true insight derived from the experience of men anywhere, for there is always the possibility that such insight may contribute to one's own self-understanding and point the way to a more inclusive truth. The three main forms in which this genial tolerance has revealed itself historically are a zest to appreciate what other religions than Hinduism have to teach, an endeavor to clarify the different paths toward the achievement of *moksha* so that every person can find most readily and follow most successfully the path adapted to his need, and a generous acceptance of much in popular religion that theologians have usually condemned.

Outstanding examples of the zest for responsive appreciation are Ramakrishna in the nineteenth century and Gandhi in the twentieth. These two great Hindu saints endeavored consciously to enter into the living spirit of each of the major religions of the world so that they might know what it meant to its own devout adherents—what Christianity meant to the earnest Christian, Islam to the Moslem, Buddhism to the Buddhist. Only thus, it seemed to them, could their own spiritual pilgrimage move toward the true ideal of perfection. And the deep reverence toward every faith which this attitude involves is well expressed by Gandhi in an address given in January, 1928:

My veneration for other faiths is the same as for my own faith. Consequently the thought of conversion is impossible. . . . Our prayer for others ought never to be "God, give them the light Thou has given to me," but "give them all the light and truth they need for their highest development." My faith offers me all that I need for my inner development, for it teaches me to pray. But I also pray that everyone else may develop to the fullness of his being in his own religion—that the Christian may become a better Christian and the Mohammedan a better Mohammedan.[2]

The endeavor to clarify the different paths toward the successful achievement of *moksha* has led in Indian thought to the recognition of a number of *margas* or "ways," the four most important of which are *jnanamarga* (the way of knowledge), *bhaktimarga* (the way of devotion), *karmamarga* (the way of dutiful action), and *rajamarga* (the way of systematic mental discipline). The thought behind this recognition is that individuals differ sufficiently so that some can follow with profit one of these ways but not the others; that no individual, however, would fail to find among them a way suited to his needs. The way of knowledge is in general adapted to those whose capacity for intellectual insight is strong; their progressive acquisition of self-comprehension can guide them steadily toward the goal of full realization of their identity with the ultimate source of all being. That realization constitutes *moksha* for them. The way of devotion is adapted to those who need a personal embodiment of spiritual perfection, capable thus of being envisioned in concrete form. Through adoring love of this ideal personality they identify more and more with him and thus are progressively transformed in the direction of the spiritual ideal he exemplifies; *moksha* for them comes when the identification has reached the point where no desire inconsistent with such loving devotion remains. The way of dutiful action takes various forms in detail; in general it is adapted to those whose spiritual attention can be held neither by a guiding principle nor by an ideal image, but can be focused upon the faithful fulfillment of responsibilities and the performance of appropriate rites. Through giving themselves to these tasks under a sense of loyalty to their social obligations, they too are gradually released from the power of self-seeking demands; when that responsiveness to duty is complete and unqualified, their spiritual transformation has been accomplished. The responsible action to which they give themselves may be simply an expression of their traditional obligations to family, village, or vocation; it may involve the fulfillment of special religious vows or some particular social task. The way of systematic mental discipline—first taught by Patanjali and usually referred to as *rajayoga*—consists of a series of steps reminiscent of the Buddhist eightfold path. Beginning with certain positive and negative moral commitments, it guides the aspirant through various stages of bodily and mental control till he becomes capable of sustained and fully unified concentration; this achievement marks the attainment of *moksha*. The literal meaning of *rajayoga* is "the kingly way to union" (with the divine), and it has been regarded by many religious thinkers as including the essential virtues of the other ways.

The generous acceptance of popular religion is revealed in the fact that while India's religious leaders have felt a responsibility to guide the masses away from primitive superstitions and immoral practices, they have been strongly disposed to recognize that the average man cannot at present appreciate the insights of the intellectual and spiritual elite. They have been willing therefore to give their blessing to the forms, even though they be very crude, through which popular religion naturally finds expression. There will be plenty of time, in other existences if not in this, for the earnest man to outgrow these crude vagaries, and in the meantime he needs them as a medium in which to satisfy the insistent religious needs of which he is now conscious. So such crudities are to be tolerantly accepted and given a place. One finds little trace in Hinduism of the trait in Western religious pioneers which is expressed in an aggressive condemnation of idolatry as an insult to the transcendent nature of deity and a practice that must be renounced by the true believer. Hinduism hospitably embraces all sincere expressions of religion. We shall note in a later section the form which this hospitality takes in the theology of Sankara.

The third fact that stands out vividly in the growth of Hinduism, especially to Western students of religion, is the concept of *avatar,* meaning "divine incarnation in human form." Christianity is familiar with the idea that a historical person can be the unique incarnation of God, loyal faith in whom is necessary for salvation. The dynamic quality of Hinduism—its responsiveness at all times to new spiritual insight and new exemplifications of spiritual leadership—leads it to the conviction that God has been incarnated not once only but many times, and that the succession of *avatars* is presumably not ended. Not only are there saints and mahatmas in each generation—men who realize a far higher level of mature insight than their fellows—but occasionally, in the course of time, there are those rarer individuals who bring a revitalized vision of spiritual reality adapted to the needs of the age in which they appear. It is to be expected, in fact, that whenever the force of a previous revelation has been spent and men are sinking into the darkness of ignorance and the impotence of inertia, such an *avatar* will come to rouse the world from its lost condition, penetrating the gloom with the light of truth and instilling renewed hope in place of fear and despair. Krishna is believed to have filled such a role in his day; who knows but that, several centuries in the future, Gandhi will be viewed as filling it in our disturbed and anxious time, being thus promoted from the high status of mahatma to the even more exalted rank of *avatar?* Mahayana Buddhism adopted the same principle in its doctrine of the savior Buddhas—periodic incarnations of the eternal Buddha-nature in the universe. Gautama was the divine savior in his day, but he is not unique; in due time Maitreya will appear as a savior Buddha filling a comparable role in some future era.

C. THE ESSENCE OF UPANISHADIC TEACHING

In view of these characteristics of Hinduism, and especially of the manifold ways to salvation which it recognizes, it is important to avoid centering attention upon one single scripture or significant individual. This would easily convey the false impression that the genius of Hinduism can be adequately disclosed in such a fashion. Instead, keeping in mind the dynamic nature and absorptive power of this religion, let us concentrate on three selections from the varied material that it offers us—one of which will clarify its basic ideas and the aspirations they express, one the way of loving devotion, and one the way of knowledge. Each of these will also help us understand a typical Hindu orientation on certain crucial problems of moral perplexity and theological interpretation. For the first, I shall turn to the central theme of one of the most important Upanishads, the *Brihadaranyaka;* for the second, to the beloved *Bhagavad-Gita;* and for the third, to the philosophy of Sankara, universally respected teacher of the system of Advaita Vedanta.

The hero of the *Brihadaranyaka Upanishad* is the sage Yajnavalkya, presumably a historical individual, about whom nothing is now known except what this Upanishad reveals. But before we trace the outline of his philosophy, it is well to sense the spiritual passion which underlies it and which animates what is distinctively new in the writers of the Upanishads in general. For there is such a spiritual passion, quite as clearly present as in their Western contemporaries, the great prophets of Judaea; and there is a significant common element in the two cases. The Vedas, as handed down in the ritualistic elaborations and commentaries of their accepted interpreters, had already congealed into a formal tradition, whose main note seemed to be insistence on the meticulous correctness of sacrifice and ceremony. The Upanishadic sages revolted against this corruption of religion, as the Hebrew prophets revolted against the mistaken magnification of ritual in Palestine.

But their revolt was guided by a different basic principle and infused with a different religious insight. Instead of asking, What constitutes true obedience to the will of God? they asked, in effect, What constitutes true sacrifice? And their answer was: it is sacrifice of one's separative, self-centered soul on the altar of the ultimate oneness of things—a oneness which they now for the first time dimly or more clearly glimpsed. And their method of clarifying this insight and revealing its power—in contrast to the aggressive preaching of men's social responsibilities by their Hebrew counterparts— was the method of contemplative retirement to the forests, where, freed from the distractions of ordinary social life, they might deepen their realization of ultimate truth and their capacity to express the spiritual energy which its apprehension releases. Only through growth in power to exemplify the peace and joy and love that union with the divine brings to those who have attained it, they were sure, will one be able effectively to mediate it to others and to become a constructive force in their lives as well as in one's own.

From the standpoint of most Westerners this conviction seems very strange. They persistently ask: Is not one who follows this route simply withdrawing from all the conditions of human well-being? What reason is there to expect that as a result of his retirement he can communicate anything significant to others? But Indian thinkers are confident that this procedure is necessary and that experience confirms its wisdom. K. T. Behanan, a Western psychologist who studied life in an Indian hermitage, came to share this confidence. He writes, "I have had the privilege of watching at close range the daily lives of more than a half-dozen yogins for over a period of one year. I can testify without any reservation that they were the happiest personalities I have known. Their serenity was contagious and in their presence I felt always that I was dealing with people who held great 'power' in reserve. If the saying 'radiant personality' means anything, it should be applied to them."[3]

I shall concentrate simply upon the central religious theme of the *Brihadaranyaka*, leaving aside its framework of mythological cosmology and many even of the philosophically significant details. The setting of the theme is as follows. Yajnavalkya has fulfilled his duties as a householder, and is ready to retire to the forest to enter upon the next *ashrama* of his career. He wishes before doing so to divide his wealth between his two wives Maitreyi and Katyayani. But Maitreyi is a seeker for spiritual truth too; she wants to know: "Even if I were to possess the wealth of the whole earth, would that make me immortal?" "No," replies her husband. "Then tell me what would bring immortality. What value would anything have to me if I do not become immortal by achieving it?"[4] So Yajnavalkya proceeds to answer her question. And his first lesson builds upon the state of mind that she has already disclosed. Yes, the things we now care for and value are not really valuable for their own sakes, but only for the sake of the eternal object of love to which they can lead us. And what is that object? Not immortality, as it is ignorantly craved, but something else.

"Verily, wealth is not dear, that you may love wealth; but that you may love the Self, therefore wealth is dear. . . .

"Verily, everything is not dear, that you may love it; but that you may love the Self, therefore everything is dear."[5]

What, now, does this mean? In the first place, it is important not to misconstrue such a statement as expressing an unfortunate self-centeredness. A misinterpretation of this sort is easy to fall into, and is encouraged even more strongly by the following comment on this passage: "The love of the Self is the basis of all other loves. One loves another because one loves the Self the most. The ultimate purpose of all loves is to rest in the satisfaction of one's own Self."[6] But if we became the prey of such a misunderstanding we should have forgotten that for Hinduism the true self of each person is the universal Self, and that in loving it we are realizing a loving oneness with all other persons. "Thy neighbor is in truth thy very Self, and what separates thee from him is mere illusion."[7]

In the second place, if this error is avoided we are prepared to discover what is basically distinctive about the Self as the object of love. It is, as Yajnavalkya proceeds to explain, that every other object besides the Self is external to the one who perceives and knows it; there is in such cases an unresolved duality between subject and object.

"When there is as it were duality, then one sees the other, one smells the other, one hears the other . . . one perceives the other, one knows the other; but when the Self only is all this, how should he smell another, how should he hear another . . . how should he perceive another, how should he know another? How should he know him by whom he knows all this? How, O beloved, should he know the Knower?"[8]

The problem for us then, as Yajnavalkya develops it on the

basis of this lesson, is to gain a vision of the ultimate, undivided reality which is in all things and from which each derives its being—the reality that is eternal because it is uncaused and has nothing outside it—and to realize that this reality is identical with the Self. "This is the Brahman, without cause and without effect, without anything inside or outside; this Self is Brahman, omnipresent and omniscient." "He who dwells in all beings, whom all beings do not know, whose body all beings compose, and who rules all beings from within, he is thy Self, the ruler within, the immortal one." "(He is) unseen, but seeing; unheard, but hearing; unperceived, but perceiving; unknown, but knowing. There is no other seer but he, no other hearer but he, no other perceiver but he, no other knower but he. This is the Self, the ruler within, the immortal. Everything else is of evil."[9] Immortality, then, is not to be sought directly; but it can be achieved by realizing the Self, for the Self is intrinsically eternal.

So much for the basic principles. Now how about the crucial practical problem? How is this realization to be gained? One who honestly probes his nature discovers that it harbors many selves, and none of them seems to be the self which Yajnavalkya is describing. "Which self, O Yajnavalkya, is within all things?" Which is the Self with the capital S?

Yajnavalkya's reply teaches the next essential lesson; it is one with which we are familiar from our study of Buddhism. This Self is "He who overcomes hunger and thirst, sorrow, passion, old age, and death. When Brahmins know that Self, and have risen above the desire for sons, wealth, and (new) worlds, they wander about as mendicants." To be sure, there is a difficult problem as to what more can be helpfully said about this Self. The meanings of the words by which we describe the objects of our acquaintance are determined by their use in the immature experience of finite individuals, confronting external things that arouse hunger and passion, grief and aversion. Naturally, the Self that permeates, transcends, and unifies such experience cannot be described in these terms. Their positive meanings are inadequate; they cannot properly be applied here. "That Self is to be described by No, no! He is incomprehensible, for he cannot be comprehended; he is imperishable, for he cannot perish; he is unattached, for he does not attach himself; he is unfettered, he does not suffer, he does not fail."[10] None the less, he is the true self of each of us, and when we comprehend this, in the joy of realized union, we have become one with the essence of reality, and every wish that is itself in accord with reality is fulfilled.

"This is indeed his (true) form, free from desires, free from evil, free from fear. Just as a man, when embraced by a beloved wife, knows nothing that is without, and nothing that is within, so this person, when embraced by the intelligent self, knows nothing that is without and nothing that is within. This indeed is his (true) form, in which his wishes are fulfilled, in which the Self (only) is his wish, in which no wish is left—(he is) free from all sorrow."[11]

But one more major lesson Yajnavalkya must teach. As long as this liberating realization has not yet come, and a person is still caught in the web of passion, of desire for this or that object, the leaving of one body at death necessarily means transmigration into another, in which the striving for liberation is continued. And the kind of body he enters will be determined by the law of *karma*. Such "a person consists of desires. And as his desire, so is his will; and as his will, so is his deed, and whatever deed he does, that will he reap. . . . A man of good acts will become good, a man of bad acts, bad. . . . According as he acts, and according as he behaves, so will he be."

"So much for the man who desires." However, his ultimate destiny of freedom from bondage is assured, no matter how long the spiritually maturing process may take. When the realization of one's true selfhood is achieved, liberating him from all these desires for finite things, transmigration into other forms of cramping and painful existence is no longer

needed. Nor will it be caused, for it is just the ignorant desire for finite existence that is responsible for its continuance.
"As for the man who does not desire, who, not desiring, freed
from desires, is satisfied in his desires or desires the Self only
—his vital spirit does not depart elsewhere; being Brahman,
he goes to Brahman. When all desires which once entered his
heart are undone, then does the mortal become immortal—
then he obtains Brahman!"[12]

The *Brihadaranyaka* is not, of course, an essay in systematic theology. Its attempt to achieve a clarification of the way
to blessedness, through the process of self-understanding and
emotional purging, does not quite forsake the realm of poetry
and of persuasive intuition for that of logical reason. The
more systematic and precise philosophies come later. But to
the Western reader this formulation has the great virtue of
disclosing the search of the Indian mind for religious truth at
the early stage where its insights are expressed in quite simple and unsophisticated form. The general framework of
thought here assumed—about the universe, about the individual seeker for saving truth, and about his way to spiritual
realization—is handed down through subsequent Indian history and is taken for granted in almost all of the serious philosophy which appears later. That there is a transcendent
source of all reality or apparent reality, incapable of comprehension by man in terms of his finite experience; that man's
destiny is union with this reality; that until such union is
achieved he passes from one form of separate existence to another, the forms adopted being determined by the law of
karma; and that this achievement is attained by a process of
spiritual growth, involving renunciation of the desires that
tend to perpetuate his separate existence and block such union
—these ideas become the common property of Indian reflection on the basic problems of life.

But, as has been noted above, within this broad framework
there are very significant differences. The most outstanding
difference that has affected religious thinking through the

ages is the difference between a nonpersonal and a personal interpretation of this transcendent reality. The religious yearning of the common man, guided more by emotional needs than by the lessons learned through abstract thought, strongly demands a personal divinity as the object of adoring devotion. He treasures the supporting and inspiring image of such a divinity, giving concreteness to the spiritual ideal which he seeks to realize, and he is not troubled by the logical or metaphysical problems which arise in the attempt to conceive the ultimate through such an image. In every generation, indeed, there have been theistic philosophers who have struggled so to interpret the personality of God that it may plausibly be identified with transcendent reality. To many thinkers, however, this struggle seems bound to be futile. Personality, they are sure, is irrevocably a limiting concept; it cannot be properly applied to the source of all being. If an entity is to be conceived as personal, attributes must be assigned him—will, or purpose, or reason, or even desire— which are inevitably haunted by these limitations and therefore cannot be rendered metaphysically ultimate or spiritually perfect.

D. THE MESSAGE OF THE BHAGAVAD-GITA

As our exposition of the *Brihadaranyaka* suggests, it is the latter of these two conceptions that has been most widely accepted among the philosophical thinkers of India, and in the subsequent course of history it has been expressed in influential form in the Advaita Vedanta to which we shall soon turn. But the former has never been without its champions, and in Indian devotional literature, as contrasted with theological systems, it has more than held its own. We shall not be surprised, then, to find that this view is the one presented, with persuasiveness and beauty, in the devotional classic that has become the favorite at all levels of Indian piety—the *Bhagavad-Gita*, or the "Lord's Song." Of course there is much else in this profound poem besides the defense of a theistic metaphysic and a clarification of the way of loving devotion. Although it too is not an essay in systematic theology, it weaves together in suggestive interrelationships all the major themes of Indian reflection on the issues of life, and thus provides the basis for an appealing religious philosophy. Widely diverse have been the interpretations given it by subsequent thinkers. In its bearing, for example, on the question whether war is ever morally justified, there is the radically pacifist interpretation of Gandhi, contrasted with the quite nonpacifist view of Tilak; and in its reference to other matters there are equally provocative differences. Where acknowledged experts disagree it is hazardous to offer one's own interpretation, but one who seeks to grasp the distinctive genius of Hinduism cannot avoid the responsibility; he must make the most earnest attempt to penetrate its message that he can, in the light of everything else that he knows about the Indian mind.

Before we follow the main sequence of thought in this poem, however, it is well to pause briefly over a few details of one of the six orthodox systems of Indian philosophy, the Sankhya. For the basic concepts of this philosophy are presupposed in the *Bhagavad-Gita*, and the reader who is unfamiliar with them finds his quest for appreciative understanding seriously blocked.

The Sankhya conceives the knowable universe as a process of interaction between *purusha* and *prakrti*, the former of these terms being translatable roughly (for there are no precise equivalents in English) by "conscious soul" or "spirit," the latter by "nature." In this interaction *purusha* is believed to be entirely passive—a registering awareness, so to speak, and nothing more—which means that *prakrti* is the active source of all the changes that take place.* Its function in this dynamic role is performed through its three "gunas"—here again is a term incapable of exact rendering in English: "con-

---

* This is a more plausible position than it sounds. Indian thought has drawn the line between soul (or mind) and body quite differently from Western thought; what we call volition and emotion are for it, in general, not essential to soul and therefore belong to *prakrti* rather than to *purusha*.

stituent property" will perhaps do, if we think of a property as not merely a kind of quality but also something that exercises force. The highest (most creative) of these gunas is *sattva*. In the physical world *sattva* reveals itself as light, spreading through and penetrating the surrounding darkness; in the world of spiritual relationships it is impartial acceptance and self-giving love, reaching into the darkness of the souls around it and creatively igniting whatever spark of responding love it can. The intermediate guna is *rajas*. This guna appears in the material realm as the active energy which brings about the varied changes that transpire; in human action and emotion it is self-seeking desire—that potent urge in all life to exploit the things in its environment, living and nonliving, so as to make them serve its needs. The lowest guna is *tamas*. In the physical world this guna is revealed as obstruction to the activity of the other two gunas—in the darkness that resists the power of light and dulls its brightness as it spreads far from the illuminating source, and the inertia which every force in nature must overcome in producing any change. In the realm of spiritual striving it shows itself in the torpor and lethargy which make us wish to stay where we are instead of steadily seeking the ideal—the laziness that constantly clogs our progress toward the ultimate goal. In the *Bhagavad-Gita* these ideas are used without explanation. The major difference of interpretation there, as compared with the Sankhya philosophy, is that the cosmic *purusha* is identified with Brahman, while Brahman in turn is transcended by the personal divinity Krishna, who becomes the ultimate source of creative power in the universe. *Prakrti* is here conceived as the instrument through which the energy of creation is exerted, and the three gunas are its agents which are responsible for the detailed nature of the effects produced.

The universal message of the *Bhagavad-Gita*, as a religious classic belonging to all civilized epochs and cultures, has been unfortunately obscured, especially to the Western mind, by the familiar translations. These tend to adhere so closely to the Indian framework of ideas that the wider bearing of the problems discussed and solutions proposed fails to emerge clearly. Also, until one catches something of that wider bearing he is likely to be overperplexed by the specific form of the question with which the discussion opens, and by the frequent challenge of Krishna to Arjuna throughout the early chapters: "So stand up and fight!" I shall attempt the difficult task of expounding the main sequence of thought in terms that will place it properly in its Hindu setting while at the same time distilling its universal and profoundly human meaning. And some glimpse of that meaning must be caught at the very beginning, in order that we may have a guiding thread to follow in the varied detail which will have to be explored.

Stated in terms of the Indian background of thought and experience, the basic theme is the spiritual meaning of *karma* (action). This is clarified by an analysis of the way of dutiful action in relation to other recognized ways to *moksha*, especially those which call for renunciation of action, and by an examination of the practical and theoretical problems that are vitally involved. Stated in terms of its universal significance, the theme is concerned with the guidance that religion can give in dealing with the fundamental moral problems of life. According to the *Bhagavad-Gita*, ethics is not an autonomous field; it can reach a solution to its own deepest questions only through the light that comes from religious insight. Just as in the field of knowledge such insight provides our ultimate grasp of reality, in relation to which the quest of science and philosophy can alone find its fulfillment, so spiritual realization provides the answer to questions concerning our moral perplexities, which without it would remain insoluble dilemmas.

The ostensible setting of this poem is the battlefield of Kurukshetra, where the armies of the Kurus and the Pandavas are lined up on opposite sides, each set for victory or death. The leaders of the two armies—Arjuna of the Pandavas and Duryodhana of the Kurus—are cousins. Each is a member of the Kshatriya or warrior caste. The substance of the poem is presented in the form of a conversation between Arjuna and the god Krishna, who appears in the role of his charioteer. And the event that precipitates the discussion is Arjuna's paralysis, involving complete inability to act, as he surveys the field of battle and suddenly realizes that what he is about to do is to engage in mutual slaughter with his own kinsmen. He slumps on the seat of his war chariot and flings aside his bow and arrows, saying, "O Krishna, now as I look on these my kinsmen arrayed for battle, my limbs are weakened. . . . What can we hope from this killing of kinsmen? What do I want with victory, empire, or their enjoyment? . . . What is this crime I am planning, O Krishna? Murder most hateful, murder of brothers! . . . Rather than this, let the evil sons of Dhritarashtra come with their weapons against me in battle. I shall not struggle, I shall not strike them."[13] In short, Arjuna is caught in a numbing moral conflict; his *dharma* (duty) as a Kshatriya requires him to fight for victory against his enemies, but his *dharma* as a man of family loyalty, with all the sentiments gathered round it, tells him to refuse to fight, risking death himself rather than the possibility of killing his kinsmen.

But, as the sequence of thought through the rest of the poem makes clear, this is merely a peculiarly vivid illustration of a more general, nay universal, moral problem, to which spiritual insight is here called upon to provide the solution. Any man may at any time confront such a conflict of apparent duties—a conflict between what is expected of him (and what he expects of himself) in one of the social roles which he obviously fills and what is expected in another. In fact, it is just this dilemma that provokes serious moral reflection in a sensitive man who is capable of it, since it reveals the inadequacy of the traditional rules of conscience by which he has been guided before. Any earnest person will be forced to confront the question, "When, as in this situation, I cannot fulfill all my duties, what is the right thing to do?" And those who are responsive to the broader perplexity involved will also face the more general problem, "How can one put himself in a position to act aright, with confidence that it is right, in any such situation that he might be called upon to meet? Can spiritual understanding help him here, and if so in what way?" It is this question that provides the unifying theme throughout the *Bhagavad-Gita;* Krishna's task is to guide Arjuna to an answer, not merely in the sense of one which he can intellectually accept but as one which he has come emotionally to realize, so that he can put the lesson into practice with the unified insight and vigor of his whole personality.

The answer is developed in eighteen chapters, and although there is no sharp break anywhere in the thought, they may be conveniently divided into three groups of six chapters each. It is wise to sketch the argument as a whole before plunging into the major details.

The first six chapters clarify in introductory fashion the perplexity posed by a conflict of moral duties, pointing out the subsidiary problems involved, explaining the part that must be played by the way of knowledge, and introducing the way of worshipful devotion to Krishna as filling a major role in the needed solution. Chapters seven to twelve develop this ideal of ardent self-surrender to Krishna, and explain who this divinity, as the proper object of such adoring commitment, really is—the embodiment of supreme perfection and the transcendent source of all reality. The last six chapters expound the conception of the universe that is assumed in this explanation, elaborating its bearing on essential cosmological, psychological, and religious questions; they conclude by reaching a final answer to the opening problem. Throughout the discussion, but especially in the first third, Krishna's technique is to force Arjuna not to forget the claims of each of the conflicting duties that he confronts, until a foundation has been established, in his understanding and motivation, that provides a real solution of any such moral perplexity. Especially is this needed in the case of his duty as a Kshatriya leader, since it is the contrary scruple that paralyzes him and renders him impotent to act. Here lies the reason for the repeated challenge "So fight!" which appears at the end of several of the early chapters; Krishna sees that Arjuna's shrinking from the action expected of a Kshatriya rests on ignorance, family sympathy, and feelings of guilt, not on true understanding, and that to refrain from his military duty because of these motives would express no growth toward spiritual maturity at all. In fact, scruples based on such motives would be quite undependable. These confused emotions vacillate; as soon as Arjuna's mind turns again to the challenge of his duty as a warrior he would very likely be swept into action as easily as he is now blocked from it by his instinctive shrinking. "If in your vanity you say 'I will not fight', your resolve is vain. Your own nature will drive you to the act. . . . You will do the very thing which your ignorance seeks to avoid."[14]

Now let us bring out the main sequence of thought more fully, doing so in the form adopted by the poem itself, i.e., a conversation between Arjuna and Krishna.

ARJUNA: "Is this real compassion that I feel, or only a delusion? My mind gropes in darkness. I cannot see where my duty lies. Krishna, I beg you, tell me frankly and clearly what I ought to do. I am your disciple. . . . Show me the way."

KRISHNA: "Your impotence to act rests on ignorance, not on understanding. Just consider: Every soul is eternal; the souls of those whom you might kill in battle cannot be slain; the time at which a soul is released from its present body and passes into a new existence is unimportant. Can you, a Kshatriya, bear the shame that will be heaped on you if you refuse to perform your duty as a man of valor? Men will call you a coward.

"So act. But realize that you cannot act aright as you now are. You need a deeper understanding and a clearer perspective in which to act. Only one who has become purged of his blind cravings—of attachment to selfish ends, and the confused emotions that it generates—can act in freedom, inward peace, and wisdom."

ARJUNA: "But if attainment of understanding is more important than rushing ahead into action, how is it that you want me to engage in such a vile act as fighting? I can't do it. But I don't see what else to do. What can save me from this unbearable conflict?"

KRISHNA: "You can't really escape action. Those who think they do, retiring from society and meditating with bodies stilled, merely control the external organs of action; that does not prove that they have mastered the inner acts of heart and mind which may still express a selfish craving. You are in such a state right now. Renounce that craving, so that you will no longer be captive either to the urge to act or to the need to refrain from acting. Then you can achieve wisdom; you will act; but the motive expressed in your action will be no self-seeking end but the loving unity of all living beings.

"So (seeing that Arjuna is still in the grip of his despairing paralysis) give up this self-centeredness, and fight!

"Don't think that what I now teach you is something new. I revealed it to the world at the very beginning of time, and I bring it again whenever saving truth is on the verge of being lost. When you understand the truth about action with the understanding that purges from all selfishness, then you can act freely and with no paralyzing sense of guilt. Some people offer to the divine the customary sacrifices, some practise various forms of strict self-discipline; but the greatest sacrifice is sacrifice of one's blind ignorance for the sake of true knowledge, the knowledge without which no self-discipline can achieve its end.

"Letting now that knowledge resolve your doubts, stand up and fight!"

ARJUNA (beginning to sense the crucial point but still confused):   "You seem to recommend both renunciation of action (in favor of gaining knowledge) and action in accordance with my duty as a warrior. How can I do both? Which is better?"

KRISHNA: "Either way can lead to salvation, but the way of engaging in action is superior. However, it must be action freed from bondage to the fruits of action—freed, that is, from domination by the longing for pleasure and aversion from pain, by the demand that this or that alluring outcome must be achieved. This freedom can be gained by the way of knowledge; it can also be gained by detaching action from any special goal. However achieved, it brings a sense of union with ultimate reality (Brahman) and it means union also with one's own supreme Self (*atman*), assuring undisturbed serenity and joy. He who realizes this state never loses it. And with it comes power to act without being tainted by action.

"The crucial lesson to master, at the present stage of your progress, is this. Since no one can escape action, some kind of action being unavoidable, and since, as long as blind craving remains, no assurance that one is performing the right action is possible, the wise course is to engage in the kind of action that will lead toward self-understanding and therefore toward freedom from such paralyzing conflicts as you are now in. Then, even though you make mistakes before you achieve full liberation, you need not be anxious. You will know that at any given moment you are acting in the best way you can; your action is expressing whatever stage of self-discipline and detachment from ignorant desire you have achieved."

ARJUNA (rising now above his paralysis and wishing to follow Krishna's counsel): "But my mind is too restless for this self-discipline. And what if I should try to master it in the way you recommend, and fail? Then I would lose both the fruits of action and the virtues of renouncing action."

KRISHNA: "Self-discipline is indeed hard, but the goal is attainable. And don't forget that if anyone fails, his earnest effort will cause rebirth in a form which will make success easier. In the end, no sincere seeking fails. The best way to progress in this quest is through loving identification with me, being absorbed in thoughts of me, seeing all things in me and me in all things, giving yourself in worshipful devotion to me.

"And as you come to know me more fully and become more deeply united with me you will not be anxious about failure. In whatever form any earnest soul worships me, I accept his devotion, make his faith secure, and guide him on his spiritual quest. To be sure, his achievement will be partial and temporary till he attains a clear vision of me, as the changeless and perfect being revealed in all finite forms but not limited by any. He who thus knows me in my true transcendent nature and adores me with complete devotion will attain freedom and eternal peace, and I will meet all his needs. Dwelling in his heart, I will destroy the darkness born of ignorance, and replace it by the light of wisdom and by power for unattached action. The way of devotion to me can thus include and perfect all other ways to salvation.

"Remember that I am present in all forms of existence, and especially in the distinctive powers and ideal qualities that each form reveals. Yet remember also that the entire universe is but the expression of a portion of myself; I am in all, and I infinitely transcend all."

ARJUNA: "Your words have removed my delusions. Now I long for the clear vision of which you just spoke—the vision of you in your infinite divine essence."

KRISHNA: "Your human eye is incapable of this. But I will endow you with supernatural sight. Behold me in my supreme glory!"

[He then gives Arjuna a vision of himself in the blazing splendor and supernal energy of his divine majesty. Arjuna is awed and terrified; and in response to his frightened plea Krishna reassumes his human form of gentleness and compassion and consolation.]

"Only your single-hearted devotion made this vision possible. Work now for me; accept union with me as your supreme goal; become my devoted follower. Then you will be free from attachment, free from hatred toward any creature; and you will become one with me."

ARJUNA (puzzled now by the major theological issue of Hindu thought): "As between those who seek devoted absorption in thee and those who seek union with the nonpersonal ultimate, which has greater knowledge of the way of blessedness?"

KRISHNA: "Those who sincerely seek the nonpersonal ultimate will come to me in their own way, but that way is arduous and painful. Those who in perfect faith and devotion seek oneness with me do best. They will soon win salvation from the sea of births and deaths. Even if they cannot attain steady absorption in me, or wholesouled commitment to me, still, if they will work for my sake and surrender all attachment to the fruits of action, they will gain peace and be loved by me."

ARJUNA: "I would now learn how to understand the world,

as it is experienced and understood by one who knows it truly."

KRISHNA: "That which is to be known is the supreme, transcendent ultimate and the various states of matter and mind through which it is revealed. One knows it at first through the three gunas of *prakrti*. His knowledge will vary in its degree of clarity or confusion according to which of these gunas dominates his mind. If *sattva* is in the ascendant it is relatively clear; if *rajas* or *tamas* is in control, much confusion is inevitably present. The quest for true knowledge must therefore be pursued by turning in any situation to the sattvic mode of understanding instead of a mode which expresses *rajas* or *tamas*. The final stage is reached when, under the guidance of *sattva*, one rises to the point where he achieves intuitive union with that which transcends all the gunas and is not conditioned by them—i.e. becomes absorbed in loving devotion to me who am the source of the three gunas.

"Do not be afraid of action, at any stage of this process. What is important is not the act itself but which guna is revealed in it. The same act may be good or bad—good if it expresses a sattvic state of mind, bad if it is the expression of *rajas* or *tamas*. This is true even of religious acts of austerity, charity, and sacrifice. So, renounce what you now see to be the root of all evil, and do your work in the world—fearless, self-controlled, calm, and full of compassion to all living creatures."

ARJUNA (at last ready for the lesson which the entire poem has been teaching): "Please explain to me then, in the light of all you have said, the difference between renouncing action and becoming detached from the fruits of action."

KRISHNA: "Becoming detached from the fruits of action is alone of true spiritual value. Nothing else brings to an end the series of rebirths. Renunciation of action, as you now realize, may express *rajas* or *tamas* rather than *sattva*. Strictly, indeed, it is impossible for one still living in the body. Moreover, you can see that it is undesirable in the case of certain acts, such as those of true sacrifice, earnest self-discipline, and compassionate self-giving. So, acting under the guidance of *sattva*, gaining knowledge and power of self-control, put away all egoism with its torpor and craving, and become one with me in adoring devotion. Thus you will rise above all obstacles, achieve inward peace, and fulfill your duty in love and joy.

"Now I have taught you the wisdom that is the secret of secrets. Ponder it carefully. Then act as you think best."[15]

The central lesson of the *Bhagavad-Gita* then is: whatever one does when he is in darkness, captive to the power of self-seeking desire, is likely to be wrong. But whatever he does when he has gained freedom from these blind forces and has realized union with God will be right and good. So far as the soul has become illumined, purged, and wholly devoted to God, it will act aright. The freedom that it seeks is not freedom from the urge to action, but freedom from bondage to selfish craving and its stormy emotions. The ideal is not avoidance of action, but selfless action in oneness with true reality.

One aspect of this lesson will become still clearer if we consider again the poem's setting. At its conclusion Arjuna picks up his arms and proceeds into battle, giving his forces inspired leadership and piloting them to victory. How is this consistent—many Western readers, and Indian readers too, have asked—with the spiritual ideal which the poem clearly teaches? One who has realized that ideal "knows that his Atman is the Atman in all creatures"; he shares "the bliss and suffers the sorrow of every creature within his own heart, making his own each bliss and each sorrow"; "When men go to war he does not regard either side as his enemies or his partisans."[16] How can Arjuna, having accepted and understood this ideal, engage in the slaughter of his kinsmen? How can the *Gita* also say: "He whose mind dwells beyond attachment, untainted by ego, no act shall bind him with any bond. Though he slay these thousands, he is no slayer."[17] There are doubtless serious problems here, and one cannot be sure of any detailed interpretation. But the basic answer to this question is clear; it is one that pacifists in East or West do well to ponder.

What is spiritually important, to the author of the *Gita*, is not an act as such but the state of mind and soul of which it is the expression. In the case of one not yet liberated, to refrain from fighting may express unacceptable motives—cow-

ardice, revulsion from blood, blind loyalty to family interests
—quite as much as to engage in fighting. These motives are
unstable, and they do not promote growth toward the
strength and assurance of true spiritual perfection—they
rather obstruct it, just as untamed martial passion would obstruct it. What is vitally important in his case is unreserved
commitment to whatever action is needed to purge his soul
of craving and the unhappy emotions of which it is the root.
Such action is always good. And while he is earnestly fulfilling this task, any other action is right if it is a genuine expression of the stage of self-discipline that he has then reached
—whether it be a deed of kindly compassion or the valorous
act of a Kshatriya warrior. When the dialogue with Krishna
ends, Arjuna has not yet become a liberated soul; he has but
gained the initial enlightenment and clarified zeal that free him
from his paralyzing confusion and start him on the path toward the goal. To attain it will require a lengthy process. As
to how he will act when that process is complete, we can only
say that whatever he does will express the perfect freedom
and love that he has then realized.*

It is worth observing that the personal theism defended in
this poem seems to imply that the liberated and devoted self
does not lose its individuality but only its self-centered separateness from others and from God. Each person is, to be
sure, a microcosm; his body and mind are a part of nature
and his self a spark of the divine. But when he has realized
devoted oneness with God, his action is still his own, expressing the unique individuality that makes him the person he is.
The *Gita* does not teach the mystic merging in the divine
through which all individuality is destroyed.

E. THE THEOLOGY OF SANKARA

In its subsequent development Hinduism has continued to
illustrate all the basic emphases and convictions above de-

* It should be noted that the author of the *Mahabharata*, of which the
Bhagavad-Gita is a part, believes that Arjuna's side was fighting a righteous
war, which because of the intransigence of the other side could not be
avoided.

scribed, while being continuously responsive to the novel forces entering India from without. The dominant belief with respect to the nature of the divine—as the nonpersonal or superpersonal Brahman—was given its most systematic theological interpretation by Sankara in the early ninth century A.D., and its capacity to arouse intense religious feeling is also shown in his thought and life.

As is the case with most ancient sages, the exact period when Sankara lived and taught is uncertain. According to the prevailing opinion of historical scholars, he was born in south India about A.D. 788, and died at the early age of thirty-two in A.D. 820. He precociously studied the Vedas and the other traditional scriptures; when he was still in his teens religious enthusiasm inspired him to renounce the world and become a *sannyasin*. He gathered a group of devoted disciples and expounded the principles of his teaching far and wide, largely in the form of debates with champions of other theological doctrines. Far from fitting into the picture of the saintly recluse, he traveled through the length and breadth of the land, establishing monastic centers for the training and inspiration of spiritual leaders. His aim was to make these centers an enduring force for the renewal and nourishment of religious life throughout the entire subcontinent; the most famous are the four widely separated monasteries at Sringeri in south India, Joshimath in the Himalayas, Puri on the Bay of Bengal, the Dvaraka in the far west. Along with these strenuous practical activities he was the author of twenty-four or more important writings, some consisting of independent expositions of his teaching, some of devotional hymns and poems, some of commentaries on the Upanishads, the *Bhagavad-Gita*, and the *Vedanta Sutra*. The document last named was a pithy summary of Upanishadic doctrine which appeared some time between 300 B.C. and A.D. 200; almost all subsequent thinkers of note found it needful to offer their interpretation of it and to square their teaching with its basic ideas. It is also called the *Brahma Sutra*.

The Western reader is reminded by the name of this document that he must become familiar with the complex meaning of the term "Vedanta," and the significance that it gradually came to have in modern Indian philosophy. Literally, it means "the end of the Veda."* As a particular term, "Vedanta" refers to a certain group of scriptures, namely, the three documents mentioned in the preceding paragraph. As a general concept, it may be interpreted in three ways. First, it means simply the portions of the Veda that were latest to be written. Second, it embodies the idea that these portions validly clarify the goal of all Vedic searching and thinking; they give its final interpretation. Third, it expresses the conviction that such an interpretation, to be adequate, will harmoniously synthesize all the varied strands of religious experience and theological insight. In Sankara's case the emphasis is on the last of these three meanings, and his historical influence is largely due to the fact that to the minds of many later thinkers his attempt to achieve this ideal seemed to be uniquely successful.

The period in which he lived was peculiarly in need of such an achievement and especially ripe for it. The upsetting waves of migration in earlier centuries had come to a temporary end; the subcontinent was settling into a stabler political, economic, and cultural pattern. Buddhism, after its vigorous challenge to religious thought in India, had entered upon its decline. Each of the orthodox systems of philosophy had had its chance to show the significance of its contribution to the deeper understanding of man's experience, and at what points it must be surpassed or reinterpreted. The perennially renewed vitality of popular religion had revealed in what ways it could be molded by philosophic insight, and in what ways it would continue to insist on its own rights—though needing, even in that respect, sympathetic theological acceptance and justification.

* The term "Veda" itself means "knowledge," especially "sacred knowledge."

Sankara's genius responded to the opportunity provided by this historical situation. His appreciative mastery of Buddhism, especially in its Mahayana forms, was so thorough that in following his thought one often feels in the presence, with little more than verbal change, of the basic position of the Buddhist nihilists or the Buddhist idealists. His attitude toward the Vedas combined deep respect for the insights of tradition with full recognition of the primary authority of living experience. The Vedas, he held, are a genuine divine revelation, supplementing other sources of truth; one who diverges from them does so at great risk. At the same time they cannot supersede the vital experience of those who, under their guidance, have climbed the path to liberation and have realized union with the divine. His attitude toward the role of reason likewise combined appreciation of its unique importance, in freeing the mind from obstructive errors and irrational superstitions, with unqualified insistence on its limitations in relation to intuitive insight into ultimate truth; such insight transcends the distinctions with which in the nature of the case reason must do its work. Perhaps the clearest indication of his comprehensive sympathy, which is shown in his hymns as well as in his systematic philosophy, appears in his attitude toward popular religion. He was sure that it must be purged of all groveling barbarisms and immoral practices; at the same time, its need for an anthropomorphic picture of the divine should, he believed, be accepted, and this idea should be harmonized theologically with that of the nonpersonal ultimate instead of being rejected as a religious error. In all these and many less crucial ways Sankara's philosophy reflects the tolerant and open responsiveness of Hinduism to all insights into spiritual truth. He made central the teachings that thinkers were more and more convinced deserved such emphasis, and he gave appropriate place for other strands whose continued appeal showed that they could not be neglected in a just and adequate interpretation of man's living experience.

The following outline of his major ideas endeavors to be faithful to the essential course of his thinking, and to expound it in the way best calculated to clarify to Western minds his solution of fundamental religious problems.[18] Parts of the exposition will be unavoidably difficult, especially for those who have taken for granted Occidental philosophical assumptions; I hope that my readers are ready for a brief intellectual tussle.

A basic difference from Buddhism in Sankara's thinking appears in the fact that he began not merely with the problem posed by human suffering but also with its positive counterpart, man's search for happiness. The concern of his whole philosophy is with "the utter cessation of suffering and the attainment of supreme bliss." And he is sure that this concern, in both its parts, is ineradicably grounded in human nature. Now the concept of "supreme bliss" reveals Sankara's conviction that man is not satisfied with happiness anyhow conceived or in whatever form it might seem to be attained. He seeks happiness that is stable and lasting. The happiness that we find ourselves from time to time enjoying is imperfect, limited, uncertain as to its continuance; the happiness that we seek is free from these defects. Now happiness as thus described is a great deal to hope for. Are we perhaps mistaken in such a quest; are we seeking more than the nature of things in this universe makes possible for man? This question can only be answered by earnest and careful examination. But in the meantime we may keep firmly in view one encouraging consideration. If human beings were not capable of perfect bliss, how can the fact be explained that we are all moved to seek it and are dissatisfied with anything less? It is not that we may safely assume that whatever we long for must somehow be attainable; it is rather that our consciousness of the limitations of the happiest experience we have already achieved implies that that consciousness itself somehow stands beyond those limitations, and is therefore capable of a happiness in which they have been left behind.

This consideration provides the key to the solution of the problem of life, as we pursue the examination in all its essential details. It enables us, for example, to state in promising form the appropriate initial question in such an inquiry: What is it that inevitably makes the best happiness with which we are already acquainted so limited, and where might the conditions be found which bring freedom from those limitations? And the answer to this question seems clear. We have been conceiving happiness as the satisfaction of desires for this or that object or goal in the external world. Now the satisfaction of such desires depends on the vicissitudes of what happens in that world; they are beyond our control, so far as concerns the certainty of their occurrence and the length of time that any desired enjoyment will last. We must submit to the causal laws that operate throughout nature, and the happiness derived from any cause lasts no longer than the time during which that cause is effectively present. As long as we identify our happiness with this kind of satisfaction it will unavoidably remain imperfect and disappointing. Is there something in the nature of our internal self, which is aware of these facts, that gives the clue to a happiness free from limitations? Is that conscious self in some sense superior to the vicissitudes of the surrounding world, and can the realization of its superiority put us in a position where we can experience the perfect bliss we seek? Let us see.

First, it is clear that the reality and essential nature of the inner self cannot be doubted, whereas with everything in the changing world outside us this is not the case. Sankara anticipates here, in the setting of his own thought, the basic steps in Descartes' analysis eight hundred years later in the West. Our perceptual illusions and hallucinations show that, so far as concerns the external objects of which the self is aware, we can never be sure that they have the characteristics they seem to have, nor even that they really exist. A shell may appear yellow because it is seen through a glass that distorts its color, and what is perceived as a fearsome snake may be really an innocent piece of rope.* We can correct these mistakes, of course, but there is no assurance that the correction is final and that by its means we have discovered an object that is absolutely real. In the case of the self, however, no doubt is possible. The very experience of doubting proves its reality; it is just the self of the doubter. Nor can we be uncertain about its essential nature. That is simply consciousness—the common, universal, ever-continuing character that is present in every cognitive experience. It is present in every awareness of the self; it is present in every awareness of objects. In and through every doubt that we may entertain about external objects, this consciousness can be discovered that is itself beyond doubt.

Second, this consciousness in its pure, essential nature is nontemporal and changeless. Our experience of change reveals that which is identical and permanent throughout the experience. The objects and events come and go; the content and quality of each arise and disappear before the mind; what was pleasant a moment ago becomes painful or indifferent now—but all through this experience there is something in us that remains constant, something that is the steady and continuing witness of these variations and transformations. The sights differ but the seeing is the same; the experiences vary but something in the experiencing is immutable.

The fact, then, that our happiness as thus far achieved is trivial, perishable, and therefore imperfect is due to our seeking it in the manifold, fluctuating, transitory objects of consciousness rather than in consciousness itself. But we are not those objects; we are the enduring, undivided, and unvarying awareness that apprehends them. It, not they, constitutes the essence of our selfhood. Our basic mistake has been in identifying ourselves with those shifting, delusive objects, and with the desires that focus upon them. To correct this mistake, we must turn away from these things and identify ourselves with the pure consciousness that we truly are, realizing to the

* These are stock illustrations in Indian philosophy.

full its essential nature. Then we shall find the lasting and perfect bliss that we have missed. Our happiness will be absolute instead of sadly limited by the transitory character of the unstable entities in which we have tried to find it.

With a third consideration the initial clarification of Sankara's viewpoint is complete. Ordinarily, when we think of consciousness, we think of a subject which is aware of this or that object as distinguished from and related to other objects. But on consideration it is clear that this is the empirical self that reflects our finite limitations; it is not the consciousness of which we have just been speaking. The mere perception of this or that changing object partakes of the distinctions and vicissitudes of the temporal realm; it is not the pure indivisible consciousness implied by the continuity of our experience as a whole, and attested by the saints of all ages who have achieved the insight and joy that the rest of us seek but have thus far missed. We have been thinking of consciousness in this its ultimate nature.

Now, as we turn to a constructive probing of the questions that can be answered in the light of these considerations, the point of primary importance concerns the concept of Brahman. This concept has not yet explicitly entered the account, but we have been implicitly concerned with it and have already solved some major problems about it. For, whatever else is meant by Brahman, the term by general consent refers to Absolute Reality. Well, we have been dealing with absolute reality, although indirectly. Our attention has been focused upon questions concerning happiness, concerning the realm of phenomenal objects, and concerning the inner self. But what we have been trying to find out is whether and how "real" happiness is possible; what is the "reality" underlying the world of unstable objects; how we should conceive the essential "reality" of that inner self. And throughout this examination a definite criterion of reality has been employed. It has been assumed that that is real which is enduring rather than transitory, changeless rather than changing, independent and self-sufficient rather than dependent on other things, and (because of these three attributes) perfect rather than imperfect.

Whatever lacks these features is only relatively real; the kind of being it possesses is intrinsically defective and incomplete. But whatever does not lack them in any respect or degree is real without qualification. So all that is necessary to clarify the nature of Brahman, as the absolutely real being in the universe, is to recognize these implications and to follow them out to the further consequences that are involved. Let us summarize what has been already found. We are assured thus far that Brahman is, that He is of the nature of pure consciousness, and that His essence is perfect bliss. But there is also a vital negative implication in what we have learned. His mode of existence, of consciousness, and of bliss, being absolute and changeless, transcends the mode in which our finite experience exemplifies the meaning of such words. Hence, while our experience in these respects points toward the ultimate reality, as it is clarified by careful scrutiny, it also falls short of it; the terms we use, gaining their meaning in our finite experience as they inevitably must, do not strictly apply to the absolutely real. What we can properly mean by ascribing these attributes to Brahman might be better indicated negatively. We can say unhesitatingly that He is not the opposite of existence, not the opposite of consciousness, not the opposite of bliss. Similarly with His unity. What we mean here is not the unity familiar in ordinary experience, contrasted with diversity or duality, but a unity transcending the distinction of unity and duality—hence a concept that is best expressed by affirming nonduality (*advaita*)* instead of unity. A helpful analogy to this situation is found in our experience of day and of night in their relation to the sun. Each of these experiences acquires meaning in its contrast with the other, and it is the light of day rather than the darkness of night that

* Hence Advaita Vedanta, as describing the form of Vedanta philosophy championed by Sankara.

provides our clue to the nature of the sun; yet, since the sun knows nothing of this contrast, for it there is neither day nor night in our sense of the terms.

Thus Sankara explained the Brahman-Atman* in its fundamental significance for religious philosophy. And the two areas that need detailed elaboration on this foundation are those of the theoretical and the practical questions that an adequate theology must answer. On the one hand, it needs to help us understand Brahman-Atman in relation to all else in our experience; on the other, it needs to give us practical guidance in the task of realizing our identity with Brahman-Atman—the realization that brings freedom and true happiness. The second of these areas is vital to any responsible theology, while the first is of deep interest to philosophy, especially in its concern for a sound metaphysic. I shall summarize briefly Sankara's answer to the questions belonging in the first area that are of crucial importance, especially to a Western reader, and then deal more fully with his solution of the practical problem.

What is quite essential to a grasp of Sankara's philosophy on its theoretical side is the recognition that one must maintain two different standpoints, and that strictly there is no logical continuity between them; the difficulty posed by this circumstance, and Sankara's way of dealing with it, must be mastered if one is to comprehend any of the major details in his system. On the one side there is the standpoint of the Absolute and of those who have realized their identity with the Absolute; this standpoint is that of ultimate truth and reality. On the other side there is the standpoint of finite experience and of man's logical reason—the indispensable tool for understanding its distinctions and relations. This standpoint is relative rather than absolute, but it is the standpoint with which we all must begin our quest for truth and happiness. Realization of the spiritual goal is thus in its intellectual

---

* The reader will recall what was said above about the ultimate identity of Brahman and *atman*, pp. 209, 238 ff.

aspect a passage from the relative and therefore false standpoint to the absolute one. Now all metaphysical explanations are made for the sake of those who are only able as yet
to view things from a relative perspective (since the liberated
ones, seeing all things in the unity of the Absolute, need no
explanation). However, if they are to be true explanations
they must be given from the absolute perspective. At least,
they must be couched in such terms as fully harmonize with
the insight that will be realized when the relative perspective
is transcended.

What this means, more concretely, is that everything must
be explained as grounded in Brahman-Atman which is the sole
and eternal reality, for this is the ultimate truth; but in order
to be intelligible to those who have not yet realized their
identity with Brahman-Atman, any explanation must be
couched in terms derived from the relative world of finitude
and change. These terms however, expressing causal, spatial,
temporal, or other relations, only have meaning *within* the
phenomenal realm—they are false when applied to the relation between that realm and the changeless Absolute.* In
short, one must maintain that the world of finite objects and
the human soul depends on Brahman, but no true and intelligible way of expressing that dependence to those who seek
to understand it is available. Strictly speaking, the task is logically impossible, and certain concepts in Sankara's philosophy derive their very significance from his attempt to deal as
best he can with this impossibility. The outstanding example
among these is *maya*. This concept expresses the fact that,
viewed from the absolute standpoint, the phenomenal world
does not exist, and is recognized as unreal when *moksha* with
its insight into ultimate truth is achieved. It also expresses the
fact that, viewed from the relative standpoint, a creative energy must be at work through which the phenomenal world
arises from Brahman. For it can arise in no other way. The

---

* The Western philosopher will at once think of a corresponding feature
in Kant's doctrine of the categories.

ultimate reason for its appearance is a mystery; we cannot explain why the changeless Infinite takes on the garb of change and finitude. There is no act of Brahman by which this occurs. That it appears in such a garb, however, is, from the relative standpoint, clear. And we must explain this fact in terms which will be harmonious with the insight that is gained when the relative standpoint is left behind. The basic term that fills this role is *avidya* ("ignorance," or "nescience"). Since it is through true knowledge that one transcends the relative standpoint, with all the ways of thinking that characterize it, the reason for the appearance of such a standpoint must lie in an inscrutable cosmic *avidya* which is reflected in the particular state of ignorance present in each person. In virtue of this *avidya*, Brahman appears to each individual under the guise of certain limiting "adjuncts" (*upadhi*). Thus the appearance of the phenomenal realm and the relative standpoint in which it appears can be understood.

At times Sankara seems fully to recognize the limitations that a philosophy dealing thus with the Absolute and the relative is under. In such passages he offers this metaphysical picture as providing merely a set of helpful analogies through which the inexplicable can be somehow clarified to a sincere seeker pending his achievement of ultimate insight. It can also, he is confident, expose the unjustified claims of other cosmologies by revealing, for example, contradictions in the concept of causality by which events in the phenomenal world are explained.

The two general problems that are probed with special care in this setting concern our understanding of the world of physical objects and the individual soul. Both arise through *avidya* and the creative energy of *maya;* however, there is a difference in the two cases because in *moksha* the phenomenal world disappears, while the individual soul does not disappear but realizes its identity with Brahman. This difference can be understood by the analogy of two familiar sorts of illusion which have been mentioned above. In the case of the rope that is mistakenly perceived as a snake, when the illusion is corrected the snake completely disappears; only the rope is left. In the case of the white shell perceived as yellow because it is seen through a tinted glass, the correction of the illusion leaves the shell; only the yellow color disappears and is replaced by the true color white. The former of these illusions is like the situation with the phenomenal world. On the achievement of true knowledge the entire realm of objects, in its spatio-temporal divisions and its structure of causal relations, disappears, and only the unity which transcends the phenomenal remains. The latter is like the situation with the individual soul. When it attains liberation, all that disappears is the set of limitations under which it has lain by its mistaken identification with the finite objects in which it has sought happiness; its true self, as one with Brahman, remains, and freedom from those limitations is realized.

It is important fully to appreciate that this does not mean that the empirical world may without qualification be pronounced illusory. It has no existence whatever from the absolute standpoint; but from the relative standpoint, which is taken for granted in the daily activities of life and in our inquiry about these matters, it is assured a high degree of reality. The objects in that world reveal an empirical substantiality and are publicly observable; neither of these statements holds of the snake that is perceived by an individual in a moment of fright, instead of the rope. Thus, if we try to include in a single picture all the distinctions that philosophy needs to recognize, we find that there are three levels of reality, not two. Brahman alone is real without qualification. Objects of illusory perception, like the snake, are completely unreal; even from the empirical point of view no reality in them remains when the illusion is removed. The empirical world itself lies in between; logically it must be pronounced neither real nor unreal. Were it real it would remain, as it stands, in Brahman, while were it a sheer unreality it could not exhibit even the relative constancy of the rope. But it must always be remembered that these levels only present themselves in this way from the relative standpoint, which is itself ultimately unreal. From the absolute standpoint only Brahman exists.

The details of Sankara's analysis of the empirical world are of great interest to a comparative study of philosophy, but we must pass them by and turn to his solution of the practical problem of life—his conception of the way through which we can realize our identity with Brahman and the incomparable bliss that it brings.

Finite objects, in their inconstant vicissitudes, are so radically different from the infinite and changeless Brahman that it might well seem incredible that a being who is really one with the latter should fall into the error of identifying himself with the former. But this mistaken identification is a fact, and any solution of the practical problem must begin with full acceptance of the painful entanglement it involves. Next, we must clearly recognize that the way to truth and blessedness does not lie in creating anything that does not now exist, nor in acquiring anything that is not now at hand. It is thus entirely different from any process taking place in the phenomenal realm. It is just the realization by the individual soul of the Self that it eternally is. We need only remove ignorance; insight into the truth then dawns. What are the steps by which this realization can most readily be achieved?

Sankara's answer to this question constitutes a form of the "way of knowledge" (*jnana yoga*), but he recognizes the preparatory need for certain disciplines such as have been emphasized in *karma yoga*, *raja yoga*, and the Buddhist eightfold path. These preliminary disciplines might be summarily described as aiming at such measure of detachment from bondage to the phenomenal realm as is necessary if the aspirant is to be able systematically to pursue the goal of liberation. While he trains himself in these disciplines, he will continue to engage in conscientious performance of the various duties of life, guided by the ideal taught in the *Bhagavad-Gita* of acting without attachment to the fruits of action.

Long and continued fulfillment of duty in steadfast adherence
to this ideal will gradually remove the deep-rooted errors in
his habitual beliefs about life and his egoistic proclivities. As
his convictions and impulses are thus purified, he becomes
more fit to pursue seriously and steadily the ultimate truth.
During this period he will presumably worship the divine in
some personal form, though realizing that it is but a symbol
of the absolutely real.

The specific prerequisites that must be established at this
stage of the spiritual quest are listed under four heads. First,
power to discriminate clearly between the real and the unreal,
the eternal and the transient. Second, freedom from control
by the longing for pleasure and shrinking from pain, so that
one becomes indifferent to both worldly and heavenly delights. Third, realization of the "six treasures." These are the
basic ethical virtues that constitute the foundation for cultivating spiritual insight. They are serenity, temperance, stability, forbearance, power of concentration, and unqualified
commitment to the spiritual goal. Fourth, an intense and
consuming eagerness for liberation. The aspirant will know
that he is advancing in the right direction as he finds himself
making progress in each of these respects.

When this preparatory stage is passed, one is ready systematically to pursue the knowledge that brings liberation. Certain steps in this process can be specified that must ordinarily
be traversed, in appropriate order, before the final insight
can dawn. The three vital steps are formal study (*sravana*), reflection (*manana*), the meditation (*nididhyasana*). By formal study is meant learning the basic teachings of Advaita
Vedanta, as contained in the ancient scriptures, under the
guidance of a *guru*. By reflection is meant the passage from a
state in which one knows the ultimate truth as a persuasive
lesson taught by his teacher to a state in which he has become
convinced of its validity for himself. The reflection consists
in drawing upon examples from ordinary life showing that
and how the unity of all things in Brahman must be the truth.

Since common experience often seems to teach the contrary, and to emphasize the dividedness of things, it helps one's conviction to see that daily life also reveals instructive analogies to the truth. By meditation is meant the crucial process whose aim is to transform into direct experience the theoretical grasp acquired through the preceding stages. A merely intellectual conviction is not enough. Erroneous habits of thought, grounded in experiences and feelings that are inconsistent with it, will not have been completely excluded from the mind. "The present step is intended to overcome them. It consists in meditating upon the central point of advaitic teaching; and when that process is crowned with success, there dawns of itself upon the mind of the contemplative the truth of the statement 'That thou art.'* The intrinsic bliss of the self, is as it were, released in its wholeness at the same time."[19] What had become an assured intellectual persuasion has through this final stage been transformed into a realization of truth by the entire personality. The culmination of the process is *samadhi,* or concentrated absorption in Brahman.

The point of chief interest in Sankara's position regarding the state of the liberated soul is whether, before the death of the body, it may engage in "action." Its immortality in the sense of deathlessness is assured through its union with the eternal Brahman. But while it is still in the body, what is its proper role so far as concerns activity in the world? Is the *jivanmukti*† superior to such action in virtue of his achieved spiritual freedom, or is he still in any sense responsible or able to accept active tasks? There are passages in which Sankara appears to answer this question by saying that the free soul cannot engage in action. But careful consideration of other passages shows that this interpretation would be a mistake. Action as such is not inconsistent with spiritual freedom; only it must be the kind of action that expresses spontaneity of love and is the natural overflow, in the form of service to

---

* I.e., "Thy real self is Brahman."
† One who has gained liberation in his present life.

the world, of the sense of oneness with Brahman and therefore of oneness with all life. It is free from any taint of ignorance, and any kind of empirical motivation. Sankara's theology, as well as his energetic practical activity, show that
among the fundamental features of Buddhism that he has
made his own is the Bodhisattva ideal of Mahayana Buddhism;
when the saint has realized with his full selfhood the ultimate
unity of truth, he returns to the realm of social action and
serves his fellows in a spirit of dedicated and universal love.

Radhakrishnan summarizes the significance of Sankara in
the history of Indian thought in these words:

> After the tumult and storm of the polemical period came the
> Advaita of Sankara, with its elemental calm and persuasiveness of
> rational conviction. . . . It grounds religious reality in the center
> of man's consciousness, from which it cannot be dislodged. The
> sole spiritual vocation of man consists in the discovery of reality,
> and not what serves our temporal ends. This discovery demands
> a complete abandonment of the egocentric and the anthropo-
> centric points of view, in an absolute surrender of man's vain and
> inordinate pride in his own importance. We must relinquish all
> attempts to envisage God in terms of our limited knowledge and
> experience. . . . Sankara has combined a penetrating intellectual
> vision into things divine with a spirit of mystic contemplation.
> With Sankara for our witness, it is impossible to say that a vigor-
> ous play of the intellect is an impediment to mystical contempla-
> tion. He also shows that freedom from external occupations is not
> a necessary characteristic of contemplative lives. He reconciles the
> personal or mystical, the institutional or authoritarian, and the
> intellectual or philosophical elements of religion with one an-
> other. . . . Supreme as a philosopher and a dialectician, great as a
> man of calm judgment and wide toleration, Sankara taught us to
> love truth, respect reason, and to realize the purpose of life.[20]

F. HINDUISM SINCE SANKARA

For two hundred years or more after Sankara the main
processes which had been going on for some time earlier
continued to characterize the course of Indian thought, and

to them was now added the expansion of his influence and the gradual absorption of his ideas. Beginning with Ramanuja in the late eleventh century, there was a period marked by efforts to harmonize the principles of Vedanta philosophy with a theistic position. In some of these cases the theism originated in the cult of Vishnu, in some cases in that of Siva, and in some cases its source lay in other forms of devotional religion. Ramanuja himself was a Vaishnavite, and so the personal God who is ultimate reality for him is often referred to as Vishnu; but in many passages He is also identified with Brahman or with Isvara. Ramanuja's philosophic position is known as "qualified nondualism" (*visistadvaita*); God is the sole reality, but the physical world and human souls are real as parts of Him. They constitute His body. When *moksha* is attained the soul does not lose its individuality; it retains its distinctive selfhood in devoted fellowship with God, and the world of physical objects does not disappear as a sheer illusion.

With the formation of the Brahmo Samaj* in 1827, a period opens in which Hinduism attempts to come to terms with the religious as well as the scientific and political ideas of the modern West. And, growing in part out of the influence of such attempts, there dawns in the late nineteenth and the twentieth centuries a sense that Hinduism has a world mission to fulfill. This mission is not to convert the world to specifically Indian beliefs, but to aid individuals throughout the world in realizing the best that their own religion offers, and in coming to appreciate the spiritual contribution that has been made by the insights of other faiths. Ramakrishna, a nineteenth-century saint, is an important figure in this development, largely through his influence on Vivekananda, who actively carried this conception to the West, and on the formation of the Ramakrishna-Vedanta Society, which maintains missionary centers in several large cities in Europe and

---

* A religious organization founded by Ram Mohan Roy, a Brahmin who also championed many social reforms.

America. The work of the Theosophical Society and the writings of the poet Rabindranath Tagore are among other forces that have furthered the same development.

It is too early as yet to predict what will happen, of significance to religion, as a result of Indian independence. But the career and teachings of Mahatma Gandhi, who was the great leader of the independence movement, are important, not only as constituting a new phase of Hinduism in which the Indian ideal of the saint is combined with the Western ideal of the reforming prophet, but also as marking a novel development in the history of civilized religion in general. As such, we shall devote a section to him in the final part of the book.

We may conclude this survey of Hinduism with a few summarizing remarks. That which is most basic in it is its mystical conception of ultimate reality and of the nature of salvation. But what is most noticeable in relation to the other great religions is its teachable receptivity. Hindu thinkers are sure that the best form of religion will be open-minded, inclusive, and constantly growing. It is not surprising, then, that Hinduism has shown the dynamic and absorptive power that it has throughout history. It is not surprising, either, that it looks back to no founder, no single outstanding individual in whom its character is uniquely embodied. It has in all ages its seers, its saints, its mahatmas, its *avatars;* and more are to be expected in the future. Each reinterprets the ancient sacred writings in his own way, and each adds his new insight to what he finds there. All these contributions are absorbed; the spiritual process which constitutes Hinduism goes on, guided by the faith that sincere searching always leads, however slowly and deviously, to truth, to God, to salvation.

PART THREE

The Religions of the West

Religion in the
Old Testament

We now come closer home. Having surveyed the provocative phenomena of primitive religions, with their radical
differences from religion as we have known it, and having
explored the distinctive ideas of the religions of the East,
we are ready to study the background of our own religious
heritage. There lie before us the great civilized religions of
the West—Judaism, Christianity, and Islam. But, already, it is
well to note that the descriptive phrase I have just used—
"religions of the West"—is not wholly satisfactory. These
faiths have spread far to the East as well as to the West—
especially Islam, which (to take an extreme example) is the
dominant religion of northwest China and of the southern
Philippine Islands. And these religions had their source, not
in what we now think of as the West, but in the Middle
East. They originated among peoples who belong racially
to the Semitic group, and in exploring their major ideas we
shall therefore in a sense be studying the Semitic religious
genius, in comparison and contrast with the distinctive genius
of Chinese or Indian religion. But Christianity and Islam have
been fully accepted by the non-Semitic peoples among whom

they have spread, and in terms of their general geographical contrast with the civilized faiths thus far examined, the religions we are now to study constitute the religions of the West. When referring to them as a group I shall therefore call them by this term.

Let us consider these religions in exactly the same spirit as the religions that have hitherto been our theme, namely, with sympathetic impartiality. We shall want to catch, first, the distinctive setting that is characteristic of these religions as a group and, second, the central ideas of each of them considered by itself. And in the case of each faith we shall want to understand and appreciate it at its best. Especially when we come to Christianity and Islam, it will be our hope to grasp what it was about them that explains their persistent and widespread appeal, in virtue of which they have satisfied the spiritual hunger of hundreds of millions of people all over the world.

The outstanding thing that at once strikes a student of the Eastern faiths when he turns to an examination of Western religion is the prominent place of personal theism. In the East, this type of religious belief has played an influential role, but on the whole it has been a subordinate role as compared with that exerted by a nonpersonal or superpersonal conception of the divine. In this statement I am thinking, of course, not of popular religion, which is highly anthropomorphic everywhere, but of the theologies through which reflective minds have related the objects of their religious devotion to everything else in their experience. In China Mo Tse, who lived about 400 B.C., founded a religion which centers around a personal divinity conceived as animated by love toward all creatures. But the sect he established exerted only a limited appeal and after a few generations passed away. The Chinese mind in its search for the divine seems to be satisfied better by the Taoist concept of *tao*—a metaphysical ultimate, but not personal—or by the Confucian concept of Heaven as a cosmic extension of the moral order realized when men respect *li* and exemplify *jen*. In India we have observed the powerful influence of personal theism as taught in the *Bhagavad-Gita* and as formulated theologically in the Vedanta philosophy of Ramanuja. It has taken many other forms too, some of which are historically significant. But, again, it must be said that among India's intellectual leaders this note has not been as prominent as that of the superpersonal concept of Brahman, which satisfies the deep mystic urge of Indian religion as no personal image of the divine quite can.

In the Western religions this situation is reversed. A definitely personal conception of God fills here the dominant role and expresses the pervading conviction. To be sure, a vigorous strain of mysticism appeared in Judaism, Christianity, and also Islam, which at times and among certain sects has been a very potent force. But the idea that God is a personal being, possessing will and intelligence and capable of love toward his creatures, uniformly provides the norm for religious thought about the divine—so much so that even the mystic theologians have usually assumed that they could identify without contradiction the transcendent One, in which the mystic seeks to lose himself, with the personal Father of the more influential theologies. This fact doubtless reveals a powerful trait of the Semitic religious mentality, and of the religious need of the peoples among whom these religions spread.

A. BASIC CHARACTERISTICS OF THE WESTERN RELIGIONS

The Ninety-sixth Psalm in our Bible beautifully expresses the basic characteristics of the Western religions—the characteristics common to dominant strains in all three of them.[1]

> Sing to the LORD a new song;
> Sing to the LORD, all the earth;
> Sing to the LORD, bless his name;
> Publish his deliverance abroad from day to day.

Tell among the nations his glory,
Among all the peoples, his wonders.

For great is the LORD and greatly to be praised;
Fearful is he above all gods.
For all the gods of the peoples are nonentities,
While the LORD made the heavens.
Honor and majesty are before him;
Strength and beauty are in his sanctuary.

Ascribe to the LORD, O families of peoples,
Ascribe to the LORD glory and strength.
Ascribe to the LORD the glory of his name;
Bring an offering and come into his courts.
Worship the LORD in holy array;
Tremble before him, all the earth.

Tell among the nations that the LORD is king;
The world also is established that it cannot be moved.
He judges the peoples in equity.

Let the heavens rejoice and the earth exult,
The sea roar, and its fulness.
Let the field exult and all that is therein;
Then let all the trees of the wood shout for joy
Before the LORD, for he comes,
For he comes to judge the earth.
He will judge the world with righteousness,
And peoples with his faithfulness.

If the picture given in this song is carefully analyzed, in the attempt to bring out features that on the one hand are common to the three great Western religions and on the other more or less sharply diverge from what we have found in the Eastern faiths, one's attention will naturally center on several points. I shall list the features that are suggested to my mind by this Psalm, realizing that statements elsewhere in the Old Testament are being drawn upon to help in their exposition.

First and foremost, the thought and feeling here expressed

are permeated by a sense of the reality of a Divine Being who is not only personal in the full meaning of the word but is also clothed in cosmic grandeur, majesty, and power—a God before whom a reverent, humble, and obedient awe is alone appropriate. The entire realm of nature He holds in the hollow of His hand; it discloses to discerning mortals something of His greatness, goodness, and wisdom, for He is immanent in it, but He also transcends it in the unapproachable mystery of His ultimate being. In the language of later theology, He is omnipresent, omnipotent, omniscient. He created everything in the universe outside of Himself. Nothing in that universe has any independent power by which it might resist or frustrate His will, and He guides it toward the destiny that His beneficent purpose has chosen.

Second, the particular aspect of God's nature which is basic to a true understanding of Him is precisely this Will by which He brings things into existence, determines their mode of action, and, when He pleases, destroys them. His Will is all-powerful; it governs all things and holds them together in the unity of the divine plan. Strictly speaking, there is no such thing as natural law, in the sense of a predictable order arising from the intrinsic properties of objects and events. So far as there is regularity in the world, it is because He has chosen to impose such measure of orderliness upon it and thus make its behavior intelligible to man. But God Himself is always superior to the law He has imposed. He can change it any time He so wills, and He can bring about exceptions to it whenever His kindly purposes so require. Hence the world in which these religions live is a world in which miracles are to be expected and sometimes happen.

Third, He is not only endowed with the metaphysical attributes just described but also embodies moral perfection. He is a God of justice, mercy, and love. Because He possesses these attributes the appropriate course for imperfect mortals is to imitate Him; we should therefore exemplify such virtues ourselves as fully as we may—but, even more basically, our place is that of trustful, submissive obedience. Since we are assured that He is just as well as all-powerful we may, and should, wholeheartedly surrender our will to His: "not my will, but Thine, be done." Confident in His goodness, our proper role is to cease from rebellious disobedience and to find our peace in the full acceptance of His will for ourselves and for history at large. And through such acceptance we find not only rest from inner conflict but also the way to creative action, as His loyal servants, in relation to our fellows and to the physical world.

Fourth, in virtue of these attributes God's major significance in the unfolding of human history becomes clear. Being just, and requiring justice of men, He fills the role of lawgiver and judge. As lawgiver He lays down commandments, which then constitute the moral laws and ceremonial observances by which His human creatures are expected to live. He enters into a covenant with the Hebrew people, involving special contractual obligations and responsibilities on both sides; and when they disobey He brings dire punishment upon them for their faithlessness—He even rejects his special relation with them and enters upon a new covenant with all peoples in which His mercy and His love are more fully expressed than His justice. In fact, these kindly attributes are already disclosed in the fact that He sends prophets from time to time to warn His wayward people and to assure them of His forgiveness if they repent.*

It is in terms of these concepts that one comes to understand the distinctive meaning of "sin" for the Western religions. Nothing quite comparable to it is present in the Eastern faiths; they are familiar with moral ignorance, with spiritual lethargy and failure, with missing the *tao* and adding to bad *karma;* but they do not know sin, in the Western sense of the word.† For sin is essentially disobedience to the com-

---

* For Christianity, of course, the supreme disclosure of His love is the sending of His Son to redeem the world.

† With some qualifications in the case of the explicitly theistic sects.

mandments which God is believed to have given man—it is rebellion against the Divine Will, upon whose power and goodness man depends. God's role as judge is partially revealed in the rewards that the course of history bestows on the righteous and the punishments that descend on the wicked; it will be finally and vividly revealed at the great judgment day which is to come. On that awe-inspiring occasion all men, living and dead, will be brought before His throne to be judged according to their deeds, and from this judgment there is no appeal. Those who have sincerely repented of their sins and turned to God in humble, obedient trust, and have heard His welcoming assurance of forgiveness, will pass to their heavenly reward; those who have remained impenitent and stubborn will be hurled into a pit of fire and brimstone, to suffer unending torment for their crimes.

Fifth, the Western religions are consumed by a prophetic passion for social justice. This passion is akin to the Confucian superior man's sense of human responsibility and to the Indian's loyalty to the *dharma* of his station in life, but it has a distinctive quality of its own. This quality reflects a readiness to identify, in loving sympathy, with the poor, the weak, the suffering, the exploited, and the courage to denounce the powerful evildoers of this world; it also reflects an assurance that in so doing one is obeying the demands of God's righteousness and love. It is this factor in the religions of the West that accounts for the aggressive reformers of each generation in history who have refused to be passive in the presence of outrageous social wrongs and have attacked them with a burning religious zeal; it explains the fact that religion in the West has been a force for reshaping social institutions so that they become more nearly instruments of justice and equality than they have been in the past. Religious faith in the Western world has not been merely faith in God's just and merciful treatment of each individual; it has in large part been a trust in the possibility of realizing a more equalitarian social good in the course of human history. The Hebrew prophets are still the outstanding historical models in this regard, and they have awakened a responsive chord in Christianity and Islam as well as among their own racial descendants.

Sixth, it is a major conviction of these religions that it is the responsibility of each disciple actively to spread to all people the truth of God's glorious rule. We have here the root of the eager missionary zeal that has been characteristic of the Western religions—and of the fanatical dogmatism which this zeal exhibits in its extreme forms. Our God is the one and only genuine God, all other so-called divinities being merely idols; and our religious faith is exclusively true, all others expressing the sad aberrations of men in the darkness of error. Right belief, not only in modes of moral action but also in sound doctrine, now becomes of central importance in religion; and one must believe sound doctrine not, as in the Eastern faiths, because it teaches the laws of spiritual growth by which one progresses toward liberation from *tanha,* but because it describes the one and only way by which God extends his saving grace to men.* Now since there is but one way, God will not hold us guiltless if we fail to spread knowledge of Him to all who might respond, and secure, so far as in us lies, their obedient submission to His holy will. It is our privilege to bring to all people the good news of God's fatherly love and forgiveness; it is also our duty to warn them of the dire punishment that lies in wait for those who refuse to believe and submit.

Seventh (although this feature is present in the above Psalm only by implication), these religions reject asceticism as spiritually unsound. Everything in the world and in human experience, except sin, is potentially good; none of the natural pleasures and delights of life is intrinsically evil. They are a token of God's benignity, just as the hard experiences that befall man are a token of His chastening, which itself ex-

---

* Cf. the statement in the Athanasian Creed: "Whosoever will be saved, before all things it is necessary that he hold the Catholic faith, which faith, except every one do keep entire and unviolated, without doubt he shall perish everlastingly."

presses an ultimately loving purpose. To be sure, all the welcome things that God's goodness provides should be consecrated to Him and be used in His service for human happiness, but when so used they are pleasing to Him. It is in virtue of this conviction that family life, with its daily sharings of work and hope, joy and sorrow, occupies a high religious place in Judaism, Christianity, and Islam—as high a place as in Confucianism, though for essentially different reasons. God saw the world that He had made, and behold, it was very good—this can be said unqualifiedly for the Western religions, although not, in general, for the Eastern ones.*

It will be important to see, as we follow the development of these religions, what form these seven features take in each of them. And we shall see also, in the course of that development, how a significant variation appears in their conviction as to what religion essentially is. Most prominent, especially in Judaism and Islam, is a legal conception—the idea that at bottom religion is obedience to the laws that God has laid down for man and which are taught in a scripture divinely revealed. In a less central place is the mystic idea that religion is the path to the goal of union with God. But in later Judaism, and becoming a very prominent strain in Christianity, a conception appears that is not identical with either of these, though its affiliations with mysticism are close. This is the idea that religion is essentially a way of overcoming evil with good, in a universe in which the central problem is the practical one of dealing with the tragic reality of evil. Certain basic Christian doctrines, at least, can only be understood in the light of this principle, and Second Isaiah had already introduced it into prophetic Judaism.

B. OUR HISTORICAL SOURCES AND THEIR INTERPRETATION

Judaism was the major source out of which Christianity and Islam as civilized religions emerged. And later Judaism

---

* It is true that certain sects in the Western religions did come to accept an ascetic strain.

itself—especially the prophetic period which was of such crucial influence on subsequent history—grew out of the Judaism of earlier times. The first thing that we must do in approaching the religion of the Old Testament is to have in mind a few important dates.

The era of the great prophets extends from about 760 to 535 B.C. Amos, the earliest of this remarkable line, preached his dramatic and gloomy prophecies near the former of these dates, and Second Isaiah, the last and greatest, was bringing new hope to his countrymen who were captive in Babylon at approximately the later date. Now the earliest preprophetic period about which we know enough so that its major events can be reconstructed with any assurance is the period five hundred years earlier, when the Hebrew tribes were establishing themselves in the fertile plains and valleys of Palestine. An important group among them had migrated to Palestine from Egypt, under the leadership of Moses, who was the first individual to give the impress of his vigorous personality on the course of development that we shall trace. It will be observed that the prophetic period—or at least its culminating phase—was simultaneous with the creative religious revolutions that occurred in China and India; Second Isaiah was a contemporary of Confucius and Buddha, perhaps also of Lao Tse. And it may be further observed that there is a similar time span—five to six hundred years—between each pair of the outstanding epochs upon which we shall now be centering attention. Moses lived about 1200 B.C.; the later prophets were preaching around 600 B.C.; Jesus and Paul were laying the foundations of Christian teaching from A.D. 30 to 60; and Mohammed's active career falls between A.D. 611 and 632. Is there some cyclical law which can explain this periodic swing of the religious pendulum in the West?

Our major question as we think of these dates of course is: What was happening during each of these epochs that is religiously significant? The difficulties in the way of answering this question are not crucial so far as the later periods are concerned; the basic data lie before us in practically unquestioned form. With regard to the earliest epoch, however, there is a serious difficulty—unless we have already resolved it by choosing between two different ways of interpreting the Bible. If not, we must now make our choice between them— and the historical picture we accept will be rather different according to which way we adopt.

The choice, in fact, is between the so-called "higher criticism," as applied to the Biblical records, and the traditional mode of interpretation among Jews and Christians, which rests on the belief that the Bible is a unique revelation from God and therefore that every statement in it is infallibly true. If we adopt the method of the higher criticism, we shall find that the preprophetic religion of the Jews was in most respects a form of primitive religion, akin to the kind of religion studied in Chapter II. Exceptional features are not absent, as we shall see, but in general this description stands. If we make the other choice, our conclusion will be that no such primitive period existed save so far as some of the Hebrews lapsed from the teaching of their leaders and fell into the degenerate practices of surrounding peoples. According to this view God had been continually revealing His truth to man ever since the time of Adam, and especially to the Jews since the time of Abraham; there can therefore be nothing in Hebrew history that would properly be described as an evolution from primitive to civilized religion. Also, from this standpoint, the great religious teacher who has been mentioned above as Second Isaiah did not exist; his doctrines are a part of the teaching of the first (and only) Isaiah who lived a century and a half earlier, since the chapters that higher critics attribute to him are included in the Book of Isaiah.

My own choice between these alternatives has already been made. It is determined by the method of sympathetic impartiality which has been followed throughout this book. In dealing with the Eastern religions a rule of interpretation has been taken for granted which, if expressed in Occidental terms, would be precisely the principle of the higher criticism. We have not assumed that any of the Eastern scriptures is a revelation from the ultimate source of truth and therefore that everything it says must infallibly be so. If, for example, the later Confucian writings attribute some statement to the Master, we have felt no obligation to accept it as actually spoken by him; only when the total historical evidence, external as well as internal, confirms the attribution would we adopt it as correct. Similarly, if we find the classics of Mahayana Buddhism putting into Buddha's mouth metaphysical statements that seem inconsistent with the earliest and more dependable sutras, we would not regard them as possessing coercive authority; they reveal what their authors doubtless believed him to have said, but not necessarily what he did say.

So, unless we are to give some special privilege to the Jewish or Christian scriptures, we shall wish to apply the same assumptions to them. The Bible will be viewed as a collection of sixty-odd writings, produced over a period of a thousand years, expressing various aims in the minds of their authors, and reflecting many degrees of knowledge or ignorance about the events with which they deal. None of its assertions will be accepted as true merely because it is in the Bible; everything that is said will be judged, in the light of all the evidence that is relevant to its truth or falsity, on the same basis as would be employed with other writings, religious or secular. When, for example, later portions of the Bible make statements about earlier ones—e.g., the references in the New Testament which assume that the first five books of the Bible were all written by Moses—we shall test such statements in the same way that other historical assertions would be tested, and we shall accept whatever the verdict may turn out to be. Hence there will be no puzzling difficulty (as would otherwise be the case) in the fact that the final chapter of the last book traditionally attributed to Moses, Deuteronomy, contains a description of Moses' death and burial, the description ending with the remark that "no man knows the place of his burial unto this day."[2] This remark clearly implies that its author lived at a later date than the events he is describing, and if we find no break in language and style as between these verses and the rest of the book, our conclusion will naturally be that the whole of Deuteronomy was written at a time subsequent to Moses' death. Similarly, we shall be prepared for other corrections and reconstructions of the historical picture given in the Bible, as they prove to be required by respect for the total mass of relevant evidence, within the Bible and without.

When the Old Testament is interpreted in this way, the most probable conclusions about its main contents which are important for our present purpose run as follows. The earliest material that attained written form is a group of songs, legends, stories, and records, contained mostly in the books of Joshua, Judges, and Samuel; they preserve a picture of the events and prevailing conditions during the period when the Hebrews were settling in Palestine and expelling, killing, or absorbing the earlier inhabitants. As we now have them, these ancient relics are embedded in later writings which give them a setting more congenial to accepted religious principles of a subsequent period, but patient textual criticism can with some confidence disentangle them from this context. The material now contained in the first two books of the Bible and the fourth, describing the creation of the world, its early history, and the story of the Jewish people down to the escape from Egypt, consists mainly of two documents which were written between 850 and 750 B.C., and were combined into one volume after the fall of the northern Hebrew kingdom in 722 B.C. Deuteronomy and Leviticus, which purport to supplement this description, were actually written much later, Deuteronomy[3] appearing in 622 B.C. and Leviticus reflecting the viewpoint of Ezekiel, who prophesied about 580 B.C. during the early years of exile in Babylon.

The whole of this quasi-historical material, along with other writings that deal with the period of the two kingdoms and the work of the great prophets, was given unity in its present form under the editorship of members of the priesthood living about 450 B.C. or perhaps even later. Their editorial work reflects a perspective which we would expect from what we know of their historical situation. They were chastened by the catastrophes which the Jews had undergone, and they accepted the general principles for interpreting them that had been preached by the prophets; but the framework into which they fitted everything was provided by the essentially legal and sacramental conception of religion characteristic of the priestly mind in the West.

C. PREPROPHETIC HEBREW RELIGION

The following account of preprophetic Hebrew religion, of the teaching of the great prophets in its revolutionary significance, and of the main events in the late Old Testament period, takes for granted the method of the higher criticism and the historical analysis of the Old Testament books just outlined.

When, on this basis, one asks what the religion practiced by most of the Hebrews previous to the work of the great prophets was like, the answer is reached by examining the oldest material embodied in Joshua, Judges, and Samuel, and allowing it to tell its story undistorted by the editorial commentary of a later age. This story, thus disentangled, indicates that what they practised was in most respects a form of primitive religion similar to that of the Semitic peoples surrounding them. Yahweh or Jehovah was their special god, but He was not the only power recognized by them as divine. They believed that other peoples had their divinities, who were quite real and needed to be dealt with when one was traveling in their territory; moreover, Yahweh was not the sole object of propitiation or worship among themselves. Their religion included animal and plant cults, household images and fetishes, sacred mountains, trees, springs, stones, and pillars; along with recognition of these potent objects there were the accompanying sacrifices, offerings, prayers, rituals, and the characteristic taboos of primitive Semitic cults.* They also practiced magic, divination, and necromancy, many of whose forms are familiar from what we have learned about primitive religion elsewhere. We find, too, the absence of any sense of moral responsibility beyond the tribe that was observed earlier to be a distinctive and prominent feature of primitive religion. Several of these features are clearly revealed in the interesting story of Micah and the Danites given in Chapters 17 and 18 of the Book of Judges, if one does not allow the story to be colored by the appalled comment of the later editor: "In those days there was no king in Israel, and every man did what was right in his own eyes."[4]

As for Yahweh himself, he was conceived to possess the main characteristics of a powerful tribal chief, plus ability to control the natural forces on which Palestine's material well-being depended. His presence is associated especially with the storm clouds, and with certain mountains, trees, rocks, and springs. Military glory is attributed to him as a god of armies and of battles. He is jealous of his prerogatives, punishing strictly and severely infractions of the taboos under which he has placed his people. Often such punishment takes no account of the difference between an overt act and the intention behind it, as when Uzzah was struck dead for reaching out to steady the ark which, on its journey home from the city of the Philistines, was jostled by the oxen pulling it.[5] He has little humane feeling for the enemies of the Hebrews, sometimes ordering wholesale slaughter of their captives, including women and children as well as men.[6] He reveals his will to his people either by direct visions vouchsafed to their accepted leaders or through simple oracles of types familiar in many early religions. Upon the Jews he is believed to have

---

* Even human sacrifices were not absent. See the story of Jephthah's daughter in Judges 11:28–40.

imposed a number of ritual requirements, some of which are connected with agricultural festivals or with commemoration of his deliverance of their fathers from the land of Egypt. He has also enjoined upon them certain moral duties, expressive of the demand for evenhanded justice within the nation.

But Judaism would not have been capable of the revolution that it later underwent at the hands of the great prophets had there not been, even at this early period, certain factors present which pointed in the direction of that transformation and made it different from the kind of primitive religion that never outgrows its crudities. Two of these factors are due, most probably, to the insight and powerful personality of Moses, and are involved in the conception of the covenant relation above mentioned into which Yahweh and the Jews entered through him as intermediary. As a result of the stirring circumstances attending their escape from Egypt and migration to Palestine, the Hebrew tribes which experienced them were sufficiently loosened from their previous religious habits, and sufficiently grateful to Yahweh through whose aid the project had been planned and consummated, so that under Moses' and Joshua's insistence they entered into a voluntary pact with Yahweh, binding their descendants as well as themselves to be faithful to it. The essence of the covenant, as interpreted by their leaders, was that on their part, in thankful remembrance of Yahweh's help, they promised to worship and obey him; on his part, he was to give them continued protection and guidance as his chosen people.

The features of this covenant relation which from the very beginning stand out noticeably in contrast with the characteristic attitudes of neighboring peoples toward their divinities were, first, the vivid sense of responsibility, personal as well as social, which it encouraged; and second, the historical consciousness which thenceforth became likewise focal in all Jewish religious attitudes and ideas. The sense of conscious responsibility was, of course, based on the conviction embedded in the story of the covenant, that before they or their fathers had done anything to merit Yahweh's favor he had singled them out as recipients of his gracious attention, delivering them from bondage and providing them a prosperous homeland in which to dwell. Since they and their children all shared in the bounty thus received, there lay naturally a personal obligation on each to remain loyal to the divinity who had chosen them, and to keep their religion free from all attitudes and acts which would not accord with such grateful loyalty. To this sense of responsibility, however feeble at times it might be, the prophets who came later were constantly able to appeal in their effort to deepen the understanding of the people as to what the covenant relation really involved.

As for the historical consciousness, it is evident that for the Hebrews at this period Yahweh was not mainly a personification of natural powers, such as sun, earth, rain, or storm, with which man must needs square himself if he is to win a secure existence (as was the case with most of the divinities cultivated by their neighbors); he controlled these powers, but he was also a being with a historical plan for his chosen people, to be carried out through their active coöperation. This means that Jewish religious experience, even at this early era, was marked by a live sense of history and of progress. It distinctly included a temporal reach, extending at least from the memorable display in the past of Yahweh's great kindness toward them to an anticipated future in which his benefits would be still more richly revealed. This historical consciousness provided the necessary background for the persistent attempt of the prophets to interpret the events and prospects of their own times in relation to the covenant between Yahweh and his people.

The third factor lies in the moral sensitivity of those who were generally accepted as the spokesmen, even in this preprophetic period, of Yahweh to his people. Instead of the shaman, possessing special magical powers to cause or avert harm to others, the Hebrews more and more recognized the "prophet"—that is, a man who foretold coming events and interpreted them in the light of their moral significance. How early the prophetic line in this distinctive sense began is a difficult question to answer; perhaps not quite as early as the time described in Judges. But by the reign of King David (about 1000 B.C.) such a personality was clearly present in a redoubtable individual named Nathan. David had committed adultery with Bathsheba and then had piled sin upon sin by ordering her husband into the army's front line so that he became a military casualty.[7] The prophet Nathan, learning of these crimes, fearlessly beards the guilty king and promises divine punishment upon him and the royal household. The Hebrew prophet is thus a man of moral insight, zeal, and courage; as we follow his line through the years we find him increasingly emphasizing the social responsibilities implied by the covenant, for justice toward all and mercy toward the poor, the weak, and the unprotected.

D. THE MESSAGE OF THE GREAT PROPHETS

The period of the great prophets, who, in full commitment to this emphasis in religion, achieved a redirection of Hebrew thought and experience which became profoundly influential through subsequent religious history, came half a millennium later than the epoch just described. As was noted above, this period extended over two centuries and a quarter, from about 760 B.C. to 535 B.C. The main circumstance which provoked this prophetic reinterpretation of religion was the gradual squeezing of Palestine between the pincers of surrounding military empires, ending in the complete extinction of independent political life for the Jews at the hands of Babylon in 586 B.C. Such a national calamity, among other peoples, had always, so far as our records show, spelled decay for their religion; it seemed clear proof of either impotence or hopeless hostility on the part of their divinities. The significance of the Hebrew prophets whose thought we now examine lies in the fact that they so profoundly revised the fundamental ideas and attitudes of their national religion in the face of this threatening calamity that the cult of Yahweh was able as a result of the political tragedy to win a new lease on life and embark on a novel course of historical development. The main sources for our knowledge of this reconstruction are the prophetic books of Amos, Hosea, Micah, Isaiah, Jeremiah, and Ezekiel, with whose thought the reader should become familiar.

The prophets were true heirs of Moses and built on the foundation he had laid in the idea of a special covenant binding Yahweh and Israel. Like him, they were men of unusual intellectual power, as is shown by the fact that they vividly foresaw the crises to come and were moved to deep and thoroughgoing reflection by them. Like him, and perhaps more than he, they were men of high moral sensitiveness; faced by the complex social relationships just coming to present a serious challenge in their day—relations of rich and poor, priest and layman, king and subject, citizen and foreigner—they dealt with the basic problems of moral responsibility, and offered conceptions of righteousness and ethical greatness that have appealed to men of similar quality in all the centuries since. Like him, they were men of pious responsiveness, in whom new insights broke with suddenness and such vivid cogency that they could not be taken as ordinary achievements but were inevitably regarded as revelations of divinity. They thus led to novel interpretations of religious duty and to transformed conceptions of Yahweh.

The central question of the prophets was: What is the meaning of this impending tragedy in our national life? And the essence of their answer was: as a people we have been faithless to our covenant with Yahweh, especially to the moral and social obligations which it involves. The inroads of foreign armies are his punishment for this faithlessness. If we turn and repent of our sin, perhaps the fatal consequence of our disobedience can be avoided; or if not, perhaps Yahweh will preserve the repentant remnant of his people, even in captivity, and some day restore them openly to his favor. It is evident that this teaching is founded on the two distinctive features of the covenant-consciousness which had been a part of Jewish religion from the time of Moses, and to which attention has already been called. It also reflects an intensification of the passion for social justice illustrated in such men as Nathan, and a bold reinterpretation of the covenant relation which makes the duties of justice and mercy of primary importance in religion.

The first of these outstanding individuals was Amos, a poor herdsman from Tekoa in Judah, who felt called by Yahweh to protest against the moral abominations and spiritual blindness which he witnessed in the northern kingdom when he traveled there to sell his wool in the markets of Bethel and Gilgal. Let us listen to his message, as the crowds who have come to participate in the festivals gather round him. He begins by denouncing Syria (at that time the major threat to the peace of Israel) for her sins, and pronouncing divine punishment upon her.

> Thus says the LORD:
> "For the three transgressions of Damascus,
> And for the four, I will not turn it back;
> Because they have threshed Gilead
> With threshing-tools of iron.
> So I will send a fire upon the house of Hazael,
> And it shall devour the palaces of Benhadad. . . .
> And the people of Syria shall go captive to Kir."
>
> Says the LORD.

> Thus says the LORD:
> "For the three transgressions of Gaza,
> And for the four, I will not turn it back;
> Because they carried into exile a whole people,
> To hand them over to Edom.
> So I will send a fire upon the wall of Gaza. . . .
> And the remnant of the Philistines shall perish."
>
> Says the Lord GOD.

Thus says the LORD:
"For the three transgressions of Tyre,
And for the four, I will not turn it back;
Because they handed over a whole people as captives to Edom,
And did not remember the covenant of brotherhood.
So I will send a fire upon the wall of Tyre,
And it shall devour her palaces."[8]

At this prophecy, delighted applause must have burst from the surrounding throng; all these were among the peoples who had opposed the Hebrews in their long struggle for a secure position in Palestine. Their eager desire for vengeance and for freedom from these threats is to be satisfied—so Amos seems to promise. But now he turns in the same vein, and with the same dramatic invective, to their sister nation, his own people Judah. The audience is sobered, puzzled, a bit anxious.

Thus says the LORD:
"For the three transgressions of Judah,
And for the four, I will not turn it back;
Because they have rejected the instruction of the LORD,
And have not kept his statutes;
But their lies have led them astray,
After which their fathers walked.
So I will send a fire upon Judah,
And it shall devour the palaces of Jerusalem."[9]

And then comes the tremendous climax, toward which all these denunciations have been leading.

Thus says the LORD:
"For the three transgressions of Israel,
And for the four, I will not turn it back;
Because they have sold the innocent for silver,
And the needy in exchange for a pair of sandals;
They who trample upon the heads of the poor,
And thrust aside the humble from the way. . . .
Behold, I am going to make a groaning under you,

As a wagon groans that is loaded with sheaves.
Flight shall perish from the swift,
And the strong shall not exert his strength,
And the warrior shall not save himself;
And he who handles the bow shall not stand firm,
Nor shall the swift of foot save himself,
Nor shall he who rides upon horseback save himself;
And the stoutest of heart among the warriors
Shall flee away naked on that day."
                        The oracle of the Lord.[10]

As his listeners gasp in stunned horror and disbelief he makes his indictment more specific; he gives it its historical setting, and proceeds with a vivid portrayal of the total destruction that he foresees as their inescapable punishment. "You are my chosen people," he reports Yahweh as saying to them, "and it is for this reason that I will punish you for your sins. I have done so before, but the punishment was evidently not enough. You have not repented and turned from your evil ways. You have brought sacrifices and offerings and paid your tithes; but to do this while continuing to indulge in evil acts is compounding your wickedness and insulting to me."[11]

Come to Bethel and transgress!
To Gilgal, and multiply your transgressions!
Bring your sacrifices every morning,
And your tithes every third day!
Burn a thank-offering of leavened bread,
And proclaim voluntary offerings, publish them!
For so you love to do, O Israelites!

I hate, I scorn your feasts;
I will not smell sacrifice in your solemn assemblies.
Though ye offer unto Me offerings of flesh and offerings of fruit.
    I am not pleased;
And the thank-offerings of your firstlings I regard not.
Put away from Me the noise of your songs;
And the music of your harps I hear not.

But let justice flow like waters,
And righteousness like an ever-flowing stream.

What is the basic sin that rouses Amos to righteous wrath in this fashion?

I know that your transgressions are many,
And your sins countless—
You who oppress the innocent, take bribes,
And thrust aside the needy at the gate.
Prepare to meet your God, O Israel.

So the doom must come, brought upon them by a God who is now conceived to be not only the lord of Israel but the creator of the universe and the omnipotent determiner of its history. It is to come through the victory of foreign armies, whose activities Yahweh is controlling so that, whatever their own aims, they are really carrying out His purpose of punishing His sinful people.

The foe shall surround the land
And strip you of your strength;
And your palaces shall be plundered.

The Lord God has sworn by His holiness
That there are days coming upon you
When they will drag you away with hooks,
And what is left of you with fishhooks;
And through the breaches you will go, each straight ahead,
And you will be cast upon the refuse heap.

Fallen, never to rise again, is the virgin Israel.

Before the day of wrath has dawned there is still hope, but only if they turn a new leaf and begin to live as befits the chosen people of a righteous God:

Seek good and not evil,
That you may live—
And that thus Yahweh, the God of hosts,
May be with you
As you have said.

> Hate evil, and love good,
> And establish justice at the gate;
> Perhaps Yahweh, the God of hosts,
> Will be gracious to a remnant of Joseph.*

Such was the fiery message of this untutored herdsman from the barren region of the Dead Sea, to whom had come a momentous vision and who had turned prophet. I shall not take the space to summarize the teachings of his great successors, save for Second Isaiah, whom we shall need to study for a special reason. They all repeat the same basic theme; they differ (as historical events develop) in the source from which they expect the punishing blow to come, in the measure of comforting hope that they promise for the future, and in many detailed matters of doctrine. They differ, too, in the emphasis laid upon various attributes in Yahweh's nature— some picturing Him as moved not merely by righteous wrath but also by a tender concern for His wayward people. The important thing for us is to draw the threads of their teaching together so that we can grasp its distinctive essence in contrast with the ideas generally prevailing in Hebrew religion five hundred years earlier. And we can do this most fruitfully by analyzing their message in terms of the first three basic characteristics by which high civilized religion differs from primitive religion. For the historical significance of the prophets lies precisely in the fact that in view of their insight these three features emerge as essential to religion in the West, just as at the same time they were emerging in the East through the work of the spiritual pioneers studied in the preceding chapters. It will be recalled that these features are (1) a sense of responsibility for justice and mercy toward all men, (2) a conviction that there is only one divine being over all the earth, and (3) a belief that the inward heart of man in its moral responsiveness is what we mean by his "soul."

---

* The promise of ultimate restoration in Amos' final chapter is regarded by most higher critical scholars as a later interpolation.

Let us consider the contribution of the prophets on the second of these first. As we have observed, earlier Hebrew thought had taken it for granted that other divinities besides Yahweh existed, some of whom, like Chemosh of the Moabites, bore essentially the same relation to their people that Yahweh did to Israel. Yahweh was believed to be stronger than these other gods, and thus able, when he wished, to encroach on their territory, but in general the scope of his activity was confined to the land within which his people lived.

When the prophets, however, ventured to think of the invasion and conquest of Palestine by armies of Egypt, Syria, Assyria, and Babylon as Yahweh's righteous discipline of His people, a different conception is necessarily involved. Yahweh must really, whether these other nations recognize it or not, be their god too; at least they and their activities are swept within the scope of His historical plan for Israel. For Isaiah, the Assyrian invader is the rod within Yahweh's hand.[12] For Ezekiel, Nebuchadnezzar is Yahweh's agent in his various military depredations, in Judah and elsewhere.[13] Nay, even the internal economy of other nations and their historical vicissitudes are controlled by Yahweh.[14] The natural outcome of this line of thought, clearly seen at least by some of the prophets, was that other gods have no genuine existence at all. Yahweh is the sole God of the whole earth, and embraces all men within His providential care. This conception is given poetic expression by Isaiah in his vision that "the whole earth is full of His glory,"[15] and as a result of the prophetic reinterpretation it found theological statement in the doctrine of creation now embodied in the Book of Genesis, where the Hebrew deity is portrayed as sole maker of the universe and omnipresent controller of its history.

The sense of universal moral responsibility is less clearly exemplified in the thought of the prophets. It would naturally take the form of a conviction that the requirements of Yahweh's law are to be practiced by the Jews in their relations with individuals outside the nation in exactly the same way as in their relations with fellow Jews. While at times this conception appears to be implicit in the prophets, it does not quite gain explicit expression. So far as we find in them an anticipation of this idea, it took its most definite form in a reinterpretation of the covenant relation between Yahweh and Israel, appearing in the suggestion of the later prophets that to be the chosen people means primarily an obligation for Israel to become a mediator of religious truth to the other nations; the Jews were selected by Yahweh not primarily to enjoy prosperity but to serve as a light to the Gentiles.[16] The most appealing statement of this transformation of a preferential covenant into a moral and religious responsibility to all mankind is made by Second Isaiah.[17]

What the early prophets did clearly exemplify was a change from an overconcern with ritual to an emphasis on the ethico-social responsibilities of the covenant. Prior to their work the prevailing notion, generally speaking, was that the various prescriptions which Yahweh had imposed on the Jews for scrupulous observance are all on the same level of importance. The obligation to respect the taboos connected with ceremonial cleanliness and to bring periodic sacrifices to the altar demands at least the same degree of careful attention as the obligation to social justice. The prophets vigorously challenged this assumption. According to them, the essence of obedience to Yahweh lies in fulfilling a man's duty toward his neighbor; in comparison with this, ceremony and sacrifice take an entirely subordinate place. Nay, as Amos insists, these rituals even become sinful if attention to them stands in the way of conscientious fulfillment of social obligations or encourages the thought that the latter can be safely neglected.* The outcome of this line of prophetic teaching was that the essence of the covenant law is exhausted in the duty of love toward

---

* In the case of Jeremiah, the prophet goes so far as apparently to maintain (7:21-23) that Yahweh had never imposed ritual requirements upon Israel at all.

one's neighbor, expressed in just dealing toward all and in mercy toward those who need special care. This thought is best summarized in a frequently quoted passage from Micah: "Wherewith shall I come before Yahweh, and bow myself before the high God? Shall I come before Him with burnt-offerings, with calves of a year old? . . . . He hath shewed thee, O man, what is good; and what doth Yahweh require of thee but to do justly, and to love mercy, and to walk humbly with thy God?"[18]

And now for the third feature, in the form given it by the Hebrew prophets. The crucial idea here is that true religion requires the replacement of a state of mind in which overt deeds are the prime object of concern by one in which the spirit or attitude behind the deed is the matter of central importance, and that it is this spirit that constitutes the essence of man's soul. Before the time of the great prophets Hebrew religion had, in general, like early religion among other peoples, taken for granted the first of these viewpoints. The inner life as such, and its varied religious possibilities, had not as yet been clearly discovered. No religious or moral distinction was drawn between what a man does and the intention expressed in what he does;* to violate a divine injunction by accident is just as serious an offense as to violate it deliberately. Obedience to Yahweh is complete if one's external acts have all conformed to his behests. But the second viewpoint is really implied by the transition just noted from a preoccupation with ritual requirements to an emphasis on ethico-social responsibilities. Ceremonial duties can be minutely prescribed in advance, and so far as a person aims merely at fulfilling them his conduct can become an affair of mechanical routine. But no such detailed direction can be a sufficient guide when one conceives himself bound to obey the law of justice or of mercy, for these are not matters of routine behavior—these are general principles, to be expressed in whatever varied ways are appropriate on each occasion as it

* Cf. the episode of Uzzah above mentioned.

arises. They reflect a constant inner attitude or purpose, a commitment to the ideal embodied in these virtues, which cannot be exhausted in any particular set of acts because it signifies a readiness to act in accordance with this ideal in any situation, actual or possible. Such an inner purpose or readiness now becomes the core of man's soul.

These new moral and psychological insights had their own effect on the prophetic conception of God; the transformation in this concept involved much more than the adoption of monotheism. Formerly, of course, Yahweh had been conceived as a fully personal divinity; he was the kind of being with whom men could make a covenant, involving reciprocal historical duties and contractual obligations. But his relation was more with the nation as a whole than with its individual members, and when the latter felt his presence the attributes of which they were apt to be conscious were mystery, power, jealousy, and august sternness; although, to be sure, an element of gracious kindliness was not absent. As a result, however, of the prophetic insistence on the necessity of an inward commitment to the moral ideal, Yahweh naturally came to be conceived as exemplifying such an ideal Himself, and as treating His children accordingly. When the repentant Israelite turns toward his divinity in sincerity and loyalty, he finds that Yahweh is already welcoming him in an attitude of generous forgiveness and fatherly love. A reverent, yet intimate, fellowship becomes possible between the individual soul and its God. Hosea speaks of Yahweh yearning for His people as a husband for an erring wife whose affection he longs to regain.[19] Jeremiah, amid the upheavals of his day and the misunderstanding and persecution to which he was personally subjected, discovers in inward communion with Yahweh a sustaining support.[20] And Second Isaiah, endowed with poetic sensitiveness to the rich possibilities of this emphasis in religion, implicitly attributes to Yahweh the infinite wisdom, unfailing tenderness, commanding greatness, and elusive wonder of an ideal personality, in whose comforting presence hope is ever reborn so that suffering loses its poignancy and tragedy its sting.[21]

As a result of these changes Hebrew religion gained a new dimension, and became in the hands of these pioneers the essential expression toward God and one's fellow men of an inner spirit, a controlling attitude of trustful and joyous love. The core of religion, as conceived from this altered standpoint, came to be formulated in the two great commandments which are now embodied in the Hebrew call to worship:

Hear, O Israel, the Lord thy God is one God:
And thou shalt love the Lord thy God with all thy heart and all thy soul and all thy mind and all thy strength;
And thou shalt love thy neighbor as thyself.

The appealing devotional Psalms, most of which were written after the period of the great prophets, reveal in poetic form the result of this radical transformation of religion. They express, with a wealth of beautiful imagery, the essence of this spiritual ideal as it came to be practiced by Jews who were responsive to the prophetic message and found in it, especially during the dark days of exile, a satisfying solace and guide.

What, in this transformed prophetic view, fills the role of the fourth major characteristic of civilized religion—the conviction that man as he naturally stands is incapable of true happiness and needs to undergo a profound conversion in order to realize it? The answer is that this characteristic takes a different form from those with which we have become acquainted in our study of the religions of the East. We meet here, in fact, another major way of conceiving this aspect of civilized religion, which became of central importance in Islam and in Augustinian and Calvinist Christianity as well as in Judaism. Confucianism taught that man's natural desires are gradually redirected and integrated under the guidance of whatever fellow feeling and sense of social responsibility are innately present in him, the goal of the process being a state in which all his emotions and impulses are unified under the control of a true moral ideal. The corresponding doctrine of the Indian religions is that man's sense of individual separateness, dominated by self-centered cravings, is purged away by persistent discipline until it has become replaced by a realization of blissful oneness with ultimate reality and with his fellow creatures.

The Western religions teach a different idea, although it has some common features with the principles of *bhakti yoga* described in the *Bhagavad-Gita*. As men and women naturally stand, tempted by the satanic powers of evil, they are in a state of disobedient rebellion against God and His law. They assert their own sinful wills instead of submitting to the rightful authority of the Divine Will. What they need is sincere repentance, and a turning away from evil in whole-souled surrender to God and in humble acceptance of His law. The conviction is that through such a conversion, issuing in loving devotion to a God of justice and love, man's selfish desires will be overcome and his sinful nature transformed. As Amos vividly taught, God hates injustice and hypocrisy, punishing it severely in all nations and especially in His chosen people; but, as the other prophets held, He welcomes and forgives all who penitently turn from their evil ways in obedient self-surrender to Him. Now this forgiveness, as experienced by men, is not simply a canceling of the guilt produced by their previous disobedience; it is a transformation of their desires so that the will to sin is no longer there, being replaced by a loving wish to be acceptable in God's sight in all one's thought and deeds.[22]

E. THE SPIRITUAL IDEAL OF SECOND ISAIAH

But the high-water mark of Hebrew prophetic religion still lies before us. What has thus far been surveyed is the common message of the prophets whose work preceded the final defeat of Judah by Babylon in 586 B.C. One would expect, however, that the overwhelming experience of that catastrophe, and of life under the somber conditions of exile, would have further significant effects in the religious thinking of those who lived through it, giving a novel note to their theology as compared with that of the earlier prophetic period. And this is the case; indeed, there is more than one new note which a full account of Hebrew religion would need to describe. In the work of Ezekiel, a prophet who wrote between 590 and 570 B.C., the chapters written after his exile to Babylon envision the future restoration of the Jews and a reëstablished temple worship; the teachings of his great predecessors provide the creed around which a priestly-oriented theology and ritual are organized.

Far more important, however, for the long-range development of religion in the West is a prophetic figure who lived a generation after Ezekiel—a man who witnessed the conquest of Babylon by Cyrus of Persia in 538 B.C. and joyfully pondered Cyrus' decision to allow a group of the captive Jews to return to their homeland and rebuild Jerusalem. This sensitive thinker and poet, whose name is unknown, was one of the greatest religious teachers of history, for his interpretation of spiritual truth carries us so far beyond that of the earlier prophets that it must be expounded as a quite distinctive philosophy. By some strange quirk of history his message does not now compose a separate book, as it must originally have done, but is contained in Chapters 40 to 55 of the Book of Isaiah, who had lived a hundred and seventy-five years before him. For this reason he is referred to by historians and theologians who adopt the higher criticism as Second Isaiah (or Deutero-Isaiah).

The question that best leads us into the heart of his thought, and with which his eager searching most likely began, is the same question that stirred the earlier prophets to their momentous reflections, except that he now puts it (appropriately) in the past tense. They had wished to understand why Israel and Judah must suffer—suffer the horrors of crushing defeat and lonely, helpless captivity. He wishes to understand this too—as an event that by his time had actually happened. But he was not satisfied with their answer. It is true, he believed, as they did, that this bitter ordeal was a punishment for sin. And he was able to view history from a perspective which appeared to confirm the bold conviction of Amos that divine punishment comes upon every nation that falls into the ways of licentiousness, cruelty, and callous injustice. He had seen Assyria, conqueror of Israel, herself punished by defeat at the hands of Babylon; he had seen Babylon, conqueror of Judah, herself punished by defeat at the hands of Persia after dominating the world scene for only seventy years.

But this was merely a part of the answer, for he had also seen something else which awoke in him a new insight into the liberating spiritual possibilities of such suffering as his people had undergone. He had been deeply impressed by the personality of Jeremiah—the great prophet who had lived in the midst of the dark events that led to the collapse of Judah and the sacking of Jerusalem in 597 and 586 B.C., and who was very likely the model of the "suffering servant" whom he vividly describes in Isaiah 53.

Jeremiah had counseled the statesmen of Judah wisely, but they refused to heed him; he was treated as a traitor, was imprisoned and tortured, and finally perished at the hands of his countrymen amid the ruins of the nation and the apparent failure of all for which he stood. But he had loved his people so deeply that he willingly shared with them the fatal consequences of their sin; though misunderstood, abused, and hated as a false Jew by those whom he served, he accepted in trust and hope the tragedy that came upon both him and them because of their blindness and folly. Those who survived in exile could see that they had judged him wrongly; that he was a man of God, a true patriot. Perhaps—so Second Isaiah at least came to believe—Jeremiah was a type of the nation as a whole, and of the spirit in which it too should bear its calamities; perhaps its role in relation to the religious need of the world is essentially like his in relation to his fellow countrymen. At first it would be ridiculed, despised, and crushed by the military powers surrounding it; but later it would be understood, appreciated, and exalted to the position of trusted teacher of the deepest religious truths. Moreover—and this is the event that crystallized in Second Isaiah's mind the new thought that was struggling toward clear formulation—the Jews had appealed successfully to Cyrus, king of the victorious Persians, for permission to return and rebuild their shattered city, especially its house of worship. He was sure that there was a divine purpose in this train of events, a purpose not glimpsed by anyone before him but pointing toward a glorious future for Israel and the world.

So he answers the question, why his people had to suffer, in this historical and prophetic perspective. And in giving the solution that he does, he answers two other questions also— one vitally important to the Hebrews of his day, the other vital to an understanding of religion in all times and places where his answer awakens an appreciative response. The first is: What does it really mean to be God's chosen people? And the second is: How can what appears to be a tragic evil become a means to the greatest good—a good that could not be realized unless that evil had occurred? He gives his answers to these questions, not in the form of a theological essay but in the garb of religious poetry; and at every point the reader feels the tremendous vigor and sustained beauty that come from the unfolding of a great vision. He has glimpsed an idea that brings comfort, instruction, purpose, hope; and he expresses it in words that fully match the thought.

I shall first state the central conviction that illumines these glowing chapters, and then add such detail as is needed to place it in the setting of his whole prophetic philosophy. The terrible calamity which the Jews had suffered, he is sure, is not a proof of special guilt on their part but rather of a specially exalted role that Yahweh is calling them to fill.

Hence it is not a sheer evil (as would be the case were it nothing more than punishment for past sin) but an experience that can be turned to a new, hopeful, creative use—for them and for the entire world. If taken aright, it can purge them of the proud, self-centered vices that had corrupted them in the past—it can point the way toward the achievement of a new national personality, moved by novel aspirations and ideal purposes, and embodying a power of self-giving that was previously beyond them. As he expounds this thought there hovers before his mind a new vision of God's greatness and goodness to them and to the world. Although it was an overwhelming evil when it came upon them, their tragic defeat was a necessary preparation for a unique spiritual role —the role of serving as a light to the nations, of atoning for the sins of the world as well as their own, of leading other peoples to the truth of Yahweh's religion, of founding an era of universal peace and brotherhood under Israel as teacher and guide. Thus their suffering, if taken not in a mood of rebellion or despair but as a means of chastened soul-cleansing, can spell hope and gladness for the infinite future and for the whole human race; an appalling evil can thus become the means to an incomparable good.

He begins with a note of comfort, of tender reassurance, of the promise that his people will be fully restored to God's forgiveness and protecting love.

> "Comfort, O comfort my people," says your God:
> "Speak to the heart of Jerusalem, and call to her,
> That her time of service is ended, that her guilt is paid in full,
> That she has received of the LORD's hand
>   double for all her sins."[23]

He describes in picturesque imagery the return of the pilgrims as they march through the desert toward the new Jerusalem that they are to build. The Lord will lead them and will give them all that they need for security along the way. So they need not be anxious or fearful; the rugged mountains and deep valleys will be made smooth, pools will appear in the desert to provide them drink and trees to give them shade, darkness will turn into light. The way will be hard and the march exhausting; even the strong young men will weary, but they that wait on the Lord shall not faint but shall renew their strength like the eagles.

Before the end of his first chapter, the theme appears that over and over again recurs—the theme of the incomparable greatness, majesty, power, and goodness of the God whose historical purpose he is here unfolding. He is the only God; beside Him there is no other. He is the one who stretched out the heavens like a curtain, who measured the sea in the hollow of His hand, who brought into being the ends of the earth. Compared to Him the whole earth is but a speck of dust; the nations are as a drop from a bucket. He heaps derisive and ironic scorn upon those who worship divinity in the form of an idol, thinking in their folly that a material image can be like the transcendent majesty who sits enthroned above the earth, casting at His will its most potent rulers from their seats. He challenges the gods of the nations: Were they able to predict the great events that have happened, or to tell their significance? Still less, has any of them foreseen the glorious new event that is to come and what it betokens for the world?[24]

But soon he begins to unfold his vision. He turns to a survey of the past history of his people, interpreting it in the comforting and hopeful perspective of his opening verses. It is true that they did sin, and very grievously; the Lord had to punish them. But now Israel's punishment is over. Her guilt is paid in full; God has blotted out her sins, and is redeeming her in love and tenderness. She must not say,

> "The LORD has forsaken me,
> The LORD has forgotten me!"
> "Can a woman forget her sucking child,
> So as not to have pity upon the son of her womb?
> Even should these forget,
> Yet I will not forget you."[25]

Indeed, all that has happened is for a loving purpose, to which Israel has hitherto been blind and deaf.

And now he is swept away by the inspiring power of his prophetic dream.[26] This purpose is a far greater thing than anyone before him had envisioned. God has a wondrous task for Israel to fulfill—a task that she was not ready for in the past, a task that she could never have carried out had she not experienced the purging fire of suffering. He will lovingly guide her in this new and privileged role. For the restoration of His people, which He has now called Cyrus of Persia to decree, is no mere reëstablishment of the Jews in Palestine as of yore; that would be far too petty a thing to justify the momentous events that God's right arm has executed. A great plan is revealed in the scattering of His people to the ends of the earth, in the shifts of empire as God's judgment falls upon one proud nation after another, and in the rise now to power (in the victory of Persia) of a leader equipped to play a part in His forgiveness and restoration as the earlier rulers had played a part in His stern and righteous punishment.

So now we are ready to consider his answers one by one. What does it mean to be God's chosen people? He did choose Israel; the faith that such is the case is not mistaken. That is the reason why her punishment was so severe. No other people could have endured it, nor could they have learned the lesson from it that God wanted men to learn. For there is a breath-taking import in being His chosen people that has not been discerned before; but if the Jews can glimpse it now their sorrows and sufferings will fade away, and they will be filled with gratitude and joy and new energy for the future. They will realize as never before the greatness and goodness of the God who is doing all this for their sake and for the sake of the world.

> He says, "It is too slight a thing for your being my servant
> That I should but raise up the tribes of Jacob,
> And restore the survivors of Israel;

So I will make you a light of the nations,
That my salvation may reach to the end of the earth."[27]

By this time Second Isaiah has introduced the new concept by which he expresses this reinterpreted relation of Israel to Yahweh. She is His "servant," who has been scattered in exile to the ends of the earth so that her return to Jerusalem will display to all nations His glorious purpose in her restoration, and make possible this new service on her part to them all. To be sure, hitherto she has been blind and deaf to this calling; but now she has been refined in the furnace of suffering and her eyes and ears will be opened. God will pour His spirit upon her so that she can fill this new role. And what is the essence of that role? To bring the light of truth to all nations, to show them the way to justice, to lead prisoners out of bondage, to establish peace and unity throughout the world in common worship of Yahweh and under the inspired leadership of His servant.

How is all this to be accomplished? Here, as we might expect, Second Isaiah answers in the words of poetry and drama rather than in those of systematic theology. But the answer is none the less crucial; it is the culmination of his message and of the whole philosophy toward which the earlier chapters point. It is given in the famous passage which begins with the thirteenth verse of Chapter 52 and ends with the final verse of Chapter 53. In the first three verses of this answer God is supposed to be speaking; He describes the role of His servant and promises its full success. Then the other peoples speak, reporting their first impressions of Israel's fate, the lessons that they had learned from it, and the spiritual interpretation that they had finally come to give. In the last two verses God speaks again, summarizing this interpretation and pledging to the servant his appropriate reward for having accepted the tragic and redeeming role in obedience, humility, and joy.

Lo! my servant shall prosper,
He shall be exalted, and lifted up, and shall be very high.

As many were amazed at him—
So marred was his appearance beyond that of a man,
And his form beyond that of the sons of men—
So shall he startle many nations,
On account of him kings shall shut their mouths;
For what has not been told them shall they see,
And what they have not heard shall they contemplate. . . .

The fruit of his suffering shall he see, and be satisfied;
Through his affliction shall my servant, the righteous one,
Bring righteousness to many,
And he shall bear their guilt.
Therefore will I divide him a portion with the great,
And with the strong shall he share the spoil;
Because he poured out his lifeblood to the utmost,
And was numbered with the transgressors,
While he bore the sin of many,
And made intercession for the transgressors.*

If now we translate this inspired poetry into the prosaic language of theology, how shall its meaning be expressed? The task is not easy. Christian theology, several centuries later, took these verses as a forecast of the sufferings and death of Jesus, in their significance for the redemption of the world. Can we recapture what Second Isaiah himself presumably meant?

When I attempt such a recapture, the interpretation takes the following form: Suffering can purify an individual or a people—if it is accepted as a just punishment and as part of a loving divine plan. This, Second Isaiah hopes and believes, is now Israel's experience, and if so the baptism that she has undergone will give her a new spiritual stature; it will awaken a new power to lose herself in loving concern for the other peoples of the world, a new capacity for leadership in the regeneration of mankind. The other nations, watching events

* Isaiah 52:13—53:12, omitting the verses in which the other nations speak.

as they unfold, at first despise and condemn her—so insignificant she looks in her impotence to protect herself from invasion, in her disfigurement as she meets defeat and humiliation. But the spiritual greatness that she has attained shines
through her agony and sorrow. They are startled; soon they
catch a reverential sense of the transfigured character that
she has come to embody. They respond to the appeal of that
character; they identify with it; it becomes their own ideal.
And as they respond and identify, they repent of their sin-
fulness and turn to Israel's God. They are reborn, and thus
in their own turn redeemed from sin without needing to pass
through the suffering that would otherwise inevitably befall
them. Israel has become their teacher and leader in the worship of God and the true path to salvation. In this way her
dire agony will not only atone for her own sin but also become a vicarious atonement for the sins of others. In her pain
she bore the pains that they would have had to bear but now
will not need to bear. She has realized a sense of loving oneness with them in their spiritual quest, which gives new
meaning to her own harrowing experience and endows it
with redemptive power in relation to the experience of others.
She has become a center of light, truth, love, and peace to
the whole world, which can now find salvation through her.

In the last two chapters of his prophecy Second Isaiah
dwells again on the new value that this vision can spell for
his exiled people. If they can see in these terms what is unfolding, all the pains that they have borne will be transmuted
into joy; though it was a bitter and unbearable evil when it
happened, their tragedy has now been transformed into a
great good which without it would be impossible—a great
good for them because it is a great good for the world. Believing them worthy of this tremendous role, God shows that
He loves them with a specially tender as well as undying
love; He sees them able to realize this new ideal of the
covenant relation, and to mediate His redeeming love to the
rest of the world. And so this inspired poet ends on the note

of wondering amazement in the presence of this vision of
God's purpose through history.

Let the wicked forsake his way,
And the unrighteous man his thoughts;
And let him return to the LORD, that he may have pity upon
  him,
And to our God, for he shall abundantly pardon.
"For my thoughts are not your thoughts,
Nor are your ways my ways," is the oracle of the LORD;
"But as the heavens are higher than the earth,
So are my ways higher than your ways,
And my thoughts than your thoughts."[28]

The Jewish people as a people were not quite able to accept such a sublime role. Indeed, no nation has yet been able
to do so; the nearest approximation to it is India's nonviolent
struggle for independence under the prophetic leadership of
Mahatma Gandhi, and the friendly and hopeful relation between India and Britain in which that successful struggle has
issued. But Second Isaiah's vision entered as a significant factor into the ideal of the postexilic prophets, some of whom
picture in analogous terms the spiritual leadership of restored
Jerusalem, with the Jews guiding other peoples to peace and
unity in worship of Yahweh.[29] And we shall see in the next
chapter how, at a critical point in Jesus' thinking, it provided
his needed clue. In its most prominent character, the religion
of postexilic Israel became a revised legalism, preserving as
much of the ritual structure of the past as could be practiced
under the altered social conditions which the Jews then faced,
and reinterpreting it in harmony with the major emphases of
the prophetic teaching.

F. BETWEEN THE PROPHETS AND JESUS

Our purpose in this book does not allow us to follow the
course of Jewish religion as it separates from its daughter-
faith Christianity and continues through history, guided by
the commentaries and philosophical interpretations of its rab-
bis and scholars. But for the sake of completing the essential
background of the emergence of Christianity, three develop-

ments subsequent to the time of Second Isaiah must be briefly noted.

One is the appearance, and powerful influence in Jewish thought and feeling, of the so-called Messianic hope. We have observed that since the beginning of their religious life the Jews as a people had been characterized by an unusually vivid historical consciousness, involving cherished memories of the past and ambitious expectations for the future. This consciousness, with special reference to its hope for blessings to come, was intensified during the exile and the partial restorations which followed it, the change being encouraged by an element in the thought of the prophets. With the possible exception of Amos, these men had not taught that the calamity of wholesale national punishment was the last word in Yahweh's dealing with His people. A "remnant" would be preserved through the period of defeat and captivity, to become the nucleus of a reëstablished kingdom, in which the divine favor would once more be made evident to the world. This reëstablishment was to be carried out—so many thought— by a scion of the house of David, who might also be equipped with supernatural powers which no earthly force could resist. In the later literature and the expectant conversation of the populace this awaited deliverer was spoken of as the "Messiah," that is, the "Anointed One." As to the nature of the coming kingdom and the work of the Messiah there were varied conceptions. Many pictured the kingdom as essentially a renewed epoch of material prosperity for Israel, accompanied by severe punishment of her oppressors.[30] Those few who were most profoundly influenced by prophetic ideas conceived it as fundamentally a spiritual achievement, inaugurating a period in which the resettlement of Palestine and the rebuilding of the Temple would make possible the mediation by Israel of the worship and love of Yahweh to all peoples.

As the preceding statement indicates, the Messianic hope was significant mainly to the Jewish nation as a nation; it possessed value to the individual only through the anticipated reëstablishment of the kingdom of which he was a member and his imaginative participation in that new national life. But the development of a satisfying personal religion after the exile naturally affected the doctrine of a future hope. For some it led to a conception of individual immortality, ghostly Sheol as the underground abode of the dead becoming replaced, for them, by the ideas of hell and heaven with which the Christian world is now familiar. Hell was pictured as a place of everlasting torment for the stubbornly disobedient; heaven as the perfect fulfillment of the blessings of filial intimacy with Yahweh, of which His faithful worshiper has gained a foretaste in this life.[31] Some added a doctrine of the resurrection of those who had died in the past.[32] The conception of a last judgment was usually connected with this teaching; at the arrival of the Messiah all the dead will arise from their graves and be judged according to their deeds in the flesh along with those then living, the righteous entering into the full joy of the kingdom and the wicked being consigned to outer perdition.

The second is that during the period now under consideration certain ideas entered Hebrew religion, or a redirection and new prominence were given to old ideas, which many scholars trace to the influence of Zoroastrianism, the religion of the Persians at the time they conquered Babylon and occupied the position of foremost world power. Among such ideas are those of a final judgment and of the resurrection of the dead, just mentioned; the conception of a host of angels and archangels attending Yahweh and serving as His agents or messengers; and the notion of a personal devil, leader of the powers of evil, who wars against Yahweh and tempts men into sin. According to the Hebrew interpretation, this devil had originally been an angel in heaven who became the instigator of a rebellion against God. He and his demonic cohorts had been cast out to the lower regions where they now carry on their nefarious activities; they are destined in time to be reduced to impotence by Yahweh's power and consigned to eternal punishment. All these ideas entered Christian thought and became part of the background of Jesus' teaching; the belief in the Messiah determined his conception of his own historic role.

The third is the beginning of the process, during this period, of committing to writing the oral traditions that were accumulating, and of developing the extensive commentaries on the oral heritage that became later known as the Talmud. This development took place both in Palestine and in Babylon; already in Jesus' day eminent scholars were engaging in this task of elucidation and detailed interpretation of the law, as revised in accordance with the message of the prophets. The two outstanding men at that time in Palestine were Hillel and Shammai, high officials of the Sanhedrin. The last-named exemplified, in general, a conservative and rigorous legalistic standpoint, but Hillel's philosophy was quite in line with the inward spirit and ethical idealism of the great prophets. His thought appears to have exercised a profound influence upon Jesus; much of the detailed teaching of the latter as recorded in the Synoptic Gospels expresses the major ideas of Hillel's moral theology.

In 1947 the first of the now famous "Dead Sea Scrolls" were discovered in caves near the shore of that inland lake. It is too early as yet to assess the bearing of these discoveries on the general picture of the development of Jewish religion during the period which we now have in mind. It is clear, however, that they provide much fuller information than had been available before on textual problems in the Old Testament and on the life, discipline, and beliefs of the Essene communities which flourished near the Dead Sea during the century and a half preceding Jesus' ministry.* Also, they indicate possible sources of many items of Jesus' teaching as recorded in the Gospels, and in some cases raise new problems regarding their interpretation.

* The Essenes were one of the four main religious groups in Palestine at this time. In general, they emphasized an ascetic and quietistic withdrawal from the world, in expectant hope of the Messiah's coming. See p. 371.

XII

Christianity

A. RELIGION IN THE HELLENISTIC ERA

The prophetic development in Judaism that we have followed constitutes the greatest single factor in the background of Christianity, so far as concerns its distinctive genius as a civilized religion. But there are many other factors too, some of which will need to be mentioned later as our story of the formation of basic Christian ideas unfolds. One of these factors is the theological orientation of the Greek philosophers, especially Plato, Aristotle, and Plotinus; another is the organizational and administrative capacity of Rome as it finds reflection in Catholic doctrine and ecclesiastical practice. In time, too, the dominant interests of European peoples in the north and west played a part in reshaping Christianity into its contemporary forms.

However, we are concerned at present with what this religion was at the time of its birth. The most important further process that must be mastered besides those already surveyed is the permeation of the eastern Mediterranean world by Greek culture in the wake of Alexander's conquests, and the free flow, within the matrix provided by that cultural unification, of religious ideas, symbols, and aspirations from all over the known world in syncretic interaction with each other.

Alexander died in 323 B.C. His unwieldy empire quickly broke up into satrapies ruled by his generals, and in the course of the following centuries they were gradually absorbed under the power of Rome. But these political and military changes did not check the steady penetration of North Africa and western Asia by the characteristic features of Greek culture. Barriers to travel and trade between one part of this wide area and another largely disappeared; the same process of intensive interaction that in our day is beginning on a planetwide scale took place at this time over that extensive segment of the world. The Jews, who had maintained political independence from 166 to 63 B.C., when they were subjugated by the Romans, clung to their established ways in religion, family life, and certain economic habits, but in other respects they too were strongly influenced by the new cultural patterns that were coming to dominate their neighbors.

What was the effect of this drastic historical upheaval on religion? Essentially, it was a threefold effect.

In the first place, it meant throughout this vast region a more or less radical disruption of the traditional religious ways that had given support, guidance, and emotional security. There was everywhere a loosening from habitual beliefs and practices; to an increasing number of people these no longer seemed adequate to their religious needs.

In the second place, it brought a deepening of the religious hunger itself, especially in the more sensitive souls. When men and women were torn from their moorings in the cozy communities and local cults which had enfolded them in the past, they became conscious both of frightening evils and of wonderful possibilities in the larger world into which they were emerging. Even at best, the old faiths more and more proved inadequate to the aspirations that were taking form in this revolutionary and challenging crisis. People were hungering for a religion which would do more than meet, on a more substantial basis, the needs that had been met by their ancient cults; they longed for a faith that would satisfy these larger hopes and release the moral and spiritual energies of which keen spirits were becoming aware.

In the third place, in this maelstrom of Hellenistic civilization, religions from all quarters, new and old, were mingling and competing with each other for the privilege of meeting this need and becoming the faith of the future. They expanded eagerly and unpredictably from wherever had been their source—in Rome or Egypt, in Greece or Mesopotamia, even in faraway Persia and perhaps India. Together they came, in confused and kaleidoscopic interaction. Some held rigidly to their past forms, but many were able to abandon what was out of tune with the yearnings of the age and to adopt ideas and practices from each other. In this process new cults were constantly appearing; most of them achieved only temporary success, but some became serious competitors in the struggle for religious survival and victory.

It was in this setting that Christianity appeared, and it was in this rivalry for the souls of men that Christianity finally proved the victor. We shall not understand it adequately unless we understand those forces in it that account for its success in a historical challenge of unequaled intensity and magnitude.

B. THE LIFE OF JESUS, AS TOLD IN THE SYNOPTIC GOSPELS

The New Testament is the source book for the origin of Christianity as a distinctive faith. It is not a large book, and its writings with a few minor exceptions fall into three groups. The primary source for our knowledge of the life and teaching of Jesus is the first three Gospels, which tell a common story and emphasize the continuity of his role with that of the earlier Jewish prophets. Then there is the Gospel of John, together with the other Johannine writings, which give a radically different picture of Jesus and enable us to appreciate those features of Christianity which led to its break with Judaism and enabled it to become a world religion. Finally, there are the letters of Paul, the thirteenth Apostle and first great Christian missionary. The book entitled the "Acts of the Apostles" may well be included with these letters, since except for its early chapters its aim is to tell the story of his missionary travels. Of these three groups of materials Paul's letters were the first to be written in the form in which we now have them, but in a clarifying exposition of basic Christian ideas it will be best to consider them last. We want at the beginning the most authentic picture possible of the life of Jesus, and this means that it is the first three Gospels rather than either John or Paul to which we shall directly turn.

But even before the details of this picture are drawn we must square accounts once more with the problem of the higher criticism, and must explain why John needs to be separated from the other Gospels. For, as it makes profound differences in our interpretation of the Old Testament whether we construe its information under the guidance of the traditional assumption of complete infallibility or under the guidance of the higher criticism, so it makes a profound difference in our interpretation of the New Testament Gospels which of these assumptions we adopt. There are four of these Gospels; each offers its own account of the Master's biography, and naturally there are interesting similarities and differences between the four stories. From the pre-higher-critical standpoint, the central problem of interpretation consisted in working out what was known as a "harmony" of the Gospels—that is, a single biography of the Nazarene teacher which would include the material from all four books without duplicating accounts of the same event.

Difficulties in this enterprise arose at two points. For one thing, descriptions which obviously refer to the same occurrence are often discrepant in some particulars. The method in such cases was to add the discrepant features to each other wherever they are not flatly inconsistent; if this proved impossible, to assume that the contradictions arose from errors by copyists of the early manuscripts. For another thing, the historical sequence of events is not always the same. This is a special difficulty when John is compared with the other Gospels, but even they do not entirely agree with each other in this respect.

For the same reason that I have followed the method of the higher criticism in dealing with the scriptures of the East and with the Old Testament, I shall follow it in constructing the story of Jesus from the Gospels of the New Testament. What does this concretely mean? Well, in the first place, it means that we shall have to consider the life of Jesus from two stand-points—that reflected in the first three Gospels and that reflected in the Gospel of John. For the two standpoints, while having much in common, are yet so radically different that it is confusing rather than clarifying to examine the pictures that they give as though they constituted a single account. And, so far as concerns the dependability of these two pictures as a source of historical knowledge, the higher critic finds that the account given in John is so obviously colored by certain meta-physical ideas absent from previous Jewish thinking but prominent in late Hellenistic philosophy that he sets it aside as in the main of little historical reliability in comparison with the account given in the other Gospels. Whatever may be the case with much of the detailed material now included in it, the book itself, according to him, is a late product, written not earlier than the second Christian century, and designed in part to meet philosophies then spreading among Gentile Christians which held that the divine Word through which men are saved is not to be identified with the man Jesus and never appeared in a tangible human form. Hence, biographies of Jesus written from his point of view depend primarily on the material from Matthew, Mark, and Luke, and follow a chronological sequence developed from their account.

But these three Gospels (known as the "Synoptic" Gospels) themselves exhibit striking similarities and differences, which suggest a very definite theory for explaining the main facts. Mark, the shortest of the three, is included almost entire in Matthew, and half of it is included in Luke. By the word "included" two things are meant. First, not only are the same events described in essentially the same manner and order, but there are also extensive coincidences in the language used, such as would hardly be expected if there were not a common source of the three accounts. Second, when the slight alterations, additions, and abbreviations in this common material are examined in detail, practically all of them are readily explained if it is assumed that Mark's version existed first and was used by Matthew and Luke, while the contrary assumption leads to puzzling difficulties. It is thus concluded that Mark's was the first Gospel to exist in substantially its present form. When, further, the non-Marcan portions of Matthew and Luke are compared, exactly the same situation appears again. Not quite half of this part of Matthew and slightly less than a third of this part of Luke reveal such identities in language as to indicate a second common source besides Mark, and a source already existing in Greek as well as in the original Aramaic. This source consists entirely of sayings and discourses of Jesus, and since nothing is known about its author it is referred to in scholarly discussions as Q.* When Mark and Q are set aside, there remains somewhat less than a third of Matthew which appears to be derived from sources unique to the first Gospel, while almost exactly half of Luke was drawn from materials used only by him.

Now when, on the basis of these results, one raises the question when and why these Gospels were written, the answer given by the higher critic, derived mainly from internal evidence, runs about as follows: Mark was written not far from A.D. 65, probably at Rome. Its selection from available narratives about Jesus and sayings by him, and its characteristic emphases, were determined mainly by the

* The first letter of *Quelle*, the German word meaning "source."

problems confronting the Roman church at that time. Q was written sometime between A.D. 45 and 65, probably in Antioch, and reflects the need felt by Gentile Christians in Asia Minor for teachings of Jesus which would provide authoritative guidance in dealing with their perplexities. Matthew was written at Jerusalem sometime in the seventies. Its typical emphases are those that would be expected of a Jewish Christian moved by vigorous hostility to the Pharisees and anxious about problems of ecclesiastical organization and authority. Luke was written last of the three, probably in Caesarea sometime between A.D. 80 and 95. Its selection of details and its emphasis are what we should expect from a humanitarian, home-loving Gentile Christian who was conscious of the main problems that were coming to affect the Gentile Christian communities.

The higher critic observes that both Matthew and Luke, in their corrections of Mark, not only improve his style but also remove implications which seem to detract from Jesus' power and insight, or which reflect upon the loyalty and good sense of the disciples. He naturally concludes that other corrections of the same sort were probably already made in the original documents of Mark and Q, so that the actual life and teaching of Jesus cannot now be recovered with complete assurance.

Hence, from the higher-critical point of view, a student of Jesus' life has to do the best he can in drawing together the threads from this varied material and reconstructing the career of one of the towering spiritual figures of history under their leading. What this means in practice is that one must form, by patient study and restudy of every detail, the most plausible total picture that he can, and then interpret each event and saying in its light. Let us leave aside then, for the time being, the account given in John's Gospel, and I will share with my readers the story which, it seems to me, is told in the Synoptics—the story I judge to be, more probably than any other, historically true.

Paradoxical as it may sound, Jesus was born about 5 B.C. The paradox arises from the fact that, when the method of computing time now taken for granted in Christian countries was established several centuries later, and the date of his birth was fixed, a mistake of a few years was made. Palestine had been under Roman mastery not quite sixty years; the Jews experienced it as a harsher, less understanding form of alien rule than any they had endured in the past, except for brief periods. Hope for supernatural deliverance by God's hand was strong; expectation of the early coming of the Messiah was intense, especially in times of unusual disappointment and tribulation.

The groups in Palestine that were religiously important included the Pharisees and Sadducees, who controlled the priestly posts of authority and prestige, and such fringe brotherhoods as the Essenes and the Zealots. The Pharisees and Sadducees were conservative champions of the revised legal system administered by the priests, the Sadducees being quite rigorous in their conformity to every traditional detail, while the Pharisees were willing to make compromises here and there in the interest of peaceful adjustment to changed circumstance. The Zealots were fanatical rebels who, in their uncompromising refusal to recognize any master except God and any tax except to the Temple, broke out from time to time in violent but futile hostility to Roman rule. The Essenes, as intimated in the preceding chapter, were nonviolent on principle. They lived in ascetic withdrawal from the world, practicing celibacy and communism,* engaging in spiritual discipline, and patiently awaiting the coming of the Messiah. And of course, besides these influential groups, there appeared vigorous prophetic individuals who belonged to no organized movement, but brought some distinctive message of guidance and hope which they were sure came from God. Such a prophetic preacher was John the Baptist, who, when Jesus had reached his later twenties, appeared beyond

* In the original meaning of the word.

the Jordan River, proclaiming the early coming of God's Kingdom and calling upon his hearers to repent of their sins in preparation for this great event. He encouraged them also to accept baptism in the river as a symbol of their transformed attitude toward God and His will for the world. John was an ascetic in his own way, and was very likely influenced by the Essenes, but he did not approve the passivity of their program; nor did he accept the Zealot assumption that the heart of Israel's problem lay in her irksome and humiliating submission to Rome.

Jesus grew to manhood in a humble carpenter's family living at Nazareth, participating no doubt in the duties of a carpenter's vocation but pondering deeply the religious and moral needs of his people. He and his family were aware of all the factors and forces just described, but did not succumb to the appeal of any sectarian dogmatism; they practiced a simple and devout piety which expressed itself in kindliness toward all men and in faithful performance of those ceremonial obligations that seemed to them important. Luke gives an absorbing account of Jesus at the age of twelve; his parents, who had lost him on a trip to Jerusalem, finally found him in the Temple, listening to the teachers and asking eager questions. Except for this incident, however, we know nothing of the inner searchings of his soul until he commenced his active ministry some fifteen years later.

He had heard of John's preaching and went out to listen to the fiery prophet, perhaps several times. Something in his own nature, and the deposit of his silent broodings over the years, responded more and more deeply to John's message. He believed that John was right—that the Kingdom of Heaven was at hand and that the important thing for all who love righteousness was inward spiritual renewal in preparation for that great event. That renewal must be deep and thoroughgoing; it must affect the whole of one's life. He submitted to baptism at John's hands, and as he emerged from the water experienced an overpowering sense of God's

favor and God's call to share in John's work. The vision
may have had even further significance to him; at least it
led him to retire to the wilderness where he could prayer-
fully ponder the call instead of moving him to start his
mission at once. We may surmise that he felt a need to
clarify the differences between his own convictions and
those of John, and that it was during this period that the
fully trustful attitude toward God that underlay all his
later life and teaching was securely established.

His three major divergences from John are of vital importance. For one thing, he could be no ascetic. Even more
than the Old Testament prophets he was sure that nature,
with all her bounty and beauty, is God's creation—to be accepted gratefully, trusted joyously, and used discerningly
in the happy service of God and one's neighbor. Nothing in
her is to be rejected as intrinsically evil, as spiritually cor-
rupting. For another, he was not satisfied with John's method,
the method of making the world come to him if it wanted
to hear his words. Jesus loved the common people, among
whom he had toiled as a carpenter; many, he knew, were too
harassed by daily burdens to travel away from home, and
many who would not be willing actively to search for spiritual truth would yet be moved by the message if it were
brought to them. He determined to carry the good news of
God's early coming to the people, wherever they were, so
that all who might respond would have their opportunity
and that none who failed to respond would have any excuse
on the awesome day of judgment. And, finally, he felt the
need of a clearer and fuller content for the crucial phrase in
John's preaching—"Kingdom of Heaven." We cannot confidently tell just what this phrase meant to John beyond the
supernatural intervention by God in the world to establish
His rulership over men. But, as Jesus' many parables about
the Kingdom indicate, he saw that it was important to
give it a more definite and spiritual meaning than John had
presumably been able to provide.

So Jesus' ministry begins. He preaches John's message, too —"Repent, for the Kingdom of Heaven is at hand"—but in this altered setting. He seeks responsive individuals wherever he can find them, and he especially seeks them in the synagogues, where he knows that sincerely pious folk would resort of a Sabbath day and would be most ready to respond to his words. He gathers a group of close disciples around him for more intimate teaching, twelve in number, and he noticeably selects them neither from persons of recognized religious position nor from sophisticated intellectuals, but from poor and humble toilers like himself—fishermen, artisans, a tax collector—and it is interesting that he includes a Zealot or two in the group. It was his constant conviction throughout his ministry that what most stands in the way of sincere penitence and wholehearted trust in God is pride of status and of achievement; those who are most like children in their innocence of such smug feelings, in their simplicity and freshness, in their open responsiveness to instruction, were the ones to whom he was sure he could appeal. He conceived that his mission was to his own people rather than to human beings elsewhere. This was not because he did not believe that God's loving purpose included the whole of mankind, nor because he thought that non-Jews were incapable of a pure will and entrance upon a right relation to God. Many of his sayings would be inconsistent with the former belief, and such beautiful stories as that of the good Samaritan would hardly accord with the latter. But he was steadily convinced that he had been commissioned to reach as many as he could of his own countrymen, preparing them for the day of God's coming in judgment. God's purpose for the world as a whole would no doubt in time be disclosed, and the role that his own people were expected to play in it would become clear, but at present the prime task was to bring about the spiritual regeneration of the Jews. This was absolutely vital it they were to fill the holy task which God was expecting them to carry out. And there was a terrible urgency in the situation, he felt; it might even be impossible to reach all the Jews before the momentous day of judgment dawned. In fact, when he sent out his disciples to share his preaching ministry he explicitly predicted that the Son of Man would appear to inaugurate God's Kingdom before they succeeded in covering all the cities of Israel.[1]

Hence it was somewhat perturbing to him (although satisfyingly instructive also) to discover, as his ministry developed, that many non-Jews responded to his teaching with sincere faith while many Jews rejected and spurned him. This gradually led him to the radical conviction—evident in several of his later parables—that in view of Israel's increasingly definite refusal to accept and follow his way, God would take from her the special role that He had called her to fill and would give it to others who were more ready to bring forth fruits meet for repentance.[2] He felt sure that the common people would respond to him, despite their blindness, apathy, and toilsome preoccupations, were it not for the fact that they were led astray by their spiritual leaders—the scribes and the Pharisees—who, in their hypocrisies and injustices, their pride of position and power, their complete failure to sense the true inward meaning of God's commandments, and their suspicion of his growing influence, were obstructing his work and making it far less effective than it could have been. Hence his consuming love and compassion for the common folk came to involve an increasingly severe and bitter condemnation of those who should be guiding them toward righteousness and a happy realization of God's forgiveness, but who instead were leading them down to the pit of destruction.

But as he spread his message, with daily prayerful assurances of God's presence, and as he felt the peace and happiness growing in his own heart as well as in the penitent and loyal hearts of those who fully accepted his teaching, a new insight came more and more to the fore—a radical insight which carries religious thinking beyond anything clearly grasped by the prophets before him. This idea is implied in many of his sayings and parables, and is explicitly taught by a very revealing passage in Luke.[3] Some of the Pharisees had asked him when the Kingdom of God would come, and Luke reports him to have replied: "The Kingdom of God is not coming visibly, and people will not say, 'Look, here it is!' or 'There it is!' for the Kingdom of God is within you." It would be a mistake to interpret this verse as meaning that Jesus gave up the belief that the Kingdom was destined to appear in external form, with a day of judgment at which the righteous would be rewarded and the wicked punished. All the evidence indicates that he continued to hold, with his predecessors, that God's righteous control of history would at the appropriate time be demonstrated in a form that is obvious to all, involving the display of irresistible political and physical power.[4] But while the earlier prophets (and perhaps Jesus himself at the beginning of his ministry) had thought of this dramatic occasion as constituting the essence of the coming of the Kingdom, this verse shows that Jesus had come to think in different terms. To put the new idea somewhat paradoxically, preparation for the Kingdom in one's heart, so far as it is sincere and genuine, *is* the Kingdom itself. That is, if any human soul undergoes true repentance and is inwardly transformed from a state of disobedience to one of trustful obedience toward God, and from a selfish attitude to a spirit of love and friendliness toward all his fellows, so far as he is concerned the Kingdom *has* come and is no longer something to be waited for in the future. He has realized the inner integrity, the filial relation to God, the spiritual brotherhood with others, that bring complete joy, peace, and happiness. He is already in the Kingdom, and nothing more needs to happen for it to be fully real so far as his individual experience is concerned. From this point of view, the external manifestations that will be displayed on the day of judgment are not the essence of the Kingdom's appearance but simply visible symbols and a dramatic confirmation of the inward reality that has already dawned. In the Gospel of John, as we shall see, this thought becomes even more central, determining the very meaning of salvation and of the spiritual life.

Almost from the beginning of his ministry, Jesus found in himself a power that he had not anticipated and which led, first to puzzled reflection, and gradually to the settled conviction that he was the promised Messiah. This was the power to heal many cases of illness, especially of the epileptic, paralytic, or psychosomatic types. His trust in God and his faith in others were so complete that they were infectious; they spread to the sufferers from such ailments, so that under the invigorating power of his faith many of the sick were cured. Jesus welcomed these phenomena for the beneficent blessing that they betokened, but he was perturbed by them. What did they mean, about himself, and about his role in history? He bade those who were healed to keep their experience to themselves, that he might not be so overwhelmed by seekers for his help that there would be no time for prayerful pondering on this problem. If the accounts given of his temptation in the wilderness are authentic, he had even then thought of the possibility that the vision at his baptism meant that he was the Messiah. But then he had rejected any assumption of miraculous power, as out of accord with true trust in God's care and guidance. Now, it seemed, God was spontaneously revealing such power through him, and in a form which he could not distrust since it showed itself in the merciful healing of those in need. Perhaps, he thought, this was God's confirmation of that more radical interpretation of his call. Second Isaiah had pictured Israel as healer of the nations through her role as Yahweh's servant; it might then be the case that the Messiah would show that he was Son of God as well as heir of David by his power to awaken such faith as can cure the body as well as bring new life to the soul.*

Soon, however, this interpretation led to a new and very

* This is my suggested reading of such material as we have in Matthew 8 and 9.

difficult problem, which perhaps explains why it was some time before he was ready openly to accept the Messiah's role and to begin giving his disciples the instruction about it that they would need to remember in the days to come. It gradually became evident that his ministry was arousing the hostility of the priesthood and of others in authority instead of winning their acceptance and support; the possibility became more and more threatening that they would find some pretext for doing away with him as a dangerous subversive. The sudden execution of John the Baptist by Herod shocked him into the conviction that if he continued his mission among his own people this possibility would become a fated eventuality.

For some time he traveled with his disciples for the most part in regions remote, not merely from Jerusalem, but even from his familiar haunts around the Sea of Galilee. How could this dire outcome of his ministry be reconciled with his being the Messiah? Not only the popular but also the more spiritual conceptions of the Messiah expected the display through him of God's power and glory; they did not at all envision his suffering death. But Second Isaiah, already the portion of Old Testament prophecy that Jesus had found most illuminating, gave him the clue to this difficult problem. Our hint on this vital point is contained in a passage in Mark which is omitted in Luke, and restated in Matthew so that the clue is there lost. "Does not the Scripture say of the Son of Man that he will suffer much and be rejected?"[5] When we interpret this in the light of Jesus' subsequent action and instruction to his disciples, the clarifying idea which it reveals, and which gave him confident orientation through the dark hours that lay ahead, was, I believe, as follows:

It was a mistake to suppose that the Messiah, in his first appearance before men, was to usher in the Kingdom in obvious, political form. His task, in this part of his career, was to preach the good news, to heal the sick, to bring comfort and hope, to persuade as many as possible to realize the essential inward conditions of the Kingdom's coming. And just as Israel had to go through the fire of suffering and defeat in order to be purified so that she could really fill the glorious future role of Yahweh's servant, so he must go through the agony of torture and death in order to be fully prepared for the Messiah's cosmic role. Moreover, just as, by her willing acceptance of the painful purification and by the transformed character which she would then exhibit, Israel could vicariously redeem the other nations of the world, so by his acceptance of rejection and suffering he could bring vicarious ransom to other individuals. They would be saved by the pouring out of his blood on the cross for them. But the Messiah's cosmic role, centering around the day of judgment when the reality of God's rule through him would be blazoned forth for all to see, is only postponed—it will not be omitted. After his death on the cross he would be raised from the dead and would ascend to heaven, whence at the appointed time he would come once more to earth, this time displaying in full measure the power and authority of God, as a recompense for his willing acceptance of anguish and humiliation in his first earthly career. As Paul expresses the same thought twenty-five years later:

And being found in fashion as a man, he humbled himself, and became obedient unto death, even the death of the cross. Wherefore God also hath highly exalted him, and given him a name which is above every name: that at the name of Jesus every knee should bow, of things in heaven, and things in earth, and things under the earth; and that every tongue should confess that Jesus Christ is Lord, to the glory of God the Father.[6]

So now he was ready to go forward, ready to complete his first earthly mission in trustful acceptance of God's will and in loving concern for his followers. He and his disciples headed toward Jerusalem, after he had made sure of their convinced faith in his Messiahship. His purpose now was to force the issue with the titular religious leaders of his people.

Knowing that he was destined to torture and death, and prepared to accept this fate in humble trust in the Divine Father, he determined upon a public avowal that he was the Messiah, in Jerusalem, at the feast of the Passover, when thousands of earnest pilgrims were gathered there. The priests and officials of the Sanhedrin would be compelled either to acknowledge him or to display their stubborn rejection of his message for all the world and all history to see. As for the common people, he understood compassionately their fickleness and the ease with which they could be misled—they would respond hopefully with hosannas to his Messianic claim, and yet, a few hours later, they would beg Pilate to release the robber Barabbas and condemn him to the cross.

His main thought, during these last days, was devoted to his disciples. He tried to make them face the dire events that he foresaw would happen; he tried to explain their significance for his fulfillment of the Messiah's task and for the redemption of the world. He tried to establish sufficient insight in them so that they could give him the sympathetic support for which he so desperately longed and could meet any future eventuality with calm assurance and devoted faith. This yearning hope was destined to be completely dashed, as events moved rapidly toward their tragic climax. The disciples could not understand how such a tragedy might be a part of the founding of the Messiah's Kingdom; their attachment to him was blind and uncomprehending. Even the three who were closest to him failed—Peter, James, and John. They showed their spiritual obtuseness on the way to Jerusalem;[7] still, in his eager longing for support just before his arrest, he leaves the others and takes these three with him to the heart-rending hour in the Garden of Gethsemane, where he prayed, "Father, take this cup from me; nevertheless, not my will, but thine, be done." He hoped that they, at least, could watch with him, share with him, give him the sense of understanding companionship with which he could undergo anything triumphantly—but instead, in their weariness, they fell asleep. And here the spiritual greatness was revealed that has made him the object of affectionate adoration for Christians ever since; when he returns from his prayer and finds them asleep he does not condemn them, instead his heart overflows in tender understanding of their limitations and their weakness: "Were you not able to watch for one hour? You must all watch, and pray that you may not be subjected to trial. One's spirit is eager, but human nature is weak."[8] And yet, perhaps he sensed that despite their dullness and blindness they would, through the very force of his loving trust in them, exemplify in the future the insight and comprehending loyalty that were beyond their capacity then.

He was arrested and tried, condemned by the Sanhedrin as a blasphemer, and taken to the Roman governor, who, with some reluctance, handed him over to a battalion of soldiers to be crucified. In the agony of the cross there was a moment of utter and unrelieved loneliness; perhaps there had been hope that God would intervene in some miraculous way to save him. "My God, my God, why hast thou forsaken me?" But the deep faith, on which he had from the beginning staked his career and his very being, came back and upheld him as the end was at hand: "Father, into thy hands I commend my spirit."

C. THE ESSENCE OF HIS TEACHING

A brief summary of his teaching, as contained in the Synoptic Gospels, will be sufficient, since in so many respects it simply continues the basic emphases of the great prophets. In fact, one may say that this continuation is the most obvious note in the message of the Synoptics, with one important addition—Jesus is identified with the promised Messiah, so that everything naturally involved in this identification plays a part. During the early months, especially, Jesus' doctrines are set in the framework of John the Baptist's preaching: "Prepare for the new order which is soon coming by divine intervention"; and this setting is never subsequently lost. As he elaborates the meaning of this message, month by month, it becomes evident that he is deepening and enriching just those elements in the teaching of the Old Testament prophets that had proved spiritually most appealing and fertile—the elements emphasized in the ethically minded Talmudic authors. This fact is most clearly illustrated in the way his teaching exemplifies the first and third of the four characteristics of high civilized religion (see pp. 107 f., 112 ff.). We may start with this prominent aspect of his religious philosophy; so far as the first characteristic is concerned, he goes beyond the explicit statements of the earlier prophets and is quite in line with one major trend in the Talmud.

While Jesus, like the prophets, recognized the special relation of Israel to God and conceived that his mission was primarily to his own racial brethren, yet on occasion he shows in clearer form than they (excepting possibly Second Isaiah) the universalism implicit in their convictions. The familiar parable of the good Samaritan is the best illustration of this. The prophets had summarized religious duty under the two heads of wholehearted love toward God and sincere love for one's neighbor on the same terms as oneself. But who is my neighbor—another Jew, or anybody that I may meet? Jesus' answer to this question, as expressed on the occasion of this parable, is clear and unqualified. My neighbor is any human being in need, whether he belong to my race or to another.[9] And the hero of the story is, surely intentionally, not a Jew.

Jesus likewise shared the prophetic insistence that matters of ritual and ceremony must be entirely subordinated to the ethico-social requirements of justice, honesty, and mercy. His scathing diatribes against the scribes and the Pharisees were mainly concerned with this point. They are exceedingly meticulous (as he describes them) in paying their tithes,

bringing their sacrifices, and observing the ceremonial obligations of the law, but this only fosters the vices of pride and
self-righteousness. So far as concerns social obligations they
are guilty of every evil in the calendar—of fraud, bribery,
extortion, even ruthless cruelty upon the poor and unprotected.[10] Unless they renounce these sins, they shall have no
part in the Messianic community but will be consigned to
the outer darkness prepared for the devil and his angels. Not
that the ritual duties are to be quite neglected. It is a matter
of emphasis; justice, mercy, and kindness are the foremost
obligations to be fulfilled, while the others are not to be left
undone.[11]

Jesus' deepening of the prophetic transition from emphasis
on external acts to inwardness in religion is particularly notable. He interprets the significance of all religious ideas in
such wise as to focus them directly upon the inner experience of the individual. In the moral life it is the intention
that counts, not the mere deed; lustful desire is just as guilty
as adultery, and is so judged by Him who sees the thoughts
of the heart as easily as any outward act.[12] One must become
clean on the inside, not merely to an external view. The
kingdom for which all longed is not an affair of worldly
conquest and material prosperity; it comes within the heart
of each individual, and the significance of its external manifestations is just that they render vivid the judgment passed
upon each man in accordance with the true state of his inward self.[13] The basic virtues for him are the virtues expressing a heartfelt commitment to the right—sincerity, truthfulness, earnest devotion to God, justice, friendliness, love.

None the less, his emphasis on spiritual inwardness did
not mean any abandonment of the conviction that the appropriate external confirmations would come also; because
God governs the world and orders the events of history,
rewards will come to the righteous, to compensate for their
past and present sufferings, and drastic punishments to impenitent evildoers. Indeed, when we follow his teaching in

detail about God, about man, and about himself, we meet the influence of this conviction in each case. Let us outline the remainder of his philosophy under these three heads.

He conceives God as the wise, just, and all-powerful Creator of the world and controller of its history. He is Absolute Will, the ruler of nature and man. Human beings are a part of His creation and hence are completely dependent creatures; but they are also His children, since they are capable of a filial relation to Him as the rest of the creation is not. However, for Jesus, as for the earlier prophets, the most vital fact about God in His relation to man is that He is lawgiver and judge. He has laid His commandments upon man, whose righteousness therefore consists in sincere obedience to these commands and whose unrighteousness (or sin) in rebellious disobedience. He is also judge. Many events in history can be discerned to constitute tokens of His good pleasure toward the obedient and His displeasure toward the wicked; but the inequities that remain from these scattered judgments will all be corrected at the last and final day of judgment. On this tremendous occasion God, through the Messiah as His authorized representative, will finally separate the sheep from the goats, admitting the former to the joys of filial intimacy with Him while unrepentant sinners are consigned to the everlasting fire prepared for the devil and his angels. Thus, to the wicked, God is a terrifying, avenging, punishing power, while to the penitent who sincerely and earnestly seek to live in humble acceptance of the divine law He is a forgiving, loving Father, with whom a trustful and filial communion is possible. Reverence, awe, and unquestioning submission to His will are, of course, expected in His children, but these attitudes may be, and in Jesus' own case were, combined with a sense of deeply satisfying inward companionship. In his own relation to God, and in his references to Him when talking with his disciples and followers, "Father" (especially "Heavenly Father") was the favorite and constantly repeated term.

As for man, he, as child of God, is capable either of disobedience (and of stubborn persistence in it even after being summoned to repent) or of wholehearted acceptance of God's will as his own will. In the Synoptics there is no systematic doctrine about free will and no problem of predestination; it is taken for granted that anyone, in response to Jesus' preaching, is able either to reject it or to repent of his past sins and to experience God's forgiveness and kindly acceptance. In the latter case he enters upon a life in which the outstanding virtues will be faith, hope, and love, and the outstanding qualities will be peace and joy.

His faith will be trust in God—a humble and complete confidence in God's justice and in His unfailing providential care of those who have put their trust in Him. There is nothing that such faith cannot accomplish through tapping God's unlimited power; it can not only cure all manner of diseases but can even say to a mountain, "Be thou uprooted and cast into the sea."[14] His hope will be the assurance of the coming of God's Kingdom, and also the cheering expectation that just as a warmhearted human father delights in bringing all manner of satisfying gifts to his children, so God will love to give all manner of good things to those who obey and honor Him. These genial tokens of the Father's kindliness will include not only the spiritual gifts whose full realization must wait for the life beyond, but also material plenty in this life as a compensation for the deprivations and sufferings that loyalty to Him will entail.[15] And the famous promises with which the Sermon on the Mount opens give a fuller picture of what this justified hopefulness includes:

Blessed are those who feel their spiritual need, for the Kingdom of Heaven belongs to them!
Blessed are the mourners, for they will be consoled!
Blessed are the humble-minded, for they will possess the land!
Blessed are those who are hungry and thirsty for uprightness, for they will be satisfied!

Blessed are the merciful, for they will be shown mercy!
Blessed are the pure in heart, for they will see God!
Blessed are the peacemakers, for they will be called God's sons!

The culminating virtue of the child of God is love—wholehearted love toward God and brotherly love toward man. Jesus places the stamp of his unqualified approval on the two great commandments in which, according to him, the law and the prophets are summarized. Love toward God will mean not only glad submission to His will but the giving of one's whole self to Him in joyful surrender. Love to man will extend toward all without exception; but it will mean special care and compassion for those who are poor, sick, weak, or unjustly treated, and special thoughtfulness in meeting their needs in a spirit of helpful service. And it will mean also a heartfelt concern for those who act as our enemies. Love, expressed in appropriate conduct as well as in attitude, must include even them. "If you love only those who love you . . . what is there remarkable in that? But . . . love your enemies and pray for your persecutors, so that you may show yourselves true sons of your Father in heaven, for He makes His sun rise on bad and good alike, and makes the rain fall on both upright and wrongdoers."[16]

In sum, to love others is to practice sincerely the Golden Rule, treating all men as one would wish to be treated in their place; and acquiring facility in realizing what this would mean in the varied situations of life. Many of Jesus' parables, particularly in the Sermon on the Mount, aim at clarifying the implications of this principle—they emphasize forgiving others, avoiding hasty judgment, readiness for acts of service, and the need of penitent self-criticism.

The two outstanding qualities, I have said, are peace and joy. When one is disobedient to God, incapable of trusting Him and loving others, he is at war with himself; he is protecting his life at the cost of losing it—i.e., at the cost of the fear and inner torment that destroy all its value. When one renounces self-will and gives himself utterly to God, he finds that "in His will is our peace"; and he joyously accepts the world, with all its evils, as the expression of God's bounty and as the theater within which His just and loving purpose is being fulfilled. The gospel is "good news," because a responding faith brings real and assured happiness here and now—a happiness that will be perfected in the life beyond, but will not be changed in the essential blessedness that has already been realized.

We come now to Jesus' teaching about himself. This is the most difficult part of the problem of interpreting the Synoptic Gospels, for when orthodox Christian doctrines on this matter became accepted, as they soon did, all of Jesus' statements in any of the Gospels were read in their light. If we follow the account given in the Synoptics without allowing it to become affected by such later doctrines, the picture given is what one would expect from the above story of his life—especially from his acceptance of the Messiahship and his reconciliation of it with his expected suffering and death. Early in his ministry, though perhaps not at the very beginning, he refers to himself as "Son of Man" and "Son of God," and these phrases become more frequent in the later months of his preaching. Each of these phrases had previously been used in a very broad sense; but by Jesus' time each had also come to carry a narrower and technical sense, referring in this latter case specifically to the Messiah. As being a scion of the line of David—who was remembered as the great king of Israel in the golden age of her glory and prosperity—he is the Son of Man, while as wielder of the divine power and authority which will bring all nations under subjection to his rule, he is the Son of God. It was his acceptance of this latter title that constituted the ground for the formal charge against him in the Sanhedrin.[17] And because of this role he came to believe that he stood in an especially intimate relation to God: "All things have been handed over to me by my Father . . . and no one understands the Father but the Son, and those to whom the Son chooses to reveal Him."[18]

Moreover, in two very brief passages it seems clear that he came to apply to himself, as the Messiah, the role of vicarious atoner for the sins of others that Second Isaiah had assigned to Israel in her role as Yahweh's suffering servant. When Jesus was led to believe that he too must be prepared by suffering, in humble submission to God's will, to carry out the full task of the Messiah, he also believed that his suffering would become a means of redeeming other people from sin. His blood would be poured out not merely for his own purification but "for many people, for the forgiveness of their sins." Because "the Son of Man has come, not to be waited on but to wait on others, and to give his life to ransom many others."[19] Just how he conceives that this redeeming process would take place is left in considerable obscurity; no more than Second Isaiah does he offer any systematic explanation of it.

The one important further point that is clear in the synoptics is that since he is the Messiah chosen by God, a loyal and devoted attachment to himself is required as a proof of one's sincere obedience to the God who sent him and of one's authentic membership in the Kingdom over which he is destined to rule. Only those who are willing to "take up their cross and follow him" through the dark fate of rejection and suffering are worthy to sit at his right hand when he returns in heavenly glory to set up the Kingdom.[20] And during the period of his absence the way to show their devotion to him is by loving service to their brothers in need. "Inasmuch as you did it to one of the humblest of these my brethren, you did it unto me."[21]

If I were to attempt a summarizing description of Jesus' personality as it is presented in the Synoptics, I should say that it blended into unity the main characteristics of his prophetic predecessors (Amos, Hosea, Jeremiah, Second

Isaiah) and added to them the natural consequences of his conviction that he was the Messiah—a humbling sense of unworthiness for that role mixed with a self-exaltation in the consciousness that it was his role none the less. His heart is fully suffused by submission to and trust in God; it burns with a passion for righteousness as the prophetic tradition had come to conceive that basic virtue, exploding on occasion in aggressive denunciation of injustice and hypocrisy, especially as displayed in the official leaders of his people. It overflows in a tender compassion for the poor, the weak, and the oppressed, to whom he is eager to bring the good tidings of the Kingdom and the comfort of his never-failing affection. In this latter side of his nature is revealed the undiscouraged self-giving that is one of the outstanding traits of every spiritual pioneer in history. And along with these qualities he illustrates the typically prophetic intellect, realizing profundity of moral insight rather than logical precision and system. True wisdom, for Jesus, shows itself in a series of glimpses into the great lessons of life, expressed in homely parables or basic principles, and connected with each other not by strands of logic, but by a dynamic spiritual intuition. In fact, Jesus distrusted the wisdom of the wise, placing his confidence rather in the innocent responsiveness of the child-like mind in its readiness to trust the goodness that lies beyond its comprehension and its willingness to let this faith guide its growing experience and provide its criterion of true understanding. He is thoroughly human in expressing impatience at the bungling of his disciples,[22] and in his readiness to dwell at times on the grandeur of his cosmic role at the day of judgment when the shame of his rejection on his first earthly career will be compensated by the demonstrated magnitude of his divine power and authority.[23] But his gracious friendliness and love for the poor and needy pervade even his portrayal of what will happen on that momentous occasion; the proof of sincere loyalty and assurance of the heavenly kingdom will not consist in words of praise to him but in whether one has practiced loving kindness toward his human brothers.[24]

D. THE DISTINCTIVE PORTRAYAL IN THE GOSPEL OF JOHN

The above portrayal is based on what we find in the Synoptics. When one turns, as it is now our responsibility and privilege to do, to the Gospel of John, one meets a radically different picture of Jesus' personality, career, and teaching. Many of the same events that occur in the Synoptics are described, and many of the same items of teaching are included, although these common elements appear in a somewhat different order. However, all this material is presented in a sharply altered perspective, in the light of which the Christian faith takes on a quite different character from that to which it would have been bound if the Synoptic picture stood alone. As we proceed with our present task this perspective will gradually take shape and attain such clarity as is needed, but we may well begin by raising a question that can hardly fail to occur to one who studies the four Gospels attentively.

How are we to explain the striking difference that appears between the account given in John and the picture just outlined, and how far is the Johannine picture authentic? My preliminary answer to these questions is that the author of this Gospel was evidently responsive to a side of Jesus' nature which was not emphasized in the Synoptic accounts, and to a phase of his teaching which they almost completely missed. This side and this phase appear most clearly in the story of the Last Supper, graphically told in Chapters 14 to 17. But when one has absorbed the disclosure in those chapters, he sees that the same picture is present in the entire Gospel, although he likewise finds many of the traits emphasized in the Synoptics, especially Matthew.

What impressed this writer most vividly was the tender and loving concern for his disciples that Jesus had shown on the occasion of the Last Supper—his ability to transcend all anxious preoccupation with the agony that he was soon to suffer and to give himself completely to them and their needs. This note is not absent in the delineation of Jesus given in the Synoptics, but with them it does not become the major theme; to the author of John it constitutes the central revelation in the light of which he interprets the significance of the entire story of Jesus' life and death.

And this is not all; indeed, it is not the crucially important step that he took. That step lies in the fact that to him Jesus' deep, undiscouraged, trusting love, especially as shown on this occasion, provided the clue to a new interpretation of the nature of God—an interpretation that departed as radically from what had been taken for granted by the prophets and the Synoptics as that conception had departed from the Mosaic notion of God. Not that John is clearly conscious of the difference; rather, his emphasis is on the continuity of his thought with that of his predecessors. Just as the prophets felt sure that they were simply giving the true interpretation of the historical relation to Israel of the God of Abraham and Moses, so this profound thinker is sure that he is giving the true interpretation of the relation of that same God to the world at large.

In terms of basic doctrine, what this altered perspective primarily involves is a new meaning for the phrase "Son of God." The author of John does not fully anticipate the later doctrine of the incarnation, with the orthodox concept of the triune God, but he is confident that Jesus as the Son of God is not only the expected Jewish Messiah but in some spiritual sense is one with the Father. In his career on earth he represented the Father as yearning to save men from their sin and doom, not to bring judgment upon them for their disobedience. In this confidence John could also identify Jesus with the "logos" of Stoic and Alexandrian philosophy—the metaphysical agent through whom the world was originally created.* This means that Jesus' career, as described in this Gospel, is conceived in cosmic proportions; he is not merely the Messiah fulfilling the Messianic role but he is also the appearance in human form of this creative and redeeming Word which has eternally existed and is divine in a full and unqualified sense. Before Abraham was born, he was, and whoever has seen him has seen God, for he and the Father are one.[25] In John then, instead of Jesus the man, meeting his troubled perplexities in trusting faith and living through the poignant tragedy of his martyrdom, we find the heavenly Son of God marching with assurance and authority through his appointed epoch of history, the divine bearer of salvation to men.

But this altered perspective also involved a radically new conception of God Himself. I have just observed that according to John, Jesus not only represents God but in some ultimate sense is one with God. This statement gives a crucial clue to the distinctive religious philosophy in this Gospel. In its light we can see why Christianity had to break from Judaism and become something far more significant than a Jewish sect. It is relevant to note in this connection that some of the "sayings of Jesus," not found in the Gospels but preserved in the writings of the church fathers or in the Oxyrhynchus papyri,† point toward the same interpretation; in fact, a few teach a kind of metaphysical pantheism more extreme than anything hinted at in the New Testament. "Raise the stone and there thou shalt find me; cleave the wood and there am I."

What this teaching means is that instead of the essentially legal conception of God, man, sin, and salvation, which formed the dominant note in Hebrew thinking and which on the whole is taken for granted in the Synoptic Gospels, we meet here an essentially mystic conception of each of these vital

* John 1:1–18. "Logos" is the Greek term which is here translated "Word."
† Discovered in Egypt about 1900.

themes. Salvation is mystic union with God in Christ, and every other Christian doctrine is explicitly or implicitly re-interpreted in harmony with this central idea. And when this reinterpretation is clearly grasped in the case of the concept of God, its bearing on the rest of the doctrinal structure can be readily mastered.

The author of this Gospel does not mean to question or deny the traditional Jewish concept of God as a person, with whom we men may have personal relations. But while retaining the atmosphere and language appropriate to this concept, his central idea is rather that God is an infinite cosmic substance of which we are parts. Through sin we have somehow become sundered from the cosmic being to which we really belong, and salvation consists in transcending this separation and regaining union with the divine whole. To remain separate is spiritual death; to find this union with the divine is spiritual life—and eternal life, because the God with whom we become one is eternal.

But this idea, quite familiar in India and elsewhere in the East, assumes a distinctive form in its Christian interpretation as given in the Fourth Gospel. God is not just the ultimate "One" of pantheistic mysticism, nor the "Good" of mystical philosophers. Earlier Jewish and Christian theology had culminated in the thought that the essence of God's nature is love toward His creation, and that the supreme mark of spiritual perfection in man is also love, toward God and his fellow men. This love had been conceived in strictly personal terms, as the attitude of a kindly father toward his children and of brothers toward their father and one another. The Gospel of John, while retaining this picture, adds the mystic conception that God is not only loving, but is love itself as a metaphysical reality. Divine love is a substantial entity in the universe—the dynamic source of love in us—and only so far as we respond to the creative self-giving which is its essence and become one with it, so that a similar power of self-giving is born in us, do we escape spiritual death and attain spiritual life. The love of God is, so to speak, an expansive, life-giving energy pervading the universe; it reaches out to seek and win us even while we are lost in our self-caused separation from God—even while we are shrinking in upon our petty finite selves in the fear, anxiety, and hate that spell death to the soul. So far as we respond to the divine love this process is reversed and we pass from death into life—we reach beyond our separate, finite, self-centered selves and expand into oneness with the infinite spirit of love as it expresses itself everywhere in the universe. The analogue in the physical world of that divine spirit is light, which by its very nature actively penetrates the surrounding darkness and which the darkness is unable to quench.[26] The oneness does not have to wait to be realized after death; it is possible here and now for those who have been reborn in the spirit and have thus become heirs of eternal life. Hence they do not need to come up for judgment on their sins; they have already passed from sin to righteousness, from death to life.[27] They are one with God in Christ.

Now the word "death" has just been used in two senses, and a vital feature of John's philosophy will be clarified if their distinction and relation are briefly explained. There is physical death, and there is spiritual death; the former cannot be escaped, but the latter can. We emerge from our mother's womb and head toward the inevitable death of the body. But this entire process of physical life is spiritual death, if it continues to express the self-centered demandingness with its fears, frustrations, and hates that it necessarily expresses at the beginning. Our task is to seize the opportunity given us by our few years of physical life to become poignantly aware that we are spiritually dead, and to find the way by which we may pass from this death into life. That is the way of being "born again"—born into the union with God which by its very nature brings spiritual life.[28] The rite of baptism in the form of immersion is a vivid symbol of this experience. To sink under the water signifies one's realization of his state as spiritual death; to rise from the water signifies his birth into spiritual life.

So, on this interpretation, Jesus Christ is far more than the Messiah who is destined to come to judge the world and establish the new kingdom. He is the Savior of the world, but the Savior in the distinctive sense of being the cosmic and historic intermediary of God's love toward man and man's responding love toward God. He is the Son of God in a unique sense, sharer eternally of the divine nature. This Son of God assumed human form in Jesus of Nazareth, to share man's sorrows and sufferings even to death on the cross, and thus to demonstrate in dramatic and appealing form the eternal, divine, self-giving to men.[29] Through him men become one with God and with each other, as the branches find a shared life through oneness with the vine. The branches need their union with the vine to remain alive and to possess creative power; the vine needs the branches through which to bear fruit.[30] This union is physically symbolized by the Christian in the holy rite of the Lord's Supper, when he eats Christ's flesh in the form of the consecrated bread and drinks his blood in the consecrated wine.[31]

The transformation which the saved Christian undergoes is spoken of as a "new birth," analogous in the spiritual career of the soul to the physical birth by which we pass from the torpid and cramped darkness of the womb into the open light. This means, of course, a novel conception of the soul. For earlier Jewish thought (and again this includes the Synoptic Gospels) man's soul had come to be conceived as the factor in his personality that is capable of either rebellious disobedience toward God or loving submission to His will, expressed in a life of justice and kindness in one's relation to others. John's conception of the soul reflects his mystic orientation. It is that essence in man which can remain in blind and stubborn separation from the creative source of truth and life or can respond to the outreach of divine love and find redemption in happy union with it. And it is important not to misunderstand the new emphasis on knowledge and true belief that appears in this Gospel. "That whosoever believeth in him should not perish but have everlasting life."[32] "And this is life eternal, that they should know thee the only true God, and Jesus Christ, whom thou hast sent."[33] It is no mere intellectual achievement that the author has in mind here, as the Western mind is prone to suppose whenever these words are used. They have the meaning with which we are now familiar in the role played by knowledge in Hinduism and Buddhism, where it means a spiritual realization by the whole personality in its responsive growth toward union with God, of which a clarified apprehension is only the intellectual aspect.

Let us summarize. The revolutionary and appealing thought in this new interpretation of religion is the novel metaphysical significance of "love" that is taken for granted in John's conception of God. This love is not simply the kindly affection that a father might feel for his child, or the tender devotion that an ideal husband might give to his wife; it is more even than the spirit of self-giving that Second Isaiah attributes to the "Servant" in his relation to the other nations of the world—whose theater remains limited to the field of human action. For the Gospel of John, love is a unifying power operating in the cosmos at large and throughout all history, seeking to draw men out of their state of spiritual death toward the eternal life that comes from union with that power and with all others who are similarly finding life and love. God is this dynamic creative power in the universe. He became incarnate in Christ, suffering an agonizing death on the cross to reveal in unmistakable form His boundless love for men, that they might be awakened to a responding love toward Him, leaving behind their spiritually dead because loveless selves, and realizing a power of similar self-giving toward others. Christ thus becomes the unique historic Savior of men—the eternal mediator of God's love to the world and of the responding love whereby men become one with God through him.

In this interpretation, a legal conception of religion is completely abandoned and replaced by a mystic conception in specifically Christian form. However much the phraseology of a legal approach may still be employed, religion is not submissive obedience to God's commands. It is the conquest, through the power of God's love as revealed in Christ, of blindness, hate, and fear in the souls of men so that, in realized oneness with the divine spirit of self-giving, they can meet whatever betides in the joy of assured faith and hope. The ideal of perfection, as exemplified in the nature of God, is likewise profoundly transformed. No longer is it the image of an omnipotent ruler of the world and authoritative enforcer of law upon His subjects, self-sufficient in His unchallengeable celestial majesty and having no need of man or wish to share in his sorrows or pains. It is the ideal of love, giving itself without stint, penetrating by its dynamic power the surrounding realm of lovelessness just as light penetrates the surrounding darkness—and seeking, by dramatically expressing its loving acceptance of man, to create a mutuality of happy giving and receiving in place of monarchical domination on one side and slavish submission on the other. It is in the light of this transformed ideal that we can understand the new note reported by John in Jesus' words to his disciples. at the Last Supper: "I do not call you slaves any longer, for a slave does not know what his master is doing, but now I call you friends."[34]

And just as love toward God is thus transformed from the devoted affection of an obedient child to a mystic identification with the cosmic power of love, so love for one's neighbor is similarly transformed. Instead of being simply a service to our brothers in the spirit of the Golden Rule, it is an expression toward all our fellows of the same self-giving that God has shown toward us—it is a loving readiness to share their sorrows and sufferings and thus to become cocreators of spiritual life with Him.

How does John conceive the way in which man is awakened by God's love? I can find only one verse which gives any clarified hint as to how Christ's suffering brings about this responsive oneness on man's part. "And I, if I be lifted up, shall draw all men unto me."[35] For a more definite theological answer, relating this spiritual birth to all else in human history and experience, we must turn to Paul, who, two generations earlier than the final writing of John's Gospel, was offering such an answer in his letters to the new churches that he had founded in Asia Minor and Greece.

E. THE THEOLOGY OF THE APOSTLE PAUL

Despite some major differences between these two Christian thinkers, much of the new orientation so appealingly expressed in John was also present in Paul; in fact, since Paul's writings appeared first, they may have been a powerful factor in leading the author of John to the final teaching which we have at his hands. In Paul's case, however, the central idea was interpreted in such a way as to meet the same religious needs that were met, after a fashion, by the so-called "mystery cults" that were rapidly spreading throughout the Mediterranean world of his day. Since he felt called to become an apostle to the Gentiles rather than to the Jews, it was historically very important that he was able to develop and formulate such an interpretation. In doing so he, like John, gave the Christian Gospel a moving appeal to large numbers of people whose background of religious thought and experience was not Jewish at all, and in this process the Gospel itself became enriched and transformed.

Paul was born into a Jewish family residing in Tarsus of Cilicia, and he was educated at the feet of Jewish teachers at Jerusalem. It was natural, then, that he absorbed a typically Jewish viewpoint so far as concerns certain basic religious ideas. His God was the Hebrew Yahweh, with His special historical relation to the people of Israel and His comprehensive purpose for the human race as a whole—Yahweh as the great prophets had portrayed His character. Jewish was his conception of sin and of law; Jewish the almost fanatical conscientiousness which led him to idealize and exalt the law so highly that it seemed impossible for any mortal really to fulfill its demands. Essentially Jewish, too, was his doctrine of the coming kingdom and of the Messiah through whose appearance it would be ushered in. And, finally, his ideals of personal and social morality—of love as the perfect embodiment of the spirit of righteousness—were entirely Jewish in their origin and meaning.

But Paul also absorbed from his Hellenistic environment, at Tarsus and elsewhere in the east Mediterranean region, religious ideas which dominated the non-Hebraic world of his day, and for which he felt a deep personal need. His sense of duty to the divinely commanded law had been too weak to enable him steadily to obey it; he had become the prey of guilt, moral impotence, and despair. He longed for salvation from spiritual corruption, and from death, which he conceived to be its inevitable effect.[36] Now one of the striking features of this stage in the development of Graeco-Roman culture was the spread and intermingling of a host of the mystery cults just mentioned, which promised personal immortality to their converts through mystic identification with a savior-god who had died and then triumphed over death by resurrection to a renewed divine life. This identification was achieved through a highly moving ceremony, such as a blood bath or participation in a sacrificial feast, which gave the initiate a vivid sense that he was purged of his former corruptible nature and had assumed the immortal nature of the god who was present, at least symbolically, in the blood or consecrated food. The gods of these cults were of varied historical origin, some having appeared first in Egypt, some in ancient Greece, some in Persia.

We meet Paul first in the Acts of the Apostles as a fanatical opponent of Christianity.[37] But he became converted to the faith he had been attacking while on his way to Damascus to continue his zealous persecution.[38] His conversion precipitated these diverse elements into a unity in his subsequent thought and gave the crucified Christ a central place among them. However in detail we interpret that experience of the great apostle, it involved an intensely moving vision of Jesus, and its outcome was a profound spiritual transformation. Paul's inner conflict was ended, being replaced by a steady glow of joy, peace, outgoing love, and of unbounded vigor and enthusiasm. He felt himself saved from sin, corruption, and death, in the sense in which his Hellenistic contemporaries who pursued the mystery cults felt themselves saved, if their zeal had achieved its desired end.

After a period of uncertainty about his career, he felt himself called to spread the new faith in the Gentile world, especially in Asia Minor, Cyprus, and Greece, where he founded a number of missionary churches. To these, during the sixth decade of the first century A.D., he wrote pastoral letters in which, along with much counsel on practical matters, he explained his conception of Christian doctrine—as it was rooted in his own experience and had gained formulation through his reflective pondering.

As we should expect, the explanation was couched in terms of the background of ideas, both Jewish and Hellenistic, which has just been sketched. The result of his reflection may be described as a remolding of the basic teaching of the Hebrew prophets into a mystery religion of personal salvation, in which the crucified Jesus of Nazareth appears not merely as the promised Messiah but also as a savior-god. Through identification with his death and resurrection, according to Paul, we may be redeemed from sin and mortality, becoming heirs and joyous possessors of an indwelling principle of righteousness and immortal life. Our old sinful nature is crucified with Jesus, and in rising with Christ we really no longer live but Christ lives in us.[39] In brief, through his genius the prophetic idea of God was united with a Hellenistic concept of salvation and with John's conviction that man needs to undergo a spiritual rebirth. The essential features of this interpretation can be presented most clearly in the form they assume in Paul's philosophy of history, which is systematically expounded in his letter to the church at Rome. This church is not one that he had founded; he planned, however, late in life to visit it and did so shortly after this letter was written.[40]

God created the world as portrayed in the Book of Genesis, and Adam as the progenitor of the human race; Adam was given the power both of obedience and of disobedience to God's commands. As a result of Adam's sin under the temptation of the devil, all his descendants fell under the control of sin too; all inherited a fleshly, corrupt, and hence mortal nature. When, therefore, God revealed the details of His law to the world, selecting the Hebrew people as a special medium of the revelation, man was unable to be faithful to it. Dominated by his sinful nature, he continued to disobey and to merit still more deeply God's displeasure; all that the law could really do in view of his corrupt inheritance from Adam was to tantalize him with an unattainable pattern of righteousness and thus make him poignantly conscious of his impotence to conform to it. He was lost in sin, guilt, and the certainty of condemnation.

But God had foreseen this tragic result, and, being moved by mercy and love as well as by justice, he had prepared a way of salvation for those whom His grace should elect. In the fullness of time Christ Jesus, a divine being and God's agent in the original creation of the world, was destined to appear in human form and carry out this plan of salvation through his death and resurrection. When he did so appear, he gave as wondrous an example of humility and obedience as Adam had given of pride and disobedience; he was "obedient unto death, even the death of the cross."[41] Just, then, as in Adam all men sinned and fell under the bondage of corruption and death, so in Christ can all be made alive, replacing their fleshly and mortal nature by a holy, spiritual, and immortal one. To be sure, not everyone is impelled to turn to Jesus in saving faith; only those whom God has foreordained to salvation become actual beneficiaries of his redeeming work. But those whom He has chosen are drawn from Gentiles as well as Jews, from the poor as well as the wealthy, from slaves as well as free men. There are no distinctions of privilege in Christ Jesus.

Faith is the inward act of submission to the transforming power of Christ; baptism is the external sign of sharing in his death and his resurrection to eternal glory; and participation in the divine nature is often symbolically reënacted in eating the bread and drinking the wine of the Eucharist. Strictly speaking, the Christian no longer lives, himself, at all. It is Christ that lives in him, and his presence is made evident in daily life by the fruits of joy, patience, purity, hope, and especially love toward God and man. To the one who thus lives in Christ all things work together for good here below, and he is blessed with the assurance of immortality in the life to come. He is free now, not only from domination by sin but also from the obligation to conform to the Mosaic Law. When a man's sinful self has been crucified and his deeds are fully expressing the spirit of Christ who lives in him, obviously he needs no external constraint in the form of a system of detailed rules. He will freely act as Christ would act; for him the old covenant has passed away.

F. THE CHRISTIAN DOCTRINES OF INCARNATION AND ATONEMENT

So much for the origins of Christianity, as they are revealed to us in the New Testament. But to understand this great religion we must consider more than its original sources. In fact, if an account of the Christian faith were to close here, it would be incomplete in two major ways. For one thing, as this religion developed historically, it was affected by the genius of all the peoples with whom it gained vital contact —the genius of Greek philosophy as reflected in its doctrinal formulations, the genius of Roman law and administration as reflected in its ecclesiastical organization, the genius of modern Europe as reflected in its later theological developments, especially in the Protestant countries. For the other, although our study of the New Testament sources has given us insight into the distinctive factors that lie at the heart of Christian experience and therefore of Christian theology, it has not shown how they came together in a unified whole. We must bring into clear relief, if we can, the living core of Christian faith as out of these factors it took form and made Christianity a religion that could triumph over its rivals and win the allegiance of the Western world.

Let us attempt this second task, leaving till the end of the chapter a brief summary of the later historical developments. It is a very difficult task; because of variations of sectarian belief I cannot hope that my portrayal will be wholly acceptable to all Christians. As we proceed, it is important to remember what was said when we were considering the transition from primitive to civilized religion, namely, that the deepest problems of the latter are those of morally sensitive souls as they find themselves and their fellows struggling in the setting of civilized life with its threatening evils and its appealing possibilities of good. We must remember, too, what the basic evils are as seen from the perspective of the Jewish prophets and from that of Hellenistic thought. The greatest evil of all is human sin—not just the burden of guilt from past wrongdoing but the continuing power of sinful desire in man's heart—and the two further evils, for which sin is ultimately responsible, are suffering and death. Finally, it is essential to remember one aspect of the fourth characteristic of civilized religion. From the typical primitive standpoint, suffering (where it is not caused by forces in physical nature) is due to the sins of other people; from the standpoint of civilized religion, each individual penitently recognizes: "I too am a source of suffering to others and to myself; I am a sinner, and cannot live in freedom and inner peace until sin and suffering as rooted in me have been overcome."

So, with these reminders, we return to the fact that, as

Christian experience, Christian feeling, and Christian thought responded to the factors above described, this living core of Christian faith gradually emerged. And it did so in such a way that one can see how and why the central idea in Christianity—that which makes it unique as one of the great religions of the world—is the idea expressed in the words "God on the cross." As subsequent generations of Christians looked back to Jesus they found their moving symbol, not in any element in his teaching or in any event of his life—not even in the open tomb from which they believed him to have risen —but in the cross on which he died. Sir John Bowring's famous hymn beautifully expresses the heart of Christian feeling:

> In the cross of Christ I glory,
> Tow'ring o'er the wrecks of time;
> All the light of sacred story
> Gathers round its head sublime.
>
> When the woes of life o'ertake me,
> Hopes deceive, and fears annoy,
> Never shall the cross forsake me:
> Lo, it glows with peace and joy.
>
> When the sun of bliss is beaming
> Light and love upon my way,
> From the cross the radiance streaming
> Adds new luster to the day.
>
> Bane and blessing, pain and pleasure,
> By the cross are sanctified;
> Peace is there that knows no measure,
> Joys that through all time abide.

This means that the central and distinctive Christian convictions are those expressed in the doctrines of the incarnation and the atonement. It is in the light of these, as they were formulated by Jesus' followers, that one may understand the appealing idea that sin and suffering can be redeemed by divine love so that although they are and remain a great evil they can lead to a good of supreme value which without them would not be possible. If one attempts to fit these doctrines into a rational metaphysical scheme, as a sober cosmological theory, he will run into perplexing dilemmas. Such doctrines do not result from an attempt at an intellectual solution of cosmological problems. They must be understood in relation to the deeper experiences of the early Christian disciples, which gave them their vital meaning. As Paul recognized, even in his day, the thought of the Messiah suffering as a criminal would be a "stumbling block" to the Jews, and the idea of God on the cross would appear rank "folly" to the Gentiles.[42]

The bare essence of each of the two convictions can be quite simply stated. According to the doctrine of the incarnation Jesus was not just a prophet, nor even merely the expected Messiah—he was God appearing in human form. According to the doctrine of the atonement, in dying on the cross he atoned for the sin of all who have penitent faith in him and turn sincerely to God in his name. Taking the two doctrines together: God was in Christ, redeeming the world by this supreme revelation of His love. But to realize the richness and moving poignancy in these ideas, we must probe much deeper than these few words can carry us.

In the first place, the conviction expressed in the doctrine of incarnation often becomes more intelligible to modern minds when it is seen in terms of the radical humanism which it involved. Before this Christian conviction was formulated, in the Western world, the divine was typically identified with some irresistible power in physical nature—like the sun or the desert storm—or with a human being who exemplified such power in his relation to his fellows, as in the case of a haughty tribal chief or an imperial ruler. To be sure, the Jewish prophets had made central a new emphasis in their insistence that God is above rather than in the forces of nature, and is the embodiment of justice and love as well as of power, but for the rest they allowed this identification, with its natural emotional attitudes, to remain.

When the conviction is adopted that Jesus was not merely a great man but was divine in an unqualified sense, a quite revolutionary step is taken. On the one hand, it proclaims to the world that the place to look for the divine is not in any natural power on which man depends for physical well-being, but in the ideal spiritual character of which man at his best is capable. From this point of view, the significance of the doctrine is not the puzzling metaphysical implication that the ultimate source of all reality made Himself into a limited human being, existing at a particular point in space and a particular period of time, but rather that the clue to what is essential in the divine nature is not cosmological power but human goodness at its best. On the other hand, it teaches that this ideal goodness is revealed, not in the man who is self-sufficient in his intellectual eminence, his political domination of others, or even his moral rectitude as conventionally conceived, but in the man who accepts his erring fellows, however bad and unpromising they appear to be, and gives himself in loving service to them. He reveals the divine who prefers to be one with others in their griefs and agonies as well as their joys and triumphs, not the person who holds aloof in self-protecting isolation from the fates that bear tragically upon his suffering brothers. It is in this form that the same spiritual vision which in Buddhism flowered in the Bodhisattva ideal became central in Christianity too. The perfection that can alone be suitably attributed to God is the perfection of loving acceptance of others in their weaknesses and their imperfection—the love that finds its joy in creative sharing with the objects of its love and thus awakening in them a similar love and a similar releasing joy. To say that God is love and was incarnate in Jesus is to say these two things, in their radical contrast with what had been generally taken for granted before.

However, in the formative period of Christian thought this humanistic interpretation was adopted only by very few groups who were theologically uninfluential. The official doctrine did not break with the earlier idea of God as radically as this interpretation would require. Accordingly, the prevailing notion was that the God already conceived as the transcendent creator and ruler of the universe became so moved by love for His creatures that at a decisive moment in time He incarnated Himself in human form to provide a way for their salvation. The metaphysical paradoxes in this view have been mitigated in theological history in various ways. So far as the notion can be rationalized, the outcome appeared in the doctrine of the Trinity. God as the ultimate divine reality exists in three persons—Father, Son, and Holy Spirit. God the Father is the God of the prophets and the Synoptic Gospels—the Supreme Being in the universe, the just judge and the gracious Father of man. God the Son is the redeeming Christ in whom the divine love for man becomes incarnate. God the Holy Spirit is Christ as continuing to live in the heart of each reborn Christian, and in the church as it fills its role of uniting all Christians in loving devotion to the Father and the Savior whom He sent.

In the second place, we can clarify the significance of these doctrines in Christian thought by seeing how the new insight expressed in them became fused in a living unity with certain very ancient and primitive ideas. The strong conservatism of religion is at this point vividly exemplified in Christian teaching. There are, in fact, three ancient ideas which play a vital part in traditional interpretations of the incarnation and atonement; their presence there enabled Christian experience to preserve precious elements from its primitive past even while it was advancing to a radically new and profound conception of God and man.

One of these is the idea given central emphasis in the Hellenistic mystery religions—the idea of a dying and reviving god, through identification with whose death and resurrection, in baptism, man can leave behind his corruptible nature and partake of a new and immortal existence. This idea doubtless gained its earliest meaning in terms of the annual cycle of winter and spring, bringing death to the vegetative forces on which man depends and then resurrecting them to new life and vigor. It is no historical accident that the birth of Christ came to be dated so that it is celebrated just after the winter solstice, nor that his resurrection is commemorated at the beginning of spring. As exemplifying this idea, Jesus for Christian thought is the dying and reviving source of life in the world, demonstrating his superiority to all the forces of physical destruction and his unfailing power to bring vitality to all who become one in faith with him.

A second is the idea of the mystic significance of a totemic sacrifice, and of the participation of a worshiping group in the renewing power of its flesh and blood. Wherever such practices prevail, centered around a totemic animal, there is present the belief that through such means the members of the group reëstablish a vital union with the divine source of strength and with each other as sharers in that living renewal. The emotional potency of this idea when clothed in a garb which gives it acceptable spiritual meaning is evident in the Catholic celebration of the Mass, and in less dramatic form in the Protestant commemoration (by the Lord's Supper) of the last meal which Jesus shared with his disciples. And that event itself, of course, preserved a significant Christian connection with the Hebrew commemoration of the Passover and the sacrifice in each household of the Passover lamb. As exemplifying this idea, Jesus is the Lamb of God whose sacrifice takes away the sin of the world and enables all who believe in him to come before God cleansed and ready for His renewing grace.

The third is the idea of the "scapegoat." As involved in many primitive ceremonies, this is one of the most widespread of religious ideas. The central thought is that the accumulated sins of the community can be loaded on some individual who is chosen for this purpose and who then bears the burden of their guilt and punishment. In most primitive groups the individual thus chosen is a slave or a criminal, but sometimes a priest or even the chief himself must assume this role. In the latter case, tradition may sanction substituting for the official scapegoat, at least before the customary chain of ceremonies ends, a common citizen or a condemned criminal. This individual then suffers for the sins of the group and atones for them by being beaten and driven off into exile or by being put to death in a prescribed manner. Thus the guilt that he bears in his person is removed or destroyed and the community is freed from its contamination. There are many illustrations of this practice all over the world; the form in which it was present in ancient Judaism is interestingly described in Chapter 16 of Leviticus, whence our term "scapegoat" is derived. At the annual celebration in May of the Thargelia at Athens two "purifying men" were led through the streets, to be whipped with rods and then driven over the border of the city, bearing the people's sins with them. In a town in modern Nigeria the sins of the tribe are periodically laid on a slave girl who has been selected some time earlier for this role. As she is led through the streets the householders come forth and discharge the year's accumulated evil of each family upon her; then she is dragged to the river, bound, and left to drown.[48] As exemplifying this very pervasive idea, Jesus is the scapegoat who, though innocent himself, bears the sins of the world and atones for them through his suffering and death.

But what gives unity and spiritual significance to these ideas in their Christian form is the distinctively Christian setting in which they are interpreted. This setting involves two crucial factors of a different order than those just described, and both are of deep emotional appeal. On the one hand, there was the moving historical fact of Jesus' crucifixion. Other persons had suffered an agonizing death for the sake of a righteous cause, but there was something peculiarly vivid and dramatic in his execution, especially when it came to be understood in the light of the new Christian concept of God. After all, Jesus could have left Judaea and carried his message elsewhere, as he was doubtless tempted to do, but he accepted and fulfilled a divine mission to his own people even though it led to his martyrdom. He was compassionately concerned for his fellow Jews, and like Jeremiah preferred to serve them even at the cost of their misunderstanding and betraying him. And he also exemplified in his own experience the other feature which was equally essential. This was the moving idea that, through love, sin and suffering can be overcome and transformed from a sheer evil into a means to a supreme good. In his case the suffering which it was his lot to undergo was so transformed; by accepting it as God's will and losing all concern for himself, he overflowed in loving oneness with others who also may have to suffer, and this brought a quality of happiness that was of supreme value. "I have told you these things," he said to his disciples a few hours before his arrest, "so that you might have the happiness that I have had, and that your happiness might become complete."[44] In their case, sin was overcome through a penitent and transforming response to the divine love they experienced in him, and whatever suffering they might need to undergo was likewise transformed so that it was experienced, not as a mere evil, but as a means to a great good.

Let us see if we can understand the secret of this twofold transformation. How is man saved from sin through Christ's death, and how is suffering transformed for the Christian from an evil into a good? Here lies the heart of the Christian solution of the problem of life.

Well, in the case of sin, many are the interpretations that have historically been offered. In the early years of Christianity it was seriously proposed that man is redeemed by a deceitful barter between God and Satan: God offered His Son as a prize to the devil to induce the latter, in exchange, to free men's souls from his control; then the devil found (in Jesus' resurrection) that he could not retain his prize. In medieval times Anselm proposed a theory reflecting feudal ideas of the duty of absolute fealty to one's lord; only the lord himself, taking the form of a vassal, can compensate for the past failure of his vassals to fulfill perfectly the requirements of such fealty. Later Catholic and Protestant theologians have offered theories which are more acceptable to the modern mind.

What was Jesus' own interpretation? If the above account of his thinking as revealed in the Synoptics is correct, his central conviction was reached through an application to himself, in his relation to other individuals, of Second Isaiah's glowing hope that Israel as God's Servant would ransom the other nations from sin. Just as the Servant would be transfigured by suffering, and realize a loving character so appealing to the rest of the world that by making it their own they would be purged of their sins and no longer need punishment for them, so Jesus would be so transfigured by his obedient acceptance of the cross that men would identify with the spirit revealed in him and thus likewise become purged of everything in their nature that obstructs the free flow of divine love through them. "I, if I be lifted up, shall draw all men unto me." That such a redeeming response can come, and has come in thousands of hearts in each Christian generation, is beautifully revealed in a familiar hymn:

> When I survey the wondrous cross
> On which the Prince of glory died,
> My richest gain I count but loss,
> And pour contempt on all my pride. . . .
>
> Were the whole realm of nature mine,
> That were a present far too small;
> Love so amazing, so divine,
> Demands my soul, my life, my all.

In brief, God's outpouring of His love in Christ's death, even while men are lost in sinful disobedience, can awaken a grateful devotion to Him which liberates them from their selfishnesses and pettinesses, and enables them gladly to live up to what He expects of them as otherwise they have been powerless to do. In His love He did not fail them; they will not now fail Him.

How is suffering also transformed for the Christian, so that, while not needlessly courted, it becomes when it does befall them a good rather than a sheer evil? The answer is simple but profound. Christ had undergone, out of love for them, the most agonizing torture. Whatever sorrow or pain unavoidably then comes to them, as a result of faithful obedience to him and service to his Kingdom, is willingly, even gladly, accepted, because through it they can realize a deeper union with him than would be possible otherwise; the Christian now has the completer experience of oneness with his suffering as well as oneness with his glory. Thus the suffering becomes transfigured into an experience that is supremely good instead of remaining one that is naught but evil. For the earnest Christian's prayer is always:

> Nearer, my God, to Thee,
> Nearer to Thee;
> E'en though it be a cross
> That raiseth me.

In a world in which pain and grief are inevitable, where in some form "there is a cross for everyone," this thought permits unavoidable suffering, however tragic and undeserved it may be, to take on a new meaning and a new value. Instead of being at best a dull frustration and at worst a despairing torment, it becomes a bearer of hope and abiding joy. The Christian experiences a positive sharing with the very heart of God, and thereby a loving oneness with suffering men and women everywhere.

The greatest evils that life brings—sin and suffering—are thus, through divine love, overcome with good. It is no wonder that "God on the cross" became the distinctive idea and moving symbol of Christian faith. To Christian experience the Cross of Calvary is the unique point in history where God fully revealed Himself to the world. In the light of the event that happened there the Christian realizes what saving union with Him means.

G. CHRISTIANITY IN THE MODERN WORLD

Since many of my readers know the story of the evolution of Christianity from the early centuries to modern times, and since reliable accounts of this evolution are readily accessible, I shall confine myself here to the barest summary of the major themes that would enter such an account were it to be developed.

It would of course explain the gradual formulation of the details of Christian doctrine, and the adoption of the creeds in which the distinctive convictions of Christian faith were expressed, showing how the philosophic perspective of the great Greek thinkers was used in this process, framed in the fundamental concepts, such as "being," "substance," "act," "cause," which they had clarified. It would tell of the early waves of missionary expansion by which Christianity spread in all directions from its source in the eastern Mediterranean, especially northward and westward into Europe; so that when through the surge of Islam it lost its dominant position in Africa and the Near East, it could continue to live and grow. It would dwell briefly on the split between the Eastern and the Western Church, which became final in A.D. 1054, and on the mystical and sacramental emphases that have been characteristic of the Eastern Church. It would tell the fascinating history of the papacy in the West, with its increasing religious and secular authority. It would describe the revival of learning that took place in the Western Church in medieval times, and the systematic reformulation of Catholic doctrine at the hands of St. Thomas Aquinas about A.D. 1270. The Protestant revolution of Luther and Calvin, with its radical revisions in theology and ecclesiastical practice, would call for careful treatment, and, following hard upon that story, an account would be needed of the long tension between Christian theology and modern science, and the persistent attempts at their reconciliation. Simultaneous with these last developments, the rapid colonial expansion of Western Europe took place, as a result of which the two American continents, Australasia, and much of South Africa became added to the Christian world.

The situation which Christianity confronts today is partly the result of this historical evolution and is partly due to the impact of the new forces that are shaking the contemporary world. Among these forces four are especially vital to an understanding of the present status of Christianity and its prospects for the future. Two are somber forces; two express the concerned effort of Christians to achieve a strengthened reorientation in face of the novel possibilities of evil and of good that loom before them.

One of the somber factors is the revolutionary awakening of the non-Christian countries in Asia and Africa. Colonial control by the Western powers has already largely been thrown off, and it appears to be only a matter of time before this process will be complete. The newly awakened peoples are eager to master the science and technology of the Christian West, but not in general its religion, which in so many cases has seemed to them inextricably allied with colonialism. The activities of Christian missionaries have been drastically limited, and even in the West secular influences are here and there eroding the foundations of orthodox Christian belief. The second somber factor is the danger that in this process of emancipation from Western domination a hydrogen war will be precipitated. The Western powers (especially America) are dependent for military bases and for vital source materials on countries that in this process are likely to become neutral or may even go over to the Communist camp. If such a war comes it will almost surely be far more destructive to the Christian than to the non-Christian world. Latin America might well escape the catastrophe, but it has thus far shown little capacity for creative leadership. Should this forecast prove correct, the net outcome of such a tragedy would be a drastic weakening of Christianity and a simultaneous strengthening of the other great religions; the spiritual claims of the former would appear dubious through its impotence to avert calamity, and the latter would gain a freer field for growth and for leadership in the task of reconstruction.

How are Christian theologians and statesmen attempting to meet the searching challenge of the contemporary scene?

The outstanding answer to this question in the field of Christian social action is the ecumenical movement. Through the centuries, generally speaking, especially in the areas of Eastern and of Protestant Christianity, the dominant tendency had been for the church to split into sectarian groups, each maintaining that its interpretation of the Bible and (in some cases) its ritual practices are alone sound. The aim of the ecumenical movement is to reverse this divisive process and to bring together all sincere Christians into a living, effective unity. The difficult problem is how to achieve this on a base which is more than the pale residuum of common doctrinal agreement, and which involves no dilution of convictions precious to each group. The Roman Catholics take no part in this endeavor, holding firmly to their claim that they constitute the only true Christian church, but most of the larger non-Roman churches have shared in a series of ecumenical conferences whose purpose is to further this movement. The most recent meeting of this kind was the Second Assembly of the World Council of Churches of Christ, at Evanston, Illinois, in August, 1954.

The outstanding answer to the question in the field of Christian theology is the vigorous trend toward an "existential" interpretation of Christian doctrine. After a brief flirtation with a scientific rationalism, which in the late nineteenth and early twentieth centuries gained considerable vogue among Protestant thinkers, Christian theologians are now turning strongly to an orientation first clearly formulated by Sören Kierkegaard in the mid-nineteenth century. Kierkegaard's teachings were neglected for two generations, but in our day they have led to the most influential philosophical movement in the West outside of the English-speaking countries and to a point of view in theology which is deeply affecting all the main Christian churches, especially in the Protestant world. By an "existential" interpretation is meant essentially one maintaining that "existence precedes essence." That is, any adequate theory of man's nature must take as primary his emotional concern with the weal and woe of his existence; the direction and meaning of his thinking in all areas except those of abstract science are determined by this concern. Each individual person exists in a threatening world, whose ultimate sentence upon him is death; his attempt to adjust to this fateful situation is inevitably haunted by anxiety, fear, hatred, guilt, and despair. So far as religion is concerned, the crucial corollary drawn is that he is helpless to save himself; least of all can he accomplish this by his reason, which in subtle or more obvious ways is itself driven by these unhappy emotions. But God, existing in His eternal and incomprehensible transcendence, has broken into human history by His incarnation in Christ; thus a way of salvation is provided through His gracious love and man's capacity to respond to it in humble faith.

We may close this chapter with a summary statement of the way in which Christianity exemplifies the four distinctive characteristics of high civilized religion. Despite the fact that the two historic emphases—on religion as obedience to the divine law and on religion as mystic union with God—have become intimately blended in Christian feeling, they are yet so different intrinsically that the form these four characteristics take in any individual's experience is largely determined by which of these emphases is dominant.

If the legal perspective is the controlling one, these characteristics take the same basic form that they do in prophetic Judaism, except that it is the revised law revealed through Christ that becomes the norm of loyal obedience. There is one God, creator and ruler of the universe, and lawgiver and judge in relation to man; we as His creatures are wholly dependent on His power, justice, and mercy. The soul is in essence that basic attitude in each of us that can either rebel or obey; the heart of true obedience consists in following the Golden Rule wherever our conduct affects the well-being of any of our human brothers. We are saved from seeking a deceitful happiness in satisfying our rebellious desires by penitently turning from them to God, who is graciously ready to forgive and accept us in virtue of Christ's redeeming sacrifice.

If the controlling ideal is that of mystic union with God, the four characteristics take the form that naturally follows from such a conviction. In this case, God is the metaphysical energy of love, eternally active in the universe at large—drawing all who can respond out of their self-centered separateness toward union with Him and a creative sharing in His love. The soul is the capacity for such love in each of us, which shows itself in seeking oneness with God and with all men through Him. Our moral responsibility toward others is expressed, not merely in just and kindly conduct toward them as separate individuals, but in a readiness to share with them in their sorrows and pains as well as in their joys, thus expressing our union with the divine love through Christ. Finally, salvation is the rebirth of the soul into another dimension of being—its emergence from the spiritual death of lovelessness into spiritual life and the new happiness which it brings.

XIII.

Islam

A. ITS HISTORICAL BACKGROUND

We turn now to the youngest of the civilized religions that have spread widely, have won hundreds of millions of adherents, and are still living forces in the world. Non-Moslems (especially in the West) usually refer to this religion by the name of its founder, calling it "Mohammedanism," but from its own point of view this is an improper description; its true name is "Islam," which means "submission to God." And "one who submits" is thereby a "Moslem."

Christianity is the prime historical example of a synthetic faith—one which gathers into the unity of its own perspective many factors of diverse cultural and religious origin. This character it showed at the very beginning, when it drew together ideas derived from prophetic Judaism, from the Hellenistic mystery cults, from Persian thought, from Alexandrian philosophy, and even from the mystic teachings of the East. Now in the course of time Islam also displayed much of this synthetic power, but at the beginning it was in its essence a remarkably simple religious faith. Its message was the message of the great Hebrew prophets and the early teaching of the Synoptic Gospels in unelaborated form, with all adornments and excrescences removed. Its conception of religion was what we have called the legal conception through and through; to be truly devout is to submit humbly to God's will and conform faithfully in all one's conduct to His revealed law. As one reads the early suras of the Koran, in which Mohammed* warns, in this setting, of the coming day of judgment, he might easily imagine himself listening to the fiery prophecies of Amos, except that a different personality is now speaking and is doing so in the rhythmic cadences of another tongue.

By the NIGHT when she spreads her veil;
By the day when it brightly shineth;
By Him who made male and female;
At different ends truly do ye aim!
But as to him who giveth *alms* and feareth God,
And yieldeth assent to the Good;
To him will we make easy the path to happiness.
But as to him who is covetous and bent on riches,
And calleth the Good a lie,
To him will we make easy the path to misery:
And what shall his wealth avail him when he goeth down?
Truly man's guidance is with Us
And our's, the Future and the Past.
I warn you therefore of the flaming fire;
None shall be cast to it but the most wretched,—
Who hath called the truth a lie and turned his back.
But the God-fearing shall escape it,—
Who giveth away his substance that he may become pure;
And who offereth not favours to any one for the sake of recompense,
     pense,
But only as seeking the face of his Lord the Most High.

When the Heaven shall CLEAVE asunder,
And when the stars shall disperse,
And when the seas shall be commingled,
And when the graves shall be turned upside down,
Each soul shall recognise its earliest and its latest actions. . . .

* Arabic scholars now generally prefer the romanization "Muhammad," "Muslim," "Qu'ran." For the purpose of this book the more familiar spelling seems best.

In the form which pleased Him hath He fashioned thee.
Even so; but ye treat the Judgment as a lie.
Yet truly there are guardians over you—
Illustrious recorders—
Cognisant of your actions.
Surely amid delights *shall* the righteous *dwell*,
But verily the impure in Hell-fire:
They shall be burned at it on the day of doom,
And they shall not be able to hide themselves from it.
Who shall teach thee what the day of doom is?
Once more. Who shall teach thee what the day of doom is?
It is a day when one soul shall be powerless for another soul: all
     sovereignty on that day shall be with God.[1]

In view of the purpose of this volume I shall deal only in
the utmost brevity with the historical and cultural background
of Mohammed's career. Arabia was a land of rugged rock
and desert, traversed by a few caravan trails; its cultural centers were concentrated along the Arabian Sea, at Yemen in
the south, and at Medina in the north. The nomads roaming
the peninsula were vigorous individualists, although controlled in a few vital matters by traditional loyalty to their
clans. Every household was under the sway of a father-sheik
who ruled more by force of personality than by the authority
of tribal custom. A few divine powers with wide areas of
control were recognized, but of greater daily importance
were the mischievous local "jinns" who at any moment were
likely to make their favoring or frustrating presence known.
Travelers, especially, did well to be very wary of them.

Until the time of Mohammed, Arabia had been practically
neglected by the rest of the world, which was indeed prepared to keep on neglecting it forever. No one expected anything to come from Arabia that was destined to exert a significant impact on human history and human culture. In fact,
Islam is the outstanding illustration of the powerful cultural
force that a new religious enthusiasm is capable of generating,
at least under favorable circumstances and when certain other

factors coöperate. Arabia exploded into history with one great outburst, in which it gave Mohammed and Islam to the world; and as a result the transformed Arabic culture and the Arabic language acquired a world significance. The word "outburst" is none too vivid; within a hundred years after Mohammed's death the crescent of Islam swept all the way from southwestern France across North Africa and the Middle East to central Asia, whence it continued to spread in more leisurely fashion into southeastern Europe, into the depths of Africa, and farther toward the remote borders of Asia. Before those whom it conquered had time to rouse themselves from their lethargy and devise countermeasures, the consuming flame was upon them. And except for the Spanish peninsula, Islam lost subsequently no important part of the territory it came to embrace in its fold, and wherever it became established human society was profoundly transformed, both by its ideals and by its established social patterns. It challenges our understanding, both on its own account and because of its interesting relation to Judaism and to Christianity.

B. MOHAMMED'S LIFE

Mohammed was born about A.D. 570 into the Koreish clan, dominant in the city of Mecca and guardians of the famous Ka'aba, center of worship and goal of pilgrims throughout an extensive region. While still a young child he was left an orphan, and came under the protecting care of his uncle Abu Talib, one of the respected leaders of the Koreish. In his teens and twenties he traveled with his uncle's caravans northward and southward, becoming acquainted with Jewish and Christian traders, who were rather ignorant about their beliefs, but from whom he learned something. It is clear from later events that he was much impressed by what he absorbed from them, and pondered it deeply. But it took a long time for these ponderings to bear fruit; he was a man who matured slowly. In his middle twenties he became employed by a prosperous widow named Khadija to manage her far-flung commercial interests; and although she was fifteen years his senior, before long they were married. Khadija was a woman of keen and loving understanding; she was deeply devoted to her young husband, trusting him fully in difficult business transactions and respecting his moods of silent and troubled preoccupation. For about a decade and a half the manner of life suggested by this description of the couple continued without essential change. Except to those who knew him most intimately, Mohammed seemed to have settled more and more fully into the character of a quiet, honest, staid business-man—a dutiful and somewhat dependent husband, and a responsible protector of the family interests.

But something else must have been going on in the recesses of his soul, a perplexed and harrassing struggle to clarify religious truth—not merely for the sake of intellectual understanding, but for the sake of a vitalizing vision of God in His transcendent and majestic being. How much a sympathetic student of religion would give to know the details of this struggle! But, as in the case of most other religious pioneers, we have to reconstruct it as best we can from what happened later, and no reconstruction can claim more than a certain degree of plausibility. A few things, however, can be affirmed with fair confidence. From Judaism there had been stamped upon Mohammed's soul the conviction of the absolute and unqualified unity of God, which as it deepened brought a fiery revulsion not only against the idolatrous polytheism of Arabia but also against what seemed to him the queer Christian doctrine of the Trinity. This doctrine involved the absurd and unseemly idea that God consists of three persons, one being the begotten son of another member of the triad. He came to believe that the God who had revealed Himself to Noah, Abraham, Moses, and Jesus was not going to leave Arabia without its revelation too; He cares for the Arabian people as much as for the Jews and will give His last and greatest disclosure in their language.

And what would be the content of this revelation? Here Mohammed's intense and puzzled brooding borrowed both from prophetic Judaism and from the Synoptic Gospels; he built upon them under the guidance of his own growing convictions. The new disclosure will warn his people of the awesome day of judgment and of the final separation of the sheep from the goats which that day will bring; it will preach the good news of God's forgiving grace and compassionate welcome to those who heed the warning. It will demand explicit acceptance of Mohammed himself as God's authentic messenger, just as Jesus had demanded acceptance of himself as the appointed Messiah. But it will avoid claiming anything more for him than this—God is one God, and no human being is divine; at best he can be a humble mouthpiece of the divine among his fellows. Finally, it will proclaim a message of justice, mercy, and brotherhood, and will apply this message to enough of the specific problems of life so that there will be no excuse for those who are all too ready to accept fine precepts in general while flouting them in their daily conduct. Mohammed's ideals of justice and mercy are those of the great Jewish prophets and the Christ of the Synoptics, adapted to the desert cultural setting of the Arabia of his day. In his vision of human brotherhood he is in line with the teaching of the Gospel of John, except that he gives it no mystical grounding. What he longed for, more and more deeply, was that Christ's earnest hope for loving unity among Christians be actually realized among his own followers; in place of the sectarian divisions and quarrels that he observed among the Christians every Moslem would really feel and act like a brother to every other Moslem.

In A.D. 611, when Mohammed was forty years old, the revelations began. He had resorted in his agonized reflections to a rocky retreat near Mecca, and one day the angel Gabriel appeared in a vision before him, saying: "Speak thou, in the name of thy Lord, who created man—created him from clots of blood!" At first he was uncertain whether the revelation was authentic, and whether he was really called to the career of a prophetic messenger of God. He hurried to his good wife Khadija, who, understanding him with firmer assurance than he did himself, gave him encouragement and support. His uncle too, though more skeptical, was prepared to stand by him in the dangerous social situation that such preaching was bound to create. So he was reassured, and the messages continued. He won a few devoted followers, but stirred up increasing hostility, as the religious and economic implications of his uncompromising monotheism became more and more clear.

As matters came to a head, good fortune smiled upon this religious pioneer, not once but many times. A delegation from Yathrib in the north (the later Medina), which was torn by internal schisms, invited him to come and be their sheik at almost the very moment when his life had become no longer safe at Mecca. The famous "hegira" (flight) to Medina, from which the Moslem world dates its calendar, took place on the 16th of July, A.D. 622,* and it was marked by breathtaking escapes from what appeared to be almost certain death. Within a few years Mohammed had established himself so strongly at Medina that he was not only able to withstand a determined attack by his Meccan enemies but could follow up the victory by a vigorous offensive against them. In 630 he captured Mecca, purged the Ka'aba of its blasphemous images and unacceptable rites, and generously extended an amnesty to all who submitted to his rule. He is the one great religious founder who achieved full success in his own lifetime as measured by his major hopes and aims. When he died in 632, all Arabia was under his firm control and Moslem influence was beginning to spread in a still wider circle. His farewell message, given just before his death, summarizes in beautiful brevity the major convictions for which he stood:

I have heard that the rumor of my death filled you with alarm, but has any prophet before me lived forever? Everything hap-

* This is the date as determined when the calendar was adopted some seventeen years later.

pens according to the Will of God, and has its appointed time which is not to be hastened or avoided. I return to Him who sent me, and my last command to you is that you remain united, that you love, honor, and uphold one another, that you exhort one another to faith, and constancy in belief, and to the performance of pious deeds. By these alone, men prosper. All else leads to destruction.

I do but go before you. You will soon follow me. Death awaits us all, let no one then seek to turn it aside from me. My life has been for your good, so will be my death.[2]

So far as Mohammed's personality is concerned, the distinctive thing about him is that he combined the characteristics of the zealous Hebrew prophet with those of a highly capable political administrator and military leader. In fact, he was the only founder of a great religion in whom these latter qualities were clearly and effectively displayed. The pacifist strain, so prominent in one form or another in the other civilized religions, has no place in the basic structure of Islam; a good Moslem must be ready to fight for God's cause against the unbelievers, and he is therefore expected to unite military valor with the more spiritual virtues which all the religions emphasize as essential. Those spiritual qualities were present in Mohammed, in high degree, and there was also something of the cheerful good humor which we noted in Confucius. "He was gentle and noble—just a man who laughed often and smiled much," said his favorite young wife Ayesha after his death. And Ayesha had not lacked opportunity to see the less attractive characteristics that her husband was capable, on occasion, of showing.

C. HIS EARLY MESSAGE

As with the Synoptic Jesus, it is helpful and clarifying in Mohammed's case, before we proceed to a topical analysis of his religious philosophy, to distinguish his early and very simple message from the more detailed teachings of the Medina period. That early message, out of which all the rest develops and on which it is built, is very similar to the common core of teaching as between the preaching of Amos and that of the Synoptic Jesus, except for the distinctive features and unique emphases mentioned above. It runs about as follows:

God is One God, beside whom there is no other. Any touch of idolatry, or any hint of polytheism—and this includes the Christian doctrine of three gods in one—is an insult to Him. He transcends the world that He created, for He sits enthroned above it in incomparable splendor, majesty, and power. A great and fearful day of judgment is coming, at which God's absolute power over the physical universe will be frighteningly displayed, and the book in which the record of all men's deeds is inscribed will be brought forward. Each person will be judged, with final judgment, and sent to his everlasting punishment in hell or his eternal reward in heaven, as the case may be. Both hell and heaven are graphically described, in terms vivid with meaning to inhabitants of a tropical desert land.

Hell truly shall be a place of snares,
The home of transgressors,
To abide therein ages;
No coolness shall they taste therein nor any drink,
Save boiling water and running sores;
Meet recompense!
For they looked not forward to their account;
And they gave the lie to our signs, charging them with falsehood;
But we noted and wrote down all:
"Taste this then: and we will give you increase of nought but
    torment."
But, for the God-fearing is a blissful abode,
Enclosed gardens and vineyards;
And damsels with swelling breasts, their peers in age,
And a full cup:
There shall they hear no vain discourse nor any falsehood:
A recompense from thy Lord—sufficing gift![3]

(Later, Mohammed came to distrust the effect of this highly sensuous imagery and to describe the joys of heaven in phrases of less voluptuous appeal.)

Now his main role is to be a warner of this terrible event, so that those who fail to heed the warning will have no excuse when the day comes and the unanswerable record is brought forth. God had sent warners before—Noah, Abraham, Moses, Jesus, and others of the Jewish prophetic line—but in general they were rejected and their message unheeded, despite the frequent displays in history of His punishing hand. Mohammed is the first such warner to be sent to Arabia, and the first to bring a divine revelation in the Arabic language.

On what basis are the sheep and the goats to be divided on the day of judgment? Here the continuity of his teaching with Amos and the Synoptic Gospels is most marked. On the one hand, the sheep must believe in him and the authenticity of his revelation. On the other, they must show, by a life of justice and mercy, that they have turned from sin and disobedience to righteousness and obedient submission to God's commands. Impartial justice is to be exercised toward all, and kindly compassion toward those who especially need help and protection—the poor, the orphans, the widows, the sick, the wayfarers. In showing such tenderness, the pious follower is most closely imitating Allah himself, for, as every sura of the Koran except one proclaims, Allah is above all else the "compassionate, the merciful."

And who shall teach thee what the steep (path) is?
It is to ransom the captive,
Or to feed in the day of famine
The orphan who is near of kin, or the poor that lieth in the dust;
Beside this, to be of those who believe, and enjoin steadfastness
     on each other, and enjoin compassion on each other.
These shall be the people of the right hand:
While they who disbelieve our signs
Shall be the people of the left.
Around them the fire shall close.[4]

But this simple and straightforward message rapidly developed into a very complex system of religious, ethical, and social teaching. Even during the Meccan period preceding the hegira, revelations came to Mohammed whose purpose was to guide his action in this or that puzzling situation; in the Medina period these become multiplied, and are mingled with the formulation of general principles on all major social problems. Thus it came about that when the revelations end with Mohammed's death, the Koran embodies a detailed moral and legal system—covering such themes as marriage and divorce, inheritance, war, court procedure, economic life, diet and sanitation—along with the more obviously religious prescriptions concerning prayer, almsgiving, fasting, pilgrimage, and the like. Following our procedure with the other great religions, I shall concentrate, in the midst of this varied series of instructions, on the central emphases which I hope will enable us to catch the spiritual genius of this religion as it went forth from the founder's hands to its conquering mission.

D. THE CREED OF ISLAM

On the creedal side, every loyal Moslem must accept, as his sincere belief, that "there is no God but Allah, and Mohammed is His messenger." These two affirmations should not only be repeated with the lips but should also be deeply and devoutly believed with the heart. Whether this is the case with any given individual or not, we cannot surely tell; only God can be the judge.

What, now, does the first of these two convictions essentially mean?

Well, the Allah of Islam is identified with the God of the Jews and the Christians, speaking now to Arabia through Mohammed. Earlier Arabian thought had known a deity named Allah, who had possessed the attributes of a "high god." He had been conceived as the dispenser of justice, He was responsible for the order of the heavenly bodies, and He was not to be represented by any image. It was easy therefore for Mohammed to think of Him as the same God that Jews and Christians worshiped. As Mohammed portrays Him, He is One God, absolutely and without qualification. He is eternal and changeless. Strictly speaking, no attributes derived from the experience of His creatures can be asserted of Him, but yet it is proper to liken Him to that which is "loftiest in heaven and earth." For the varied wonders and the marvelous bounty of nature are signs of His power, wisdom, and kindliness—signs in the sense of giving true hints to the responsive soul while falling far short of providing a clear revelation of His transcendent being. Under the guidance of such signs, we may truthfully say that God is all-knowing and all-wise; in relation to both nature and man, He is almighty will, the lord and controller of all that happens. There is no natural law except so far as God has imposed orderly ways upon the sun, the stars, and other phenomena in the world. With special reference to man, what this doctrine means is that God has decreed for each individual whatever career and destiny await him—for the good, that he shall repent, submit, and enjoy his reward; for the wicked, that he shall persist in stubborn disobedience and meet his dire punishment in the fire of hell. Through His chosen apostles He reveals His will to men and warns them of the judgment to come.

One might think that such a transcendent and awful God would seem to His worshipers very distant—far removed from the daily, earthly cares and toils of men. As a matter of fact, this is not the case. One of the distinctive achievements of Islam in comparison with the other great religions is its success in bringing home to pious Moslems, wherever they may be and whatever they may be doing, a sense of the constant presence of God. This is partly due to its uncompromising insistence on the divine unity; all the feelings that in a nonmonotheistic faith are dispersed among several divine beings are for it concentrated upon the one and only God. It is partly due to the constant reminders that Islam provides of the reality of the divine, and the frequent incitements to a reverent realization of that reality; five times each day, even when he is busy with his worldly occupations, the Moslem responds to the call to worship by prostrating himself toward Mecca in a posture of humble and total submission to God. It is partly due to Islam's rejection of any mediating functions between man and God—of priest, or church, or sacrament—that might become an obstruction rather than an aid to the individual's vivid realization of the divine. Whether these explanations are adequate or not, of the fact there is ample testimony. R. V. C. Bodley writes:

> One of the strongest impressions I had when I first lived with Arabs was the "everydayness" of God. He ruled their eating, their traveling, their business, their loving. He was their hourly thought, their closest friend, in a way impossible to people whose God is separated from them by the rites of formal worship. . . . Nothing was begun or ended or promised or invoked without God being called upon to help or witness or receive thanks.[5]

My own acquaintance with the Moslems of north India entirely confirms this description. In a crowded railway compartment in the winter of 1947 most of my fellow passengers were Moslems—and not excessively devout ones, I am sure. They were traveling on various errands—some to fulfill a family responsibility, some to complete a business transaction, some on professional duties. I was struck by the fact that each of them had a living sense of satisfying companionship with God in such simple events as the journey they were then taking; they referred to His presence so naturally and spontaneously, yet with such obvious piety and reverence. The majestic Ruler of the universe was also, to them, a gracious comrade in the daily vicissitudes of life.

"And Mohammed is His messenger." The word I have here translated "messenger" is the Arabic *rasul*, which is often rendered by such English terms as "prophet," "mouthpiece," "apostle." It is well to free ourselves from the misleading theological associations of these latter words, and "messenger" is a simple, straightforward medium for presenting to modern Westerners the essential thought. It is an especially good term for suggesting clearly the negative implications of the role claimed for himself by Mohammed. He is no divinity, in any sense whatever, but only a messenger of the Divine. He has no supernatural power—he can perform no miracles and is not immune from illness or death. He wields no authority over others, save on matters specifically revealed by God as falling under his lawmaking power. He does not know what God knows, as, for example, the time when the day of judgment will dawn. In relation to God he is as completely humble as any other human being should be. On the positive side, he is essentially a warner of the great judgment to come and a bringer of glad tidings to those who respond to the warning. And—very important, of course—he is the first official warner to the Arabians and the last divinely appointed warner to the world at large.*

As we follow Mohammed's statements about himself from the Mecca into the Medina period, we find what might be expected from the altered role that he was called upon to fill. The function of warner recedes into a subordinate position; his chief task now is to be a systematic lawgiver for the growing and increasingly complex Islamic society. As he fills this function there is increased emphasis in the revelations on "obeying God and the apostle"—although here, too, he is concerned to assert the modest limits of his own responsibility in contrast with the absolute authority of God. "Whoso obeyeth the Apostle in so doing obeyeth God; and as to those who turn back from thee, we have not sent thee to be their keeper."[6] Also, in the Medina period, certain special privileges are allotted him which are not enjoyed by other Moslems; he is allowed, for example, a larger number of wives than the four whom the ordinary Moslem may marry. I shall not attempt to discuss the difficult and complicated problem of Mohammed's motivations in accepting these privileges; this

* In the Koran this is taught by implication rather than by direct assertion. In the later history of Islam there were groups that attributed to Mohammed a quasi-divine status and supernatural powers.

problem can only be resolved by a thorough and impartial study of all the relevant records in the light of the customs then affecting the status of Arabian women.

We come now to the Koran itself, which is a collection of all the revelations disclosed to Mohammed during his lifetime and preserved for posterity. In many respects it is unique among the sacred books of the world's religions. According to Moslem conviction, it is a copy of an eternal book existing in heaven,* of whose communication to men the angel Gabriel is the agent. It is written in the Arabic language, and it must be accepted as a revelation from God, although, according to its own statements, most men will not believe. Several interesting claims are made about itself. It makes quite plain, for example, all that it reveals, so that no man has any excuse for rejecting it. It is consistent with itself and there is a reason for repetitions where they occur. One passage states that an earlier revelation may be canceled by a later one;† this led to animated theological discussion as to which statements in the Koran shall be regarded as superseded in accordance with this passage. Keen psychological insight is reflected in the assertion that every new revelation increases faith in those who already believe, and adds doubt in the minds of the doubters. And one of the main purposes which led God to reveal Himself in the Koran is to clear up what men dispute about, along with the purpose of guiding believers in the right way of life. Lastly, it confirms the validity of the Jewish and Christian scriptures, which means that for Moslems the relation of the Koran to the Bible is essentially analogous to the relation, for Christians, of the New to the Old Testament. Mohammed is the last and greatest of the line of authentic messengers whose earlier revelations are given in the Christian Bible.

Soon after Mohammed's death, Islam took a step which

---

* According to some schools, it is that eternal book itself.

† "Whatever verses we cancel, or cause thee to forget, we bring a better or its like." *Koran*, trans. J. Rodwell, New York, 1909, p. 349 (Sura 2).

textual students of the scriptures of other religions often wish their own predecessors had taken. Already there had appeared divergent readings and variant traditions as to what, exactly, Gabriel had communicated in some of his disclosures to Mohammed. Foreseeing the divisive danger in this situation, the Caliph Abu Bekr commissioned Zaid, one of Mohammed's most loyal and intimate disciples, to collect and compare all these variations, and to issue an authoritative text, which thereafter could not be questioned. This Zaid did. His task was completed in the course of a few years, and all copies were destroyed which diverged in any respect from the standard copy which this process of editing had established. Thus Islam has been saved throughout its history from two of the difficulties haunting other religions that have appealed to an authoritative revelation from God. Christian sects have disagreed, for example, as to just which writings should be regarded as constituting the sacred scripture; in the case of the Koran this problem was avoided by the basic and unquestioned dictum that only the messages communicated to Mohammed himself were to be accepted as God's revealed will. And when Christian theologians investigated the history of the Biblical texts, they found a number of variations in the ancient documents at their disposal, with no clear indication in many cases as to which is most likely to be the original reading. A similar problem that would otherwise have puzzled Moslem scholars was averted by Zaid's fulfillment of his assigned task and especially by the destruction of all materials that might later have raised questions about the decisions made.

E. ITS RELATION TO JUDAISM AND CHRISTIANITY

I have just remarked on the fact that Mohammed regarded himself as the last in the line of authentic divine messengers whose revelations are given in the Old and New Testaments. This brings up for fuller consideration the interesting question of Islam's relation to Judaism and Christianity. From the Christian standpoint, its younger rival has historically been regarded as the arch-heresy and Mohammed as the great "impostor"; Christians have never forgiven Islam for robbing them of North Africa and the Middle East, and especially for securing possession of the sacred places associated with the life and death of Jesus. The crusades are on many accounts an instructive phenomenon in the history of the great religions. From the Mohammedan standpoint, however, Jews and Christians are to be treated with special consideration, for they are worshipers of the one true God; they are partial believers in the saving faith, and must not be confused with the pagans who are wandering in total error. In fact, until some years after the hegira, Mohammed taught his followers to face toward Jerusalem when they prostrated themselves in daily prayers; only when the majority of the Jews at Medina stubbornly refused to accept his claims did he begin to think of Mecca as the holy center of Moslem devotion and initiate the practice of facing in its direction. As Islam expanded its military and political control, Jews and Christians were of course expected to live peacefully and submissively under Moslem law; but no further pressure was to be brought upon them, and they were to be given the privilege of paying a special tax as a substitute for the tithe collected from pious Moslems.

Whom did Mohammed have in mind as constituting the line of major apostles that preceded him? The list varies, and it is interesting to observe that none of the great figures of the creative period of Hebrew prophecy is regarded as of special importance. The ones most frequently mentioned are the early heroes of Jewish lore—Noah, Abraham, and Moses —and, very significantly, Jesus of Nazareth. Mohammed loves to dwell upon those episodes in the preprophetic period of history which exhibit God's righteous punishment of those who rejected his messengers and flouted His revealed decrees; the more catastrophic judgments of 722 and 586 B.C. appear to be ignored. The dire events in the earlier period he uses as warnings to the stubborn disbelievers of his own day.

For Jesus of Nazareth Mohammed felt a very deep admiration and respect. Indeed, he believed far more of the Christian doctrines about Jesus than Christians have usually realized. Bodley summarizes this common core of teaching as follows:

Mohammed said that he (Christ) was the greatest of all prophets. He was convinced of his miraculous powers, that he was the Word proceeding from God, that he was the Messiah. He accepted the Immaculate Conception and believed that the birth of Jesus was a miracle. Before the end of the world, Jesus would return and slay Antichrist. After that, there would be universal peace. Christ would then die and be buried beside Mohammed.[7]

Why, then, did Mohammed not become a Christian? The gap which remained seems surprisingly small. The answer is that he was unable to believe that Jesus was the incarnation of God in human form, and he was likewise unable to believe that one individual can in any justifiable sense atone for the sins of others. Thus the points at which he diverged from the Christian faith were, after all, quite basic, and the divergence expresses not merely an intellectual disagreement but also a moral revulsion. Just as Christian thinkers were never quite able to appreciate the spiritual reasons which prevented most Jews from becoming converts to Christianity, so Mohammed and his followers were unable to penetrate the experiences which underlay the doctrine of the incarnation of God in Christ.

For Mohammed's very intense conviction, the unity of God—absolute and unqualified—is the foundation of all true religious faith. Hence the Christian doctrine of the Trinity—this bizarre idea of three gods in one—seemed to him a blasphemous error; it was a covert form of polytheism, however disguised. Moreover, the relationship that Christians conceived to obtain between the first and second members of the Trinity aroused his moral misgivings; it is very unseemly to believe of God that He should beget a son. We are not to suppose, I am sure, that Mohammed took this phraseology quite literally; however, to his religious feeling, even an analogical use of such a term as "beget" derogates from the absolute perfection of the one divine being. That this is the basic reason in his mind is indicated by the fact that he does not reject the Christian doctrine of the virgin birth; it is one thing (and wholly to be expected of the chosen Messiah) that he should be born in a miraculous manner, but it is another (and quite impossible) thing to hold that he is the begotten son of God. It was undoubtedly Mohammed's essentially legal conception of the relation between God and man that led to his revulsion from the doctrine of atonement. He never comprehended the idea that the love of one individual might so transform another that the latter becomes free from sin and guilt; his interpretation of the doctrine was entirely legal, not at all mystical. When each individual stands before the judgment seat of God he stands on his own feet and is inescapably responsible for his own record. No one else can pay the penalty for his disobedience and his failure to heed the divine warning; no one else can appropriately intercede for him. Such notions would weaken the absolute responsibility that each man has for his own conduct, and would compromise the awful finality of the great day of judgment.

The Christian reader of the Koran will not only ponder these drastic criticisms but will also observe with interest certain particular ideas which at one time or another were evidently in Mohammed's mind. Like Jesus' disciples during the weeks preceding his death, Mohammed could not believe that crucifixion was to be the destined fate of the Messiah. He held accordingly that Jesus was not really crucified, but that "God took him up to Himself"; in some unexplained manner a "likeness" was substituted for him on the cross. He also maintained—and we have seen that this could be plausibly supported so far as the Synoptic Gospels are concerned—that Jesus did not claim to be divine, but only the expected Messiah. And there is one passage in which he seems to have believed that Jesus' mother Mary is in Christian eyes one of the members of the Trinity.

F. THE SOCIAL GOSPEL OF ISLAM

But along with these critical notions about Christianity there is another which Mohammed emphasizes; it has been mentioned above, and now we must consider it with some care. If I am right, it is in large measure the clue to the distinctive historical genius of Islam. The criticism is that Christianity has divided into a number of quarreling sects, whereas unity and brotherhood are among the essential marks of true religion. Now the significance of this emphasis has been obscured to non-Moslems by the fact that Islam, like other religions, has generated its own deep cleavages (especially that between the Shiites and the Sunnites) and by the circumstance that in many Moslem countries there are stark economic disparities between the rich and the poor. But such failures fully to exemplify an accepted ideal are present in all religions; when one examines the situation more carefully, he finds a significant achievement to the credit of Islam. Gandhi, after becoming well acquainted with all the great religions, acknowledged himself increasingly impressed by the practical emphasis of Islam on equality and brotherhood; his coupling of the Koran with the *Bhagavad-Gita* during the later years of his life was in part an expression of this feeling. It was not merely due to the fact that the schism in India which he so longed to heal was a schism between Moslems and Hindus.

If one surveys the comparative achievement of Islam on this point with appreciative impartiality, what he finds, I think, is somewhat as follows. Before Mohammed's day the Bedouin of Arabia was a strange compound of democrat and haughty, independent aristocrat. He was a democrat in the sense that he respected courage, strength, and merit wherever and in whomever he found them; he allowed no questions of social prerogative or status to stand in the way. Bodley, in describing the Arabian nomads, says (with some exaggeration), "The chief and the shepherd meet on an equal footing. . . . No one is better than anyone else, except by outstanding merit. The deserts of the Arabs are the only places in the world where democracy is really put into practise."[8] He was a haughty aristocrat in his firm conviction that the group to which he belonged was the noblest among all peoples, and he therefore jealously restricted his devotion and sense of loyal belonging to his own clan. Mohammed, by the forceful appeal of his personality and his capacity for moral leadership, succeeded in achieving a super-clannish unity, on a basis of essential equality, among these liberty-minded and redoubtable nomads—a unity which, because its bond was enthusiastic acceptance of him and his cause, could in principle be extended as far as his appeal was able to reach. And it is clear that, along with his power of practical chieftainship, he possessed the prophetic human qualities that win enduring affection and trust on the part of others. He felt and showed compassion for those to whom life was a struggle, remembering his own early years as an orphan. He aimed at realizing, in Islam, a community where there is security, without dependence, for all, and where each one who submits to the divine sovereignty feels respect for every other as his equal. And according to Bodley, "this democratic spirit has been carried to all parts of the world where Islam has penetrated, and has been made applicable to nations as well as to individuals."

Of course this ideal was not carried out unqualifiedly in the details of Mohammedan law and custom. No more than the Christianity of the Pauline letters did the Islam of the Koran do away with the idea that men are superior to women, or that slaves may be properly retained in their servile position. But wherever this religion spread, it not only preached but in large measure practiced the conviction that all sincere Moslems are equal before God. It rejected special privileges of race or caste; it set up no special spiritual hierarchy of priests or monks as compared with laymen. When Moslem pilgrims flock to Mecca from all over the world, they lay aside their special garb and don the seamless white robe which makes each indistinguishable from every other pilgrim and proclaims to all the world that he is just one devout follower of Allah and nothing more. It is no wonder that Hinduism in India, after the Islamic invasion, found a large proportion of its lower-caste and outcaste adherents enticed away by Islam, which made them feel accepted on a more equalitarian basis.

How did it come about that Islam proved able to practice this ideal of equality and brotherhood as fully as it has? If we can answer this question, another feature in the distinctive genius of this faith besides those already discussed will become clear. And there is something about both the basic religious and the characteristic ethical attitude fostered by Islam which, I think, provides the answer.

On the one hand, there is the Moslem conception of God—as a cosmic being of transcendent, overwhelming majesty. He is the ruler of the universe, before whom man is nothing. In His awesome presence man lies submissively prostrate, and the differences between one person and another fade into insignificance. All are equally humbled before the all-powerful and all-knowing Allah. No one can witness the Friday noon service in a great Mohammedan mosque, when thousands of men fall in unison on their foreheads toward Mecca, without a vivid sense of the equalizing effect of the Moslem creed, with its incomparable exaltation of the divine being. Where God is consciously recognized as All, the pretensions of one human being in comparison with another dissolve as of no account. In Protestant Christianity, Calvinism produced something of the same effect, and became a powerful support of modern Western democracy for the same reason.

On the other hand, the ethical attitude that was encouraged in the Koran remedied one of the serious weaknesses of Christian ethics as taught in the New Testament. The emphasis of

Christian moral teaching fluctuated between insisting on the heavenly ethic of the Sermon on the Mount, together with the commandment in John that we should all love one another, and accepting the ethic of temporary compromises with the ways of worldly law and politics. The ideal envisioned was so high that when it was taught as a law, expecting strict obedience, men inevitably fell short of its demands, and in their discouragement looked for guidance to principles far less exacting. Thus Christians, summoned to "love your enemies" and finding themselves unable to practice the command, turned to the easier implications of the principle, "Render unto Caesar the things that are Caesar's, and to God the things that are God's." Hence the prevalence in Christian history of the idea that while one's inner obedience to God's will should be unqualified, his activities in the various institutions of which he is a member may be guided by the standards customarily recognized in the way those institutions function. Thus Christians have easily tended to accept, without any sense of serious conflict between such acceptance and their Christian loyalty, the ways of secular life in such matters as economic competition, racial privilege, war, patriarchal family control, and unjust legal precedents from the past.

Islam has on the whole avoided any such dualism. It has avoided it, in large part, by combining a kindly realism in dealing with human longings and limitations with the firm principle that the rules inculcated in the Koran are to be conscientiously practiced here and now. They are not to wait for the supernatural establishment of the divine kingdom, being replaced in the meantime by a system of accommodating compromises with the ways of an unregenerate world. Although the Koran envisions a high social ideal, and gives the devout and discerning Moslem every encouragement to live up to it more and more closely, it does not command the exemplification of this ideal as though it were a law. The realistic principle, repeated in several passages of the Koran, is, "We will not task a soul beyond its ability." But he is expected to live up to the standard that lies within his ability. Detailed rules are laid down, guided by the concepts of justice, mercy, humane consideration, and conscientious fairness, which the loyal Moslem is expected to practice in daily life. They lift his conduct above the impulsive, biased, and self-centered behavior of the mass of men, while not insisting, as a matter of law, that he conform to the ideal that the most alert and tender conscience will glimpse. Thus he is asked to go as far as the average man can go in meeting the concrete situations and obligations of social life in an attitude of equality and a spirit of brotherhood, while growing as he does so toward a fuller exemplification of the perfect love and tenderness that the saintly character embodies.

When one examines from this viewpoint the detailed regulations of the Koran, one discovers what this general description would lead him to expect. Slaves are not freed and accorded social equality, but their status is improved as compared with what it was before Mohammed's day, and especially in the matter of basic security and protection. They are to be given equal treatment in such practically important matters as sharing in the food supply of the family and in being provided with adequate clothing. Similarly in the case of women. It is explicitly proclaimed that "men are superior to women," but Mohammed achieved a vast improvement in the accepted rights of women as compared with the situation which had earlier obtained—where the absolute power of father and husband was unquestioned and where unwanted baby girls were buried alive without qualms.* The Koran assures to women protective rights on marriage, divorce, inheritance, and the like—in general, providing that a female heir inherits one-half as much as a male heir under the same circumstances. The way in which, through the pervading spirit of Mohammed's social teaching, Islam hopes that these

* Likewise cruelty to animals—even the cursing of camels and cocks—is proscribed.

rules will be affected by the ultimate ideal appears best, perhaps, in the Koran's provisions regarding marriage. A faithful Moslem may marry as many as four wives. But Mohammed is at pains to insist that he must not marry more than one unless he can give them equal tenderness and consideration. And the sympathetic reader of the Koran will not fail to note the insistent emphasis that is laid on such important personal and social virtues as cleanliness, avoidance of intoxication, generosity in business, impartiality in judicial decisions, and systematic protection for orphans, widows, travelers, and those who are sick.

In short, the Moslem social ethic combines a high ultimate standard with a set of rules which recognize human weakness and are accommodated to the differences as well as to the similarities in social situations. Love is the supreme ideal—and yet the average man is not really expected to love his enemy, only to treat him with respect, chivalry, and fairness. Justice and compassion are to be practiced toward all, and love and tenderness toward those who are close to us by ties of family connection or friendship. Equality and brotherhood are to be exemplified toward other Moslems, of whatever race, rank, or calling, and toward non-Moslems, too, so far as the attitude of the latter does not prevent their realization.

However, we meet here an important question, on which the teaching of Islam is ambiguous. Under what conditions may the earnest Moslem decide that believers in other religions are not so acting that the attitude of brotherhood toward them may be appropriately expressed? The whole problem of the "holy war," which has troubled non-Moslems through the centuries, is involved. The answer is that, partly because of altered circumstances in Arabia during the period of Mohammed's revelations, the relevant messages in the Koran vary; thus Moslems find justification either for exercising compulsion upon disbelievers or for treating them with a considerable degree of tolerance and generosity. The Koran explicitly teaches that only defensive war is permissible; but there are also passages clearly implying that it is a duty to make war upon disbelievers until they submit to Moslem rule and pay tribute, or even (in the case of idolaters) until they become converted to Islam.[9] As one would expect, Moslem practice through the centuries on this matter has followed no uniform pattern, but the emphasis has often been on chivalry and tolerance; in fact, the influence of Sufism (which will soon be discussed) has been in the direction of treating non-Moslems in the same spirit of love that is properly expressed toward fellow believers.

And the characteristic rejection of asceticism in the Semitic religions pervades the Islamic attitude toward life and the world throughout. All the potentialities that we find in the world and in ourselves are to be accepted and enjoyed as God's bounty to His children; none is intrinsically evil. Hence restrictions in the Koran on our use of the good things of life and the satisfaction of our natural desires are specific, few, and in certain cases temporary. Take for example, the matter of diet. As against the many taboos on food characteristic of earlier Arabian religion and imposed by religions elsewhere, the frequently reiterated principle of the Koran is that God gave all the pleasant things that man can eat for him freely to use and enjoy. There are a few items from which he must always refrain: pork, blood, anything that dies of itself, whatever has been offered to idols—and intoxicating liquor. The major temporary restriction—imposed in the interest of spiritual self-discipline and to show that every physical good should be subordinated to loyal obedience to God—is the fast during the month of Ramadan. On every day of this month of the year all faithful Moslems eat nothing and drink nothing from dawn till darkness, and indulge in no sexual gratification. And Mohammed's thoughtfulness of those in special need is beautifully revealed in these regulations. Those who are sick when Ramadan begins may postpone the fast until they are well, and any who are on a journey may wait until they return home.

Were I to expand this exposition of the original teachings of Islam in fuller detail, one intriguing task would be to show how the Koran brings out with unusual vividness certain problems which through the centuries have perplexed thinkers of all three of the great Western faiths.

Perhaps the most prominent of these is the problem of human responsibility and divine predestination. In the Koran there are many passages which teach or imply unequivocally that every man is responsible for his deeds, and especially for his acceptance or rejection of Mohammed's revelation from God. At the last judgment he will be called to account for his exercise of this responsibility on the assumption that he was free to choose the right or to succumb to the wrong. But when the question under consideration is how to explain the fact that some men choose the right and some the wrong —and this question is often dealt with in the Koran—the doctrine of predestination is consistently taught as the answer.[10] It is true that there is one passage which states that "whatever betideth good is from God, and whatever betideth evil is from thyself,"[11] but this verse hardly intends to reject the doctrine, fundamental to the whole Islamic perspective, that God is the sole ultimate cause who determines everything to happen as it does. Hence the reason why some are moved to choose the good and some yield to temptations of evil must in the end lie in the determining decree of God. Many are the passages in the Koran which affirm this consequence without flinching.

How are these assumptions of personal responsibility and moral freedom to be reconciled with the unqualified assertion of divine predestination? It is no wonder that Moslem (as well as Jewish and Christian) theology has struggled manfully with this dilemma, and that many keen solutions have been proposed. One observes with interest the fact that a solution widely accepted in Judaism and Christianity was not easily available to Moslem theologians, namely, the doctrine that God gave man complete freedom to choose either good or evil.

Many explicit statements in the Koran seemed to contradict this idea and could hardly be ignored.

G. *THE EARLY CENTURIES OF ISLAM*

I shall not take the space for an extended account of the significant developments in Islam from the period of its origins to the present day. The following sketch aims merely to underline those features of the story that one who has read the above pages should have in mind if he is to understand the picture presented by Islam in the modern world. For most Moslems, through the centuries, the heart of their religion has lain in following the basic precepts and observances which from the beginning have encouraged their sense of the living reality of God and of their brotherhood with each other. These features consist mainly of the five daily prostrations in adoration of God, the frequent recital of the Moslem creed, the giving of alms to provide for the poor and needy, the fast during the month of Ramadan, and the pilgrimage to Mecca sometime during one's lifetime, with the privilege thereafter of assuming the title *hajji.** Of course, only a small minority of those who live far away from Mecca can afford such a costly trip; none the less, the number of pilgrims who come to Mecca each year runs into the tens of thousands. Along with these basic continuities, however, there have been certain significant developments that could not have been anticipated at the beginning of this religion's career and which make the living situation of Islam today a different affair from what it would have been without them.

Catholic Christianity has its pope, who claims spiritual authority over all Christians, but whose sovereignty has never been accepted by the whole of Christendom. Islam throughout the greater part of its history has had its *caliph*—regarded as "commander of the faithful," besides ruling as political

* "One who has made the pilgrimage." The title is actually used in many Moslem countries.

sovereign over an important part of the domain of Islam. But there have at times been rival contenders for the caliphate; there have also been varying conceptions as to the nature and degree of the caliph's authority; and there have been different theories as to the rule of legitimacy in the historical succession from Mohammed. This last point naturally introduces us to the outstanding cleavage within the Moslem world which confronts the historical student. Despite Mohammed's earnest desire that a spirit of unity be preserved among his followers, and the extent to which this desire has been satisfied, groups did divide from each other on doctrinal or practical grounds, and these divisions have been as complex as those exhibited by any other great religion.

The sharpest and broadest cleavage has been that between the Sunnite and the Shiite Moslems, the former comprising a large majority of all believers, but Shiah constituting the dominant form of Islam in Iraq and Iran. It also has some strength in Pakistan and north India. According to the Shiites, the legitimate succession from Mohammed is through Ali, Mohammed's cousin and son-in-law, who actually ruled as the fourth caliph, and then through the twelve *imams* who were contenders for the headship after Ali's reign, the last of whom passed away in A.D. 878. The Shiites attribute to the *imam* the same spiritual authority and essential infallibility that Roman Catholics do to the pope. An influential doctrine in Shiah (though not universally held) teaches that the last *imam* did not die but is preserved alive in some secret place; at the appropriate time he will return as the *mahdi* to restore justice throughout the world and establish the supremacy of Islam. Many have been the claimers to the mahdiship in Islamic history.

H. MYSTICISM AND THE THEOLOGY OF GHAZZALI

As founded by Mohammed, Islam was as completely free from any touch of mysticism as a religion well could be. It exemplified a legal conception of religion throughout. But the appeal and power of mysticism in civilized religion are strikingly shown in the fact that during the second century after Mohammed's death an explicitly mystic note became articulate and steadily gained influence; before long it had succeeded in imposing an indelible stamp on the Islam of succeeding centuries. This is the more surprising in that it involved a pretty radical change, at that late date, from what had been the basic emphasis on obedience and submission to God as constituting true piety—as radical a change, in essence, as that achieved by the Johannine perspective in Christianity. The Moslem mystics are generally known as "Sufis," a term originally meaning "wool" and referring to the coarse garb adopted by the ascetic forebears of the mystic movement. Contrary to what one might expect, the historical influences which underlay Islamic mysticism do not seem to have come from the East (except in the case of the later Indian Sufis) but from Christian mysticism, and the framework in which it attained its intellectual interpretation was mainly provided by the Neoplatonic philosophy.

This circumstance is largely responsible for the fact that the Sufis not only exemplify the general mystic conviction that salvation consists in the attainment of union with God, rather than in submission to His kingly authority, but also emphasize love as constituting the essence of the divine nature. In harmony with this emphasis, they teach that love of God and of others in God is the supreme mark of spiritual perfection. "It is in the love of God that man loses himself and finds the fulfilment of his being. Love is the principle and motive of Sufi ethics; it is, as Jelal al-Din says, 'the remedy of our pride and self-conceit—the physician of all our infirmities. Only he whose garment is rent by love becomes entirely unselfish.' He who loves God supremely sees God in all His creatures, and expresses this divine love in all his dealings with them."[12]

All the distinctive characteristics of mystical religion, in East or West, naturally followed from this foundation and are exemplified in the Sufi form of Islam.* This even includes the tendency in mysticism to transcend all sectarian distrust and to recognize spiritual unity with sincere seekers of God in other religions—contrasting vividly with the exclusive claim to religious truth taught in the Koran and characteristic of early Islam. From this point of view religion becomes a positive evil if it allows its varying creeds and rites to divide men from each other. Ibn Arabi is quoted as saying, "There was a time when I took it amiss in my companion if his religion was not like mine, but now my heart admits every form. It is a pasture for gazelles, a cloister for monks, a temple for idols, a Ka'aba for the pilgrim, the tables of the Law, and the sacred book of the Koran. Love alone is my religion, and whithersoever men's camels turn, it is *my* religion and *my* faith."[13]

How did mysticism affect the developments through the centuries in Moslem theology? The perennial issue here, as in the case of Judaism and Christianity when they sought to appeal to intellectually alert men, has been the issue of faith and reason. Granting a fundamental place in religion for faith in the sacred authority of revelation, how far may its deliverances be appropriately rationalized and systematically related to a philosophical interpretation of the world? How much trust may the devout Moslem place, in dealing with religious ideas and beliefs, in the methodical, logical use of reason? The most influential school of rationalist theologians, during the early centuries of Islam, were the Mutazilites; they were opposed by the defenders of a simple faith who distrusted any attempt at philosophical inquiry into religious questions,† and before long also by the mystics, who insisted on the ultimate necessity of transcending both authority and reason by a superrational intuition.

As a result of these debates Islam was ready, four and a

* Even the Buddhist concept of Nirvana appears and plays a significant part. Its Arabic equivalent is *fana*.

† The extremer among these taught that "he who seeks religion through theology becomes a heretic." See A. S. Tritton, *Islam*, London, 1951, p. 35.

half centuries after Mohammed's death, for the work of the
great thinker al-Ghazzali (A.D. 1058–1111), who occupies a
similar historical position in Islamic thought to that of Sankara in modern Hinduism and Thomas Aquinas in Catholic
Christianity. In fact, so far as the analogy with Christianity is
concerned, Ghazzali was an Augustine as well as an Aquinas; he reached his certainties after a torturing struggle with
skepticism and a desperate effort to square himself with all
the main alternatives that the thought of his age offered. Like
Augustine, he found that his final intellectual solutions could
be worked out only on the basis of a profound inner experience. In virtue of the intellectual aspect of this experience,
Ghazzali became convinced, both of the central tenets of the
Moslem creed and of the validity of an essentially mystic
interpretation of them. The book in which these solutions are
systematically expounded is entitled *The Revival of the Religious Sciences.*[14]

Al-Ghazzali was sure that the rationalizing theologians
were wrong in assuming that religious truth can be systematically demonstrated; any demonstration rests on certain ultimate premises and fails to convince all who reject them. He
saw also that the arguments of those who defended some
source of infallible authority inevitably moved in a circle;
the authority must be true because it is a revelation from God,
and we know it is from God because what it says is true. As
for the mystics, he was sure that the heart of their interpretation of religion is right; God is love, and only as every
aspect of religious life and thought is permeated by the spirit
of love does it really express devotion to God and true communion with Him. But the mystics, too, were wrong so far
as they insisted on any particular intellectual interpretation of
their experience; in fact, the deepest religious experience cannot be intellectually described at all.

What role, then, can reason helpfully fill in this situation?
Ghazzali's answer to the question is essentially that of Sankara in India and of the "existentialist" Christian theologians

today. It is a modest role, but a very important one none the less. Reason can help the seeker for religious truth to avoid misleading errors; it can guide him toward the purging of his soul from all that is not God; it can show how everything in experience and the religious life should be interpreted if it is to express through and through the love of God. Ghazzali's *Revival* is the result of a systematic effort to write a theology which would successfully fill this role. Its profound historical influence is due partly to its complete penetration by the spirit of loving communion with God and partly by its success in interpreting the manifold details of Moslem faith and practice in harmony with this spirit. As a result of Ghazzali's memorable achievement, the same transformation took place in a large segment of Islam that had occurred in Christianity during its early years through the insight of John and Paul. For those who could respond, a strictly legal conception of religion was replaced by one in which the mystic approach is dominant and in which God becomes the cosmic spirit of love instead of the lawgiver and judge.

I. ISLAM IN THE WORLD OF TODAY

I shall pass over entirely the vicissitudes of Moslem history between the time of al-Ghazzali and our own day. What is happening to the religion founded by Mohammed in this stirring twentieth century? Well, Islam, like the other major faiths, is endeavoring to adjust itself to the complex challenge of the contemporary world scene. The forces of conservatism are very powerful, perhaps more so than in any of the other great religions. But the impact of new factors cannot be escaped. A commission appointed some years ago by the Faculty of Theology at the University of Istanbul reported that the first reform needed in Turkey was a reinterpretation of the Koran such as would harmonize it with modern ideas and would accord with the method of science. Similar statements have appeared in other Moslem lands. In line with this suggestion, Moslem thinkers, especially in Egypt, Pakistan,

India, and Indonesia, offer new philosophical interpretations from time to time, but so far as I can tell the novelties are either not very radical or have failed thus far to win widespread influence. It would seem that the story of Islamic theological reconstruction in our revolutionary age is mainly a story of the future. The Islamic countries are slowly becoming industrialized, and are more and more eager to learn from the science and technology of the West. The women are gradually discarding the veil. Most Moslem peoples have lived through the experience of colonial control by one or another Western power; like many other lands they are now in process of throwing off that control and asserting their national independence. There is some readiness for sympathetic collaboration with each other, but no such sense of spiritual union has appeared as would portend a united front on international issues.

Let us close this survey of Islam by a summary statement of the way in which it exemplifies each of the four main characteristics of the living civilized religions.

An essential monism is revealed, of course, in its conception of the one true God, who is the sole creator of all that exists and the controlling power in all that happens. The acceptance of moral universality appears in its conviction that God has laid down in the Koran certain laws that are obligatory upon the conduct of all, and has disclosed an ideal of spiritual perfection that is valid for all. The virtues making for unity and brotherhood stand at the heart of this ideal. The discovery of the soul as something inward and invisible, unlike any physical object or process, is revealed in its insistence that what decides salvation or damnation is not any outward act as such, but whether or not there is sincere inner obedience to God and sincere love for Him. And the doctrine that man cannot find true happiness merely by satisfying his desires as they naturally press upon him, but must undergo a radical transformation in order to attain it, is present in the basic concept of "Islam" as essential to salvation. We human beings are naturally oriented around our own wills as the determinative force in our conduct; but the true good, here and hereafter, can only be found by complete and wholehearted submission to the Divine Will as the ultimate control over our lives. To do what God wills instead of what our own impulses lead us to will is the key to dependable peace and blessedness for man. In the case of those who have accepted a predominantly mystic interpretation, salvation means the purging of our souls of all that separates us from God, and becoming absorbed in the divine love so that it flows through us in every thought, word, and deed.

PART FOUR

Religion in the Present and the Future

XIV.

A Summary,
Comparison, and Forecast

A. THE NATURE OF RELIGION IN THE LIGHT
OF ITS HISTORY

Were it my purpose merely to write a descriptive story of religion the account would close with the preceding chapter. But I hope that, while being faithful to the vital facts, what I have written will contribute not merely to a historical but also to a philosophical understanding of religion. If it is to fill such a role, we shall not wish to bring the narrative to an end at this point. We shall want reflectively to ponder, under the guidance of a few summarizing and comparative questions, the panorama that has unfolded; we shall want to cast a glance toward the future. Our closing chapters will deal with these themes.

And we might as well plunge right into the heart of the summarizing task with the first question. What is the significant place and function of religion? What is its distinctive role in human life, the role that clearly belongs to it and is not filled by science, or art, or philosophy, or any of the other major aspects of man's cultural life? In Chapter I we considered this question, and decided that the appropriate place to give a direct answer is at the end of the book rather than at the beginning.

455

Our procedure throughout commits us to answer in terms of man's seeking and man's experience; we rejected the temptation to assume that we could give God's answer to the question. At the same time it has seemed clear that these two modes of approach are by no means irreconcilable with each other. If God is real, has He not been revealing Himself to man in and through man's humble search for Him—not the search of some single sect, but of all sincere seekers for religious truth in all places and times?

First, let us give the best general answer that we can—one applicable to all forms of religion everywhere. And it is evident from the whole course of our study that such an answer will inevitably be very abstract and thin; all the concrete richness disappears when one takes no account of the differences between primitive and civilized religion and tries to formulate a definition that applies to religion wherever it appears. Then we shall want a summarizing statement applying to primitive religion—that is, to those prominent forms of it that we needed to discuss because of their provocative and clarifying contrast with the great civilized religions. Finally, we shall try to articulate a synoptic view of these civilized religions, in the light of our patient study of each of them, thus completing, with the relevant material before us, the anticipatory characterization given in Chapter IV.

The basic general truth is something like this. Through his religious responsiveness man (1) discovers a power (or powers) in the universe through which his most insistently challenging needs can be met, and (2) establishes an effective relation to it so that those needs, in greater or less degree, are met. The distinctive object of man's religious feeling—i.e., the divine—is then that power (or those powers), and man's soul is the dynamic core of his nature that feels those needs and actively pursues the quest for their satisfaction.

So much for the necessarily meagre general answer. But for our purposes such an inclusive definition is relatively unimportant. Let us turn at once to the difference between primitive and civilized religion, for the major needs that provide the clue to our understanding in the one case are quite distinct from those that provide the clue in the other, especially when we think of the great living civilized faiths. Our central concern has been to understand these differences, not just to concoct an abstract formula that will hold of all religion.

The major (though not the only) need in primitive society which finds religious expression is the need of winning the help of those forces on which man depends in his effort to assure continued existence and physical well-being. He is weak; life is precarious; he lacks accurate knowledge of nature's ways. So the main divine powers recognized by primitive religion are identified with such forces; and with the growth of science such divine powers gradually fade into limbo. They are replaced by natural energies which man increasingly believes he can control by mastering the verifiable laws of their behavior.

What is the corresponding major need in civilized society? Well, instead of anxious preoccupation with the fickle subhuman forces of nature, the center of emotional attention more and more becomes the struggle for security and supremacy among various social groups—between one nation or race and another, between the few rich and the many poor, between rulers and ruled, between one vocation with its special interests and others. And these struggles also go on within every soul; each person identifies himself in feeling and action both with narrow, selfish concerns and also with the welfare of all his fellows.

Now the persistent need which civilized religion confronts in this situation is twofold. On the one side, it is to find a way of resolving this social and inner conflict, through the aid of whatever mysterious powers can be discovered that give insight into the right solution and dependable support in the quest for its realization. On the other side there is the even more significant positive urge that is the counterpart of this search. This urge, as it reveals itself more and more in the history of civilization, is what we call the undying aspiration in man. It is the effort to envision and fulfill newly awakened possibilities, of which man could be only vaguely aware when his attention was mainly absorbed in the task of maintaining himself against the uncertain forces of physical nature. Stated in broad terms, these possibilities are (1) a rich, dynamic integrity within the soul of each individual person, (2) a harmony of loving understanding between every man and each of his fellows, and (3) an expanding creative union between himself and that which is most real in the universe within which he has his being. As he grows in each of these directions, civilized man becomes aware of a kind of satisfying fulfillment far superior to and incomparable with the happiness gained merely by appeasing the desires that (except for meagre and transitory intimations) filled his consciousness before these possibilities were clearly glimpsed.

The prime concern of high civilized religion is this searching and exploring aspiration of man as it takes form through the insight and example of the spiritual pioneers of history. The faith which it everywhere expresses is the conviction that there are resources in the universe in virtue of whose creative presence nothing but the greatest conceivable fulfillment in each of these three directions is good enough for man —and good enough for all men, without regard to distinctions of sex, race, color, or tongue. Neither science, nor art, nor philosophy, nor politics, nor any other broad phase of man's cultural life makes this aspiring search its distinctive concern, although each of them draws inspiration in its own way from this spiritual faith. Here is the role of religion in civilized society; it accepts the responsibility to guide this hopeful quest toward its fulfillment. Without the part of his nature that such religion reveals, man in civilized society would not be fully man.

Of course, along with this searching and exploring urge there is a strongly conservative note in religion. For this reason many adherents of the civilized faiths do not yet clearly appre-

ciate what religion at its best and greatest can be. Were they
to do so, these faiths would break sharply with every aspect
of primitive religion that is incompatible with their deepest
visions. At any given time the theology of a civilized religion
is always a confused mixture of ideas which reveal a quite
primitive orientation and ideas expressing keen spiritual insight into man and his universe; the mixture gradually struggles toward consistency and clarity under the guidance of the
latter. The process takes time.

How does civilized religion perform this distinctive role?
In answering this question, let us continue to fix our eyes on
what is common to all the great civilized faiths.

An adequate answer would need to include four assertions.
First, each civilized religion achieves, in its own way, an intuitive vision of the ideal of character and principles of conduct which, if they could become effective in human life,
would end the divisive conflict within man and between
men, replacing it by creative harmony and brotherhood.
Second, it abandons the purely primitive notion of divine
power; instead, the divine is located in the realm of mystery
that haunts man's search for this ideal and for fulfillment
of the rich possibilities that such a search reveals. This requires that the divine be no longer conceived as an aggregate
of natural forces, but as essentially embodying this ideal in
its two dimensions of moral perfection and metaphysical
unity. Thus dawns the vision of the One God of wisdom,
wholeness, and love. Third, it provides a way by which this
search can be progressively satisfied in the earnest experience of men and women, and opens resources of spiritual
power for removing whatever obstructions block the path.
In both these respects the solution varies in detail from one
faith to another, since successful fulfillment does not occur
in the same way in all individuals and all social groups. Moreover, no religion can really achieve a synthesis of all valid
ways, even though it may consciously try to do so; inevitably it makes its own special emphasis, which reflects

an insight that is limited rather than truly universal. Fourth, it offers the world a radiant and inspiring example of the new vision it has caught. Indeed, we are now in a position to see, more clearly and fully than we could at any earlier stage of our study, the unique role filled by the pioneering leaders of the civilized faiths. To those who came after them they communicated both the new insight they had gained and also the transforming energy by which that insight could become effective in the lives of others. This they did partly by their teaching, but still more by their exemplification of the ideal which lies at the heart of their message.

We can see how significant this role is if we consider as an illustration the ideal of love—supreme mark of spiritual maturity for all the great religions. Thinkers could have defined and preachers might have taught, till doomsday, the concept of "self-giving love," but the listening world would not have known what these words mean. It would never have experienced anything but possessive, demanding, self-seeking love, except in the limited forms of family affection or devoted friendship. By "love" people would have meant the highest moral ideal that had thus far clearly come within their ken; they could not have conceived any meaning for it that lay beyond their meager experience. But when people not only heard the words but saw, in Confucius, Buddha, Jeremiah, Jesus, Mohammed, Gandhi, the reality which the words expressed—the free, compassionate responsiveness to others and the joy, peace, and strength intrinsically flowing from it—they understood the words, and were more and more moved in their own feeling and conduct to identify with the ideal thus exemplified. The meaning and the way to realize it came home to them together.

Without such pioneers as these the world would have continued to live in spiritual blindness and numbness; but their appearance threw human history into a divine unrest which could never be ended until other men too had realized the true meaning of love and had shared the enriched experience it can bring. For, even while wandering in darkness, they can see dimly that this is the mature ideal for man and that the happiness to which it leads is the only stable and enduring happiness possible in the world as it really is.

The most radical form taken in civilized religion by this response to a radiant and dynamic personality appears in the deification of their founders by Mahayana Buddhism and by Christianity.* These two individuals became to their followers such unique sources of spiritual insight and transforming power that Buddhists and Christians found what was most divine in their universe as a whole revealed in the personality of their founder. Here, they were convinced, is God—here is the incarnation, within human history, of the divine reality which in its full and infinite meaning transcends history.

But I am well aware that it is hard for modern men and women to see religion as filling any such creative role as I have attributed to its great pioneers. What are the main reasons for this difficulty? Well, the basic reason lies in the failure of most people to distinguish clearly enough between the adventurous first-hand religion of these spiritual geniuses and the second-hand religion of their followers. Thus there is a strong and persistent tendency to identify religion solely with the latter. Now, although some followers in each generation realize the same revolutionary experience that their master did, in general these two kinds of religion are very different. For the pioneer, religion is essentially a creative exploration into new and hazardous territory where he has to clear his own path; he has left behind the security, protection, and comfort that adherence to traditional ideas and practices brings. The religion of his successors is second-hand, not in the sense that it is insincere or a mere echo of his vital experience, but because its chart is already at hand in the interpretation of his adventure that he has taught them. So far as that chart is a good one, they often depend on it so

* And in the Hindu concept of *avatar*.

completely that they lose the sense of perilous searching; their religion consists in finding security and comfort in the now safe itinerary that he has explored for them. Of course such dependence varies greatly in degree, but surely any conception of religion that would reduce it to this second-hand type would be a very inadequate conception. To bring out the crucial point in extreme form, it would be like describing the enterprise of science as it is exemplified by the obedient laboratory assistant, without giving a central place in one's picture to the work of a Galileo, a Newton, or a Pasteur.

A further reason, closely connected with this, lies in the fact that in the course of religious history ecclesiastical institutions are born which reveal the vices of all powerful organizations. The priestly mind strongly tends to hold essential to religion whatever conditions are required to preserve the institution he administers, and because of his position of authority this assumption exerts wide influence. But in falling into such an attitude he forgets that in its original form his religion needed none of these conditions, and therefore that it would be a mistake to count them essential. It is precisely when this mistake has been made on a serious scale that a living prophetic revolution has to break open the ossified church with a revitalizing vision of what religion must and can be. Not for long will men live without a faith expressing their aspiring hopes and interpreting with insight their deepest experiences.

We may be sure, then, that high civilized religion will continue to fill this distinctive role, either through the dynamic growth of the forms in which it already exists or through the birth of new faiths better adapted to the needs of the modern world.

B. RECURRING TYPES OF CIVILIZED RELIGION

Now let us raise a different question. Throughout our study we have been careful to respect the cultural and historical setting within which each religion appeared. We wanted sympathetically to let it tell its own story; we were determined to avoid imposing on it the strait jacket of our own theological assumptions. If we have realized the virtues of that method, it is our privilege no longer to be bound by its limitations. It is now important to ask: What recurring types of religion can we discern—types that cut across the great civilized cultures and are exemplified in each of them, or at least in more than one? That there are such types we are already aware. Of course it is not easy to identify them in an impartial and clarifying way. I think none the less that we may helpfully recognize four discernible types; each of them, as I shall describe it, emerges full blown only in civilized religion and appears in primitive societies merely in rudimentary form. The fact that these types exist testifies to diverse religious needs that are rooted in human nature as such, irrespective of the way it is molded by this or that set of cultural forces.

The most obvious, I should think, of these recurring types is mysticism. In all three broad areas of the civilized world surveyed by our study this has been a conspicuous form of religion. In Hinduism it is most prominent. There we found it so strong and pervasive that it determines the main currents in philosophy; the most widely accepted interpretation of the universe among India's intellectual leaders is an essentially mystical interpretation. But Taoism reveals a powerful mystic strain in the Chinese temperament, and the vigorous influence of the Gospel of John shows that the religious spirit of the West also responds to the mystic call and finds satisfaction in a mystic view of the divine. Moreover, Islam, developing for a hundred years or more in the almost complete absence of any mystic element, found it necessary to make a hospitable place for Sufi mysticism, which thereafter became a transforming current in the Moslem world. It would seem from these facts that no civilized religion can hope for enduring success unless it satisfies the mystic urge in man.

Another recurrent type, exhibited all over the civilized world, is the one described in Hindu literature as the "way of loving devotion." The *Bhagavad-Gita* has won its strong appeal to the Indian mind because of its beautiful portrayal of devotion to Krishna as the perfect solution of the perplexed individual's quest. And the decisive role of man's idealizing imagination in the way of devotion is clearly illustrated in the *Gita*. Although this divinity was originally a historical person with many weaknesses and foibles, the Krishna of the *Bhagavad-Gita* is portrayed as the ideal of spiritual perfection; he has almost completely lost contact with his historical namesake. In Christianity, Jesus of Nazareth so closely exemplified the spiritual ideal to his followers that he was readily identified with the Christ who is the object of loving devotion for millions of earnest hearts in the West. In China the need for this type of religion was not adequately met by any of the native faiths, and here is surely a major reason why Buddhism became the spiritual force in China that it did. In the devotional sects of Mahayana Buddhism, Buddha himself, in the form of Amitabha, becomes the prime object of loving attachment and satisfies the need in much of Eastern Asia for a religion of earnest faith in a personal divinity. Judaism and Islam, because of their august monotheism which forbade identifying the divine with any human figure, however idealized, were unable to meet this powerful urge in the same way. But neither could they ignore it. What happened in their case was that they managed to bring the Sovereign God of the universe sufficiently close to man so that he was experienced by the pious Jew or Moslem as a daily companion and friend, toward whom the same adoring sentiment could be felt. Clearly a religion that fails to meet this deep longing will find it hard to achieve lasting influence in any civilized society.

A third recurrent type, especially strong in the Occident, is the way of obedience to the divine law. Among the Western religions this is bound up with a theistic view of God, and a psychology which regards will as the dominant faculty in both God and man. From this standpoint God is believed to have imposed detailed commandments, ceremonial and moral, and the essence of true religion is for man to renounce his rebellious self-will, expressed in disobedience to these commands, and to submit sincerely to God's will. We have noted more than once the vital influence of this idea in Judaism and Islam, and the fact that it has been a significant strain in Christianity too. But the need to conceive religion in this way has not been absent in the Eastern faiths; however, because of their different framework of thought, it appears in another guise. Instead of being associated with the notions of "will" and "law," its closest affiliate in Indian theology is *dharma* and in Chinese thought *li* or *tao*. In terms of the former of these concepts, to be truly religious is to fulfill the rites and functions of one's station in life and to accept the duties of one's caste; in terms of the latter, it is to respect the proprieties that in any situation a sensitive man will recognize and to follow the true laws of spiritual growth. It would seem that this need also is a strong one; it is the phase of civilized religion that is most clearly continuous with the similar phase in primitive religion.

There is one important recurring type not yet mentioned. We may call it briefly "the way of the Golden Rule." The center of emphasis in each of the three types just sketched is the individual person in his relation to the divine. But the center of emphasis in a civilized religion may lie in man's practical role as member of a social order, the divine power being interpreted in a significant relation to that order. This basic conception of religion is dominant in Confucianism; but it constitutes a popularly influential strain in several other religions, notably Christianity. Many Christians will say, "I am not much on theology; my religion is to follow the Golden Rule." In Confucianism, to be a superior man is to fulfill one's moral responsibilities toward the various social groups (especially the family) to which one belongs, and their spiritual significance is realized by conceiving the moral order of society as part of the wider realm of right relationships regulated by Heaven. The central principle which gives guidance in fulfilling this social role is the rule to do unto others, not as they are doing to you, but as you would that they might do to you were you in their place. This emphasis, too, in some form can hardly be neglected by any civilized religion.

Consideration of these types reveals the further point that no great civilized religion exemplifies a single type only; even if it appears to do so at the beginning, in the course of time it takes forms which enable it to satisfy other needs too. This happens either as a result of interaction with other religions or by the unfolding of further resources within itself. Every great faith thus comes to fuse in its own distinctive way two or more of these types. The fusion has usually taken place without specific intent; Hinduism is the one living religion in which the quest for such inclusiveness is a consciously adopted principle.

It would seem, then, a justified forecast that each of these four types of religion will continue to live and adapt itself to changed circumstance, at least as long as the basic conditions and problems of civilized society remain.

But I see no reason to suppose that civilized religion must be restricted to these types. Our study has amply shown that religion is as dynamic as any other phase of human life; this appears most vividly in the transition from primitive to civilized religion, but to a discerning eye it is revealed everywhere in religious history. Nothing has happened, surely, to extinguish the creative spark in religion; it is today a growing aspect of man's quest for fullness of life as much as in any earlier period. New sects spring up from time to time; how do we know that one of them may not grow into a world-wide faith, perhaps even taking a form that would not quite fit any of the types above described? In this case it would very likely, in its initial stages at least, appear something else than a religious movement; only gradually would its religious character become clear as it shows its capacity to meet the human needs that other religions have met.

This seems to be an intriguing possibility. In fact, it may be more than a possibility. Let us ponder, in the setting of this suggestion, a challenging and timely question.

C. IS COMMUNISM A RELIGION?

Were we wrong, perhaps, in speaking of Islam as the youngest of the great civilized religions of the world? Has another one risen in our own day? All thinkers in the modern world are aware that communism is an economic and a political system; is it also a religion? One is tempted, of course, to answer this question by a flat no—remembering the hostility of communist leaders toward the established religions with which they are acquainted, and their avowed atheism. But any reader of the preceding pages will know that such considerations are not by themselves conclusive. Early Buddhism was atheistic—or at least agnostic, with respect to the reality of God as religion has usually conceived Him—and it involved such a radical revolution in what many in Buddha's day considered essential to religion that to not a few it must have seemed positively irreligious.

So we must probe the question quite seriously. And there should emerge from the probing both a fuller understanding of the meaning of our key word "religion," in its potentialities for the future, and also a sharper appreciation of the features which distinguish the Western religions from those of the East. For, if it turns out that communism may properly be called a religion, there is no doubt that it belongs with the Western triad of religious faiths—Judaism, Christianity, and Islam.

Why do I assert this so confidently? Well, on careful examination communism reveals all—or, perhaps we had better

say, almost all—of the distinctive features of the great Western faiths of the past in their contrast with the religions of
the East. Let us follow up this clue.

In the first place, communism claims to offer, wherever it
goes, an appealing social ideal of liberation from aristocratic
iniquity and colonial exploitation—an ideal whose pursuit
promises justice and equality and hope for the downtrodden
masses of the world. Now we have seen that this is one vital
note in the preaching of the Old Testament prophets, one
note in what the coming of the Kingdom meant to the
Synoptic Jesus, one vital note in Mohammed's message to the
poor and ignorant Arabians whose status he helped to ele-
vate. In the second place, communist thinking is marked by a
vivid sense of the reality of history, and of an inevitable law
governing the way it develops. According to the Marxian
dialectic, social evolution necessarily passes through a certain
sequence of stages in its march toward the ideal society
which is destined to be realized in the future. Now as one
looks at the religions of the past from this point of view,
he can hardly help observing that the Western religions—
and only they—have shown any such sense of the significance of history and offer any such social promise for the
future. The Eastern religions speak their message of hope to
the individual; but when it comes to an interpretation of
worldly history they conceive it as a ceaseless repetition of
cosmic cycles, or even as a shadowy appearance—ultimately
illusory rather than real. In the third place, communism
believes that there comes a crucial moment in history when
punishing judgment falls upon the forces of evil—in its
terminology, the "revolution," which has already happened
in the communist countries but which still waits to be realized
on a world-wide scale. On this decisive day of judgment
the wicked capitalists who are responsible for the pains and
miseries of mankind will be toppled from their seats of power
while the hitherto oppressed toilers achieve their triumph
and receive their reward. One can hardly miss the similarity

of this denouement with the judgment day of the earlier Western religions, when Satan with his cohorts will be consigned to destruction while the poor and faithful followers of the way of righteousness will pass to their merited paradise in the kingdom of equality and brotherhood. And in the fourth place, how about the communist conception of this kingdom of equality and brotherhood? It looks suspiciously like the kingdom of God on earth promised by the past prophets of the Western religions, whose establishment will inaugurate the "millennium"—a new era of justice, peace, and happiness such as well-disposed men have always sought, but which has hitherto never been realized. In communist terminology, this new social order is the "classless society," whose appearance ends the unhappy struggles for power between classes, and establishes a community in which each freely gives to others what his talents can produce and freely receives from others what he needs for life and growth.

In the fifth place, the efforts of communists to spread their creed over the world are marked by the same aggressive and fanatical fervor that has characterized the earlier Western religions in the heyday of their missionary enthusiasm. For it is bound up with the same dogmatic conviction which says, when frankly expressed: "Ours is the saving truth, and the only saving truth. All who refuse to accept it are wandering in darkness and error; their minds are clouded by the blind pursuit of self-seeking ends. Join us, or else be lost in the convulsive destruction destined to overtake the wicked who persist in impenitent hostility to the ideal goal that history will surely realize." Now, as we have seen, this attitude is radically alien to the tolerant teachableness characteristic of the Eastern religions; even Buddhism, the great missionary faith of the East, spread through Asia not by any dogmatic claim to final truth but by inviting its converts to rediscover, under the guidance of their own experience and reason, the saving insight that it brought. But this claim to the exclusive possession of truth has, generally speaking, characterized the missionary activities of Christianity and Islam, deeply convinced, as their propagandists have been, that salvation required acceptance of their message as the unique and final disclosure from God to man.

To these provocative parallels must be added a sixth, which is of special interest. One of the most perplexing features of the judicial "purges" in Russia and the "brainwashing" achievements in China is the readiness of many who have been subjected to these rigors to confess their errors—some even wildly exaggerating the faults of which they are guilty— and to demand appropriate punishment for their crimes. Such phenomena will continue, I am sure, to constitute an insoluble puzzle if we think of communism in merely political terms and refuse to recognize its religious character. But when the latter takes its place in the picture, the explanation becomes obvious and simple. One merely needs to recall the way in which religion—especially Western religion, with its emphasis on God as authoritative judge—has sought the spiritual transformation of rebellious souls by inducing an experience of penitent conversion. What happens in that experience? Conscience-struck by a sudden realization of the terrible abyss of error into which they have fallen and of the sad consequences to others of their sinful deeds, fearful of the punishment in hellfire which they now see justly awaiting them, convicted souls turn away in revulsion from their past way of life; they purge their hearts by a full confession —sometimes public confession, as in the case of the Oxford movement—acknowledging themselves miserable sinners before God and wholly dependent on His merciful grace. As the outcome of this emotional upheaval they experience a release from the burden of sin, and give themselves in unqualified commitment to the new way of life that is now accepted as alone true and good.

The converted adherent of communism, especially when his conversion has been skillfully fostered by the purging techniques, evidently undergoes a similar emotional purge.

He is seized with guilt at the thought that he has opposed the way of liberation and justice for the downtrodden masses of the world; he accepts as right the threat of liquidation if he were to persist in his unjust ways; through confession of his heinous errors he feels himself released from the burden of guilt; and as a result of this series of steps he is overcome with a sense of gratitude toward the inscrutable power which instead of punishing him forthwith has compelled this inner revulsion and liberating awareness. That communism has been able to induce this kind of experience in its own way, and to orient toward its ends the emotional convulsion produced, is clear testimony to a genuinely religious dimension in communist psychology, and to the deep significance of the parallels already drawn. And again the comparison is obviously with conversion phenomena familiar in Western religion rather than with the spiritual realization characteristic of the East.

So, in all these respects, a surprisingly full and clarifying parallel can be drawn. We come, then, to the crucial differences—and the answer to the question raised at the beginning of this section depends on how those differences are interpreted in their bearing on the meaning of "religion." Most obvious, of course, is the difference with respect to belief in God. To the earlier Western religions such belief is basic; but communism rejects it, not merely as a piece of superstition but also as a peculiarly offensive way of exploiting the masses, benumbing them to the earthly injustices under which they live in the comforting illusion that divine compensations will be their lot hereafter. But we must examine this situation; perhaps the contrast is not as stark as it seems to be. What is the practical and emotional meaning of faith in God to the earnest Christian or Moslem? Well, in many cases what it essentially means is a confidence that the course of history is guided by an invisible power which is leading events toward a kingdom of justice and happiness for all who accept the truth and give themselves to its

service. Now communism has this confidence too; only it
calls that invisible power, not "God," but the "dialectic of
history." The difference is that instead of conceiving the
controlling force as a transcendent, personal deity, communism conceives it as an impersonal and immanent, but
none the less inevitable, law governing the historical process.
Is this difference sufficient, in the presence of all the common
factors mentioned above, to justify our saying that where
faith in this guiding power takes the one form we have a religion, and where it takes the other, no matter what important
similarities obtain, we do not have a religion?

Perhaps the really significant difference lies not in the
presence or absence of the word "God," but in something
else. If communism is a religion, it has thus far marked, in at
least one important respect, a return from civilized to primitive religion. In typical primitive religions the individual is
treated as a pawn, to serve the religious security of the
community. He has no intrinsic worth which must at all
costs be respected. If the high priests select him as a needed
sacrifice to appease some threatening power, he is sacrificed
without compunctions about his own fate; if they decide that
he is the needed scapegoat for the accumulated guilt of the
tribe, he is condemned to exile or death without regard to
what this means to himself. Now such readiness to make the
individual a mere means toward the achievement of an accepted social end has been a part of the totalitarianism of the
communist view; an agent of communist policy will ruthlessly
sacrifice any individual, himself or another, to serve the ends
of that policy whenever the decisions of the dictators so
require. He will even frankly turn man's concern for truth
upside down; the beliefs of his fellows as to what is true
become instruments to his communist ends instead of being
allowed any moral value on their own account. So convinced is he that what people now call "truth" is nothing
but the product in their minds of capitalist exploitation that
he is ready to manipulate their ideas himself, wherever he

can, toward the goals of his own faith; if it would help communist strategy for people to believe this or that, he will persuade them so to believe. He rejects as superstition the notion of an objective truth with which our thinking ought to accord. But the civilized religions (including the earlier Western faiths) have not, in basic conviction, at least, been led into any such self-deception and ruthlessness. There have been approximations to it in all their major sects, but in general these religions have committed themselves to the freedom of reason to seek the truth, and to an ultimate respect for each individual, as an end and not merely a means to some end beyond himself. This belief in freedom, and in respect for the individual as of priceless worth, is expressed in the frequently repeated verse of the Koran: "Let there be no compulsion in religion"; and the practical way of following these convictions, in missionary work, is adoption of the method of loving persuasion, rejecting every hint of force. Perhaps in the light of this important consideration, the answer to our question should be that communism is a religion, but in this crucial respect it is a reversion to primitive religion, leaving behind one of the major insights and remarkable achievements of the civilized faiths.

However, a further word must be added. It is evident that since Stalin's death in 1953 the guiding ideas expressed in the decisions of communist leaders have undergone a radical change, which has affected more or less drastically communist policy on many matters. In revulsion at the high-handed tactics of Stalin and in their eagerness to woo the noncommunist areas of the world, they have rejected monolithic dictatorship in favor of the principle of collective responsibility; they have allowed a greater measure of independence to dissenting individuals and groups; they have moved nearer to the way of coöperation with satellite peoples as contrasted with the way of forcing them to toe the party line. How enduring these changes will prove to be, and how dependable the attitude they seem to express, we do not yet know. But many if not all of them point in the direction of fuller respect for the individual in a communist society and his right of free judgment. There is still a wide gulf to bridge, of course, before this respect reaches the point where it accords with the Anglo-Saxon ideal of individual liberty.

If this should prove to be a permanent change it will mark a most significant development for all aspects of life in the communist areas of the world. So far as religion is concerned it will mean that, if communism may rightly be called a religion, it is now beginning in its own way the process of evolution from primitive to civilized religion with regard to the outstanding feature in which it has thus far exemplified the former rather than the latter.

D. RELIGION LOOKS TOWARD THE FUTURE

It is obvious that in discussing such questions as these we are no longer describing the history of the past nor are we merely making comparisons in the present. We are trying to look ahead and predict the course of religion in the future. This is a rather ambitious undertaking.

But why not?—as long as we are fully aware of the daring nature of what we are doing. In a philosophical study of religion I believe that one should not shy away from such a challenge. He will make mistakes, but even when he goes astray discerning readers will find the role of religion clarified by his suggestions.

However, one would do well not to be too ambitious. As I see it, one may profitably attempt two things in the presence of such a challenge. He may offer a few general observations on the way in which religion grows from any present state into any future, and he may examine certain specific events in the contemporary scene to judge their effect on the direction in which religion is moving. In the present section I shall propose some general comments about the growth of religion, leaving the second task to the final chapter.

Whatever may be the case with primitive religion, civilized religion grows in two ways. On the one hand, religious thinkers, in their search for what is deepest and loftiest in reality, adopt ideas from nonreligious phases of man's experience wherever they promise to clarify that search. On the other hand, earnest followers of one religion learn from the prophets and sages of other faiths, taking account in this way of a wider range of religious experience than they had been able to before.

Not much can be said about the first of these ways, beyond illustrating it from religious history in the past. So far as the future is concerned, who knows in what unexpected corner of life some spiritual explorer will find a clue by which to articulate for himself and communicate to others a fruitful insight that he has gained?

But it is clear that most of the growth that has taken place thus far in the civilized religions has taken place in this way. Religious feelings, of course, are as such incurably unstable and incommunicable. If stability in religious experience is to be achieved, these feelings must be informed by cognitive awareness, interpreting them in words with dependable meanings which can be shared between one earnest seeker and another. And only on the basis of such stability can growth occur, as words like "soul," "faith," "love," and others are given new meanings to accord with the deeper insights that spiritual pioneers from time to time gain. Now many words that for us are charged with spiritual meaning began their career by filling a nonreligious function. As they promised to be serviceable for the expression of religious truth they were adopted and used in that way; the changed meaning gradually became widely understood and in time even taken for granted.

"Heaven" at first meant just the overarching blue sky,

with whatever strange powers it seemed to possess. As civilized thinkers began to clarify the spiritual ideals of secure protection, of impartiality, and of dependable order, the celestial realm provided a natural symbol and model of these increasingly significant virtues. Firmly associated with the search for these high values, heaven could gradually become the object of reverent trust that in time it became— for the Confucian, and also for the Christian who prays not merely to "Our Father" but "Our Father in Heaven."

Similarly with this now sacred concept of "father" as applied to God. Originally a father was just a male progenitor, with whatever vices and foibles he might show along with his virtues. Perhaps the ideal of wise and kindly fatherhood was more closely approximated among the Jews than among other civilized peoples. At any rate, when the great prophets and the Synoptic Jesus found their deepening experience of God leading them away from the qualities of a natural power or a mighty ruler toward more humane and generous virtues, their search and insight were clarified by thinking of Him as the ideal father. Thus they could give durable meaning to their new vision and communicate it to others.

Likewise with the very instructive concept of "spirit." In the beginning it meant the process of breathing—the most obvious token of the difference between a living and a dead body. A strange process it is. Invisible and intangible, it appears to have its source deep within the living body; and yet it actively relates that body to the outside world. In virtue of these qualities the word "spirit" could undergo the transformation that it did. It proved just the needed term when the pioneers of civilized religion discovered an invisible inward reality in themselves which constituted the core of their moral selfhood—a reality whose dynamic liberation marked the difference between spiritual life and spiritual death. And in this case the transformation was so radical that at its end all reference to any physical process was left behind.

Nor did religious inquirers disdain to make use of the concepts of speculative philosophy. When Plato clarified the notion of the "eternal" in the sense of that which is super-temporal, he did not know that he was serving the needs of Christian and Islamic theology. When religion found its idea of the "everlastingness" of God inadequate to its needs, it adopted his word to express the conviction that God not only exists at all times but transcends the entire realm of the temporal. When Aristotle defined his abstract metaphysical concept of "being," he did not know that "the Supreme Being" would in time become a phrase of religious as well as of philosophical use. But this also happened.

Religious searching is not proud; it is ready to seize on any phase of man's experience that promises a clue for the helpful expression of any insight it has caught. And if the clue succeeds, another word will gradually be transformed in meaning so that it becomes a sharable symbol of spiritual reality. What will be the next important word to go through this refining crucible? We cannot tell. One would have to be a creative pioneer in religion to answer this question. All that we can say is that as long as religion remains alive adventurous seeking will go on, and with it the process of articulating what is found in any available language that proves suitable.

So let us turn to the other way in which civilized religion grows. Followers of one faith may learn from the deep experiences of other faiths, so that their spiritual wisdom gains in richness and in power to meet the varied religious needs of men. Whenever this happens, theology is challenged to achieve a more inclusive synthesis than it had been able to achieve before, providing a just and adequate interpretation for all facets of man's religious insight.

We face today a provocative challenge and an unparalleled opportunity for such a synthetic vision. Interaction between the great religions of the world is rapidly growing; on the increase also is the readiness of their adherents to learn from each other and to embody the lessons learned in their religious thinking. Such interaction has, of course, occurred throughout the past history of civilized societies, but on a limited scale. In China Confucianism and Taoism have been in living contact with each other from the very beginning, and each has been profoundly modified by the impact of Buddhism after that religion was introduced from India. In the West there has been continuous interaction, on the fringes at least, between Christianity and Islam; both have been strongly affected by Zoroastrianism, and Judaism has been influenced by them both. Now, for the first time in history, all the religions have been thrown into intensified interaction with each other, in virtue of the same forces that compel increased interaction all over the earth in economic, political, educational, technological, and artistic spheres. The whole world is a single melting pot, in all these areas, as it never was before. Religion will surely be as deeply affected as any other phase of human life; and the process would seem to be a cumulative one. What does this betoken for the future?

The galvanizing effect of this intensified interaction is likely to be momentous. Even without considering this process, I ventured to suggest in our opening chapter that religion may still be in its youth, with the greatest part of its history lying ahead instead of behind. If the human race avoids suicide, science is surely still in its youth, with its most revolutionary discoveries lying ahead. Philosophy is still in its youth; the breathtaking insights that could do for modern thought what Plato did for the experience of the Greeks may not as yet have even been glimpsed. Art is still in its youth; the inspiring creations that will appear when future artists, freed from their obstructive fears and rebellious iconoclasms, come to share these insights cannot now be imagined. So with every other phase of cultural life—political structures, economic habits, educational policies, even modes of recreation and of relaxation. So, too, with religion.

Of course, these new forms, in religion as elsewhere, will grow out of the best that has been realized in the past and the present. We always move toward the future from where we are, not from somewhere else. And that means, in religion, that men and women all over the world will start from where each now is, not from where we, with our particular sectarian faith, would like them to start.

And is this not a wonderful and exciting fact? Should it disturb us that earnest seekers have found many and varied paths to the spiritual goal, and that these paths have been isolated enough from each other so that each has had a chance to show what its distinctive powers and resources are? Religion would have been a far poorer thing than it is if there had been just one way all over the world, limited in the scope of its vision and incapable of growth through friendly interaction with other ways. But happily these mani- fold ways have made their appearance, each with its own distinctive genius; and now their inevitable interaction with each other gives us and our children the chance to bring them together in a single panorama of man's search for the divine. Through our responsive appreciation and wise understanding we can sift the good and the true in each, and unite it in dynamic fertility with the good and the true in all the rest. This process will be a gradual and natural one; no attempt artfully to concoct a synthetic religious insight could possibly succeed. It will take its own forms as it gains reality in the hearts and minds of seekers who are eager not to miss any possibilities of spiritual greatness that might be glimpsed and progressively realized.

And it will be a continuous process. Men are diverse; and they will follow diverse approaches in their search for the divine. The finitude of each individual will limit his vi- sion, even as he grows through learning and sharing toward an ever completer vista of spiritual truth. But this diversity is good, not bad—provided we renounce any lurking urge to proselytize each other in favor of a loving acceptance of everyone's sincere searching. Where such acceptance is absent, diversity of faith is the source of destructive conflict. Where it is present, such diversity not only enriches the religious scene—it holds open the prospect of infinite growth through the sharing of each other's insight.

But now, can we make this look toward the future more concrete? If such is our wish before ending our study, we must turn from glowing prospects in general to specific trends in the contemporary scene. The concrete future grows out of the concrete present. So broad principles alone will not help us here. We must survey the confusing maelstrom of events in the world today with selective discrimination, guided by the lessons learned from the history of the past. What events shall we pick as especially significant? What signs tell us whither civilized religion is moving?

Another chapter is needed—and it will be the final one— to deal with this theme.

Religion Faces the
Contemporary Scene

In responding to the challenge with which the last chapter ended one might roam far and wide. I shall resist the temptation to do this. What is most likely to help in clarifying the nature of civilized religion and forecasting its future is to concentrate on a few events of obvious importance. I shall, then, discuss two situations whose bearing on the history of religion may prove to be very great. Each will need to be expounded at some length if we are to be able to think fruitfully on the question that is of prime concern to us about it. In the first case the question is: What contribution toward the evolution of civilized religion is being made by the movement Mahatma Gandhi has initiated in India? And in the second: What is the relation between psychotherapy and religion, and how is the latter likely to be transformed through the influence of the former? Whatever conclusions the discussion may reach, our understanding of religion should be deepened and enriched by thinking together about these questions.

A. MAHATMA GANDHI'S RELIGIOUS PHILOSOPHY

The fact that civilized religion can still show creative vitality is strikingly revealed in the movement, now reaching hopefully to every continent, that has its source in the life and work of Gandhi. In its basic emphases this movement reminds us of the doctrines taught by the great religions of the past—especially the doctrines in which their ideal of spiritual maturity is revealed. But it clarifies this ideal in a significant way; and it also aims at producing a revolution in political, economic, and social life, reconstructing society in such a way that every aspect of it will be harmonious with, and indeed express, true religious wisdom. Its provocative feature in this latter role is that the revolution it produces is a nonviolent one; the means employed are thus fully consistent with the vision of the end to be attained, namely, a loving community of all men and women.

I shall introduce Gandhi's philosophy, first by a few comments on his general perspective, and then by a brief survey of the formative period of his career.

The matrix of Gandhi's experience and thought, in religion as elsewhere, lies in the long historic tradition of India. His concept of God is basically in line, so far as concerns its theistic orientation, with the concept appealingly taught in the *Bhagavad-Gita*. But his teaching about God, as about other religious themes, involves much more than a simple theistic faith, and it is embedded in an activistic religious philosophy which consciously aims to guide social and political change. He thus embodies the Jewish-Christian ideal of the prophet and the Islamic ideal of the political reformer as well as the traditional Hindu ideal of the saint. This circumstance illustrates the fact that while his religious perspective is grounded in the basic ideas of Hindu thinking, he has been more responsive to the insights and values of other religions than one would expect merely from the tolerant open-mindedness of Hinduism itself, and has in remarkable degree exemplified them in his own person.

The distinctive feature of his philosophy, however, lies not in any particular doctrine but in the new kind of "experimentation" to which his whole life has been committed. The subtitle of his autobiography[1] is "the story of my experiments with truth," and an explanation of this phrase cannot avoid including an outline of his entire religious viewpoint. What he has in mind is a conception of "experiment" which contrasts sharply not only with the conception familiar in the West but also with that prevailing earlier in his own land. The West usually means by "experiment" the kind of activity which the scientist carries out in his laboratory, in his quest for truths about the external world—truths which, when discovered, can guide manipulation of that world in the interest of satisfying human desires. In pre-Gandhian India another kind of experiment had been carried on through long centuries—experiment with one's inner selfhood, aiming at the discovery of truths by which self-centered desires can be conquered and salvation from bondage to them achieved. Gandhi was acquainted with these forms of experimentation and accepted them; the former he believed has a relative value because of the human misery it can help to relieve, as in the science of medicine, and the latter is absolutely vital to the spiritual progress of every individual. But what he was distinctively concerned about was a third kind of experimentation—an experiment with the application of religious truth to the solution of vast and difficult social problems. As every reader is aware, the specific purpose which guided the most widely known among these experiments was the purpose of achieving Indian unity and Indian independence from Britain, the latter being successfully fulfilled and the former resulting (thus far, at least) in failure. But the general principles exemplified in these experiments are of much wider significance; if loving devotion to truth can operate not only in the saving transformation of the individual but also as a constructive force in meeting political and economic problems, it is clear that religion has an unlimited role to play in human history, the possibilities of which have as yet been hardly more than glimpsed.

Before we embark on a systematic exposition of Gandhi's

major convictions, a few references to the way in which they took shape in the course of his career will be of value.

From very early in his life he accepted with profound seriousness the Hindu ideal that one should search for religious insight wherever he might find it; so he studied the various sacred scriptures of the world, especially the Christian Gospels, and he read deeply in such writers as Tolstoi and Thoreau. His whole life thereafter was committed to the principle that there is rewarding and saving truth in all religions, and that it is therefore not merely presumptuous but sacrilegious to attempt to convert the adherent of one faith to another; what one should do is rather to help him realize more fully the spiritual riches that he has thus far missed in his own religion. When consecrating a temple in New Delhi he said, "It must be the daily prayer of every adherent of the Hindu faith that every known religion of the world should grow from day to day and should serve the whole of humanity."* Thus, far from competing with one another, different religions should help each other fulfill the highest spiritual promise of which each is capable.

What did he find to be the heart of the message taught by all the great religions, as it gradually took form in the crucible of his own experience and reflection? First, that love (implying an unqualified refusal to harm others) is the true way of life, the way to be uncompromisingly practiced by all who dare to believe it, come what may. Second, that in following this way one must constantly be open to a fuller realization of what it involves, both in general and in its application to

* Quoted in T. M. P. Mahadevan, *Outlines of Hinduism*, Madras, 1940, p. 7. Note also the following statement made by Gandhi to a group composed of adherents of various religions (quoted in Fleming, *Ways of Sharing with Other Faiths*, New York, 1929, p. 198): "So we can only pray, if we are Hindus, not that a Christian should become a Hindu, or if we are Musalmans, not that a Hindu or a Christian should become a Musalman, nor should we even secretly pray that anyone should be converted, but our inmost prayer should be that a Hindu should be a better Hindu, a Muslim a better Muslim and a Christian a better Christian. . . . I would not only not try to convert, but would not even secretly pray that anyone should embrace my faith."

any specific situation. Especially must one ever be in search of a deeper self-understanding, thus continually purging himself, through honest awareness, of any lurking motives that are inconsistent with the spirit of love. Now the initial lesson that he learned in this manner, while facing the entrenched power of race prejudice in South Africa in the 1890's, was that love must not take the form of a merely passive attitude in the presence of social iniquity. There are situations in which it must show itself as nonviolent resistance to evil, courageously practicing civil disobedience to political authority. There are times when the social institutions under which men live are so radically unjust, depriving them of freedom and crushing their dignity as human beings, that moral and spiritual progress is impossible without defying those institutions. Every effort should be made with persons in power to reach a peaceful solution, but "situations sometimes arise when one side to a dispute shows itself so obstinate and unyielding, so unwilling to agree to any compromise, that the other party is obliged to look for some effective way of showing that to it the continuance of the 'status quo' is intolerable."[2] In such cases one must defy such institutions for his own self-respect as well as his concern for others; there is no hope of a constructive change except through determined opposition.

However, since this defiance is moved by loving concern for the freedom and dignity of all, not just liberation or power for oneself, it must be expressed in such a way that one becomes no cause of harm to those whom he opposes; whatever suffering occurs as a result of one's defiance must fall on himself, not on anyone else. Gandhi was convinced, in brief, that love is not merely the valid ideal to guide our personal relationships; it is also the effective force behind a dynamic program of social reform. It can transform the institutions of society, and because it is love it does so in such a way as to express no hostility toward men who are instruments of social authority; they too are capable of being transformed by love and won to willing coöperation, and should unfailingly be treated on that supposition.

The reader will observe that in adopting this position Gandhi explicitly abandoned a widely accepted interpretation in India of the law of *karma* and its role in transmigration. This interpretation involved the belief that one's present status in society is part of the inevitable effect of one's conduct in previous forms of existence; hence it should be accepted rather than changed, however much misery and humiliation that status might bring. From this standpoint it would be impious to attempt a radical transformation of social institutions and established practices; the appropriate way is faithfully to fill one's place in society and to progress thereby toward one's own spiritual perfection. Now Gandhi did not reject the basic belief in causality implied by the idea of *karma;* one's past is still with him, and he cannot escape responsibility for his moral state in the future. But he did reject the implication that it is one's duty passively to accept evils that might be changed for the better—evils bearing harshly upon others as well as himself. In fact, if he does not do what he can to change them, he will increase rather than decrease his guilt in the future. In short, there are social conditions so completely incompatible with national self-respect and the personal dignity of everyone involved that the first step toward spiritual progress is to refuse to accept them—such as subjection to a foreign power and the traditional abasement of the "untouchables." Spiritual growth in the individual and the renovation of society toward the ideal of a loving community go hand in hand; neither can really be separated from the other.

When Gandhi turned from Africa to India and inaugurated his civil disobedience campaigns there, it was under the guidance of this clarified yet constantly developing religious conviction. The struggle to free India from Britain was the expression of a thoroughgoing spiritual revolution, with its own essential ideal of a perfected society, and every step taken was in his mind determined by its relation to this spiritual transformation. So far as concerns the social aspect of the revolution, "his objective was to create, out of the oppression of colonial rule and economic exploitation, not a dictatorship of the proletariat, nor even a democratic tyranny of the majority, but a community of equal citizens joined in the pursuit of the common good." Or, more fully, he sought a "moral, nonviolent revolution in all the departments of life of a big nation, at the end of which caste and untouchability and other such superstitions must vanish, differences between Hindu and Muslim become things of the past, and enmity against Englishmen or Europeans must be wholly forgotten." A social revolution must be designed to produce a "casteless and classless society," with decentralized, democratic "village republics."[3]

The vital features of this religious and philosophic perspective are succinctly revealed when we consider Gandhi's main aim in his practical relations with each of the three groups whom he was endeavoring primarily to influence and whose coöperation it was essential to elicit. With his followers, the aim was that they become absolutely committed to the way of nonviolence, and sufficiently trained in its practice so that they could be trusted to exemplify it no matter what risks or suffering they might have to undergo. More than once he called off a particular campaign when his followers proved unable to avoid retaliatory violence, postponing further efforts in that sector till he believed that those who must participate were fully ready for their ordeal. With the Indian public in general, especially in the villages, his aim was to develop a basic sense of self-respect, and to foster courageous initiative in solving harassing problems of village life that need not wait for independence. Thus when it came they would be ready not only for self-government but also for the steady evolution of efficient self-government, from the level of the village to that of the nation as a whole. With the British political authorities (and others whom he found it necessary to oppose), his aim was not merely to resist them but to resist them in love, so that at every step there would be the maximum possibility of winning them away from injustice to a willing coöperation with what is true and good. This meant aiding them in every constructive activity the government embarked upon; and when opposition was necessary it meant a constant recognition of the difference between a person's unjust acts, which must be resisted with all one's strength, and the person himself, who is capable of something better and should always be treated in accordance with that moral faith. Indeed, commitment to the method of nonviolence is a way of saying to an oppressor, "I cannot and will not accept your unjust acts, but I am ready for the consequences of my resistance to fall on me rather than on you, for I have faith that you are better than your acts, and even in my resistance I shall always treat you with friendliness and love."

That this assured trust is not futile has been proved many times in Gandhi's career. When he was still in Africa one of Premier Smuts' secretaries said to him: "I do not like your people and do not care to assist them at all. But what am I to do? You help us in our days of need. How can we lay hands upon you? I often wish that you took to violence like the English strikers, and then we would know at once how to dispose of you. But you will not injure even your enemy. . . . And that is what reduces us to sheer helplessness."[4]

With this biographical sketch as background, we are ready for a systematic account of Gandhi's developed religious philosophy. Its basic principles are evidently those of truth and loving rejection of violence; when he came to see their interrelations fully it was clear that truth rather than nonviolence is the primary principle. The third major idea, marking the distinctively novel element in Gandhi's convictions, is *satyagraha* (a term left untranslated for the moment), which must be understood in its relation to the two others. Let us consider these principles in order.

The reader will realize at once that to understand the meaning of "truth" for Gandhi we must leave the atmosphere of Western science and philosophy, and place ourselves in the context of Eastern thinking. What Gandhi was concerned about is not truth as a set of verified propositions about things and events, but truth as a fundamental orientation of the inner self—i.e., truthfulness. And this truthfulness is shown, not primarily in ability to apply the method of science to the details of the physical world, but in an absolutely honest facing of oneself, and a full acceptance of whatever such utter honesty discloses. When truth gains meaning for a person by this route, he is in a position to discover the deeper truths about others, in such a way that loving understanding can helpfully apply them toward the achievement of mutual happiness. He can also explore truths about the environing world, viewing the latter not merely as a set of events to be artfully manipulated but as a theater within which the highest possibilities of man might be realized. Such utter truthfulness is for Gandhi the foundation of everything—in religion, in morals, in statesmanship, in economic life. Our attempts to determine what is right and good are likely to be mistaken unless they are grounded in this commitment to truth, and in any event they must always be ready for correction by it. "We do not always know wherein lies our good. That is why it is best to assume that good always comes from following the path of truth."[5] What this means is that a searching honesty is always likely to uncover blind or selfish motives in one's pursuit of what appears good, and that only the new vision of good that has been liberated from such motives by self-awareness is a stable and trustworthy guide.

What Gandhi found disclosed about himself by this truthfulness was that he was no *guru*, no prophet or saint, no infallible teacher. He was simply a man "who blunders from error toward truth," always trying to learn by his mistakes and courageously applying each insight in daily life as well as his frailty permitted. And this conviction about truth in Gandhi's mind inescapably required a thoroughgoing acceptance of democratic methods and an unqualified respect for the processes of persuasion as contrasted with those of compulsion. He had "no desire to conquer his adversaries by force. . . . He wished to convert them, or rather, he wished to communicate with them, to persuade them, or to be persuaded by them, of the truth." When it expresses this spirit, "pursuit of Truth requires a recognition that no one man, no one party, no one class, no one race has the whole Truth; that since all human views are partial every view should be given free expression, should be considered and respected, even as it should often be rejected and resisted. Men must be free to seek the Truth, he said, and the Truth shall make men free."[6]

It will be noticed that in this quotation the word "truth" is capitalized. This brings us to one of the very fundamental features of Gandhi's philosophy. When, according to him, one is called upon to give an accurate verbal definition of God, the proper way to respond is to say that "Truth is God."[7] This is more correct than to say (what is right, of course) that God is Truth. What he means, I think, is that the being we properly conceive as "God" is the being who looms more and more clearly before our vision, as the ultimate object of adoration and trust, when we follow the way of unflinching truthfulness, just as the true referent of the word "good" is the purposive goal of action that takes form as we follow this path. However, this does not mean that Gandhi has rejected theism. It is legitimate, he believes, and not falsifying, to personify the Truth which is God and thus give it satisfying vividness to our religious feelings. "As we cannot do without a ruler or a general, names of God such as King of Kings or the Almighty One are and will remain more usually current. On deeper thinking, however, it will be realized that *Sat* (Reality) or *Satya* (Truth) is the only correct and fully significant name for God."[8]

It would be a mistake to suppose that by this identification Gandhi thought that one could substitute the abstract term "Truth" for "God." This would be to replace religion by philosophy. He holds it very important, not only that one commit himself without reservation to Truth, but also that he believe, with all the depth of his being, that Truth is God. Otherwise his conviction will lack the emotional energy and sustaining devotion needed to carry him through whatever ordeals await him in the path of social action—especially the sacrifice that he may be called upon to make as a result of his nonviolent resistance to evil.

So much it is essential to say about truth before specifically considering nonviolence. But to Gandhi's insight the two are intrinsically bound together. Truth—if it is really the utter truthfulness above described—inevitably leads to the rejection of violence; and on the other hand, "a perfect vision of truth can only follow a complete realization of nonviolence," and is impossible without it. Why is he sure that this is so?

In its basic meaning, nonviolence is identical with love, except that it is negative in form and is taken as an attitude to be seriously practiced, not only in one's personal relations, but in dealing with all the social problems of life—political, economic, educational, and the rest. Unless one practices it thus he has not realized love in its full outreach or committed himself to it without condition; moreover, to practice it is to express the true nature of man—"Nonviolence is the law of our species as violence is the law of the brute."⁹ Or—and here we meet a fuller statement of the principle which underlies Gandhi's entire philosophy—"Only truth quenches untruth; love quenches anger; self-suffering quenches violence. This eternal rule is a rule not for saints only, but for all."¹⁰ Gandhi is sure that this is a law for man, not in the sense that all people practice it, but in the sense that only so far as it is practiced is evil in human experience overcome with good, and the great potentialities of man fulfilled.

Can we discern the vital connection between truth and nonviolence more precisely? Yes, according to Gandhi—by tracing with clarifying insight the relation just suggested, in either direction. On the one hand, it is obvious that wherever passions explode in violence the attitude of open, responsive, patient truth-seeking is blocked. One cannot discover more truth about a person or an object when he is consumed by a hostile impulse to injure or destroy. More important, truthfulness about oneself requires full awareness of one's blind hostility and destructive urge for what it is, and this is completely impossible when one is possessed by it and swept into action under its control. We can thus see that the only kind of action consistent with the attitude of utter truthfulness is nonviolent action.[11]

On the other hand, the truthful man, so far as he is really truthful, cannot long remain violent.[12] For if he is honest he will come to know two things: first, that the hostile impulse he feels is not just righteous indignation (as he would like to believe) but proves the presence within himself of the same evil that he is so eager to destroy in his enemy; and second, that the inevitable effect of violence in human relations is more violence, so that the net result is more tragic than before, whereas it is possible for love to overcome hatred and to build in its stead enduring friendship. The practical corollary of the first realization is that if one is to treat any other person as an enemy, he ought by the same token to treat himself as an enemy; when one sees this clearly, he sees that as long as any pugnacious drive remains in him he is indeed his own enemy. The practical corollary of the second realization is that if one wishes his action to be truly creative, he must commit himself absolutely to the way of nonviolence, whatever consequences this may entail for himself. Gandhi is so confident that honest understanding of reality and avoidance of self-deception lead in this direction that he maintains with calm assurance:

"Nonviolence is the greatest force at the disposal of mankind. It is mightier than the mightiest weapon of destruction ever devised by the ingenuity of man."[13] He said this before the invention of the hydrogen bomb, but there is every reason to believe that he would say it with equal conviction now.

Thus truth and nonviolence, however different they may

superficially seem to be, are two sides of the same spiritual ideal; truthfulness is the searching, open-minded aspect of love, and love is truthfulness in feeling and action. Neither can be really separated from the other.

So we come to Gandhi's third fundamental principle, which is derived from these two and which is unusually difficult to translate—*satyagraha*. A literal English equivalent for this word would be something like "firmness in devotion to the truth"; it has been rendered variously, "soul-force" being a frequent but hardly adequate translation. The essential idea, however, follows directly from what has been said above. It is that love is not just an abstract ideal nor a valid guide merely in personal relations; it is a power in the world, creatively transforming social institutions and the way in which they work. And it is power in another sense, too. It can be practiced by the strong but not by the weak. If in any situation the only practicable alternatives are violent struggle and weakly submitting to evil, violence is the preferable way; for according to Gandhi, "cowards can never be moral." "I do believe," he said, "that where there is only a choice between cowardice and violence, I would advise violence." But when one becomes capable, without reservation, of expressing love in action, and sees the inevitable corruption that comes from violence, there is never any need to make such a choice. "The nonviolence of my conception is a more active and more real fighting against wickedness than violent retaliation, whose very nature is to increase wickedness."[14] *Satyagraha* is thus simply an extension to the social arena, and especially to the field of political relations, of the law of love which we take for granted as validly applicable within the circle of the family. "It is this law of love that silently but surely governs the family for the most part throughout the civilized world. . . . The doctrine of *satyagraha* is merely an extension of the rule of domestic life to the political."[15]

Now this application of the law of love to the wider arena of all social relationships is for Gandhi a quite general principle; it means the progressive reconstruction of every phase of man's cultural life so that it will become a consistent expression of the spirit of love.

Happily, in most situations this reconstruction can proceed without leading to active conflict with governmental authority or other wielders of entrenched power. Generally speaking, government is good, and is on the side of the forces which make for justice and human dignity. But not always; and then *satyagraha* may require the practice of civil disobedience. To be sure, even when a law or authorized power bears unjustly on some group of men and women, civil disobedience is not an automatic consequence of *satyagraha*. The seeker for truth and love will often still obey rather than disobey because, knowing that laws normally operate for the welfare of society, he does not wish to encourage the flouting of established rules of social order. "But there are occasions, generally rare, when he considers certain laws to be so unjust as to render obedience to them a dishonor; he then openly and civilly breaks them, and quietly suffers the penalty for their breach."[16]

Gandhi's adoption of this determined pacifism reflects his twofold conviction (1) that this is the way in which love overcomes evil with good in intolerable social situations, and (2) that if any group follows this way with undiscouraged "firmness in devotion to the truth," in the long run its power will be irresistible. By love, all men and women can be won to the way of truth and love; it is only needful realistically to remember that they are the prey to outbursts of uncontrolled violence when mastered temporarily by blind fury. For this reason, in any given situation one who practices *satyagraha* may fail; and he must be ready to suffer or die himself for his conviction, if need be. Should it so happen, he will be buoyed by the knowledge that his cause will triumph in the end because it is grounded in truth. Such suffering will sometimes indeed turn the hearts of those who have succumbed to the fury of injustice; in any case it will have some moving and transforming influence on those who witness the loving sacrifice, which will not be lost. "The appeal of reason," said Gandhi, "is more to the head, but the penetration of the heart comes from suffering. It opens up the inner understanding in man."[17] This conviction found expression in Gandhi's various fasts, by which he sought to accomplish through his own suffering a desperately needed change that could not be brought about in any other way.

One feature of Gandhi's concept of *satyagraha* is not well understood in the West; it has been mentioned above, but an explicit emphasis on it will not be superfluous. The idea of nonviolence is familiar from Jesus' teaching in the Sermon on the Mount, but the idea of nonviolent *resistance* to evil is not familiar, except in the specific form of conscientious objection to military service. Now this concept is absolutely vital to *satyagraha*, as Gandhi understood, taught, and practiced it. For him, evil in social relations is not to be accepted in passive submission; if it is evil enough it must be resisted with all our strength. "Non-coöperation with evil is as much a duty as coöperation with good."[18] Here is where Gandhi shares the mantle of the Hebrew prophets in their determined and fearless protests against social injustice. But evil must be resisted in such a way that the greater justice achieved will be stable and enduring, and the evildoer not just checkmated in his aggressive exploitation but won to friendship and the willing acceptance of truth. Confronted then in an unbearable situation by any agent armed with social authority and power, one practices "nonviolent resistance," and each of the two words in this phrase is of equal importance. It is resistance because it expresses absolute refusal to accept the evil or to coöperate with it; it is nonviolent resistance because it involves no use of force. The resister is prepared to suffer himself whatever pain or loss may come as a result of his refusal to submit to wrong.

It has been said, of course, that Gandhi's program succeeded as well as it did against Britain because the British have a live sense of fairness and of chivalry toward opponents. Would the method work with a more ruthless imperial power? The answer presumably is that with a different foe Gandhi would follow a somewhat different way, promising more effectiveness in that situation, yet it would always be a way of fearlessness and of love. "We must devise ways of love whereby everyone will come to realize his kinship with us. This leaves no room for war, nor even for violence in guarding friends."[19] For Gandhi's whole philosophy is grounded on a faith in the reality, the absolute value, and the power of love. "Through love we become aware of the greatness of reality, our peace of mind increases in spite of suffering, we become braver, more enterprising, and the evil within us shrinks from day to day."[20] Such love shrinks the evil outside us, too, for it expresses itself in an undiscouraged friendliness without slavish submission, which in the long run has its effect.

The fact that Gandhi's philosophy seeks nothing less than a spiritual transformation of human life, and is flexibly adapted to any kind of social problem where entrenched injustice must be constructively met, is revealed in the program of land reform (*bhoodan*) now being carried forward by his followers. In fact, the St. Paul of the movement he initiated is Vinoba Bhave—India's "walking saint," who has already persuaded the well-to-do landowners to part with several million acres of their possessions for the sake of the landless peasants. Vinoba is a very different type of personality than Gandhi; he is an ascetic scholar and hermit saint turned into a missionary prophet, and his religious philosophy reflects these qualities as well as the fact that his background is more exclusively Hindu than Gandhi's was. He is more concerned even than Gandhi that the wealthy sinners he calls to the altar of sacrifice will be saved rather than stirred to embittered opposition. And he has pretty completely avoided the temptation of the traditional religious leader to let his followers become devotedly attached to himself; he refuses to bring any pressure on others to adopt his ideas, and is concerned that everyone who comes to him for guidance find his own truth and his own spiritual vocation.

But, so far as one can see at present, his main contribution to the Gandhian faith lies not in these variations, but rather in the vivid way in which through the *bhoodan* movement he has clarified the basic principles that he and Gandhi hold in common. They are both seeking to inspire a total "revolution in love." That is, they conceive the economic, political, and educational transformations that they are fostering, not only as valid reconstructions within these areas of India's cultural life, but also as phases of a spiritual revolution whose aim is to awaken men everywhere to the realization that all aspects of human culture fulfill their role only when their activities actually accord with the vision of man's high destiny that the great seers have caught. Hence such an economic process as the industrialization of a "backward" country should be guided, not by the idea of a maximum use of the machines that modern man can invent, but by that of their optimum use, in the light of a clarified ideal of human well-being. "A machine that is helpful at one time or place may be harmful at another . . . no set formula can be laid own. We should therefore have neither blind infatuation for the machine nor blind opposition to it. Service of man should be the sole test."[21]

Hallam Tennyson summarizes the significance of Gandhi and Vinoba in the spiritual evolution of India in these words:

India, then, for matriarchal, historical, geographical, and spiritual reasons, still honors the saint above the film star, the political boss, the baseball hero. . . . But the type of saint that India honors has changed. After centuries of meditative sloth the *sannyasins* have come down from Himalayan peaks, emerged from forest hideouts, stripped themselves of ashes and excrement, in order to endure the rigors of love in the all too human dust from which their forerunners shook themselves free. For this, Western virtue can claim its own share of credit. . . . Western virtue has been crossed with Indian vision. It is this that has given birth to the most exciting and important spiritual movement of our time. . . .[22]

The world is looking to India in wonder and hope. Will Tennyson's final assessment prove to be right?* Already the Gandhian principle of nonviolent resistance to evils that crush the freedom and violate the dignity of man is spreading, and is guiding movements of constructive protest in widely separated parts of the world. Under the leadership of Manilal Gandhi, son of the mahatma, natives and Indians in South Africa have been organized in nonviolent protest against the segregation program of the South African government. General Rondon in Brazil, with a group of assistants trained in the Gandhian way, has succeeded in removing the hostile fear felt by Indian tribes in the Matto Grosso jungles, so that they have been pacified and won to willing coöperation with those who are ready to teach them the arts of civilized culture. The motto courageously adopted by General Rondon and his men was "We shall die if need be, but we shall never kill."[23] In Montgomery, Alabama, the way of nonviolent resistance to intolerable discrimination on the city buses has been practiced by the Negroes of the community, no longer willing passively to accept the humiliating status of second-class citizens. Shortly after his arrest the leader of this movement, Rev. Martin L. King, Jr., said to his followers:

If we are arrested every day, if we are exploited every day, if we are trampled over every day, don't ever let anyone pull you so low as to hate them. We must use the weapon of love. We must have compassion and understanding for those who hate us. We must realize so many people are taught to hate us that they

---

* A statement from General Douglas MacArthur, quoted in Chester Bowles, *The New Dimensions of Peace*, New York, 1955, p. 161, gives a relevant and sobering judgment: "In the evolution of civilization, if it is to survive, all men cannot fail eventually to adopt Gandhi's belief that the process of mass application of force to resolve contentious issues is fundamentally not only wrong but contains within itself the germs of self-destruction."

are not totally responsible for their hate. But we stand in life at midnight; we are always on the threshold of a new dawn.[24]

Other exemplifications of the Gandhian vision in action will doubtless appear, and perhaps with increasing success. It may well mark the most significant development of religion in our time—a development in which self-giving love proves its divine reality and its creative power not merely in the spiritual transformation of individuals but also in the moral regeneration of society. Perhaps it will save the civilized world from suicide through a hydrogen war.

B. RELIGION AND PSYCHOTHERAPY

The movement just examined is the outstanding illustration in the contemporary world of the way in which forces at work within the current of religion as it has come down from the past may lead in new and promising directions. The outstanding illustration of a force impinging on religion from the outside, which yet is likely to elicit from it a constructive response and to guide a more or less radical development in the fulfillment of its role, is psychotherapy.

Only a cursory consideration is needed to discover that the basic function and goal of psychotherapy and religion are the same. To a purely rational approach, religion often appears a kind of philosophy, offering its alternative answers to traditional philosophical perplexities, but a more balanced view quickly sees that this is but the intellectual aspect of a far richer and deeper role, namely, the healing of troubled souls. The essential task of religion is to help people solve the problem of life, in its emotional and volitional as well as its intellectual involvements, and by solving it to become fully and happily adjusted to the realities of the universe. And its guiding conviction is that until a person has achieved such a solution he is a sick rather than a healthy soul—a source of spiritual corruption to himself and to others. Now this is the task of psychotherapy, too, as the very word indicates. To be sure, psychotherapists are apt to say so in somewhat different language—their aim, as they would express it, is to help people resolve disturbing conflicts and achieve the serenity, energy, and wholeness that only such an integration can bring —but there is no vital difference in what these two modes of statement mean.

Moreover, there is a common goal as well as a common problem. In both cases, what the solution essentially requires is an emancipation of the sick soul from bondage to its childish self-centeredness and a realization of its hitherto obstructed power to love—whose free and full expression is the distinctive mark of human maturity.

What does this striking identity of aim and goal betoken for the future of religion? Does it mean that, just as applied science in its already familiar forms solved the major problems of primitive religion so that the divine powers of primitive man lost their reality, applied science in the form of psychotherapy is now ready to solve the basic problem of civilized religion, so that the supernatural entities of the civilized faiths will also disappear? The outcome is hardly likely to be as radical as this; but the mere mention of such a comparison shows the drastic possibilities of the impact of psychotherapy on religion. So the question we are now to consider is a serious one. And a linguistic comment is needed at once. The term "psychotherapy" is very broad in meaning; it covers any form of counseling whose purpose is the healing of souls. What is at issue today is the relation between religion and psychotherapy as oriented in the psychoanalytic psychology developed by Sigmund Freud and his great successors. When I use the term in what follows, it is psychotherapy in this narrower sense that I have in mind.

Before we embark on the clarifying analysis that will alone enable us to reach conclusions, a brief survey of the divergent background of psychotherapy and religion, as it affects their approach to their common task, is in order.

The Eastern religions, especially Buddhism and Hinduism,

quite obviously accepted the responsibility of healing sick souls. Their great pioneers conceived the task of religion as that of liberating man from bondage to self-centered craving (*tanha*) and thus making him a source of true and dependable well-being to himself and to others. They realized that the process of liberation is normally a long and difficult one, and they attempted to provide a structural and dynamic analysis of human nature such as would give effective guidance in it. Thus were formulated the psychological concepts that they found indispensable; and thus appeared also such theories of the essential stages of growth toward freedom as are expressed in the Buddhist eightfold path and the Hindu systems of yoga.

The Western religions attacked the task in the terms provided by the theistic presuppositions of their theologies. To be sure, the mystic strain which has not been absent from them provides its own way of dealing with this human need, which is more akin to the spiritual techniques of the East. But the dominant solution has been reached on the conviction that man is responsible to a personal God who is his authoritative lawgiver and judge. Viewed from this standpoint, man naturally is in a state of sinful rebellion against God, proudly asserting his own self-centered will in opposition to God's commands, and his salvation consists in a penitent revulsion from this defiant willfulness; he becomes transformed into a state of obedient acceptance of the Divine Will. Such acceptance alone is true freedom, and it can only be realized through the experience of divine grace and forgiveness. The psychological concepts involved in this way of thinking are hence those of sin, guilt, repentance, and forgiveness. The fact that they increasingly seem irrelevant or meaningless to modern Westerners, while the human problem which underlies them is as poignant as ever, partly explains the growing appeal of psychotherapy, which attempts to meet this need by the aid of an entirely novel set of concepts and a somewhat different theory of human nature.

Psychoanalytic therapy is grounded in the framework and the characteristic attitudes of Western science, theoretical and applied. When it originated in the pioneering work of Freud it was a branch of medicine, promising a more adequate method than was then available for treating hysteria and related diseases. As was natural in this setting, Freud began to analyze its problems in terms of the medical and physiological presuppositions with which he was familiar; only gradually, as he found some of these assumptions leading into blind alleys, did he come to depend on the psychological concepts suggested by his clinical discoveries. In no case, so far as I am aware, did it occur to him that any help might be derived from the experience of religion or from the ideas through which it had been interpreted. In the long run this was a fortunate circumstance, since it meant that psychoanalytic therapy was established on its own foundation as an independent response to human need; thus when the time became ripe for a constructive adjustment between it and religion, each could profit from the lessons learned by the other in the highest possible degree. Freud soon found that the same principles that led to permanent cures in the treatment of hysteria were also successful in cases of anxiety and obsessional neurosis; he likewise found that they did not succeed with the more deep-seated conflicts in paranoia and schizophrenia, where the patient had lost the capacity to distinguish reality from unreality. This limitation has since been shown not to be an absolute one.

The chief point at which, in view of this background, psychoanalytic theory threw new light on general problems in the philosophy of science concerns the postulate of determinism. How are we to reconcile the universal derivation of effects from their causes, as taken for granted by science, with the moral freedom required by a religious view of man? Freud had no doubt about the validity of the postulate; psychoanalysis can achieve its results only by assuming that there is an antecedent determining cause for everything that happens in the mental and emotional life of man, including even the dreams, fantasies, and casual associations that are ordinarily taken as entirely accidental.[25] But he learned also that when these causes are located and made the objects of conscious awareness, freedom becomes possible in the only sense in which a reasonable man would desire it—namely, liberation from the compulsive need to repeat the acts that conflict with the individual's ideal of himself as a mature person. The patient becomes aware of the way in which the cause of such a compulsion appeared in his past experience; he sees that its appearance represented a choice that was adopted then but is now unacceptable in his quest for self-fulfillment; through these realizations he can relive the experience in a more constructive way and choose the acceptable alternative instead.

With these considerations in mind, we are ready for a more systematic examination of the framework of psychoanalytic theory.

This framework involves a dynamic and developmental concept of human nature, which was taken for granted by Greek psychology and is assumed in Confucian and Buddhist thought, but has hitherto been generally rejected by modern Western psychology. Many schools of the latter have conceived it as their task simply to analyze man's conscious experience into its elements and the ways in which they can be combined; some have even explained it in terms of accompanying physiological changes or observable behavior. In neither of these cases is any question raised as to whether the person studied is in a healthy or sick state, and whether such a consideration does not require an entirely different kind of analysis than would otherwise appear appropriate. In view of its origin as a branch of medicine, the psychoanalytic theory of man could not help raising this question and making it the central clue to the understanding of human nature which it worked out. From this standpoint, man is in an essentially dynamic but inevitably checkered process of growth from the pristine torpidity of the unborn babe to the state of full and mature adjustment to reality. In this process there are many and serious ills to which he is subject, arising from the impact of the surrounding world and especially from the traumatic emotional experiences undergone when a small child; the interaction between these and his innate dispositions determine what happens at each stage of his growth.

If he is especially fortunate in his parents and in the successive contingencies that he meets, he may grow toward responsible and integrated selfhood in more or less regular steps. In this case he will escape the neurotic disturbances into which he would otherwise be likely to fall. But in most cases this does not happen. Certain groups of his emotions become fixated at some childish or adolescent level, while physically and intellectually he moves on to such adulthood as is then possible; or they may even, in anxiety and fear, regress to a state of infantile dependence with its demand for protection, comforting sensations, and the immediate satisfaction of elemental drives. If these fixations and regressions are not too serious he may still live acceptably in society and fulfill his minimal responsibilities, although the inner conflict between the childish and the more mature self will take its toll and he will not realize the effectiveness and happiness that he might. If they are more serious, even this achievement will be impossible. The sufferer will have to withdraw from, or never undertake, the normal responsibilities of life, and can usually only be restored by intensive treatment under a competent psychotherapist. There is, of course, no guarantee of cure, for it requires the willing and effortful participation on the part of the patient, and of this he may be incapable.

The goal of the treatment is restoration to unobstructed progress toward mature living with all its satisfactions and fulfillments. Since this process requires that one assume a social orientation toward himself, success is possible only so far as the patient can transcend the impulsive and self-centered demandingness of the child and realize an attitude of loving understanding in his relations with others; this realization is experienced as a release from the lower self that had threatened to engulf him into the higher self that he can wholly accept. In Freud's words, "a neurotic who has been cured has really become a different person, although at bottom of course he remains the same—that is, he has become his best self, that which he would have been under the most favorable conditions."[26]

So much for the general picture of man in the light of psychoanalytic theory. The next step in clarifying this perspective further is to examine the meaning of the concepts in which its major doctrines are expressed. I shall deal first with the concepts which have become current coin among various psychoanalytic thinkers and then illustrate briefly one of those which are under serious dispute.

The process of growth to emotional maturity is a passage from domination by the "pleasure principle" to full control by the "reality principle." What this means is very simple. Each human being begins life as a baby, demanding immediate satisfaction of his needs when and as they arise, and unable to understand, accept, or tolerate the painful tension which is experienced when they remain unappeased. Emotional maturity requires that he fully and unqualifiedly accept reality —that is, become able without repining to postpone pleasurable satisfactions as he gains power to judge distant consequences in comparison with immediate pleasures and to choose the larger good. One whose emotions have thus been adjusted to reality can endure what would otherwise be painful frustration in the interest of the more mature enjoyments that are only possible in this way. Since they reflect a growing understanding and acceptance of reality, these enjoyments are richer in quality than the immediate gratifications of the child; they constitute "happiness" or "bliss" rather than "pleasure." And since the reality which he thus accepts includes the needs and interests of other members of society, which in loving understanding he makes his own, the world to which he has become emotionally adjusted is nothing less than the inclusive physical and social environment in which all men and women move toward the fulfillment of their varied potentialities.

The factor in human nature which drives toward the immediate gratification of a felt demand, and which opposes any attempt to control it in the interest of the larger good, is called the "id." The factor which comes to operate within each person as the surrogate of society's standards of right conduct is the "superego." The third factor generally accepted in an analysis of human nature from this point of view is the "ego," but it is more difficult to define precisely. Generally speaking, the ego is that part of one's make-up which can serve the well-being of the whole self through the use of prudential reason and the lessons of enlarging experience. It can refuse to submit to the imperious demands of the id, and it can criticize the voice of the superego—not merely in self-justifying rebellion, but in growing wisdom. Thus it can use and rechannel the energy of both these forces toward its own fulfillment.

To describe the earliest stage of life in terms of these concepts and their affiliates, this stage is one in which the individual is fully absorbed in love of himself—he is in the state of "narcissism." Gradually he grows in the experience of "object-love," first by responding to the smile of his mother and expressing gratitude for protective care, and then in the various ways in which, at each age, such object-love normally awakens. But this growth is precarious and checkered. Many demands of the id do not easily accept frustration and postponement, and even when they appear to do so their energy does not at once become an instrument for the expression of mature love. Frustration breeds hostility toward those who fail to give the satisfactions demanded; but as the child emerges from babyhood he finds that not much of this hostility can be safely expressed and "got out of his system." The threat of punishment is too portentous. So the hostility, with the persistent demands accompanying it, must seek compensatory

expressions that are safer—and not only safer but more acceptable to the conscious self, since the latter includes the
superego and is strongly moved by the need for social approval. What then happens? So far as concerns the drive for
satisfaction of bodily tensions, which make up almost the
whole of the infant ego and form a powerful part of any
ego which has not achieved full maturity, narcissistic "fixation"
or "regression" is always possible. That is, if one fails to find
a love relation to another person through which they are
adequately gratified, and fails to gain sufficient maturity so
that he wishes to give as well as receive, he will gratify these
demands on his own, and thus remain at the narcissistic emotional level, or regress to it, while physically and intellectually
he is growing toward adulthood.

This situation engenders "conflict," and the individual feels
the deep anxiety of a threatened split of his ego into two irreconcilable parts. For one who is physically adult moves in
a society which expects of him a minimum degree of emotional
maturity, and one who is intellectually adult will consciously
accept moral and social ideals which narcissistic behavior
flouts. The only way in which he can live with himself in
this situation is either to accept an actual split, which is then
likely to be incurable, or else to exclude from awareness the
part of himself that is unacceptable to his conscious self. The
latter process is called "repression." It is a canny device of
self-deception. However, the part thus excluded does not pass
out of existence; the urges and emotions which compose it
continue to operate at the unconscious level. But since they
are still a part of him, they cannot be kept in complete isolation from consciousness. Their effects here and there appear
at the conscious level, in the form of hysterical behavior, of
dreams, of vague anxiety, and of the various obsessional performances which are substitute satisfactions of the repressed
demands and which the conscious self can neither control nor
wholly accept.

These phenomena constitute the symptoms which guide the

therapist in his task of curing the patient. By their aid he can draw up into consciousness the hidden processes which have resulted in the appearance and compelling power of these substitute satisfactions. Once such an awareness has been gained, the patient can relive the earlier traumatic experience under the guidance of a conscious and fully accepted ideal of himself; he will no longer need the compulsive behavior that had resulted from the repression, and is freed from bondage to the disturbing symptoms of conflict. So far as concerns that anxious and enslaving situation, he has been cured. What happens is precisely similar, in its fundamentals, to what happens in man's commerce with physical phenomena when his conscious understanding of the facts involved passes from the state of primitive magic to that of rudimentary science. When still in bondage to the former he is compelled to fancy an eclipse as the swallowing of the sun or moon by a voracious celestial animal, which he must drive away from its prey by the beating of drums or the offering of a compensatory sacrifice. As soon as he becomes aware of the regular laws governing eclipses, so that he can predict their occurrence, this picture fades away from his mind and he is freed from the compulsive need to spend his energy in that futile fashion.

Philosophers and psychologists in the Western world have been so long accustomed to assume that consciousness is the defining characteristic of "mind" or "self" that they have found it very difficult to accept the idea that there are unconscious mental processes. Whatever is not immediately available to conscious introspection cannot be a part of the mind, they think. But when one takes the dynamic perspective of the medical man's approach to personality, there is no room for doubt as to the reality of the facts thus described. Here is a process which begins in the conscious self and ends in the conscious self; its unconscious part is reflected in emotional disturbances of the conscious self which disappear when that hidden segment is brought into conscious awareness. The whole process clearly belongs to the mind or personality which lives through it. In fact, the remedial treatment cannot get under way until it is accepted as so belonging. If the patient refuses to recognize that these unconscious processes are taking place in him and holds himself not responsible for the effects produced, the lifting of them to conscious awareness is impossible and healing of the conflict cannot be achieved.

This is such a crucial point that we shall consider two simple illustrations of the phenomena that constantly turn up in the practice of psychotherapy.

An adult man, otherwise able to meet the situations of life in a normal way, finds that whenever he is in the presence of a person representing social authority (even though one much younger than himself) he quakes in his boots, and is unable to assert any independent judgment or to meet this disturbing person on a level of equalitarian give and take. He has all that he can do to maintain a surface equanimity until he leaves the presence of the authority figure. If, now, this distresses him enough so that he seeks psychiatric treatment, what will almost inevitably turn up is some early experience —more likely, a series of experiences—in which he was cowed by a dominating father and possessed by an anxious fear of punishment if he did anything else than meekly submit to his father's will. But this submissive dependence, and desperate fear of disapproval, with the resulting hate and hostility toward the frustrating father, cannot be accepted by his conscious self since they are entirely out of harmony with his ideal of himself; they are repressed therefore to the unconscious level. However, they do not pass out of existence. They continue to operate as unconscious causes, producing these distressing and unacceptable symptoms whenever he is with a person in authority, who is therefore associated in his feelings with his father. When this causal pattern is dredged up from the unconscious so that he sees it for what it is, the first decisive step toward release from these unhappy and hampering symptoms is taken. The cure will become complete when, under the guidance of this clarified awareness, he can reject what remains in him of the childish need for authority, and can commit himself emotionally to the independence from both submissiveness and domination that is characteristic of true maturity.

Or consider a woman married to an energetic man who always has a dozen irons in the fire and is extraordinarily competent in everything he undertakes, even when he engages in household chores that ordinarily fall to her. She is deeply in love with him and is consciously an entirely devoted wife. But she is troubled by frequent dreams in which she is fighting with her husband, sometimes being defeated in the struggle, but often forcing him to knuckle under. The explanation of these dream adventures, if it were to be reached through psychotherapy, would doubtless in essence be very simple. Her love for her husband is thoroughly genuine, but like all finite human love it is "ambivalent." That is, it is mixed with childish feelings of inferiority, of frustrated competitiveness, of inability to keep up with his manifold activities—and these feelings inevitably engender a persistent hostility toward the husband who arouses them. Such feelings, however, are quite unacceptable to her conscious self, which pictures itself as the ideally loving and devoted wife. Accordingly they have been repressed to the unconscious level. But they have not disappeared; in this case they find an outlet in these troublesome dreams and frequent tension headaches. The cure, of course, is to become aware of what is going on, to accept the ambivalence as genuinely there, and under the guidance of this discerning acceptance to realize the integrated self which will no longer feel the disturbing hostility. Presumably such a self would be unreservedly proud of her husband's manifold talents and happy in his achievements; it would also include a new respect for herself and a fuller appreciation of the areas in which her skill and competence are displayed. Thus she achieves a sense of emotional equality with him and a liberating power of mutual giving and receiving that had never quite been possible before because of the haunting presence of her repressed hostility.

Once a course of therapy is undertaken, how does it proceed? What further conditions are essential to its success? Well, the therapist must have worked through his own emotional problems sufficiently so that his attention and concern can be entirely patient-centered; if, as the patient's tensions pour out, he is preoccupied with emotional reverberations from similar difficulties of his own, he cannot perform his function. In this patient-centered orientation the two basic roles that he must constantly fill are as follows: (1) He must be ready to give the complete acceptance, support, encouragement, and painful stimulation that at each stage the patient needs for the most rapid progress toward his goal. (2) He must be able also to make himself a tactful and understanding mirror of whatever the patient reveals as he grows in self-awareness, interpreting it in terms which the patient can accept as his own clarified insight into the meaning of his experience. As Freud succinctly describes this latter function: "Our therapy does its work by transforming something unconscious into something conscious, and only succeeds in its work so far as it is able to effect this transformation." "The change that is decisive for a successful outcome . . . lies in the preclusion of repression, so that the libido cannot again withdraw itself from the ego by a flight into the unconscious. It is made possible by changes in the ego ensuing as a consequence of the analyst's suggestions."[27]

The most critical problem likely to arise in the course of therapy, which tests the analyst's capacity to lead his patient through to a genuine cure, is the problem posed by the phenomenon of "resistance" and the way it is interwoven with the process of "transference."

To medical men, accustomed to expect ready coöperation from their patients, the undeniable appearance of resistance came as a great surprise.* Therapists found, as they embarked in any given case on this quest for health, that their patients

---

* Although every medical man of wide experience finds that he must allow for qualifications of this readiness.

not only wanted to get well but also wanted to remain sick. They not only wished to bring to consciousness material that had been repressed in the unconscious but they also wished to keep it hidden there and adopted clever devices for obstructing, to this end, the healing efforts of the therapist. However, the explanation of this circumstance was very simple. Until a fundamental cure has been achieved, the same conflict that disturbed the patient and led him to the analyst remains in him and cannot but show itself. Now it is a conflict between the mature part of his being that is seeking health and wholeness and the childish part that, having become fixated in a state of dependence, demandingness, and hostility, wants to remain there. Hence this childish self resists the healing steps undertaken by the therapist and blocks him in every way that it can. The competent therapist knows, of course, what it is up to and realizes that for a time he must support the drive toward wholeness, and induce the patient to wish more strongly to be cured. His technique here is the same that he employs elsewhere; he encourages the patient to become aware of his resistance and why he is engaging in it, so that conscious realization of what he is doing can gradually free him from the need to resist.

As this stage develops, the phenomenon of transference will make its appearance, and may mislead the unwary therapist, or one insufficiently purged from the need to control others, into thinking that a cure has been achieved. The patient now coöperates willingly with the analyst and seems eager to bring up the deeper dredgings that prior to that point he has desperately kept buried. What has happened? The answer is that an important and necessary stage in the healing process has been reached, but it is by no means the final cure. In gratitude to the therapist for his acceptance, patience, and trust, and in a new surge of strength on the part of his hitherto feeble ideal self, the patient has transcended his self-centered fixation sufficiently to identify with the therapist and to share to some extent the social perspective that the therapist represents. It is only a step in this direction; like a child, he is being good mainly to please the loved parent. So this is not the final cure, because it is essentially a state of dependent attachment to the analyst. He is beginning to leave his narcissistic childishness behind, but he has not yet realized his own individual selfhood. The therapist's task now—which requires complete self-abnegation on his part and an unfailingly patient-centered commitment—is to lead the patient to outgrow his need for dependence and submissive attachment so that he may realize his mature self, capable of its own independent valuations and its own independent judgments on whatever issues arise in his unfolding experience.

The concepts and principles above explained have, generally speaking, become accepted by all psychoanalytic thinkers. Besides these there are of course concepts which reflect differences between psychoanalytic schools. I shall only mention one of these, as a significant illustration; it is the Freudian term "libido."* As a result of his clinical experience in depth analysis Freud found himself led to the confident conviction that the energies of the id are not really as pluralistic as at first sight they seem to be. They are more or less disguised forms of sexual energy, whose presence from earliest childhood betrays itself to a discerning eye. It constitutes, he became sure, the basic drive in all the constructive and destructive activity of man. In his terminology this drive is called the "libido." The essential reasons, in his view, for the failure of other thinkers to recognize this important truth are two: (1) the fact that this is the area where, on everyone's part, the most determined and persistent repressions into the unconscious take place, so that here self-deception is most easily possible; and (2) the failure of most people to distinguish clearly between the sexual and the reproductive functions. He is sure that an unhorrified and unprejudiced consideration of "abnormal" sexual behavior, whether in children or in adults, will demonstrate the necessity of such a distinction, and that

* Note the quotation on p. 511.

when it is made the pervasive role of sex becomes clearly evident. Other schools of psychoanalysis are not convinced that the evidence for these conclusions is adequate; in their view, either no such monolithic drive exists or if it does its core must be described in other than sexual terms.*

By what criterion does the therapist tell when the cure that he seeks has in essence been achieved? This crucial question is not easy to answer. Psychoanalysts vary considerably on this matter; for practical reasons they have to accept different answers in the case of different patients, and for theoretical reasons they have differed among themselves in the concept of "mental health" that they have adopted. A generally valid answer would perhaps be this: the therapist's goal is attained when the hidden causes of the patient's conflicts have been brought to his clear realization so that an enduring liberation from their unacceptable effects has been achieved. Just as the medical practitioner regards his task as finished when the disease has been overcome and the patient has been restored to his former health, so the psychoanalyst has completed his job when his patient has attained the state of wholeness that he would have realized had the conflicts never appeared.

But there are important further issues involved in this question which can best be clarified by confronting the major problem that remains. As matters now stand, what is the relation between psychotherapy and religion, and what significant contributions can each make to the other as they seek the fulfillment, in the future, of their soul-healing function?

So far as concerns influential thinkers in the Christian churches, the present attitude is one of hesitant and tentative readjustment of ideas under the challenge of psychotherapy and its obvious success. Books by Protestant authors are being published, pointing the way toward a reconciliation of psychotherapy with their religious convictions; Protestant

---

* For instance, Adler holds that the "will to power" or "striving for superiority" is the basic drive; Jung appeals to a dynamic expression in each person of the life energy which is channeled variously at different stages of growth.

pastors in increasing number are realizing that they are willy-nilly psychotherapists and are inquiring how to use, in their counseling of troubled persons, such analytic techniques as are consistent with their Christian beliefs about the cure of souls. The Roman Catholic Church has thus far withheld any official commitment on the issues involved. It seems reasonable to expect that it will not accept any present psychoanalytic theory, but that on the other hand the time is likely to come when every confessor will be systematically trained in a Catholic adaptation of successful therapeutic methods. As for the religions of the East, there is as yet almost no contact with Western psychotherapy. A few analysts are now practicing there, but so far as I know they have not yet glimpsed any significant relations between their principles and those reflected in traditional spiritual disciplines. When this awareness has clearly dawned, however, on both sides, we may confidently expect a fertile give and take between the psychological presuppositions of religion and psychotherapy alike, leading to a far-reaching and constructive result.[28] Indeed, it may well be that the most promising interaction between the two will take place in that area, and that the future synthesis of psychoanalysis and religion will be an achievement of the East more than of the West. As was remarked above, the degree of readjustment required for such a synthesis there is far less, and should be much easier to work out, than in the West.

As one surveys the scene today, with sympathetic and appreciative impartiality, what would seem to be the major contributions that psychotherapy can make to religion and religion to psychotherapy?

I shall begin this concluding analysis with the first half of the question. What major contributions can psychotherapy make to religion? The answer is, several. If we think first of religion as it has been exemplified by its past pioneers, there are two important lessons to be learned. One is emphasized when we note the fact that with rare exceptions the founders of religious faiths have encouraged a dependent attachment to themselves on the part of their followers instead of guiding the latter toward their own independent selfhood. In psychoanalytic terms, they have been content to leave their disciples in the stage of "transference," where affection and trust have become focally lodged in themselves; they have failed to realize that a fully self-giving love would work through this stage to the achievement of an individual spiritual maturity which would be freed from any such dependent attachment. Here the essentially patient-centered orientation of the medical man has a vital contribution to make, as contrasted with the master- or teacher-centered orientation characteristic of religion. When the Holy Spirit "leads to the full truth," that truth will make free those who know it from submissive attachment to any religious leader as well as from every other form of cramping dependence.

The other lesson is revealed in the fact that while the great pioneers of religion have been fully responsive to spiritual truth wherever they could discover it, they lived in an age which was hampered by many superstitious notions. Their framework of thought could not reflect the ideals of thoroughness, responsibility to evidence, exactitude, and patience that characterize the modern scientific search for truth. Psychotherapy is free from any obligation to perpetuate those historical limitations, and can proceed, both in its theoretical quest and its practical applications, under the full guidance of these scientific ideals wherever they are relevant. This contribution will be especially important in the case of the Western religions, but the Eastern ones too will find their open-minded devotion to truth illumined and enriched by what the scientific mentality can offer.

If we think, second, of religion as it becomes structured in ecclesiastical institutions, three further major contributions from psychotherapy can be learned.

One is freedom from the need to be loyal to any detailed set of theological doctrines, such as a typical organized church has adopted. A school of psychotherapy has its basic beliefs, of course, which may be more or less structured into a theoretical system; but its patient-centered commitment, together with its scientific tentativeness, prevent it from erecting these beliefs into fixed dogmas to which one must, come what may, be loyal. They are, instead, hypotheses growing out of clinical experience, and are subject to revision whenever further discoveries, or insight into new interpretative possibilities, suggest the need of revision.

Another contribution is the rejection by psychotherapy of dogmatic moralism in its treatment of sick souls. The spokesmen of a church are usually prone to pronounce condemnatory judgment on persons who have wandered from the straight and narrow path of moral rectitude as their doctrines conceive it, and in this Pharisaic severity they are supported by the champions of customary morality in general, who pounce with the same harshness on any who violate the familiar social norms. Hence those who most need help find it hard to come to these self-righteous defenders of traditional moral rules; they know that they are likely to meet stern censure rather than loving understanding. The first principle of psychotherapy is full and unqualified acceptance of the patient, however serious the moral confusion into which he has fallen. His therapist must have the power and patience that are needed if there is to be no atmosphere of blame or reprobation; only in such an atmosphere can he pour out freely his rebellious hostility to the social norms along with all his other tangled feelings. Through the therapist's aid he can thus achieve a liberating awareness of the superego in himself as well as of the bumptious drives that have refused to cower before the superego. Contrary to popular opinion, this does not mean that the competent therapist will approve—not to say encourage—any flouting of society's standards. It does mean that he recognizes fully the relative character of these standards as contrasted with the absoluteness they usually claim. But what it means primarily is that he has wholly learned a lesson taught by the greatest religious teachers of all ages—that a person in deep trouble cannot be helped unless he is lovingly accepted as he is. He must know with assurance that his acceptance is not conditioned on his becoming more righteous or obedient than he now is. Only through such a releasing experience can he come to realize the true nature, both of the motives driving him to reject society's rules and also of the need for social order which in his community had found fumbling expression in those rules.

A third and equally important contribution is awareness of the need for progressive correction of the spiritual ideals that have been adopted by religious groups. These prized ideals reflect such deep-seated emotional presuppositions that except under the impact of deep therapy they are likely to be adamant against all change. Hence the history of religion reveals the tragic misapprehensions and needless hostilities that it does. Not to mention the fanatical conflicts between followers of different religious pioneers, there is the sad fact that those who respond to the active ideal of loving service tend to depreciate the contemplative ideal of the hermit saint, and vice versa; likewise the champions of prophetic religion and of sacramentarian religion sadly misunderstand each other. The Hindus, with their recognition of the different yogas, each being suited to its own kind of religious temperament, have done much to meet this situation in a wise and generous way. But it can only be fully met by a deep and steady probing that forces a person to perceive clearly the motives that lie behind his commitment to whatever ideal he has adopted. Such a radical, eye-opening discipline religion rarely provides; in the case of institutionalized religion it would be safe to say that it is not provided at all. But psychotherapy, if it performs its proper job at the submerged levels of a person's experience, is equipped for just this purpose. It can thus foster an achievement without which religion will continue to be a source of conflict as well as of peaceful harmony in the world —namely, a state in which religious people, through fully understanding themselves, will fully understand and accept each other, breaking down once for all the walls that have separated them. The significance of this contribution can hardly be exaggerated.

I shall illustrate this point by reference to an issue that has troubled thinkers of the Eastern faiths and which seems not yet to have been clearly resolved. What is the crucial criterion by which one can tell whether genuine union with the divine has been truly realized? Is it complete contemplative absorption, in which all distinctions have been excluded so that one is merged in an undifferentiated, blissful unity? Or is it a perfectly loving acceptance of all persons, in which the walls of fear that have separated one from them are removed and a dynamic unity of comprehending compassion is achieved? Psychotherapy can surely clarify this issue. Any trained therapist is well aware of the fact that a sense of satisfying emotional oneness can be realized in either of two contrary directions: by withdrawing from the world and its frustrations through a return in feeling to the cozy and protected seclusion of the womb, or by expanding toward full responsiveness to the actualities and infinite possibilities of reality. The former is the ultimate form of regression; the latter is mature fulfillment. Now there is much about the way of contemplative absorption, when it is made an end in itself, that suggests close similarity to this withdrawal into the state which precedes birth. Would this be a correct interpretation? The only way to tell, so far as I can see, is for the hermit saints who seek *samadhi* to become fully conscious of their own motivations in the way that would be encouraged by intensive Western psychoanalysis. If those motivations prove wholly acceptable, in a realized perspective which includes awareness of all these considerations, the analogy will be rejected as unsound. If they are not wholly acceptable, then psychotherapy will have provided in its own way a significant confirmation of the other form of the mystic ideal. Understanding love will appear more clearly than ever the essential mark of true spiritual oneness, and meditative mind control will become a major means toward its realization, not an end in itself.

These lessons that religion may learn from psychotherapy are of the very highest importance. If religious leaders really master them, a far-reaching step will have been taken toward freeing religion from the main limitations that have handicapped it in the past. It will gain the power to fill, more efficiently and boldly, the high role that the civilized faiths have attempted to fill. It will face the future with a more confident and conquering hope.

Now let us turn to the second part of the question. What major contributions can religion make to psychotherapy? Two, I think, and they are also very important.

One of them may be clarified by considering the difference between the "restoration of health" and "ideal health." The medical man's concern is essentially with the former of these aims; he knows that what most people accept as a healthy condition is far from the perfect state that they might realize, but he does not regard it as his function to prod them into the pursuit of any such distant goal. Now the fact that the psychotherapist came into his role in the light of a medical background naturally led to the adoption of the same attitude on this point. To be sure, he could not avoid noting that when normal people are observed in the light of the principles which guide his treatment of emotionally disturbed patients, they obviously appear at least semineurotic; neurosis becomes a matter of degree rather than an absolute difference between the mentally sick and the mentally well.[29] Also, the emphasis of psychotherapy on freedom from hostility and fear as the essential mark of the restoration of health implies a definite ultimate ideal of what true sanity is—an ideal that is far from being realized by the vast majority of "normal" people. But the approach above mentioned, together with the fact that rarely is it possible for the psychotherapist to continue treatment beyond the point where the main resistances and the special problem of transference have been worked through, have led to the general assumption that his goal is an assured cure of the neuroses that disturb his patient rather than the latter's achievement of ideal health. What this usually means in practice is the regaining of the patient's power of successful adjustment to the expectations of social life in the community in which he will presumably function—with all the limitations of its customary perspective and its cultural background.

The great religions have accepted no such modest goal. If their aim were to be expressed in medical terms, it would be to envision and clarify the supreme, universal ideal of mature well-being for man—of full adjustment to the infinite whole of reality—and to preach the good news that this ideal can be realized by all men. Then their further practical task is to encourage people unceasingly to pursue it, to guide them step by step toward its realization, and to teach them the systematic wisdom about life and the world which is the intellectual articulation of this vision. Far from being satisfied with successful adjustment to the cultural ways accepted in a given society at a given time, religion stands in judgment on every such culture. It criticizes every divergence from the way of life that would be exemplified by an ideal society of ideal personalities in full dynamic harmony with the universe and its divine ground.* The uncompromising affirmation of great religion is that all men are spiritually sick, not just those who have fallen into some neatly describable neurosis. The gap between the fulfillment achieved even by the normal person and the tremendous possibilities envisioned by the pioneers of religion is so great that a mere non-neurotic adjustment to this or that society's expectations is too petty an accomplishment to be called a soul cure. One can begin to speak of a genuine cure only when an individual is shaken loose from such a paltry notion of his goal and is consciously, purposefully, and

* Eric Fromm discusses this theme provocatively in his recent *The Sane Society*, New York, 1955, indicating by implication what a psychotherapeutic orientation would become when it fully makes its own the ultimate religious ideal.

hopefully seeking the divine kingdom that never was on land or sea.

Here lies one vital contribution that religion can make to psychotherapeutic theory and practice. Psychotherapists will usually, no doubt, for compelling practical reasons, find it necessary to stop far short of the achievement of any such state of ideal health in their patients; but so far as their guiding theory fails to take full account of religious insight here, it will prove inadequate to its essential role. Nothing less than true health is really health, for any individual or any society.

The other contribution is one whose consideration brings us back to the very fundamentals of religious thought. Although many psychotherapists hold a positive religious faith, and some psychoanalytic thinkers, e.g., Jung and Fromm, have endeavored to square their theoretical foundations with religious ideas, it is amply evident that psychotherapy as such can fill its function without explicit commitment to any traditional conception of God. Freud, in fact, explained away such conceptions as illusory. Does this mean that psychotherapy can really get along without any religious convictions? Or would such an idea be mistaken; is an ultimate conviction in a divine reality presupposed by the very nature of psychotherapy?

Certainly no sectarian concept of God is presupposed; and it may be that many psychoanalysts shy away from any religious commitment because they cannot envision a nonsectarian concept of God. Is this a conclusion that we must adopt? Or does the whole process of psychotherapy imply a nonsectarian concept of divine reality, whose acceptance and clarification as such would aid the therapist in filling the total role that it is his task to fill?

I am sure that the latter is the right alternative, and that it is the confusion caused by our sectarian divisions and hostilities that obstructs the full acceptance of its truth. Those who rebel against the unhappy consequences of these divisions and hostilities find it very easy to fall into the skeptical relativism about religion that is so influential in our time. And I am sure that many who have followed the account of the various religions of the world in the preceding pages will have been perplexed by these divergences, and even perhaps will assume that the thoroughly humanistic approach that we have adopted implies the acceptance of such a skeptical conclusion. It is time to confront the basic question here frankly.

Do the variability and relativity of men's ideas about the divine, so obviously displayed in the above pages, show that there is nothing *really* divine in the universe—that what we call "God" is merely a projection onto the cosmos at large of our diverse subjective hopes and dreams? No, this conclusion does not follow; what does follow is that the reality of the divine is a far richer reality and its truth a far more inclusive truth than would be the case if man's religious experience were limited to some single sectarian view.

Consider any physical object with which we are familiar —the sun, for example. In different parts of the world, and at different times, people have perceived the sun very differently, although there have of course been common features in these pictures. Some have perceived it as a genial celestial power, others as a fiery, scorching foe; some see in it an unpredictable and hence disturbing phenomenon, others a prime example of the regularity of nature. Those who live in the equatorial regions perceive its annual movements in a quite different pattern than those who live near the poles, and neither experience is similar to that of inhabitants of the temperate zones. And the theories by which it has been interpreted have been even more variable. It has been a red-hot rock, a divine light-giving substance, the central body of our solar system, a concretion of nebular dust, the generator of heat through atomic fission, and a hundred other things; what the science of five hundred years from now will conceive it to be we can hardly dare to imagine. Yet we do not construe this variability and this shifting relativity as implying that there is no sun—that what we call "the sun" is just a projection of our subjective feelings of warmth and perceptions of light. We are sure that the sun exists as an objective fact, else none of these feelings and perceptions would have lasted longer or shown more dependability than a fantasy of the imagination. And we are sure that progress toward more adequate knowledge of the sun will be achieved by building upon the most clearly attested truths that have now been gained, boldly revising them as further relevant data and new possibilities of explanation come within our ken. In this way and in this alone will we learn better what the sun really is.

So with the truth about God, except that He cannot be perceived by the organ of physical vision; He is the object of a spiritual perception which is none the less a discloser of reality for using our whole growing and maturing experience as its instrument of vision and not merely our eyes. Such a conception of divine reality is implicit in the whole enterprise of psychotherapy; it merely needs to be given its appropriate name and seen in its full historical setting. The truth about God, as we continue step by step our discovery of it, will contain all that is true and good in the accumulated insights of each of the great religions, and much more. It will free those insights from their lingering hostilities and dogmatic limitations, and it will add to them all that has not yet been, but might be, envisioned in the undying aspiration of the human spirit toward the greatest and best it can glimpse.

NOTES

CHAPTER I. GUIDEPOSTS IN OUR QUEST FOR RELIGIOUS UNDER-
STANDING (pp. 1–30)

1. C. P. Tiele, *Elements of the Science of Religion*, New York,
   1899, Vol. II, p. 142.
2. J. F. Clarke, *Ten Great Religions*, Boston, 1895–1898, Vol.
   II, pp. 233 f.
3. Sermon, "Sinners in the Hands of an Angry God," Jonathan
   Edwards' *Works*, Worcester, 1809, Vol. VIII, p. 167.
4. H. E. Barnes, *The Twilight of Christianity*, New York, 1929,
   pp. 41 f.
5. Quoted in H. Höffding, *Philosophy of Religion*, London,
   1906, p. 337.
6. Quoted in P. Smith, *Age of the Reformation*, New York,
   1920, p. 625.
7. Quoted in T. R. Glover, *Progress of Religion to the Christian
   Era*, New York, 1922, p. 137.
8. Kahlil Gibran, *The Prophet*, New York, 1943, p. 89.
9. St. Bernard of Clairvaux, *De Consideratione*, Bk. V, Chap. 11.
10. J. E. Carpenter, *Comparative Religion*, London, 1913, p. 148.
11. Gandhi may not have used just these words; they are taken
    from brief condensations of his thought in *The Walden
    Round Robin*, February 21, 1948. Exact quotations express-
    ing a similar idea will be found in selections from Gandhi, ed.
    N. K. Bose, Ahmedabad, 1948, p. 224.
12. Quoted in S. Radhakrishnan, *Religion and Society*, London,
    1947, p. 69.
13. J. Wach, *Types of Religious Experience*, Chicago, 1951, p.
    231. Source not given.
14. E. B. Tylor, *Primitive Culture*, London, 1903, Vol. I, p. 424.
15. F. D. E. Schleiermacher, *The Christian Faith*, Edinburgh,
    1948, p. 16.
16. Matthew Arnold, *Literature and Dogma*, New York, 1873,
    p. 21.
17. R. H. Lowie, *Primitive Religion*, London, 1925, p. 42.
18. R. H. Codrington, *The Melanesians*, Oxford, 1891, p. 191.

19. F. B. Jevons, Introduction to the *Study of Comparative Religion*, New York, 1908, p. 110.
20. See my article under this title in *The Philosophical Review*, January, 1953, pp. 41 ff.

CHAPTER II. PRIMITIVE RELIGION (pp. 33–72)

1. See, for example: Ruth Benedict, *Patterns of Culture*, Boston, 1934; R. H. Lowie, *Primitive Religion*, London, 1925; Paul Radin, *Primitive Religion*, New York, 1937; W. F. Calverton, *The Making of Man*, New York, 1931, Part V; H. L. Friess and H. W. Schneider, *Religion in Various Cultures*, New York, 1932, Chap. II. There are also more detailed studies of particular primitive societies, dealing with their religious as well as other aspects.
2. See the discussion of this possibility in F. B. Jevons, *An Introduction to the History of Religion*, London, 1904, pp. 114 ff., 154 ff.
3. *The Golden Bough* (one-vol. ed.), New York, 1953, p. 824. Read also Chap. IV.
4. Habbakuk 1:16.

CHAPTER III. FROM PRIMITIVE TO CIVILIZED RELIGION (pp. 73–104)

1. See especially Kellogg's *Genesis and Growth of Religion*, New York and London 1892; Lang's *The Making of Religion*, London and New York, 1898; Schmidt's *The Origin and Growth of Religion*, London, 1931.
2. See Lessing's *The Education of the Human Race* (1780); Herder's *Ideas Toward a Philosophical History of Mankind* (1784).

CHAPTER IV. THE GREAT RELIGIONS OF CIVILIZED MAN (pp. 105–125)

1. Euripides, *Bellerophon*, Fragment 292.
2. See T. R. Glover, *Progress of Religion to the Christian Era*, New York, 1922, p. 53.
3. John 15:11.
4. John 10:10.

5. *Dhammapada*, Chap. XV, in Lin Yu-tang (ed.), *The Wisdom of China and India*, New York, 1942, pp. 340 f.
6. John 3:1–8.
7. *The Golden Bough* (one-vol. ed.), New York, 1953, p. 86.
8. H. Spencer, *Principles of Sociology*, New York and London, 1912, Vol. I, p. 242.
9. See pp. 132 ff., 407 ff.
10. Quoted in A. G. Widgery, *The Comparative Study of Religions*, London, 1923, p. 340.

CHAPTER V. THE NATIVE RELIGIONS OF CHINA (pp. 129–152)

1. *The Chinese: Their History and Culture* (3rd ed.), New York, 1946, p. 70.
2. Lin Yu-tang (ed.), *The Wisdom of China and India*, New York, 1942, pp. 1063 f.
3. A. Forke, *The World Conception of the Chinese*, London, 1925, p. 72 (quoting Wentze, VI, 27r).
4. H. G. Creel, *Sinism*, Chicago, 1929, p. 36.
5. *Ibid.*, p. 132.
6. S. Radhakrishnan, *Religion and Society*, London, 1947, p. 50.
7. See *The Wisdom of China and India*, p. 811.

CHAPTER VI. CONFUCIANISM (pp. 153–184)

1. Lin Yu-tang, *The Wisdom of China and India*, New York, 1942, pp. 851 f.
2. Lin Yu-tang, *The Wisdom of Confucius*, New York, 1938, pp. 80 ff.
3. *The Wisdom of China and India*, pp. 811 f.
4. S. H. Wang, *The Chinese Mind*, New York, 1946, p. 14.
5. *The Wisdom of China and India*, p. 831.
6. *Ibid.*, pp. 834 f., 849.
7. *Ibid.*, p. 831.
8. *Ibid.*, p. 849.
9. *Ibid.*, p. 848.
10. See K. S. Latourette, *The Chinese: Their History and Culture* (3rd ed.), New York, 1946, p. 629.
11. Hamlet, Act I, Scene 3.
12. *The Wisdom of China and India*, p. 840.
13. *The Wisdom of Confucius*, p. 257.

14. *Ibid.*, p. 199.
15. *The Wisdom of China and India*, pp. 860 f. Cf. Whitman's remark in his "Song of the Open Road": "I and mine do not convince by arguments, similes, rhymes; We convince by our presence."
16. *The Wisdom of Confucius*, pp. 108, 129 f., 104; cf. also pp. 125 f.
17. *Ibid.*, p. 184.
18. *The Wisdom of China and India*, pp. 817, 847.
19. *The Wisdom of Confucius*, pp. 258 ff.
20. *Ibid.*, p. 184.
21. *The Wisdom of China and India*, p. 769.
22. Creel, *op. cit.*, pp. 81 f.
23. *The Wisdom of Confucius*, p. 182.
24. *The Wisdom of China and India*, p. 782 (my own translation).
25. *The Wisdom of Confucius*, p. 280.
26. *The Wisdom of China and India*, p. 782.
27. *Ibid.*, pp. 770 f., 784.
28. *Ibid.*, pp. 775 f.
29. *Ibid.*, p. 767. My own rendering.
30. *Ibid.*, p. 814.

CHAPTER VII. TAOISM (pp. 185–201)

1. *Tao Teh Ching*, translated by Lin Yu-tang in *The Wisdom of China and India*, New York, 1942, Chaps. I, XIX (reversing the order of the lines in XIX). See pp. 583, 592.
2. *Ibid.*, Chap. VIII.
3. *Ibid.*, Chap. VII.
4. *Ibid.*, Chap. XXII. Cf. the corresponding maxim in the Christian gospels: "Seek ye first the kingdom of God and His righteousness, and all these things shall be added unto you."
5. *Ibid.*, Chaps. XXXVI, LXVII.
6. *Ibid.*, Chap. XV.
7. *Ibid.*, Chap. XXV.
8. *Ibid.*, Chap. I.
9. *Ibid.*, Chap. XXII.
10. *Ibid.*, Chaps. XXXIII, XXV, LXIV, LVII, LIX, XXXVII.
11. *Ibid.*, Chap. XLIX. Cf. Chaps. LXII, LXIII.

12. Quoted in Lin Yu-tang, *The Wisdom of Laotse,* New York, 1948, p. 181. I have used an earlier translation.

13. *Ibid.,* pp. 33 f.

14. *Ibid.,* p. 238.

15. *The Wisdom of China and India,* pp. 686 f.

CHAPTER VIII. THE BACKGROUND OF HINDUISM AND BUDDHISM (pp. 202–216)

1. Lin Yu-tang, *The Wisdom of China and India,* New York, 1942, p. 6.

2. *Yajur-Veda,* II, 1.

3. In Book VII of the *Republic.*

4. Paramhansa Yogananda, *Autobiography of a Yogi,* New York, 1951, p. 66.

5. *Rig-Veda,* X, 129.

6. For an interesting parallel between the form this remolding took in Tibet and medieval Christianity, see J. F. Clarke, *Ten Great Religions,* Boston and New York, 1898, Vol. II, pp. 73 f.

CHAPTER IX. BUDDHISM (pp. 217–268)

1. For a brief discussion of the problem of dates in early Buddhism, see E. J. Thomas, *Early Buddhist Scriptures,* London, 1935, pp. xx ff.

2. *Mahaparanibbana Suttanta,* as translated in the *Sacred Books of the Buddhists,* ed. T. W. and C. A. F. Rhys Davids, London, 1910, Vol. III, p. 173.

3. Quoted in A. R. Wadia, *Religion as a Quest for Values,* Calcutta, 1950, p. 136.

4. Subhadra Bhikkhu, *The Message of Buddhism,* London, 1922, p. 83.

5. *Ibid.,* pp. 78 f.

6. *Digha Nikaya,* II, 278. (See *Sacred Books of the Buddhists,* Vol. III, p. 312.)

7. Lord Chalmers, *Buddha's Teachings* (Harvard Oriental Series, No. 37), Cambridge, Mass., 1932, p. 211.

8. See P. T. Raju, *Idealistic Thought of India,* Cambridge, Mass., 1953, pp. 223 f.

9. Quoted in A. G. Widgery, *The Comparative Study of Religions,* London, 1923, p. 351.

10. Chap. XI.

11. Quoted in H. Höffding, *Philosophy of Religion*, trans. B. E. Meyer, London, 1906, pp. 302 f.

12. St. Paul's Epistle to the Galatians, 5:22, 23.

13. The passage from the *Majjhima-Nikaya* is in Sutta 63. See my *Teachings of the Compassionate Buddha*, New York, 1955, pp. 32–36. The briefer quotation, also from the *Majjhima-Nikaya*, is taken from S. Radhakrishnan, *Indian Philosophy*, London, 1927, Vol. I, p. 382.

14. *Udana*, VIII, 8 (quoted from a German translation by J. B. Pratt, *The Pilgrimage of Buddhism*, New York, 1928, p. 30).

15. George Eliot, *Romola*, Epilogue to Part III.

16. Thornton Wilder, *The Bridge of San Luis Rey*, New York, 1927, p. 29.

17. Vagga 1, Sutta 8, as translated by Chalmers, *op. cit.*, p. 37.

18. Quoted in Wadia, *op. cit.*, p. 132.

19. Quoted in G. F. Moore, *History of Religion*, New York, 1916, Vol. I, p. 287.

20. *The Wisdom of China and India*, New York, 1942, p. 326.

21. As quoted in C. H. Page, *The Chief American Poets*, Boston, 1905, p. 329.

22. M. Anesaki, *History of Japanese Religion*, London, 1930, pp. 53–54.

23. See the selection from this sutra in my *Teachings of the Compassionate Buddha*, pp. 161 ff.

CHAPTER X. HINDUISM (pp. 269–317)

1. Quoted in S. Radhakrishnan, *The Hindu View of Life*, London, 1927, p. 92.

2. Gandhi, in a talk to the Federation of International Fellowships, January, 1928 (quoted in S. Radhakrishnan's Introduction to *Mahatma Gandhi*, London, 1949, pp. 340 f.).

3. K. T. Behanan, *Yoga, A Scientific Evaluation*, New York, 1937, pp. 244 f.

4. *The Upanishads*, trans. F. Max Müller in *Sacred Books of the East*, London, 1879–1910, Vol. XV. My references are to N. Macnicol's edition in *Hindu Scriptures*, London and New York, 1938. See p. 62.

5. *Ibid.*, p. 63.

6. Swami Krishnananda, *The Realization of the Absolute*, Rishikesh, 1952, pp. 27 f.

7. Swami Sivananda, *All About Hinduism*, Rishikesh, 1947, p. 170.

8. *The Upanishads*, p. 64.

9. *Ibid.*, pp. 67, 75 f.

10. *Ibid.*, pp. 72, 83.

11. *Ibid.*, p. 93.

12. *Ibid.*, pp. 96 f.

13. *The Bhagavad-Gita*, ed. Swami Prabhavananda and Christopher Isherwood, New York, 1944, Chap. 1, pp. 31–34.

14. *Ibid.*, Chap. 18, p. 129.

15. This concluding verse is in *ibid.*, Chap. 18, p. 129.

16. *Ibid.*, Chaps. 5, 6, 14; pp. 57, 67, 110.

17. *Ibid.*, Chap. 18, p. 122.

18. I am drawing in this outline upon such works as S. Radhakrishnan, *Indian Philosophy*, London, 1929–1931, Vol. II; M. Hiriyanna, *The Essentials of Indian Philosophy*, London, 1949; S. S. Suryanarayana Sastri, *Life and Teachings of Sankaracharya*, Madras, 1941; *The Cultural Heritage of India*, ed. H. Bhattacharya, Madras, 1943, Vol. III; H. Zimmer, *Philosophies of India*, New York, 1951; Swami Nikhilananda's Introduction to his translation of Sankara's *Self-Knowledge* (*atmabodha*), Madras, 1947; and others.

19. Hiriyanna, *op. cit.*, p. 172.

20. Radhakrishnan, *op. cit.*, Vol. II, pp. 655–658.

CHAPTER XI. RELIGION IN THE OLD TESTAMENT (pp. 321–363)

1. I am using here the Smith and Goodspeed translation.

2. Deuteronomy 34:6.

3. Its discovery, according to this interpretation, is described in II Kings 22.

4. See, for example, Judges 17:6.

5. II Samuel 6:6–7.

6. See, for example, Judges 20:23—21:24, where even their fellow tribesmen the Benjaminites were treated in this way.

7. II Samuel 12. See also the story of Elijah and Ahab somewhat later, given in I Kings 21.

8. Amos 1:3–10.

9. Amos 2:4–5.
10. Amos 2:6–8, 13–16.
11. The passages that follow are from Chapters 4 and 5, with the eleventh verse of Chapter 3 and the twelfth of Chapter 6.
12. Isaiah 10:5–11.
13. Ezekiel, especially Chapters 23–33.
14. This doctrine is specifically taught in Amos 9:7.
15. Isaiah 6:3.
16. Zechariah 8:20–23.
17. Isaiah 53; note especially verse 11.
18. Micah 6:6–8.
19. Hosea 11; also 2:14—3:5.
20. Notice the language of Jeremiah's prayers in Chapters 14–16.
21. Consider from this standpoint especially Isaiah, Chapters 49, 55.
22. The reader may wish to peruse again the *Bhagavad Gita* to discover passages expressing a similar idea.
23. Isaiah 40:1–2.
24. Isaiah 41:22–24.
25. Isaiah 49:14–15.
26. Isaiah 42:9–10.
27. Isaiah 49:6.
28. Isaiah 55:7–8.
29. See Zechariah 8, especially the concluding verses.
30. Zechariah 12–14.
31. The Book of Enoch, especially Chapters 24–27 and 91.
32. Daniel 12:2.

CHAPTER XII. CHRISTIANITY (pp. 364–417)

1. Matthew 10:23.
2. Matthew 21:43.
3. Luke 17:20, 21.
4. Matthew 25:31–46.
5. Mark 9:12.
6. Philippians 2:8–11.
7. Matthew 16:21–23, 20:17–28.
8. Mark 14:37–38.
9. Luke 10:25–37.

10. Matthew 23.
11. Matthew 23:23–24.
12. Matthew 5:27–28.
13. Luke 12:29–33, 17:20–21; Matthew 25:31–46.
14. Mark 11:23.
15. Mark 10:29–30.
16. Matthew 5:44–47.
17. Matthew 26:63.
18. Matthew 11:27. Cf. also the parable of the vineyard in Matthew 21:33–44.
19. Matthew 26:28, 20:28.
20. Matthew 16:24–28. Cf. also Matthew 19:18–19, 28–29.
21. Matthew 25:40.
22. E.g., Mark 9:17–19.
23. Matthew 24:29–31, 25:31–33.
24. Matthew 25:40, 45.
25. John 8:58, 10:30.
26. John 1:4–5, 8:12.
27. John 5:24.
28. John 3:1–8. Cf. I John 3:14: "He that loveth not his brother abideth in death."
29. John 1:14–18, 3:16–17.
30. John 15:1–8.
31. John 6:51.
32. John 3:16.
33. John 17:3.
34. John 15:15.
35. John 12:32.
36. See Romans 7:7–25.
37. Acts 7:54—8:3.
38. Acts 9:1–9.
39. Galatians 2:20.
40. See Romans, Chapters I–XI.
41. Philippians 2:8.
42. I Corinthians 1:23.
43. J. E. Carpenter, *Comparative Religion*, London, 1913, pp. 206 f.
44. John 15:11.

CHAPTER XIII. ISLAM (pp. 418–452)

1. The *Koran*, trans. J. Rodwell, New York, 1909, pp. 31 f., 44 f. (Suras 92, 82).
2. R. V. C. Bodley, *The Messenger*, Garden City, 1946, p. 332.
3. The *Koran*, p. 52 (Sura 78).
4. *Ibid.*, p. 35 (Sura 90).
5. Bodley, *op. cit.*, p. 86.
6. The *Koran*, pp. 419 f. (Sura 4).
7. Bodley, *op. cit.*, p. 90.
8. *Ibid.*, p. 16.
9. The *Koran*, pp. 358, 419–422 (Suras 2, 4).
10. *Ibid.*, pp. 172, 198, 207, etc. (Suras 16, 17, 45).
11. *Ibid.*, p. 419 (Sura 4).
12. G. F. Moore, *The History of Religions*, New York, 1919, Vol. II, pp. 445 f.
13. Quoted, *ibid.*, p. 450.
14. Other important works of al-Ghazzali are an autobiography and *The Collapse of the Philosophers*.

CHAPTER XV. RELIGION FACES THE CONTEMPORARY SCENE (pp. 481–524)

1. Published first in 1927–1929.
2. Letter from Mr. Horace Alexander (a lifelong friend of Gandhi) to *The Times* (London), September 5, 1955.
3. Chester Bowles, *The New Dimensions of Peace*, New York, 1955, pp. 139 f., 151 f.
4. Quoted, *ibid.*, p. 144.
5. *Teachings of Mahatma Gandhi*, ed. J. P. Chander, Lahore, 1947, p. 562.
6. See Bowles, *op. cit.*, pp. 139 f.
7. *Teachings of Mahatma Gandhi*, p. 551.
8. *Ibid.*, p. 551.
9. *Ibid.*, p. 409.
10. *Ibid.*, p. 562.
11. *Ibid.*, pp. 557 f.
12. *Ibid.*, p. 557.
13. The *Harijan*, July 30, 1945. Quoted in S. Radhakrishnan, *Religion and Society*, London, 1947, p. 237.

14. Quoted in Bowles, *op. cit.*, pp. 141 f.
15. *Teachings of Mahatma Gandhi*, pp. 495 f.
16. *Ibid.*, p. 498.
17. Quoted in Bowles, *op. cit.*, p. 142.
18. *Teachings of Mahatma Gandhi*, p. 391.
19. Adapted from Gandhi in the *Walden Round Robin*, February 7, 1948.
20. *Ibid.*
21. Hallam Tennyson, *India's Walking Saint*, New York, 1955, p. 182.
22. *Ibid.*, p. 191.
23. See an account by Scott Seegers of this venture in loving pacification in *The New York Times Magazine Section*, January 29, 1956.
24. Quoted in *The New York Times*, February 24, 1956.
25. See, for example, his *General Introduction to Psychoanalysis*, trans. Rivière, Garden City, 1943, pp. 95 f., 245 f.
26. *Ibid.*, p. 378.
27. *Ibid.*, pp. 248, 396.
28. One important book has thus far appeared, *Mental Health and Hindu Psychology*, by Swami Akhilananda (see Bibliography).
29. See Freud's comments on this matter, *ibid.*, pp. 397 f.

BIBLIOGRAPHY

This list includes only books in English which, in the author's judgment, will be found of special value to the general reader for further study.

A. Books Dealing with the Entire Field, or More Than One Part of It

Ayres, Lew, *Altars of the East*, New York, Doubleday and Company, 1956.

Browne, L., *This Believing World*, New York, The Macmillan Company, 1926.

Ferm, V. (ed.), *An Encyclopedia of Religion*, New York, Philosophical Library, 1945.

Ferm, V. (ed.), *Religion in the Twentieth Century*, New York, Philosophical Library, 1948.

Finegan, J., *Archaeology of World Religions*, Princeton, Princeton University Press, 1952.

Friess, H. L., and Schneider, H. E., *Religion in Various Cultures*, New York, Henry Holt and Company, 1932.

Haydon, A. E., *Biography of the Gods*, New York, The Macmillan Company, 1942.

Haydon, A. E., *Modern Trends in World Religions*, Chicago, University of Chicago Press, 1934.

Moore, G. F., *The History of Religions*, 2 vols., New York, Charles Scribner's Sons, 1913, 1919.

Noss, J. B., *Man's Religions* (rev. ed.), New York, The Macmillan Company, 1956.

Widgery, A. G., *Living Religions and Modern Thought*, New York, Round Table Press, 1936.

B. Books on Primitive Religion

Benedict, R., *Patterns of Culture*, Boston, Houghton Mifflin Company, 1934 (repr. in paper-bound ed., New York, New American Library, Mentor M89).

Boas, F., *The Mind of Primitive Man*, New York, The Macmillan Company, 1911.

Calverton, V. F., *The Making of Man* (esp. Part V), New York, The Modern Library, 1931.

Frazer, Sir J. G., *The Golden Bough* (one-vol. ed.), New York, The Macmillan Company, 1953.

Goode, W., *Religion Among Primitives*, Glencoe, Ill., Free Press, 1951.

James, E. O., *The Beginnings of Religion*, London, Hutchinson & Co., 1948.

Jevons, F. B., *Introduction to the History of Religions*, London, Methuen and Company, 1896.

Lowie, R. H., *Primitive Religion*, London, George Routledge and Sons, 1925.

Moore, G. F., *The Birth and Growth of Religion*, New York, Charles Scribner's Sons, 1926.

Radin, P., *Primitive Religion*, New York, The Viking Press, 1937.

C. BOOKS ON THE CHINESE RELIGIONS

Bonsall, B. S., *Confucianism and Taoism*, London, The Epworth Press, 1934.

Chan, W. T., "Chinese Philosophy, a Bibliographical Essay," *Philosophy East and West*, January, 1954, pp. 337–358.

Chan, W. T., *Religious Trends in Modern China*, New York, Columbia University Press, 1953.

Chang Chung-yuan, "The Concept of Tao in Chinese Culture," *Review of Religion*, March, 1953, pp. 115–132.

Creel, H. G., *The Birth of China*, New York, John Day Company, 1937.

Creel, H. G., *Chinese Thought from Confucius to Mao Tze-tung*, Chicago, University of Chicago Press, 1953.

Creel, H. G., *Sinism*, Chicago, University of Chicago Press, 1929.

Fung Yu-lan, *A Short History of Chinese Philosophy*, New York, The Macmillan Company, 1948.

Giles, H. A., *Chuang Tzu—Mystic, Moralist, and Social Reformer*, Shanghai, Kelly and Walsh, 1926.

Hughes, E. R., *Chinese Philosophy in Classical Times*, London, J. M. Dent and Sons, New York, E. P. Dutton and Company, 1942.

Lang, O., *The Chinese Family and Society*, New Haven, Yale University Press, 1950.

Latourette, K. S., *The Chinese: Their History and Culture* (3rd ed.), New York, The Macmillan Company, 1946.

Lin Yu-tang, *The Wisdom of China*, London, M. Joseph, 1949.

Lin Yu-tang, *The Wisdom of Confucius*, New York, The Modern Library, 1938.

Lin Yu-tang, *The Wisdom of Laotse*, New York, The Modern Library, 1948.

Lyall, L. A. (trans.), *Mencius*, New York, Longmans, Green and Company, 1932.

Reichelt, K. L., *Religion in Chinese Garment*, trans. J. Tetlie, New York, Philosophical Library, 1951.

Waley, A. (trans.), *The Analects of Confucius*, London, Allen and Unwin, 1938.

Wang, G. H., *The Chinese Mind*, New York, The John Day Company, 1946.

Wei, F. C. M., *The Spirit of Chinese Culture*, New York, Charles Scribner's Sons, 1947.

Yeh, G. C. K., *The Confucian Conception of Jen*, London, The China Society, 1943.

D. Books on Hinduism and Buddhism

Arnold, Sir Edwin, *The Light of Asia* (many editions available; see Lin Yu-tang, below).

Bhikkhu, Subhadra, *The Message of Buddhism*, London, Kegan Paul, Trench, Trubner and Company, 1922.

Brewster, E. H., *Life of Gotama the Buddha*, London, Kegan Paul, Trench, Trubner and Company, 1926.

Burtt, E. A. (ed.), *The Teachings of the Compassionate Buddha*, New York, New American Library, 1955, Mentor MD131.

Chalmers, Lord, *Buddha's Teachings* (Harvard Oriental Series, Vol. 37), Cambridge, Harvard University Press, 1932.

Eliot, Sir C., *Hinduism and Buddhism*, 3 vols., London, Routledge and Kegan Paul, 1921.

Hiriyanna, M., *The Essentials of Indian Philosophy*, London, Allen and Unwin, 1949.

Keith, A. B., *The Religion and Philosophy of the Veda and the Upanishads*, Cambridge, Harvard University Press, 1920.

Lin Yu-tang: *The Wisdom of India*, London, M. Joseph, 1949.

MacNicol, N. (ed.), *Hindu Scriptures*, London, G. M. Dent and Sons; New York, E. P. Dutton and Company, 1938.

Morgan, K. W. (ed.), *Religion of the Hindus*, New York, The Ronald Press, 1953.

Nehru, J., *The Discovery of India*, New York, The John Day Company, 1946.

Prabhavananda, Swami, and Isherwood, C. (trans.), *The Bhaga-vad-Gita*, New York, Harper & Brothers, 1944 (repr. in paper-bound ed., New York, New American Library, 1954, Mentor M103).

Pratt, J. B., *The Pilgrimage of Buddhism*, New York, The Mac-millan Company, 1928.

Radhakrishnan, S., *The Hindu View of Life*, London, Allen and Unwin, 1927.

Radhakrishnan, S., *Indian Philosophy*, 2 vols (rev. ed.), London, Allen and Unwin, 1929–1931.

Radhakrishnan, S. (trans.), *The Principal Upanishads*, New York, Harper & Brothers, 1953.

Rhys Davids, C. A. F., *Buddhism*, New York, Henry Holt and Company, 1912.

Smith, F. H., *The Buddhist Way of Life*, London, Hutchinson & Co., 1951.

Suzuki, B. L., *Mahayana Buddhism* (enl. ed.), London, David Marlowe, 1948.

Thomas, E. J., *The History of Buddhist Thought* (2nd ed.), New York, Barnes and Noble, 1951.

Ward, C. H. S., *Buddhism*, Vol. I, *Hinayana;* Vol. II, *Mahayana*, London, The Epworth Press, 1947, 1952.

E. Books on the Western Religions

Andrae, Tor, *Mohammed, the Man and His Faith* (trans. Menzel), London, Allen and Unwin, 1936.

Bodley, R. V. C., *The Messenger*, Garden City, Doubleday and Company, 1946.

Buber, M., *The Prophetic Faith* (trans. C. Witton-Davies), New York, The Macmillan Company, 1949.

Burtt, E. A., *Types of Religious Philosophy* (rev. ed.), New York, Harper & Brothers, 1951.

Corbishley, T., *Roman Catholicism*, London, Hutchinson & Co., 1950.

Edman, I., *The Mind of Paul*, New York, Henry Holt and Company, 1935.

French, R. M., *The Eastern Orthodox Church*, London, Hutchinson & Co., 1951.

Gibb, H. A. R., *Modern Trends in Islam*, Chicago, University of Chicago Press, 1947.

Goodspeed, E. J., *A Life of Jesus*, New York, Harper & Brothers, 1950.

Hurgronje, C. S., *Mohammedanism*, New York and London, G. P. Putnam's Sons, 1916.

Klausner, J., *From Jesus to Paul*, New York, The Macmillan Company, 1943.

Klausner, J., *Jesus of Nazareth*, New York, The Macmillan Company, 1925.

Koran, trans. R. Bell, 2 vols, Edinburgh, T. and T. Clark, 1937–1939.

Koran, trans. J. Rodwell, London, J. M. Dent & Sons, New York, E. P. Dutton and Company, 1909.

MacDonald, D. B., *The Religious Attitude and Life in Islam*, Chicago, University of Chicago Press, 1912.

McGiffert, A. C., *History of Christian Thought*, 2 vols. New York and London, Charles Scribner's Sons, 1932, 1933.

McGiffert, A. C., *Protestant Thought Before Kant*, New York, Charles Scribner's Sons, 1911.

Nicholson, R. A., *The Mystics of Islam*, London, G. Bell and Sons, 1914.

Oesterley, W. O. E., and Robinson, T. H., *Hebrew Religion, Its Origin and Development*, New York, The Macmillan Company, 1937.

Parsons, E. W., *The Religion of the New Testament*, New York, Harper & Brothers, 1939.

Patterson, C. H., *The Philosophy of the Old Testament*, New York, The Ronald Press Company, 1953.

Rashdall, H., *The Idea of Atonement in Christian Theology*, New York, The Macmillan Company, 1919.

Scott, E. F., *The Literature of the New Testament*, New York, Columbia University Press, 1932.

Scott, E. F., *The First Age of Christianity*, New York, The Macmillan Company, 1926.

Smith, J. M. P., *The Prophets and Their Times*, Chicago, University of Chicago Press, 1925.

Tritton, A. S., *Islam*, London, Hutchinson & Co., 1951.

Walker, W., *A History of the Christian Church*, New York, Charles Scribner's Sons, 1918.

F. BOOKS DEALING WITH THE THEMES OF PART FOUR

CHAPTER XIV

Bennett, J. C., *Christianity and Communism*, New York, Association Press, 1948.

CHAPTER XV

A

Datta, D. M., *The Philosophy of Mahatma Gandhi*, Madison, Wis., University of Wisconsin Press, 1953.

Fischer, L., *The Life of Mahatma Gandhi*, New York, Harper & Brothers, 1950.

Gandhi, M. K., *Autobiography*, Washington, Public Affairs Press, 1948.

Tennyson, H., *India's Walking Saint*, New York, Doubleday and Company, 1955.

B

Akhilananda, Swami, *Mental Health and Hindu Psychology*, New York, Harper & Brothers, 1951.

Freud, S., *General Introduction to Psychoanalysis*, trans. J. Rivière, Garden City, Garden City Publishing Company, 1943.

Fromm, E., *Religion and Psychoanalysis*, New Haven, Yale University Press, 1950.

Outler, A. C., *Psychotherapy and the Christian Message*, New York, Harper & Brothers, 1954.

Roberts, D. E., *Psychotherapy and a Christian View of Man*, New York, Charles Scribner's Sons, 1950.

Sherrill, L. J., *Guilt and Redemption*, Richmond, John Knox Press, 1945.

Van der Veldt, J. H., and Odenwald, R. P., *Psychiatry and Catholicism*, New York, McGraw-Hill Book Company, 1952.

Index